HEINRICH HEINE

A Biographical Anthology

THE GITELSON
LIBRARY

The publication of this volume by The Jewish Publication Society of America was made possible by the Nehemiah Gitelson Fund, established in loving memory of Nehemiah Gitelson (1853-1932), scholar, rabbi, talmudic teacher, and merchant.

The present work is the fifth issued under this Fund. The first, *The House of Nasi—The Duke of Naxos*, the second, *Prince of the Ghetto*, and the third, *Pilgrims in a New Land*, were published in 1948. The fourth, *The Jews, Their History, Culture and Religion*, was published in 1949.

HEINRICH
HEINE

A Biographical Anthology

Edited by

HUGO BIEBER

English translations made or selected by

MOSES HADAS

Philadelphia

THE JEWISH PUBLICATION SOCIETY OF AMERICA

5717–1956

PREFACE

It is right and fitting that a word of tribute be expressed here in memory of the late Dr. Hugo Bieber, the author of this book. Born in Berlin, Germany, in 1883, he became a historian of German literature and author of a number of works in this field; he was also the literary director of a German book guild. The transformation of Germany in 1933, from the home of culture to the citadel of Nazism, compelled him to go to France; and in 1940 he came to the United States.

Since he had made a special study of Heinrich Heine and had written a number of books on the subject, it was natural for the Jewish Publication Society to turn to him when it decided to prepare a volume on the German poet. The German manuscript was completed in 1948. It was then turned over to Dr. Moses Hadas, Professor of Greek and Latin at Columbia University. Dr. Hadas undertook this task in spite of a very busy schedule and devoted himself to it far beyond what was expected of him. The Jewish Publication Society takes this opportunity to express to him its heartfelt gratitude for his unfailing cooperation.

Dr. Bieber's own introductory and explanatory remarks are in Dr. Hadas' translation, but for the selection from Heine's writings, large recourse was had to existing versions. Dr. Bieber saw and approved the translation.

For the use of copyrighted versions of a number of poems (to be found in this volume on the pages indicated below), acknowledgment and thanks are due to Mr. Louis Untermeyer, and to Harcourt, Brace & Co., publishers of *The Poems of Heinrich Heine* (New York, 1923): Lyrical Intermezzo, pages 136, 137, 138, 139, 140; Book of Songs, "Home-Coming," pages 146, 150; "A Tour in the Harz," pages 181f.; "Peace," page 211; "Poem to Charlotte Embden," page 143. Acknowledgment and thanks are likewise due to Professor Howard Mumford Jones, for selections from his book *The North Sea* (Open Court Publishing Co., 1916): First Cycle 2, page 51; Second Cycle 6, page 209.

In the case of the prose much has been borrowed from the translations edited for the Camelot Series by Charles Godfrey Leland (Hans Breitmann). Many of these translations are anonymous, and all have been more or less revised by Dr. Hadas; names of individual translators are therefore omitted. Next to the Camelot Series, largest use has been made of Gilbert Cannan's version of Gustav Karpeles' *Heinrich Heine's Memoirs from his Works, Letters and Conversations* (Heinemann in London and Henry Holt & Co., Inc. in New York, 1910). Borrowings more or less extensive have also been made from John Snodgrass' *Religion and Philosophy in Germany* (London, 1882), I.B.'s *Buch LeGrand of the Reisebilder* (London, 1884), Elizabeth Sharp's *Italian Travel Sketches of Heinrich Heine*, and Kate Freligrath Kroeker's *Poems Selected from Heinrich Heine* (various translators). A considerable proportion of the poems, for which no translation or no adequate translation was available, was rendered by Dr. Hadas.

For a variety of reasons the publication of the volume had to be delayed. In 1950 Dr. Bieber passed on to his eternal reward. It is a great pity that he did not live to see the completion of this book. May it help keep his memory alive.

CONTENTS

HEINRICH HEINE
A Biographical Anthology

INTRODUCTION

Heinrich Heine's grave in the Montmartre cemetery in Paris was destroyed in March 1941 upon the order of Adolf Hitler. From 1856, when the poet died, until its destruction, the grave had been visited and strewn with flowers by thousands and myriads of visitors from all countries. Now no trace of it is left. As the prophet Habakkuk says, the stones shall cry out. Heine's monument has been ground to dust; but though it is itself no longer visible, its message is clear. At the pinnacle of his military triumphs, the dictator of the Third Reich acknowledged by this barbarous act of destruction that he regarded a dead poet as a dangerous opponent eighty-five years after that poet's death, and that the poet's memory must be effaced if his own system of totalitarian oppression was to survive.

National Socialism and its Fuehrer had not forgotten that Heinrich Heine had foretold their advent precisely a century before Hitler's rise to power and had warned civilization against that rise. At the close of his book on the history of religion and philosophy in Germany, Heine declared that the German spirit as represented in its outstanding figures had entered upon a development which must lead to conflict with western civilization, and that a revolution would take place in Germany which would far surpass previous revolutions in cruelty and horror. Even before Heine's prophecy became grim reality, German nationalism of all shades had recognized an irreconcilable enemy in Heine and had sought every means to discredit him. They were not content to degrade the human personality of the poet, but wished to depreciate his poems in the eyes of the world and above all in the eyes of the German people.

But neither pre-Hitler nationalism nor the Nazi agitators succeeded in their design. Again and again they were frustrated by the realization that outside Germany respect for German poetry rested principally upon the popularity of Heine's work. But they were more incensed that the Germans themselves, however they might judge Heine's character and opinions, would not surrender their love for his verses.

The Nazi regime burned Heine's books. But at least one poem of Heinrich Heine even the most ruthless rule of violence could never banish from the memory and the hearts of the German people. The grossest brutality of *Gleichschaltung* could not prevent Heine's *Lorelei* from being read, sung and printed in popular song books as before. Authorities had to content themselves with omitting the name of the poet and tolerating the poem as "a popular song of unknown authorship."

The fall of German nationalism and the termination of Nazi rule have not put an end to contention concerning Heine. It is true that the larger number of those who vilified Heine was recruited from among opponents of liberalism and democracy. But even men who have fought gallantly for freedom and progress are to be found among Heine's antagonists. Frequently, if not always, differences on the subject of Heine have cut across party alignments. By his literary productions as by the manifestations of his private character, Heine has aroused enthusiasm or indignation in followers of very diverse political, religious and aesthetic tendencies. This fact demonstrates that the political conflict which is a factor in contention concerning Heine opens only one of several vistas which afford approach to the problem of Heine.

Conflict regarding Heine began as soon as his earliest verses appeared. It has endured to this day, and there are many indications that it will continue far into the future. Seldom has a quarrel about a poet been waged with such passion; never with such passion so long maintained. Compared with it, controversies concerning Byron, Victor Hugo, Zola, Ibsen, and even Richard Wagner, are brief episodes. In the cases of these men, public opinion was agitated for only a decade, or at most a generation. Then ensued calm or oblivion, or the debate was adjourned to the narrow circles of specialists or amateurs. But in the strife on Heine divergences in literary criticism have reverberated in the passions of large sections of the population for over a century, and have been constantly stimulated by political, religious and social differences. Literary considerations alone, no more than political considerations alone, cannot suffice to explain the partisanship of Heine's devotees and his opponents.

Nor is the conflict concerning Heine merely a domestic German matter. The fascination of his poems has radiated across national boundaries, and the ideas expressed in his prose writings have influenced the cultural life of diverse peoples. From the beginning the conflict has been complicated by problems of a general nature and has involved debates on broad human issues and cultural ideologies. Always the Heine issue has transcended the realm of aesthetic evaluation, though the affirmation or denial of Heine's artistic worth has provoked heated controversy on the nature of poetry. The issue has been and continues to be joined for and against the ideas of the French Revolution of 1789 and its interpretation, but it also concerns the artist's right to question an accepted ethic. Above all, Heine's Jewish origin made it inevitable that controversy over him should involve controversy over Judaism also. Heine's adversaries made his Jewishness responsible for all the poet's artistic, political and religious attitudes which displeased them. Plaintiffs against Judaism have often cited passages from Heine's writings to prove that the influence of Jews is harmful to modern civilization and must be guarded against. But neither was the attitude of Jews to Heine by any means uniform. Leaders of German Jewry like Gabriel Riesser and Berthold Auerbach declared solemnly that Heine was an apostate who had nothing in common with Judaism and only broadcast false concepts of Jewish character. On the other hand, Heinrich Graetz, the classical historian of the Jews who did not regard apostasy lightly, represents Heine as a Jew who remained faithful to his people. Others have even regarded Heine as a Jewish nationalist. These were in turn refuted by yet others, who claimed him for the Jewish Reform movement. Nor were there lacking converted Jews or atheists of Jewish origin who invoked Heine as their model. Despite this diversity of Jewish opinion concerning Heine, the preponderant majority of non-Jewish critics has always included Judaism in its bill of complaints when it has condemned Heine.

Numerous readers have honored Heine, of course, and loved his writings without inquiring into their author's descent or allowing his participation in ideological controversies to spoil their pleasure. Prince Metternich, who for more than thirty years after the Congress of Vienna sought to suppress all revolutionary movements, caused Heine to be kept under surveillance and persecuted by the police; but he himself was a constant and delighted reader of Heine's poems. As a statesman Bismarck was an uncompromising opponent of all the ideas for which Heine fought, but Bismarck declared that the author of the *Buch der Lieder* was the greatest German lyric poet and that only Goethe could be named in the same breath. Many who have been enchanted by Heine's artistry in language but have vigorously opposed his political writings have sought to escape the dilemma by taking Heine the thinker and fighter less seriously than Heine the poet. But such a solution prevents adequate understanding of Heine's personality. No clear-cut partition between Heine's poetry, thought and action is possible. In the preface to the second edition of his *Buch der Lieder* he has quite justly observed: "But I must remark that my poetic compositions have stemmed from one and the same thought as my political, theological and philosophical writings, and that the one cannot be condemned without withdrawing all approval from the other."

If Heine deduced all his poetry and prose from one uniform source, it is by no means his intention to imply that the "one thought" he speaks of remained consistent at all periods of his life. Even less would he deny that his thoughts and feelings were often at variance and criss-crossed in sharply conflicting tendencies. From the *Buch der Lieder* to the last confessions of his *Matratzengruft*, Heine's poems reveal divergences of mood. In his prose works, too, Heine frequently remarked on this conflict, which often impelled him to alienate or injure people who were in agreement with him on many decisive problems of life.

Heine was not a simple man. One who cannot conceive of

human greatness without noble simplicity or harmonious tranquillity, or one who, with Schopenhauer, regards genius as "supreme objectivity," cannot recognize Heine as great or a genius. But in the course of time other human qualities besides the classic ideal of humanity have gained recognition. And in this development Heine has a towering share.

Men of rich psychological experience who were themselves not without their eccentricity, like Théophile Gautier and Gérard de Nerval, have said, after years of friendship with Heine undisturbed to the end, that they had never encountered a man in whom so many opposites were manifested as in the author of the *Buch der Lieder*. The singular mixture of artistic self-discipline and license, of rationality and enthusiasm, of dispassionateness and extreme sensitivity which characterizes Heine's spiritual composition will furnish many an enigma even to the psychologists of the future.

Heine's spirit was the battleground of incessant contrast and conflict. For a man of lesser gifts this might have proved very dangerous and have produced neurotic stagnation. Other poets have been shattered by far slighter inconcinnities. In Heine, these serious inner antagonisms were the source not only of his melancholy but also of his wit and humor. From them his creative genius took fire. They set his imagination and his perceptivity into motion and afforded him psychological experiences which remained an alien world to other poets and thinkers, including many of Heine's critics, whose organisms were more simply constituted. They sharpened his perception for social wrong, for inadequacies in state, society and civilization, and they spurred his battle-glee.

Heine was perfectly aware of these manifold internal conflicts at an early stage, and he took them into account to the day of his death. They were conflicts between instinct and intellect, between imagination and feeling, between aesthetic pleasure and moral judgment, between his vital interests and his preferences and distastes. In one of the most important of his self-analyses Heine called himself a fool who was a glowing partisan of reason in the eternal war between folly and reason, although he would have prospered better if he had fought on the side of folly. He expressed the same thought in his *Confessions*, and so defined his historical position more precisely: "Despite the war of extermination that I waged against Romanticism, I always remained a Romanticist at heart, and that in a higher degree than I myself realized." His deepest inward craving was to lose himself in revery or historical contemplation, to enjoy beauty, and to forget reality in the happiness of love. His life and his poetry alike show that revery, love, beauty, contemplative pleasure dominated his feelings and afforded him rich enjoyment. But they also show something quite different. The poet of the *Dream Pictures* was also the poet of disillusionment; the herald of revolution was also the ironic critic whose scornful laughter is never silenced even in the midst of profound emotion and possession; who senses in advance the transitoriness of beauty and can break a tragic mood with barbed wit. The lyric poet who overhears the secrets of rose and lily, butterfly and nightingale, is also the acute observer of the advance of new social and economic forces.

Heine perceived social and economic change more clearly than almost all the poets of his age, and he paved the way to understanding for many an analyst of society, Karl Marx not the least. He was profoundly convinced that the new forces—finance, industry, technology, the proletariat—had irresistible historical right on their side. He perceived that resistance to the progress these forces pioneered, was not only hopeless, but would corrupt those who resisted. But his feelings collided with his insight, and the same Heine who never wearied of declaring bitter war against the defenders of tradition, who was a steadfast antagonist of aristocracy and clergy, who was the author of mordant occasional poems against royalty, and whose *Song of the Weaver* German workmen adopted as one of their classic battle hymns—this same Heine mocked the tendentious poetry of the liberals, expressed his apprehension of the spread of communist associations, disdained the manipulations of the financiers, had great misgivings as to the effects of modern industry and technology upon life.

Even if Heine denied Romanticism he retained his kinship with it. In his spirit the most brutal impressions of reality were associated with myths, legends, fairy stories. Even when he depicts contemporary men, economic innovations, political constellations or everyday street scenes, and with precise accuracy, he finds his metaphors in the field of ancient, Indian, Celtic, and Nordic mythology; and to discover or enunciate contemporary truths he employs a veil woven out of the similes of the dream world and the realm of pixies. But the Heine who wanders so happily in the remote past, in mythical pre-history, in the exotic landscapes of wonderland, never loses sight of what is immediate, of the social need of the time, of the demand for a just social order. The claim of the disinherited for a minimum livelihood, which he designates "the great bread and stomach question," is to him more important than the survival of art and poesy upon which his own heart centered. These demands of the proletariat he always gave his warm advocacy, though he entertained the liveliest fears of proletariat rule. The man who revered the antique statuary and the Gothic cathedrals, which inspired his imagination, remained the consistent foe of inherited privilege and the obsolete order. Heine, whose verse celebrates the glory of the Homeric heroes, of medieval chivalry, of the grandeur of Napoleon, was one of the first Europeans to recognize that the ancient symbols of heroism and nobility could not express all that is significant to modern man and, even less, offer compensation for abiding unhappiness and injustice.

This complicated spiritual constitution predestined Heine to discover the contrasts and contradictions in the living actuality which he observed and to expose them either with angry accusations or with detached wit. Out of his own inner conflicts Heine realized that, to be adequate to modern life, poetry requires a broader frame of reference and a larger objectivity in expression than did either the classic or romantic concepts and forms which were available when he began to write. Heine's own peculiar spiritual constitution enabled him to look upon the world and man, art and culture, without prejudice, and to depict them with a justice which was felt to be unexampled not only in German but in European literature as a whole.

Similarly unexampled was the emotional richness with which

Heine reacted to reality. His melancholy was metamorphosed into an evocative exuberance. His capacity for sensual enjoyment was enhanced along with his contempt for the world. His nervous sensitivity strengthened his sense of the comic. His skepticism refined his psychologic analysis. Heine's example has found many imitators; nevertheless the originality of his perception and his language enthralls even the modern reader.

More than one contemporary critic complained bitterly that accepted notions of what is humanly valuable and artistically essential had been shattered by Heine. Modern critics, too, have deplored the fact that the period of "pure" poetry ended with Heine. But they cannot deny that Heine has contributed more than any other modern poet to change the social function of poetry and the position of the poet in our civilization. Broad masses have come to embrace poetry because they perceived that the modern poet speaks to them, too, when he expresses his own personal feelings, that he understands and shares their needs and anxieties, their wishes and aspirations. That is what Heine has achieved, though he also composed poems which suggest polarity to mass interests.

As soon as Heine's first poems appeared, his followers no less than his opponents instinctively sensed that the relation of the public to these lyrics must be quite different than to poetry previously known. When, at the age of thirty (1827), Heine collected his youthful productions in the *Buch der Lieder*, this impression had become general and inevitable. Soon it took root over all Europe, and then across the seas. With a candor which seems forthright even today these poems reveal the personal nature and position of their author. They communicate not only his emotional life but also his private and prosaic embarrassments. The mocking or melancholy echoes of the author's passing mood are mingled with satiric criticism of his epoch. The poet's plaints concerning his unhappy love for a girl who does not appreciate his worth are interpenetrated by complaints against society and politics. Their melodious language moves suddenly from sad harmonies to flashing wit. The poems are at once songs and epigrams. Heine's artistry could compass gentle transitions or stark contrasts with equal mastery. It operates by allusion, and never mystifies the reader even when it is silent on non-essentials. Frequently it enables the reader to divine that the words which are the means of expression are in contradiction to the feelings which are their end. But even in such cases Heine's language remains clear, and unerringly leads the reader to the effect intended. As dramatist Heine had no success. As novelist he never got further than fragments. But many of his short poems contain whole novels. Others sketch a complete drama with absorbing action in a mere handful of verses. Heine's dramatic sense is triumphant in his ballads such as *The Grenadiers, Belshazzar, Sir Olav, The Rogue of Bergen, The Battle of Hastings*. In this department he is recognized as acknowledged master even by critics who are cold to his lyrics.

His *Buch der Lieder* laid the foundation for his worldwide reputation, and this reputation has not been extinguished to this day. To be sure, all Heine's verses do not convey the freshness which Heine's contemporaries felt. Much in them has been rendered trite by his imitators. Much he himself repeated too often. With his poetry Heine broke through the traditions of sentiment and of form. But as artist he was not a thoroughgoing revolutionary; no artist has ever been. Language is a means of communication. The user of language may break with tradition at individual decisive points, but not completely if he wishes to be completely intelligible. Even radical innovators of our own day, in Europe as in America, have not been able to break completely with prevailing convention. The originality of individual devices produces an acoustic illusion which for a time evokes an impression of freedom from all previous traditions. But after a few years this impression vanishes, and in 1940 we perceive that the revolutionaries of 1930 employed traditional devices as frequently as did their predecessors of 1920 and earlier. Heine no more evaded this principle than did Goethe, Byron, Victor Hugo or T. S. Eliot. After more than a century has elapsed since the appearance of the *Buch der Lieder*, much which struck its first readers as novel has become trite. But even more is as fresh and vital today as when it first appeared.

A further result of the contrasts which dominated Heine's personal feelings, his poetry, and his criticism of life, is that he was indeed a fighter but never a partisan. He frequently proved embarrassing to groups which fought with him for a common goal, and despite a strong feeling of solidarity he almost always emphasized his own exceptional position as a poet. At times he suffered from his isolation; but he would seldom surrender his detachment from groups constituted on the basis of origin, religion, nationality, or community of ideas. He sympathized with democracy and remained an irreconcilable foe to any aristocracy of birth or position. But he was acutely uncomfortable in any situation in which the will of the majority was sole arbiter and he cherished a strong distaste of social egalitarianism. If Heine had known the remark of the Autocrat of the Breakfast Table— "I go politically for equality and socially for *the* quality"—he would have recognized a precise statement of his own point of view. On the basis of his observation of the political events in Europe he soon reached the conviction that the rights of the individual could best be protected by a compromise between a democratic parliament and a hereditary monarchy, provided that the monarch would dissolve all ties with the aristocracy and the clergy. In this view Heine persisted throughout his life. The view has often been misunderstood and has brought him the enmity of monarchists and conservatives as well as the suspicion of the democrats. Heine's heart beat in time with the revolutionary popular movements in Greece, Poland, Italy and Spain. To him the German struggle for constitutionalism did not seem radical enough. Attempts at republican insurrection in France found him sympathetic. But his understanding always demanded a strong government which would not be driven by the masses but retain leadership in its own hands. He remained a constitutional monarchist, although this position was not in consonance with his feelings, and although republican radicalism attracted him much more. He could not reconcile himself to a prudent policy of compromise between opposing tendencies and interests such as was advocated particularly in the thirties of the nineteenth century, not even after he had come to realize its usefulness.

For only rarely did Heine judge political systems, measures, and personalities exclusively from the point of view of political expediency. He was one of the first men in Europe whose concept integrated political development with social, economic, artistic, religious and philosophical development. This is the basis of the strength and the attractiveness of Heine's political writings, but also a source of error in his criticism of contemporary policies. Frequently he is in error because he employs aesthetic criteria in judging contemporary politicians.

So Heine's regard for Napoleon I is strongly if not exclusively conditioned by aesthetic considerations. In Napoleon he saw the hero who consummated the French Revolution, and he laid greater emphasis upon those measures of Napoleon which were in accord with the Revolution than with those which destroyed republican institutions. Frequently Heine's glorification of Napoleon was at the same time a protest against the new order in Europe initiated by the Congress of Vienna and against the reactionary policies of the German government. Heine never forgot that his personal career had been diverted from its original direction by Napoleon's fall, for after the Emperor's defeat Heine became a Prussian subject and access to office was now impossible for him as a Jew. But aside from such practical considerations, Napoleon's historic stature as a manifestation of human genius intrigued him. The outward appearance of the victor of Marengo and Austerlitz, the expression of energy in his countenance, the monumental utterances of his bulletins made Napoleon a genius, in Heine's sight, who stood beyond good and evil. "My homage is not to the actions but to the genius of the man," Heine said in his *Travels*. The deeds he sacrificed to criticism; he believed that the grandeur of the historical phenomenon must be acknowledged without consideration of moral or political evaluations.

The principle of judging men independently of their moral and practical activity Heine frequently followed in his personal intercourse also. He wished to weigh his friends and foes "purely as phenomena." For that reason he frequently bestowed loyal friendship upon individuals of dubious morality, even men whom he knew to be tricksters and traitors, because some quality in their bearing or speech pleased him. Even more frequently did he persecute with hostile mockery and malicious contempt persons whose irreproachable character and undeniable services to the cause of freedom he had on occasion freely acknowledged. Both these tendencies have injured Heine in the opinion of contemporaries and of posterity. Only few of his friends could permanently tolerate Heine's habit of disregarding his feelings of justice, of using every opportunity to bring his trenchant wit into play, and of seeking to ridicule his opponents' physical infirmities as tirelessly as their weak or strong arguments. But the same Heine who so frequently violated all rules of fairness and even of decency when his appetite for mockery or vengeance was aroused, often generously supported opponents who had fallen into need. "He reviled with his mouth, he gave with his hand," says the German dramatist Heinrich Laube, who was bound to Heine by a friendship of many years' standing, though interrupted by disagreements.

In Heine's poetry and prose as well as in his letters and conversations a strong inclination to caricature is frequently to be observed. The trait is very noticeable, and is implicit in Heine's temperament. But as with all great caricaturists this tendency of Heine's to exaggerate and destroy is bound up with love of truth and the courage to express truth. Heine was very well aware that his cant to caricature was related to his intellectual capacity of associating ideas and phenomena far removed from one another; and both elements, delight in association of ideas and joy in caricature, frequently produced a more sharply limned perception of truth and reality, but also frequently falsified the true state. There can be no doubt that Heine was often seduced by this tendency to perpetrate injustices to men and ideas. Not always did he observe the boundary which separates comic distortion from complete falsification. But he also had a lively feeling that simple truth unadorned produces a stronger effect than the most artful circumlocutions. He knew that on occasion what the situation demanded and what the heart suggested must be uttered forthrightly without adornment, without simile or metaphor, without exaggeration or distortion. Accordingly Heine wrote like a journalist as well as like a poet. One may argue whether or not he always gave proper consideration to opportunities to forego witty or pathetic embellishments. But it is indisputable that, often enough, he uttered truth unadorned and by so doing moved his readers deeply, particularly in his last poems. The alternation between the play of association of ideas and the undisguised and immediate expression of feeling and conviction constitutes one of the principal charms of Heine's verse and prose.

Even when Heine regarded life and reality with sobriety his reaction was one of pathos. Many ideas and convictions he recognized as illusions, and he suffered gravely from the destruction of these illusions which he himself occasioned. The advance of his intellect contradicted his instinctive inclinations and his basic spiritual needs. But aware as he was of this cleavage he never consciously evaded it. The poems of his last years are a resounding lament over the loss of illusion, but never is the wish for a restoration of the past expressed. And in this Heine differs sharply from the German Romantics who desiderated a return to the Middle Ages.

Even in the *Buch der Lieder* Heine showed how clearly his sight was capable of penetrating people, how explicitly he could expose their hidden characteristics and their secret feelings. In the works of his later period Heine retains an astonishing acuteness in divining seemingly insignificant symptoms which indicate a change in cultural conditions and which were ignored by the majority of his contemporaries. This acuteness has little in common with that of the scientific investigator who coolly and objectively assembles his data before he draws general conclusions and who seeks to avoid yielding to any prejudices. Heine's intuitive acuteness is inspired above all by love and hate, by longing for a future which would actualize his desires, and by horror of developments which seemed hostile to his ideals. Heine never ceased emphasizing the cleavage between the cultural conditions of his age and his own personal views of a life of energy. Recognition of this cleavage determines the tone of his contemporary criticisms and his judgment of the peoples who in his sight were destined to carry out the most important cultural mission—Germany and France. It was also decisive in determining his attitude to Judaism and Christianity.

Heine was the most important intermediary between the cultures of France and Germany that the history of these two peoples had known. He regarded it as one of the most important tasks of his life to foster peace between Germany and France and to promote mutual and abiding understanding between them. Heine devoted much of his time and energy to carrying out this task, and was never distracted from it by accusations and suspicions on the part of German nationalists.

Although Heine broke with the traditions of German poetry in many respects, his poetic productions are rooted in the spiritual life of Germany. There are far fewer imitations of foreign models in Heine's poetry than in the works of Goethe or of the German Romanticists, to say nothing of the foreign influences upon German poets of the seventeenth and eighteenth centuries. Heine not only mastered the German language, but loved it and regarded its expressive and musical qualities as far superior to English and French. He felt exiled in spirit where German was not spoken. This feeling overwhelmed him in England and in Italy, and did not leave him even in France, where he lived from 1831 until his death. For a long while he was convinced that German philosophy was superior to the thought of all other peoples, and that it alone adequately comprehended the development of world history and the spirit of the age. On this point Heine changed his mind in the last years of his life. But to the end he insisted that the poetry of no other people attained the artistic heights of German song and that German song alone was true poetry. In private and public confessions Heine emphasized that he had gone to school to Goethe, Uhland, Wilhelm Mueller, Fouqué, and the collections of old German folk songs. He took artistic account of the contrasting effects of the echoes of this old poetry with the peculiar modern content of his own verse; and actually those of Heine's poems which were created as folk songs, are indeed clearly distinguishable by their conciseness and compactness from the older poems which are generally much more prolix and which lack Heine's quality of concentration. But aside from any calculation of effect, Heine instinctively produced the same melancholy melody; for his own concept of the poetic agreed with that of the folk song, even though it was much richer and embraced within the realm of poesy, areas of life which almost all his German predecessors had avoided out of dislike, shame, fear, sluggishness or stupidity.

And yet Heine saw in the Germans, not only a nation of poets and thinkers, but also a nation of Philistines as timorous as they were aggressive, as ignorant of the world as they were hostile to culture. He excepted neither the devotees of absolutism nor the champions of democracy. Indeed, the German democrats seemed to him even more awkward and dangerous than the conservatives. With mordant irony Heine mocked the despots of Germany, great and small, and their minions, but neither did he spare the opposition, whom he charged with want of energy, courage and farsightedness. He vigorously opposed every effort to unite Germany under Prussian hegemony. One poem of Heine directed against the king of Prussia was regarded as so insulting that it was forbidden until 1918 and could not even be included in the scientific editions of Heine's works. But Heine feared worse things of a republican victory in Germany than of the German monarchists. His experience as a student in German universities had led him to the conclusion that even those Germans who were politically on the left paid only lip-service to ideas of freedom, democracy and cultural progress, and in actual fact pursued power politics more ruthlessly than the contemporary statesman of the German right. On the right as on the left Heine discovered a deeply rooted hostility to western civilization. Heine was the first to pursue, in his books on the history of the German spirit, this process of resistance to western European ideas as it manifested itself through the centuries until his own day. He begins with the "elemental spirits" in which he demonstrates traces of pagan Germanic ideas surviving into the Christian epoch, and argues that Christianity had never penetrated life in Germany as deeply as it had done in other countries.

These reflections are set forth in his books on *The Romantic School* and *On the History of Religion and Philosophy in Germany*. In Luther's reformation Heine sees the first attempt to establish in Germany a national religion to rival international Christianity. The philosophy of Kant, Fichte, and Hegel completes the process of de-Christianizing Germany, in Heine's view, and thereby destroys the last barriers which Christianity had erected against Germanic joy in battle. "In Germany a drama will be enacted in comparison to which the French Revolution will seem to be an innocent idyll." Whether it would be the crown prince of Prussia or the leader of the German democracy who would rule, Heine foresees that the Germans would "fill the world with horror," and he warns Germany's neighbors to prepare their defenses.

As a poet Heine is rooted in the spiritual life of Germany. But as a champion of liberty Heine was decisively influenced by the ideas of the French Revolution of 1789. He connected his impulses deriving from France with his knowledge of German philosophy and history, and by this connection developed his own peculiar views concerning man's position in society and concerning the conditions and dangers of civilization. But even in thinking these ideas through he never surrendered the point of view of the German poet. Events out of French history, events in world history inspired by France, mingle with Heine's personal feelings, and their interpretation is the point of departure of his judgments on political values.

Heine lived to be fifty-nine years old. Almost twenty-five of these years, from June 1831 until his death in February 1856, he spent in France, with the exception of two journeys to Hamburg. His removal to France marks an important division in Heine's life. From this time on he was conscious that he was living in the closest proximity to the focal point of European events and tendencies, and at the same time, as an exile, he felt all of the disabilities of his isolation in heightened measure, until the serious illness which banished him to his "mattress crypt" for eight years completely effaced the distinction between exile and cosmopolis.

But Heine's removal to Paris was not the beginning of his relationship to France. From his early childhood onward he sensed his cultural affinity with that country, and until his young manhood he felt politically connected with France also. French soldiers occupied his native Duesseldorf until 1814. The city was ruled by Napoleon's brother-in-law, Murat, and then came directly under Napoleon's administration. The preponderant majority of the Rhenish population desired to belong to France permanently, and even when Prussia annexed the region it retained French judicial procedures and legislation, until the German civil code was introduced in 1900. Even after the end of the First World War there was a desire for the return of the Rhineland to France. Heine had good cause to complain that these events had transformed him from a French citizen to a Prussian subject. For this change lost Heine the political rights which France guaranteed its citizens without distinction of religion, and hence also the prospect of public office unless he went over to Christianity. Later Heine took this step and felt it as a personal humiliation his life long, whatever, in the course of time, his thoughts concerning Judaism and Christianity might have been. He never ceased reflecting that he would have been spared such humiliation and that his career might have taken a quite different turn if Napoleon had been victorious in Russia, at Leipzig, or at Waterloo. Several years before Heine left Germany, he associated himself with a group of German politicians whose goal was a renewal of the Napoleonic Rhine Union, and even from Paris he campaigned for this "French party"; but he soon realized that its strength was too slight to withstand the nationalist movement.

The immediate ground for Heine's emigration was his grave apprehension that he would be arrested. But along with this fear, he cherished a desire to witness in Paris, where the July revolution had broken out in 1830, the progress of a new French Revolution which would bring France, and with it Europe, a great stride nearer the political ideal. Heine's faith in the revolutionary mission of France lasted for almost a decade. Then came disillusion and resignation. His ideal was the realization of the ideas of the Revolution of 1789 by a man who should possess Napoleon's merits without his faults, who would unite republican freedom with the splendor of imperial rule. But such a man never came. Instead there was a growth of socialism and communism, which filled Heine with the gravest forebodings for the survival of civilization.

Heine was acquainted with almost all the founders of European socialism, and with many he was on terms of personal friendship. But only one socialist system, Saint-Simonism, seemed to him promising, even if for a brief period, and left perceptible traces in his view of life. In contrast to proletarian socialism the Saint-Simonists rejected social equality, advocated gradation of men according to their cultural merits, entrusted the restoration of social justice to an elite of technicians, scholars, bankers, or artists, and did not entirely exclude a princely ruler from government.

Much as Heine feared proletarian socialism, as a phenomenon it engaged his interest. He was convinced of the transitory victory of a proletarian revolution. The remoter future he imagined as a tragedy in three acts, beginning with a Franco-German war which would result in the destruction of civilization, passing then to a social war which would end with the victory of the have-nots over the haves, and then as the ultimate reaction, the strengthening of absolutism or Bonapartism.

Until 1840, the French were for Heine the chosen people of the revolution whose arms would liberate the other peoples. Then it would become the nursery of communism, which terrified Heine and at the same time fascinated him. "Communism is the grim hero for whom a great if only transitory role is destined in the modern tragedy," says Heine in *Lutetia*. Only briefly did Heine set his hopes upon Napoleon III. Very soon he turned from him in disillusionment.

Enthusiasm for the Revolution did not make Heine a republican. He admired Danton and Robespierre, but he saw "no inconsistency in the fact that I love this republic enthusiastically without in the slightest desiring this form of government to be introduced again." But faith in France's revolutionary mission often misled Heine to a false judgment of French policy and to a false estimate of the distribution of power in Europe. While this faith brought to an end Heine's preference for the French people, it did not terminate his interest in France. Heine's concept of history was strongly influenced by Voltaire, Thiers, Mignet, and Augustin Thierry. Beyond this, French cultural life left him cool. The classic drama of the French held little for one who revered Shakespeare. He rejected the French Romanticists for the most part. He set little value upon the French language as a poetic medium.

The starkest contrast is to be found in Heine's attitude to Christianity and Judaism. His expressions on this subject brought him more bitter enmity than his most venturesome political challenges. Heine's relation to Christianity reveals a chief trait in his general opposition to ruling forces, and the contemporary situation contributed considerably to his concentrating his opposition to Christianity as a religion as well as to the Church.

As long as the war which ended with the defeat of the Emperor was waged against Napoleon, when Heine was eighteen years old and awakened to self-awareness, the front of what he considered the opposition was neither united nor clear in its goals. Men fought in the name of the right of self-determination of peoples against a world dictatorship, but they fought also for the restoration of ancient dynasties against upstarts, for the expansion of national power against the might of France, for the retention of old privileges against the ideas of the French Revolution. Only a diminishing number of those immediately participating in the battle were in position to define with any clarity how far the war was being waged against the person and dictatorship of Napoleon, against the traditional power politics of France, or against revolutionary innovation. Even smaller was the number of those, either contemporary witnesses of the event or belonging to posterity, who were capable of formulating such distinctions. After Napoleon was decisively defeated at Waterloo, a strong alliance was formed among the victors between the dynasties and the opponents of revolutionary ideas, among whom the Christian churches occupied a dominant position. Whereas during the eighteenth century, before the outbreak of the French

Revolution, the "enlightened despots," despite their political conservatism, were rather cool to the Christian religion and sought to limit the rights of the Christian churches, a close alliance between "throne and altar" was proclaimed and translated into actuality after the fall of Napoleon. The revolutionary events had convinced monarchy and clergy of the solidarity of their mutual interests, and they gave one another support in their propaganda for dynastic loyalty and for churchly orthodoxy as well as in the struggle against innovations in the realm of politics and culture; these were branded as revolutionary even when they had nothing to do with subversive tendencies. Above all, the monarchic governments and the churches were at one in their resistance to liberalism and democracy. For this attitude they found a strong footing in the literature of the age, which was everywhere dominated by Romantic tendencies. The Romantic literature of Germany championed political and religious conservatism with the greatest energy and persistence. French Romanticism declared for a similar conservatism for a decade, but then went over to the camp of the political opposition. In England, Byron protested against these reactionary tendencies with a vehemence whose echo was heard throughout Europe and not least by Heine. Other influential English poets sympathized with the Romanticists of the continent and supported the conservatism of their own government.

In Napoleon, Heine saw, particularly in his youth, the man who actualized the Revolution, and in his fall, the defeat of freedom and democracy as well as grave damage to Heine's own private interests. In his protest against the defeat of Napoleon he was most deeply impressed by the alliance of "throne and altar." In this alliance he saw the essence of all reactionary tendencies which hampered the development of liberal institutions as well as his own career. But in the alliance the "altar" seemed to him a stronger and more dangerous force than the "throne." The political reaction which was represented by the dynasties and their cabinets provoked Heine's sarcasm. The pressure which the strengthened churchly orthodoxy exerted over spiritual life evoked his emotional antagonism. Heine thought little of the governments, cabinets, bureaucracy and police, even of the armies, in which reactionaries and revolutionaries of all shades saw the main support of their regime. He believed that the reactionary governments with all of their physical means of power could not survive without the help of the Church and would fall as soon as the Church lost its influence on the masses of people.

It was from this point of view that Heine persistently fought Christianity as a state Church. His strongest opposition was to Roman Catholicism; in Protestantism he saw a compromise of the Church with worldly reason. His opposition awakened in Heine a vivid sympathy with everything that Christianity vanquished, suppressed, or oppressed—with classical and Germanic paganism, with the Moors in Spain, with the victims of Christianization in Africa and America, with the martyrs of the Inquisition. Insofar as Heine in his youth took the part of the Jews, he did so because the Jews had suffered the greatest and longest oppression and persecution by the Church and still suffered from the consequences of the Church's dominant position in the state. But Heine had begun his campaign against Christianity as a "born contemner of all positive religion." Along with Christianity he rejected Judaism, and if he deplored the fall of Islam in Spain he was far from any predilections in favor of Mohammed's religion. He opposed a development in world history which brought Christianity triumph over other religions and dominion over Europe and the parts of the world colonized by Europe, and he rebelled against any tendency to reaffirm and continue this domination which had been shattered by enlightenment and revolution. Heine remained an antagonist of the Christian State-Church until his death, although his views of the character of the Christian religion altered along with his views of Judaism. This struggle he regarded as much more important than the battle concerning the form of the constitution of the state. From a victory over the State-Church he expected not only security for freedom of conscience but also salutary effects in morality and riddance of wrongs in all concerns of life.

From his conversion until his return to Judaism, Heine waged ruthless and bitter war against Christianity; he blamed it not only for religious oppression but also for overrating the spiritual at the expense of the sensual. This viewpoint Heine first developed in the *Reisebilder*, and then enlarged upon in Paris, after his emigration from Germany, in the broad historical perspective of his books on Germany. For many years this theme was of paramount importance, which it never wholly lost, because in Heine's poetry spirit and sensuality are indissolubly intertwined, and by very reason of their close relationship always in conflict with one another. Heightened sensuality and spiritual intensity incited Heine to poetic creativity. But when he stood outside the poetic creative process and reflected upon their effectiveness, spirit and senses became for Heine irreconcilable poles.

In this stark opposition of spirit and senses Heine was by no means alone. Many important poets and thinkers, before, during and after his time, experienced the same conflict. Modern criticism is not adequate to the psychologic and philosophic basis of this stark antithesis between spirit and sense. Heine was forced to convince himself that no satisfactory explanation of the most important problems which agitated him was to be attained on this basis. Nevertheless this antithesis exerted a powerful force of attraction upon his spirit even later.

Heine's ideal was a civilization in which the life of the spirit and sensuality were in harmonious equipoise so that both could attain unhampered development. He thought the Judaeo-Christian view of life disturbed this harmony. In Judaism and Christianity he saw religions which denied the world, which advocated asceticism and contempt of the senses—surely a one-sided view —and to combat this suppression of the senses he believed it was necessary to war upon exaggerated spiritualism until, when the Judaeo-Christian religion had been worsted, the original balance between spirit and senses should be restored. He expected that such a result could be achieved by a new religion whose creed would be compounded of ancient Greek paganism and modern pantheism, of rationalism and sensualism. At the same time he expected, under the influence of Saint-Simonism, that this religion would bring a solution of social problems.

But only for a few years did Heine persist in this point of view.

Experiences, events, and studies of various kinds brought him
to the realization that Hellenism, sensualism, and pantheism
were not capable of maintaining themselves in the reality of life.
He found his way to Judaism which he had so long falsely conceived as an ascetic religion which denies the world. Concomi-
tantly his attacks on Christianity also gradually decreased.

The historical relationships and the common ground of Judaism and Christianity long preoccupied Heine, but on this subject
he never attained the clarity which he so often shows elsewhere.
At one time Judaism is for him the classic religion of art-hating
asceticism, and Christianity only a weakened form of the same; at
another time he sees in Christianity the accentuation and complete development of the ascetic tendencies which are perceptible in Judaism only in germ. Undoubtedly Heine was misled in
his historical conception of both religions by his exaggerated
emphasis upon their ascetic character.

Heine would not have been Heine if he had not felt a tension
with regard to Judaism which expressed itself in strong contradictory attitudes. In general Heine had a true estimate of the
logic of unalterable facts; but he was not the man to be inwardly
content with unalterable facts. Certainly he is not to be counted
among the idealists or illusionists who refuse to recognize the
actualities of life because they do not correspond to their own
fundamental requirements; but he was never able to reconcile
himself to an actuality which did not correspond to his wishes,
even though he prudently accommodated the course of his life
to such actualities. Heine's philosophy of history assumed that
the destinies of individuals as of peoples are determined by laws
of causality; but this assumption never prevented his personal
feelings from branding such laws as unjust.

The fact that Heine was born a Jew at once distorted and enhanced his self-awareness. He early discovered that his Jewish
origin made his way difficult everywhere, and not least in his
literary career; but he felt that this disability confirmed his claim
to be spokesman for all that were oppressed and defamed.

Heine's reaction to the fact of his Jewish origin sharply out-
lines the conditions and influences upon which his importance

for the modern spirit rests. Whenever Heine took a stand on the
fate of the Jews and on Jewish tradition, he always gave utterance to the problems which particularly affected his personality
at the moment of utterance. As the problems changed, so did his
attitudes to Judaism, but so, too, did Heine's concept of his own
character and his personal claims. Whenever he discussed the
inner contradictions and the abuses of his age and of modern
civilization, he found himself faced with "the Jewish question."
At times he attempted to thrust it into the background of his
consciousness; frequently the Jewish problem was completely
amalgamated with other great questions which engaged Heine's
spirit; but even more frequently he felt himself constrained to
concentrate upon the fate of the Jews without digressions and
with exclusive attention upon their past, present and future.

But this reflection upon the problem of the Jews was made
difficult for Heine by circumstances for which he cannot be
made responsible. He sprang of a family which had dissolved its
inward bonds with Judaism, even if it had not broken with Judaism externally. He grew up without religious education. His
mother, the only human being whom he loved and honored
without reserve, had filled him with distaste for Judaism and hostility to its teachers. Until the last period of his life he was virtually without any knowledge of Jewish history and religion
drawn from Jewish sources. After he had long been dependent
upon writings on Jewish questions composed almost exclusively
by Christian or free-thinking opponents of Judaism, he only
gradually and with great difficulty attained to an independent
judgment of Jewish history, in which, however, the traces of anti-
Jewish influences never wholly disappeared. It was only the grave
illness which he had to endure, which opened up to him an
understanding of the Bible as a source of Jewish spirit and for
the people of the Bible.

In Heine's youthful letters there are to be found only disparaging remarks on Jews and Judaism, or expressions of complete
indifference on religious questions. What allied him to Judaism
without, however, uniting him with it, was his dislike for Christianity. The disabilities and persecutions to which the Jews were

exposed aroused his sympathy. But at first this had no different coloring than his sympathy for the vanished paganism of the Greeks, or for the Moors who were expelled from Spain. His feeling of solidarity was first aroused when he was confronted with the necessity of formally separating himself from the Jewish community and allowing himself to be baptized in order to be able to follow a civic career after the completion of his juristic studies. Heine made available his objections to the coercion of conversion to the efforts of the *Verein fuer Kultur und Wissenschaft der Juden*, whose members strove, but with inadequate forces, for an intellectual, moral and social regeneration of German Jewry. In his discussions with the members of this association, who were far superior to him in knowledge, Heine learned aspects of Jewish history which had previously been unknown to him. Even then Judaism held nothing for him as a religious force. His enthusiasm was not for the Bible but for the Jewish martyrs of the Middle Ages in Germany and Spain, who brought him to the realization that even Jews could be heroes. But if the heroism of Jews who preferred death or exile to change of faith moved him, the belief, the cause for which these martyrs suffered, left him untouched. What interested him was the picturesque aspect of medieval Jewry, not its inner force. It was in this frame of mind that Heine began his novel, *The Rabbi of Bacherach*. But the peculiar situation in which the author found himself prevented its completion. At every step Heine felt himself frustrated by his lack of Jewish knowledge. Aside from information which Zunz and Moser, the outstanding members of the *Kulturverein*, communicated to him by word of mouth or letter, Heine could resort only to Christian sources. He was even more hampered by the certainty that the novel which was to be written to glorify the Jewish past could not be completed before his own baptism. And so the *Rabbi* remained a fragment which was later enlarged but never completed.

It was not the conversion, but rather the campaign against Christianity which Heine waged with the greatest abandon after his conversion, that alienated Heine from Judaism for many years, although he was doubtless seriously hoping that his campaign would abolish all discrimination against the Jews. But the position from which he launched his attack upon Christianity brought him into sharp opposition to Judaism. Against the personal God of the Bible he proclaimed pantheism; against the Jewish moral law, unrestricted enjoyment of life; against the exaggerated value placed upon the spirit, "rehabilitation of matter." He divided mankind into "Nazarenes" and "Hellenes," into art-hating ascetics and lovers of art who enjoy life, and he numbered himself among the "Hellenes."

This pagan hedonism did not long maintain sole dominance of Heine's spirit, though it was never entirely forgotten. Keener observation of political, social, and economic events taught Heine that peoples, like individuals, could not base their existence upon aesthetics and sensuality alone.

In 1838, Heine began a gradual return to Judaism. In 1840, he led a great journalistic campaign on behalf of the Jews of Damascus, who had become victims of the blood superstition. On grounds of foreign policy the French government took no measures against the persecutors but even favored them, and Heine risked his own safety by his attacks on the French premier. In 1845, Michael Sachs' book on *The Religious Poetry of the Jews in Spain* opened a vista into the cultural life of Judaism. Under the profound impression made by the testimony of these Jewish poets who gave expression to their religious sentiments, Heine composed his *Romancero*, a work of far greater significance than the *Buch der Lieder*. It was while he was in the midst of this work that the sickness struck which banished Heine to his "mattress crypt" until his death. During his illness Heine read the Bible, the Old Testament, again and again, and through it rediscovered his ancestors' faith in a personal God. But Heine's return to God by no means implies reconciliation to the world. The songs of the *Romancero* and the poems written subsequently are fearful accusations against fate, terrifying eruptions of anguish at his own and humanity's misery, but they also contain noble reflections on the transitoriness and dubious worth of beauty and glory, the injustice of success, the illusion of happiness. Closely interwoven with these accusations are the glorification of the living spirit, rapture at the magic of beauty, which does not forfeit its power even when its brevity is recognized, joy in the pleasure of the moment even when the illusion of the senses is perceived. These poems no longer have the pregnant conciseness of the *Buch der Lieder*, but Heine's language has gained in energy and vigor of expression. Richness in visions and ideas has grown incomparably.

The road to Judaism which Heine had to travel was long. First he was distracted by anxiety concerning a civic profession. Then he believed that Judaism could not be combined with his life as an artist. Not only did his sickness bring Heine back to the God of his fathers; faith in God enabled Heine to endure his horrible disease and preserve the resilience of his spirit. Eye and hand had both failed when he wrote his last poems, composed in sleepless nights. His physical debility hampered his poetic productivity but did not paralyze it.

Heine never excluded his artistic sensibility when he took position on the facts, events, and problems of real life. But he lived in no ivory tower, as so many poets who have guided life by an aesthetic gauge have done. The convictions to which he attained in pondering religious and philosophical questions, as a political observer and campaigner, as eyewitness of social and economic processes, as interpreter of the cultural changes of his epoch, penetrated his poetic consciousness deeply. More than once these convictions changed, but they cannot be isolated from his artistic development. Their justice may be questioned, but not the righteousness with which Heine advocated them, even when he gave free rein to the play of his fantasy and his wit. In many another great poet active participation in philosophical or religious discussion has absorbed poetic creativity. But Heine, as his later compositions in particular show, was able to steep his contemplative and his polemical moods in poetry.

The outward obstacles due to Heine's Jewish origin, and the inner conflicts caused by his reflections on his origin, developed in him a new form of self-awareness and afforded him access he had previously not possessed to hidden strata in the human soul. They enabled him to judge European civilization with a freedom

from bias denied to non-Jewish poets and thinkers of equal
stature, because they were more closely bound to tradition and
could afford to be indifferent to prejudices of birth. But such
accidents of origin and position would have made Heine little
more than a literary curiosity if his artistic eminence had not
carried him through his antithetical situations and discovered for
his inner contradictions a form free of contradiction. To his peculiar composition he owes his faculty of giving expression to
extremely complicated psychic states in clear language and with
a refined simplicity, which enabled many of his poems to pass
from mouth to mouth and to serve as popular songs. Few artists
have polished their work as carefully as did Heine and have
tested the sound, accent, and expressiveness of every word before
they released their work for publication. And very few indeed
have succeeded, as Heine did, in conveying an impression of
unpremeditation, even of artless naturalness. It is this clarity and
simplicity which have won Heine's poetry recognition outside of
German-speaking countries. For a similar reason no other poet
has so richly inspired musical creativity. Heine's poems have
been set to music by Schubert, Schumann, Brahms, Hugo Wolf,
and many other more or less distinguished composers. It is estimated that some five thousand printed songs follow texts of
Heine.

Even greater was the incitement to and influence upon poetic
production that emanated from Heine. The history of modern
German literature is completely unintelligible if Heine is excluded. From him political poets like Ferdinand Freiligrath and
Georg Herwegh learned to employ verse as a satiric or pathetic
campaign medium; though neither of them can compare with
Heine's unerring wit. From Heine the important lyricists of the
post-Goethe epoch, like Theodor Storm, Gottfried Keller, Friedrich Hebbel, and countless minor poets like Geibel and Greif,
learned to shape song as an expression of subjective mood. But
none of them achieved Heine's union of ease and conciseness,
intensity and calm. Although the German lyric after the nineteenth century in many ways returned to the Romantic tendencies which Heine opposed, or yielded to the influence of French

symbolism, Heine's lyric has remained the model for free, easy-flowing, simple, and at the same time striking and gripping expression of an individuality; in every succeeding generation it has aroused love and hatred, but always it has remained interesting.

Heine's influence on German literature reaches much further than lyric. Richard Wagner has given full treatment to one of Heine's stories in his opera *The Flying Dutchman*. Wagner's *Tannhaeuser* is also influenced by Heine's poem on the same theme. A remark in Heine's writing on art criticism sufficed to open a new vista into feminine psychology for Friedrich Hebbel, the most important German dramatist of the post-classical period, and to make his tragedy *Judith* a pioneer work in modern German drama. From Heine the modern psychological novel learned to deduce activities of the soul from slight physical manifestations, or to present the inner history of a man by a bare description of a glance, a mouth, or a hand. For psychology and the art of language Friedrich Nietzsche learned much from Heine and honored and praised him as an "artist to his finger-tips."

Beyond the range of German-speaking countries also, poetry received fresh impulses from Heine. Above all in Dutch literature, which stands on a very high intellectual and artistic level, every new movement throughout a century has invoked Heine's ideas and poetic creations for theoretic justification. In the poetry of Italy and Spain, of the Scandinavian countries, of Russia, Poland, Hungary, and Rumania, literary groups and individuals have been encouraged by Heine to strike out on new paths. In France, too, traces of Heine's influence are perceptible from Théophile Gautier to Verlaine. In England, Heine has affected personalities as basically diverse as Tennyson, George Meredith, and Shaw. George Eliot and Matthew Arnold demonstrate that Heine did pioneer service in the cultural life of England. In America, Longfellow was the first to recognize the importance of Heine. He was followed by a distinguished succession of poets and critics—William Dean Howells, Marion Crawford, Emily Dickinson, and others—who have kept the memory of the author of the *Buch der Lieder* and the *Reisebilder* alive.

Traces of Heine's contributions to the shaping of the modern spirit are to be observed in very diverse manifestations of cultural life. By the melodic and stimulating expression of his personal moods and his general views, Heine has opened a new approach to the apprehension of reality. His acute criticism of life and his deep insight into the complicated structure of human character and modern civilization have pointed a new direction for psychology and have enriched understanding of inevitable and avoidable conflicts between the individual and society. The intimate relationship of Heine's poetry with his political, religious and philosophical writings has sharpened our sight for the close bond between art and life, even if Heine was himself in error. By his redintegration of the pantheist faith, which he avowed for many years with extreme passion, and by his return to the personal God of his fathers, Heine demonstrated that he possessed the moral strength openly to acknowledge error and that truth rated higher with him than prestige. Heine was by no means free from human weaknesses, but he never represented himself as better than he was.

In the period which has elapsed since Heine's death modern civilization has undergone numerous and basic changes. Much that aroused Heine's mockery and ire has vanished and been forgotten. Much that he advocated is now assumed as obvious. But many decisive problems with which he wrestled have remained real and will continue, in the foreseeable future, to occupy men's thoughts and arouse their emotions. Threatening perils which are as yet far from being allayed were foreseen by Heine. Even yet defenders and foes of freedom and of justice give keen attention when Heine's name is mentioned. For, despite all his inner conflicts and contradictions, Heinrich Heine fought unequivocally for justice and freedom his life long, and it is that fight, principally, that has brought him enmity after his death.

———

Several years before his death Heinrich Heine destroyed the bulky manuscript of his memoirs. In the last years of his life he began to write new memoirs, but these do not extend beyond the description of his childhood. Then death snatched the pen from his hand. But much autobiographical information is to be found in Heine's poetry, prose and letters. These data are here combined in a unified picture to present Heine's own interpretation of his life and work. The reliability of this information has often been underestimated. In many instances scientific investigation has confirmed, by the discovery of new documents, that Heine told the truth even when what he says seems dubious. In other instances he did indeed transmute actual events or present imaginary experiences if his artistic purpose demanded it. Stories which are demonstrably invented are not included in the present collection. Yet the editor has not limited himself to such descriptions as are literally and factually true in every detail. The reader must not expect to see in every sentence of Heine a strictly historical report, but frequently a reflection of truth in the spirit of the poet.

I

CHILDHOOD AND YOUTH

An early biographer of Goethe, who devoted his whole life to the study of that poet, was heartily ridiculed because he annotated a remark of Goethe's concerning a very personal matter with the comment, "Here Goethe is in error." The comment seemed to illustrate the presumption of a desiccated literary historian to be better informed concerning the inner life of a great poet than the poet himself. But the poor man did not deserve the ridicule. He did not wish to cast doubt on Goethe's feelings when he made the remark in question, but only to show that the poet's memory of past events in his life was not accurate when he put the remark to paper. That actually was the case. Even great men are subject to lapses of memory, especially when they employ such words as "never" or "always." What we call memory is not a scientifically constructed recording machine. It is a transforming, selective and rejecting force, deeply rooted in instincts and impulses. This transforming force is at its strongest in poets and artists. They are no less great when their memory deceives them.

Attempts to correct Heine's own autobiographical data must similarly incur the risk of being ridiculed, for there are persons who cannot imagine under what conditions Heine looked back upon his life and what circumstances enable the historian to recognize the statements of the poet as being in many cases in error. The historian's ability to do so by no means makes him superior to the poet. His position is different from Heine's. Heine wrote about his earlier life for the most part without having documents before him. He had to rely upon his memory, which frequently functioned superbly, frequently failed, sometimes reported facts faithfully and sometimes altered them greatly. Thanks to the industrious labors of earlier investigators, the historian has at hand

32

many documents which were not available to Heine. He can draw upon sources of which Heine did not and could not know. If he is thus better informed on many events in Heine's life than is Heine himself, at least at the moment of writing, he may claim no special credit for himself. But he can justly put forward another claim: Precisely the man who accurately establishes the conditions under which Heine expressed himself on his own life will feel entitled, and indeed obligated, to demonstrate that Heinrich Heine in his autobiographical statements generally told the truth as far as it was available to him, except when special considerations compelled him to transform the truth or when poetic purposes demanded such transformation.

But critical remarks on Heine's views concerning historical events, political occurrences, philosophical ideas and religious experiences cannot be divorced from criticism of his autobiographical statements. These views are inextricably blended with the events of Heine's life. In many quarters such criticism will doubtless expose the editor to greater suspicion than will the correction of biographical errors. But without such criticism, correction of biographical data must remain incomplete and frequently even unintelligible. Here, too, criticism must not imply depreciation of Heine's cultural contributions, even when that criticism takes exception to his views. Since Heine's death, scientific research has made immense advances in all the areas which interested Heine. Even years before his death, his illness made it impossible for the poet to follow such advances. Repeatedly he complained from his sickbed of the lack of books, and the state of his eyes prevented his reading. Even greater changes of general views have been occasioned by events in world history during the past century. All of these changes must be taken into consideration to obtain an accurate picture of Heine's standpoint and his contribution. They permit us to recognize Heine's historical limitations. It is nevertheless astonishing how often, with his imperfect tools, Heine recognized and pointed out the character of his age, how often he saw into the future correctly.

Samuel Johnson praised the author of the Seasons because his work contained "No line which dying he could wish to blot."

Heine did not hold such a view of his own production, though he was fully aware of the worth of his work. He polished his writings carefully. He frequently expressed dissatisfaction with his books after their publication and emended them in later editions. Like all great masters of style he recognized that the artist's self-criticism could not be silenced by popular success of his works.

Even less was Heine satisfied with all that he had done or omitted to do in life. Many of his deeds he would gladly have rendered undone. In moments of depression he spoke of his existence as:

> Failure in love, failure in life.

In other moods he comforted himself:

> Great follies have I committed—
> With cleverness I fared worse.

The avowal:

> In my own breast, I have with death
> Played the dying warrior's role

reveals the truth of his life with much greater clarity and precision than the poet realized when he wrote the verse. In actual fact he was a warrior long lingering in death, after joy in playing a role had long vanished. The gallantry with which Heine endured his horrible suffering reveals a human grandeur of a different sort than the longing and pride of his youth had promised.

From his Youthful Passion Heine traversed the road to his "mattress crypt." This road passed over pinnacles of happiness. Happiness did not silence melancholy. Unhappiness did not render humor mute. Heine's autobiographical expressions show how these contrasting moods interpenetrated his life and his poetry.

————

Heine was born on December 13, 1797. His father, Samson Heine, and his mother Peira, later Betty, van Geldern were married at the beginning of February 1797 according to the Jewish rite. Their eldest son was named Chaim, after his deceased pater-

nal grandfather, or, in German, Herz; but even as a small child
he was given the name of Harry, which he changed to Heinrich
at his baptism, which took place in 1825. Harry had a sister and
two brothers: Sarah, later called Charlotte (1800-1899); Gottschalk, later called Gustav (1805-1886); and Meyer, later called
Maximilian (1807-1879).

At Heine's birth, Duesseldorf belonged to the Palatinate, and
in 1806 it became the capital of the Grand Duchy of Berg, which
was ruled by Napoleon's brother-in-law Murat. In 1808, it came
under the direct administration of Napoleon, and in 1814 it
became Prussian.

After the annexation of Duesseldorf, the Prussian government
immediately introduced obligatory military service and con-
scripted youths born in 1797. Heine's parents exempted their
eldest son from military service by making him two years younger
than he actually was. They were able to do so because the birth
and circumcision registers of the Jewish community in Duesseldorf had been destroyed by fire some years before. Consequently
Heine found it necessary to give 1799 as his birth year in official
statements; in private remarks he repeatedly gave his correct birth
year as 1797.

The last moon beams of the eighteenth and the first red dawn
of the nineteenth century played about my cradle.
                        —Thoughts and Reflections (about 1854)

I was born at the end of the skeptical eighteenth century, and
in a town where not only the French, but also the genius of the
French, ruled during my childhood.
                                            —Memoirs (1855)

In my childhood I breathed the air of France.
                                        —To Philarète Chasles,
                                        Paris, January 11, 1835

I shall only say that the date of my birth is not exact in my
biographical records. Just between us, this error seems to have

arisen by reason of a wilful mistake committed in my favor at
the time of the Prussian invasion, in order to exempt me from
service to his majesty the King of Prussia.

—To Saint-René Taillandier
November 3, 1851

Ancestry

Heine was descended on both his father's and mother's sides
of old and respectable Jewish families whose merits are reported
in the annals of several Jewish communities of Germany. But
Heine never learned about these documents. What he knew of
his forebears he drew from information provided by his parents
and his maternal relatives.

The tradition of his paternal family in particular was extinguished for Heine. It was illuminated only many years after the
death of the poet by scholarly researchers. The Heine family
resided in Bueckeburg, the capital of a small principality. From
there, Isaak Heine visited the Leipzig fair; his presence at the fair
in the year 1697 is attested. His son, Aaron David Simon Heine,
who died in 1744, lived in Bueckeburg and Hanover. He was
regarded as a devout and charitable man and attached great value
to the religious education of his children. His eldest son, Heymann Heine, originally called Chaim Bueckeburg, was the poet's
grandfather. His first marriage was to Edel Gans, who died in
1757, his second to Mathe Eva Popert, the daughter of the respected banker, Meyer Schamschen Popert and his wife Frum-
met, née Heckscher, in Altona. Of Heymann Heine's second
marriage six sons were born: Isaak Heine, who removed to Bordeaux in France and there became a successful banker; Samson
Heine, the father of the poet; Salomon Heine, the Hamburg
banker and one of the richest men of his time; Meyer Heine, who
later resided at Schwerin in Mecklenburg; Samuel, who died
young; and Herz (Henry) Heine, a respectable broker in Hamburg. Heymann Heine died, apparently in straitened circumstances, in 1780. His widow subsequently married her widowed
brother-in-law, David Bendix Schiff; she died in 1799. Judah Loeb
Heine, younger brother of Heymann, remained in Bueckeburg,

where his son and grandson were court bankers until the middle
of the nineteenth century. When Heine sojourned in Bueckeburg in 1843 "in order to examine the citadel of his race" (Germany, Ch. 19), he was not aware that kinsmen bearing his name resided there, and occupied influential positions.

Once when I was a little boy, at the time when I spent my working days at the prim school of the Franciscans, and the Sabbath at home, I seized an opportunity to ask my father who my grandfather was. He answered my question, half laughing, half cross: "Your grandfather was a little Jew and he had a long beard."

Next day, as I entered the class-room where I found my schoolmates gathered together, I made haste to tell them the great news that my grandfather was a little Jew and had a long beard.

Scarcely had I made the communication than it flew from lip to lip, and was repeated in every different tone of voice to an accompaniment of mimic animal cries. The boys jumped over tables and benches, tore down from the walls the multiplication tables, which toppled down to the floor among the ink-pots, and they laughed, bleated, growled, barked, croaked—a pandemonium, in which the refrain was my grandfather, who had been a little Jew and had a long beard.

The master of the class heard the noise and came into the room blazing with anger and asked who was the creator of the uproar. As always happens in such a case, every one attempted feebly to exculpate himself, and at the end of the inquiry, it came about that luckless I was pitched upon as having caused the whole bother by my communication concerning my grandfather, and I paid for my offense with a considerable thrashing. . . .

Nor did I forget the name of the master who beat me so unmercifully: his name was Father Dickerscheit. . . .

Together with the name of the man who gave me my first beating there remained in my memory also the cause of it, my unlucky genealogical communication; and the influence of those early youthful impressions is so profound, that whenever I heard tell of little Jews with long beards, an uncanny recollection of it all crept over my back. "A scalded cat fears the boiling kettle," says the proverb, and it should be easy to understand that I have, since that time, had no great inclination to receive more particular information concerning my doubtful grandfather and his pedigree, or to make, to the great public as to the small, any communication so fraught with consequence.

I will not, however, pass unmentioned my paternal grandmother, of whom also I have little to say. She was an extraordinarily beautiful woman and the only daughter of a banker at Hamburg, celebrated far and wide for his wealth. The circumstances lead me to suspect that the little Jew, who led the beauty from the house of her opulent parents to his own dwelling-place, Hanover, must have possessed admirable qualities besides his long beard, and must have been very respectable.

—Memoirs

The poet knew a great deal more of his maternal van Geldern family than of the Heine family. The van Gelderns had played an important role in the history of the Jews at Duesseldorf and of all the lower Rhine, as in the economic life of the city and the province, for many decades. Heine's oldest maternal ancestor was Israel Jacobs, who presumably immigrated to Duesseldorf from Geldern and was highly esteemed as the court Jew of the Duke Wolfgang Wilhelm von Juelich-Berg. He died in 1650. His son Joseph Jacob van Geldern, called Juspa by his coreligionists, was the financial agent of the Elector Johann Wilhelm and his right hand in matters relating to finance. During the war of the Spanish Succession, in which the Elector participated, Juspa as "military provisioner" financed the pay and maintenance of the Palatine troops. In 1705, he shared in the administration of the Banca di Affrancationi which was directed by Christian bankers and whose principal office was in Cologne. His business relationships extended to England, Holland, France and Austria. He built himself a palace and bestowed a synagogue upon the Jewish community in Duesseldorf, of which he was president. He was married to Brunella Levi, and died in 1726. After his death, his widow continued the business, but she was unable to meet the competition of the Italian banks, and in 1733 was forced to enter bankruptcy; all the real property of the family was sold at auction. Juspa's son, Lazarus van Geldern, who was active in Vienna from 1716 to 1725, married the daughter of Simon Michael (Simon Pressburg), the Jewish coiner of the Emperors Leopold I and Joseph I and president of Hungarian Jewry. He succeeded his father as the Elector's financial agent and also as president of the Jewish community, but could not achieve his father's business success. In 1760, he was forced to appeal for a moratorium, and all his possessions were sold under the hammer. His sons, Simon and Gottschalk van Geldern, were more interested in scholarship than in business. Concerning the eldest son, Simon, Heine has spoken in some detail (p. 62, below). The second son, Gottschalk van Geldern (1726-1795), the poet's grandfather, studied medicine and obtained the doctorate in 1752. As "the Jewish doctor" he was highly esteemed, but nevertheless forced to mortgage his property in order to support his family. Gottschalk's sons also studied medicine. Joseph, the eldest (1765-1796), was court physician to Prince Karl Theodor of Bavaria; the second, Simon van Geldern (died 1833), influenced the cultural development of the young poet (p. 59, below). Gottschalk had three daughters: Brunella (Braeunele), who was married to Abraham Samuel; Johanna, who remained a spinster; and Peira (Peierche), the mother of the poet.

In his memoirs Heine described the history of his maternal ancestors in considerable detail on the basis of oral tradition. But his brother Maximilian, who endeavored to conceal the Jewish origin of his family, destroyed more than twenty fascicles of the manuscript, which were devoted chiefly to Heine's Jewish descent, after the poet's death. Only the following section, which has no connection with Judaism, escaped destruction.

When I entered the university my father's affairs were in a very sad state, and my mother sold her jewels, necklace and earrings of great value, to assure my maintenance for the first four years at the university.

I was indeed not the first of my family to have devoured

precious stones and gobbled pearls at the university. My mother's
father, as she once told me, tried the same trick. The jewels
which decorated his deceased mother's prayer-book had to defray
the expenses of his sojourn at the university when his father, the
old Lazarus van Geldern, was impoverished by litigation with a
married sister concerning an inheritance—Lazarus, who had inherited a fortune from his father of whose greatness an old great-
aunt used to tell me so many wonderful things.

To me as a boy it always sounded like tales from the *Arabian
Nights* when the old lady spoke of the great palaces and the Persian carpets and the massive gold and silverware which the good
man, who had been so respected at the court of the Elector and
Electress, so lamentably forfeited. The great hotel in Rhein-
strasse was his city house; what is now the hospital in Neustadt
also belonged to him, as did a castle at Gravenberg also—and at
the end he scarcely had a place to lay his head.

—Memoirs

In my father's beauty there was a weak, characterless, almost
effeminate quality. . . . But I do not mean to say that he was
less than a man; that he often proved to the contrary in his youth,
and indeed I am a living witness to it. Let it be understood that
the expression casts no slur; I had in my mind only his physical
appearance, which was not rigid and stiff but rather soft and
tender. The contour of his features lacked definiteness, and was
mistily vague. He was stout in his later years, but even in youth
he seems never to have been thin.

In this conjecture I am confirmed by a portrait, which was lost
in a fire in my mother's house, representing my father as a young
man of eighteen or nineteen, in a red uniform with a powdered
bag-wig on his head. The type of beauty expressed in his features
called to mind neither the severe and chaste ideality of Greek
art, nor the spiritual and visionary style, impregnated for all that
Pagan joy, of the Renaissance: no, the aforesaid portrait bore
rather the character of an age that had no character and loved
beauty less than prettiness, daintiness, and coquetry; an age that
brought insipidity even into its poetry, the sweet age of the

rococo with all its flourishes, which is called the age of the bag-wig, and wore for token not on its brow but on the back of its head a bag-wig. . . .

It is, perhaps, worthy of remark that even in his later years my father remained faithful to the old French mode of powder, although he had the finest hair conceivable. His hair was fair, almost golden, and of a softness such as I have only found in Chinese floss-silk. . . . The red uniform in which the counterfeit of my father appears in the aforesaid portrait betokens his official capacity in Hanover. My father was in the train of Prince Ernest of Cumberland at the beginning of the French Revolution and accompanied him on the campaign in Flanders and Brabant in the capacity of a store-master or commissary. . . .

In that campaign were begotten many of my father's tastes from which my mother was able only gradually to wean him. For instance, he was easily induced to play high, and he used to patronize dramatic art, or, rather, its votaries, and he had a passion for dogs and horses. . . . In my father's camp days was also begotten his boundless love for the soldiery, or rather for playing at soldiers, and his delight in that gay, idle life, in which spangles and scarlet caps conceal the emptiness inside and tickled vanity can strut as courage. . . .

What happiness then for my father when the citizen army was raised at Duesseldorf and, as an officer, he could don his fine dark-blue uniform, with sky-blue satin slashings, and march past our house at the head of his column. . . .

Unbounded love of life was a predominant characteristic of my father; he was a seeker after pleasure, gay and sanguine. In his mind was constant festival. . . . There was always blue sky for him and brightness, lightheartedness and tantara! Careless he was and never gave a thought to the day that was gone or the day that was to come. . . .

Indeed he was a great child with a child-like naïveté, which dull psychologists might easily take for simplicity, but it often betrayed in some subtle expression a most remarkable perception.

He would divine with his mental feelers what it took wise men much time and pondering to grasp. He thought less with his head than with his heart, and he had the dearest heart conceivable. . . .

Of all men he was to me the most beloved on this earth. He has been dead now for more than twenty-five years. I never thought that I must one day lose him and even now I can scarcely believe that he is indeed lost to me. . . . There has never been a night when my father has not been in my thoughts and when I awake in the morning I often seem to hear the ringing sound of his voice like the echo of a dream. . . .

Many people have their hearts in the right place, but they do not know how to give, and it takes a long while for the heart's will to find its way to the pocket; the interval between the good intention and its execution creeps slowly along like a post-snail. But between my father's heart and his pocket there was an express railroad. That the operation of this railway did not enrich him must be obvious. . . .

It is remarkable that this man who was so bad at advising himself was yet shrewd enough in practical things when it came to giving others in some difficult situation good advice. . . .

I was accused of blasphemy, and my father delivered the longest homily that he ever made. It sounded something like this: "My dear son! Your mother makes you study philosophy with Rector Schallmeyer. That is her affair. For my part I have no liking for philosophy, for it is sheer superstition, and I am a merchant and need my brains for my business. You can be as much a philosopher as you please, but I ask you not to say in public what you think, for it would injure me in my business if my customers were to hear that I have a son who does not believe in God: the Jews especially, would buy no velveteen of me, and they are honorable people and pay promptly, and do quite rightly cling to their religion. I am your father and therefore older than you, and therefore more experienced: you must believe me when I tell you that atheism is a great sin."

—Memoirs

Though Heine's characterization of his father is not without criticism, filial love prevented him from uttering the full truth. According to the testimony of the physicians who treated him,

Samson Heine suffered from epileptic seizures. In 1819, he suffered a complete mental breakdown. He was placed under guardianship and his brothers Salomon and Henry undertook his care. His mental confusion was now and again interrupted by sane moments but remained incurable. The months which the poet spent with his father after the outbreak of his mental disease gravely affected his nervous system, which was very delicate from childhood. Although Heine did not suffer from epilepsy, the cramps which later afflicted him in Paris were similar to his father's attacks. Heine doubtless knew that his own disease was inherited from his father, but he never uttered a word on the subject beside the remark that his attacks of the cramps were often like his father's. After his father's death he frequently mentioned him with love and honor in letters to his family. Nor did he admit that, even before his illness, Samson Heine was never able to support his family without the assistance of his brothers. The father was completely without means when he came to Duesseldorf in 1796 and there won the love of Peira van Geldern. The administration of the Jewish community therefore denied him the right of settlement. Peira van Geldern overcame this objection by appealing to secular officials and procured a government order to the rabbi to receive Samson Heine into the community. The energy of Heine's mother came to the rescue when the father failed in the management of his business. But eventually she too was unable to avoid bankruptcy (1819).

To my Mother

(1)

I have been wont to bear my head on high,
  Haughty and stern am I of mood and mien,
  Yea, tho' a king should gaze on me, I ween,
I should not at his gaze cast down my eye.
But I will speak, dear Mother, candidly:
  When most puffed up my haughty mood hath been,
  At thy sweet presence, blissful and serene,
I feel the shudder of humility.

Does thy soul all unknown my soul subdue,
Thy lofty soul that pierces all things through,
And speeds on lightning wings to heaven's blue?
Or am I racked by what my memories tell
Of frequent deeds which caused thy heart to swell—
That beauteous heart which loved me, ah! too well.

(2)

Thee had I once in a mad dream forsaken,
 And then I longed to roam the wide world over
 To see, perchance, if I might Love discover,
And, with embraces loving, Love awaken!
 I made my search for Love thro' all the ways,
Before each door with outstretched hands implored,
Like any beggar, alms from Love's rich hoard.
 Men sneered, and froze me with their scornful gaze,
But in my love-search never ceasing, ever
For Love, still Love, I sought and found it never;
 Then turning once more homeward, sick with care,
Thou didst come forth to meet me—was I dreaming?
For oh, behold! in thy deep eyes lay gleaming
 Love, the long sought-for, sweetest Love, was there.
       —The Book of Songs

My Mother . . . was in the greatest fear that I might become
a poet—that was the worst, she used to say, that could happen
to me. The notions bound up with the name of poet in those
days were not particularly honorable, and a poet was a poor devil
out-at-elbows, who supplied occasional verse for a few shillings,
and in the end died in the hospital. . . .

My mother had in her mind great, ambitious projects for me,
and her whole plan of education was directed to that end. She
played the chief part in the history of my education, she mapped
out the programs of my studies, and even before my birth she
had begun her plans. I followed her express wishes obediently,
but I confess that she was to blame for the unfruitfulness of most

of my endeavors and strivings in civic employment, for it was never in accord with my nature which, far more than material circumstances, decided my fate.

The stars of our fortune are in ourselves. At first it was the splendor of the Empire that dazzled my mother, and when the daughter of a hardware manufacturer of our neighborhood, a friend of my mother's, became a duchess and told her that her husband [Marshal Soult] had won many battles and would shortly be promoted to kingship—ah, then my mother dreamed for me of the most golden of epaulettes or the most elaborately embroidered office at the Emperor's Court, to whose service she designed to devote me. Therefore I had to pursue a course of such studies as would promote such a career, and although quite enough attention was paid to mathematical science at the *lycée* and I was properly crammed by dear old Professor Brewer with geometry, statics, hydrostatics, hydraulics and so forth, and though I swam in a sea of logarithms and algebra, yet I had to take private tuition in such mental exercises as would set me on the way to becoming a great strategist, even, if need be, an administrator of conquered provinces.

However, with the fall of the Empire my mother was compelled to renounce the glorious career which she had dreamed of for me. The studies pursued to that end came to a stop, and, marvelous to relate, left not a trace in my spirit, so alien were they to it. It was only a mechanical attainment, which I cast aside, like so much useless lumber.

—Memoirs

In this connection I often recall a conversation I had with my mother about eight years ago when I visited the old lady, then already an octogenarian, in Hamburg. When we were speaking of the schools in which I spent my boyhood and of my Catholic teachers, she let slip an extraordinary remark. . . . We spoke a good deal of our dear old Schallmeyer who was made rector of the Duesseldorf *lycée* in the French period. . . . My grandfather had once saved him from a very grave illness. In consequence the old gentleman frequently spoke to my mother about my education and future career, and it was in these conversations, as my mother later told me in Hamburg, that he advised her to devote me to the service of the Church and to send me to Rome to study Catholic theology in a seminary there; Rector Schallmeyer assured her that he would be in position, through influential friends among the highest ranking prelates in Rome, to advance me to some important Church preferment. While my mother told me this she regretted that she had not followed the counsel of the spiritual old man who had so early understood my true nature and correctly grasped what spiritual and physical climate might be most appropriate and wholesome for it. Now the old lady is sorry she rejected so reasonable a suggestion, but at that time she dreamed of lofty worldly dignities for me. Furthermore she was a disciple of Rousseau, a strict deist, and it seemed to her quite wrong to put her son in the cassock which displeased her so when worn so clumsily by German priests. She did not know how differently the Roman abbots wore their cassocks, with what grace and what coquetry they shrugged their shoulders clad in the black silk mantles which are the pious uniform of gallantry and preciosity in eternally beautiful Rome. . . . In the end I might have risen to the loftiest post of honor, for although I am not by nature ambitious I should not have turned down a nomination to be Pope.

—Confessions (1854)

Now my mother began to dream of a brilliant future for me in another direction.

The house of Rothschild, with whose head my father was acquainted, had already at that time entered upon its fabulous prosperity; and other princes of banking and industry had arisen in our neighborhood, and my mother declared that the hour had come when a man of brains could attain an incredible height in business, and could raise himself to the loftiest pinnacle of temporal power. She resolved, therefore, that I should become a power in finance, and I was set to study foreign languages, especially English, geography, book-keeping; in short, all the sciences relating to commerce by land and sea, and to trade. . . .

A celebrated merchant with whom I was to become *un apprenti millionaire* was of the opinion that I had no talent for business, and I laughingly confessed that he was very probably right.

Shortly afterwards there came a great business crisis and my father, like many of our friends, lost his fortune. The mercantile bubble burst even more quickly and lamentably than did the imperial, and my mother now had to dream up another career for me.

She now thought I must by all means study the law. She had noticed that in England for a long while, but in France also and in constitutional Germany, lawyers were all-powerful, and in particular, by reason of their habit of public speaking, advocates played principal roles of loquacity and thereby rose to the highest offices of state. My mother's observations were quite correct. . . .

I concluded my accursed legal studies but I could never resolve to make use of my attainment and, perhaps because I felt that others would easily outsoar me in pettifogging, I hung my juridical mortar-board upon a nail. My mother put on a gloomier face than usual. But I was now a grown man at an age to forego maternal guardianship.

The good woman had grown older and since, after so many fiascos, she had given up supervising my life, she regretted, as we noticed above, that she had not devoted me to a clerical career.

Now she is a matron of eighty-seven years and her spirit has not suffered from age. She had never pretended to mastery over my true thoughts and for me she was always compassion and love personified.

Her faith was a strict deism, quite suitable to the dominant direction of her reason. She was a disciple of Rousseau, had read his *Emile*, suckled her own children and education was her hobby-horse. She herself had had a bookish education and studied along with one of her brothers who became a distinguished physician but died young. Even as a quite young girl she was required to read Latin dissertations and other scholarly writings to her father, and she often astonished the old man by her questions.

Her reason and her sensibility were wholesomeness itself; I inherited no feeling for fantasy or romance from her. She had a dread of poetry, as I have mentioned, tore from my hands any novel she found, permitted me no visit to the theater, forbade me any participation in folk plays, watched over my associations, scolded housemaids who told ghost stories in my presence—in a word, did everything possible to remove me from superstition and poetry.

—Memoirs

A number of Heine's mother's letters, written before her marriage, in German language but with Hebrew characters, are preserved. These confirm what Heine says of the cultural interests of his mother. They also indicate a lively participation in current events and in German patriotism. Betty van Geldern understood Latin, Hebrew, English and French, but had no sure mastery over these languages. Nor is her German free of faults in grammar and syntax. Her inclination towards the ideas of Rousseau and of the German enlightenment alienated her from traditional Judaism. Her quarrel with the Duesseldorf rabbis, Salomon and Abraham Scheuer, concerning Samson Heine's admittance to the community (see p. 43, above) accentuated this conflict. Later, too, she appears to have been involved in further disagreements with the rabbinate. Her eldest son she allowed to be educated in a Jewish elementary school for only a short period, but then permitted none of her children instruction in the Jewish sense, although the French school administration prescribed that Jewish children should receive religious instruction from teachers of their own community. None of her sons became bar-mitzvah. The daughter was given to the family of an evangelical pastor to be educated. But, on the other hand, her "strict deism" forbade her conversion to Christianity. She was buried in a Jewish cemetery. But, as the poet wrote her in a letter dated May 7, 1853, in her "disinclination towards the Jews" she went much further than seemed to him proper. And so Heine grew up without knowledge of Jewish religion and Jewish history. Only at an advanced stage of his studies, in Berlin, did he begin laboriously to acquire a knowledge of Judaism from Jewish sources. What he knew of Jewish history, religion and ethics in his childhood and early youth was influenced either by his Christian school, or by the concept of history, particularly Voltaire's, characteristic of the enlightenment. Both gave him a badly distorted picture. Heine's father was at first inclined towards Jewish orthodoxy, but was later persuaded by his wife to join the Freemasons. His schooling, his reading and his mother's influence kept young Heine far from Judaism, although the outward connection with the Jewish community was maintained intact. The fashion in which Heine as an eight-year-old, according to his boyhood friend Joseph Neunzig, exploited the Sabbath laws according to his own convenience—once he refused to help in extinguishing a fire, alleging the Sabbath as the reason, and another time he bit grapes from an arbor with his teeth because plucking was forbidden on the Sabbath—is no proof of pious observance but rather of skeptic slyness. Only one component of Jewish tradition remained vital in Heine's family. That was the strong coloring of their colloquial language by Hebrew and Judaeo-German words. Until the end Heine used such words in letters to his mother, to his brothers and sister, and to certain Jewish friends, with relish. He was also able to write cursive Hebrew and used it for confidential communications in German. The Hebrew language remained foreign to him.

Despite the ironical criticism with which Heine describes his mother's educational endeavors, he not only loved her but revered her intensely. The exiled poet's longing for his mother finds expression in gripping verses (see p. 43, above). After he was afflicted with his fatal illness he was most anxious that his mother be kept in ignorance of his suffering.

Growing Pains

To Sister

> My child, we were two children,
> Small, merry by childhood's law;
> We used to creep to the henhouse,
> And hide ourselves in the straw.

We crowed like cocks, and whenever
The passers near us drew—
"Cock-a-doodle!" they thought
'Twas a real cock that crew.

The boxes about our courtyard
We carpeted to our mind,
And lived there both together—
Kept house in a noble kind.

The neighbor's old cat often
Came to pay us a visit;
(We have made the very same speeches
Each with a compliment in it.)

After her health we asked,
Our care and regard to evince—
(We have made the very same speeches
To many an old cat since.)

We also sat and wisely
Discoursed, as old folks do,
Complaining how all went better
In those good old times we knew;—

How love, and truth, and believing
Had left the world to itself,
And how so dear was the coffee,
And how so rare was the pelf.

The children's games are over,
The rest is over with youth—
The world, the good games, the good times,
The belief, and the love, and the truth.
                    —Book of Songs, "The Homecoming," 38

Childhood Memories

The beautiful world-old legends
That oft in my boyhood
By neighbor children were told,
When in the summer twilight
Through the quiet story we huddled
On the stone steps by the house-door—
Our little hearts all aflutter,
And eyes as round as saucers—
Meanwhile the older maidens,
Peeping through the fragrant flowers,
Sat across in the opposite window,
Their rosy faces
Smiling and moon-bewitched.

—"The North Sea," First Cycle, 2

When I was a boy I always experienced a hot longing when
beautifully baked *tarts*, of which I was to have none, were carried
by, wafting their fragrance; later I experienced the same sort of
prickly feeling when beautiful ladies, modishly decolletée,
strolled past.

—Travel Pictures, "North Sea," 3

In childhood days when yet I wore
Childhood's simple pinafore,
To infants' school my footsteps turned
Where first my ABC's I learned.
I was the only boy, the only one,
In that birdcage of a room.
Girls a dozen, darlings all,
Like birdies there did peep and call,
All atwittering, all atrilling,
All most woeful in their spelling.
Dame Hindermans sat sedate,
Spectacles on long nose, in state,
(Rather 'twas an owl's beak we spied)

Her little head bobbed from side to side,
And in her hand a birchen rod
Wherewith her tiny brood to prod—
The tearful, wretched little mite,
Whose spelling would not come out right.
　　　　　　　　　　　　　　　　—"Citronia"

If I now inquire: What is God? what is his nature?—it is something I had already inquired as a little child: How is God? what is he like? In that childish time I could gaze upwards at the sky during whole days, and was sadly vexed at evening because I never caught a glimpse of God's most holy countenance but saw only the gray, silly grimaces of the clouds. I was quite puzzled over the astronomical lore with which in the period of the "enlightenment" even the youngest children were tormented, and there was no end to my amazement on learning that all those thousand million of stars were spheres as large and as beautiful as our own earth and that over all this glittering throng of worlds a single God ruled. I recollect once seeing God in a dream far above in the most distant firmament. He was looking contentedly out of a little window in the sky, a devout hoaryheaded being with a small Jewish beard, and he was scattering forth myriads of seed-corns, which, as they fell from heaven, burst open in the infinitude of space, and expanded to vast dimensions till they became actual, radiant blossoming, peopled worlds, each one as large as our own globe. I could never forget this countenance, and often in dreams I used to see the cheerful-looking old man sprinkling forth the world seeds from his little window in the sky.
　　　　　　　　　　—Religion and Philosophy in Germany, 3

There was a time when I devoutly kissed the hand of every Capuchin I met on the street. I was a child, and my father left me in peace, knowing well enough that my lips would not always be content with Capuchin flesh. And in fact I did grow bigger and bigger, and kissed pretty women.
　　　　　　　　　　　　　　　　—Elementary Spirits

At that time rulers were not so beset with cares as now, their crowns being grown more firmly to their heads, and at night they even covered these with a nightcap, and slept peacefully. The nations slept quietly at their feet, and greeted them in the morning with a "Good morning, father!" to which they gave answer, "Good morning, my dear children!"

But suddenly all this was changed. One morning when we awoke at Duesseldorf, and were about to say, "Good morning, father!" lo! he had departed. Everywhere there was heaviness of heart, a funereal air pervaded everything, the people crept silently to the market to read the long paper placard on the door of the town-hall. The weather was dull; nevertheless, spare tailor Kilian stood looking at the placard mumbling to himself with thin trembling lips, in his nankeen jacket which was only meant for home wear, and with his blue woollen stockings so carelessly put on that they showed his puny bare legs. An old pensioner from the Palatinate read it in a higher key, and at many of the words a bright tear trickled down his honest white beard. I stood by him and wept, and asked him why he wept. He answered, "the Archduke desires to express his thanks"—and after a pause he continued, weeping still more bitterly—"for the long-tried fidelity of his subjects, and releases them of their allegiance. . . ."

I, however, went home weeping and mourning over the Archduke's proclamation. My mother was in despair; I knew what I knew, and would not be convinced to the contrary. I went to bed in tears and dreamed that the world was coming to an end. . . .

When I awoke the sun was shining through my windows as usual. I heard the sound of drums in the street, and when I entered our sitting room and said good morning to my father who was in his white dressing gown, I heard the nimble hair dresser, whilst doing his hair, had told him to a hair every particular of the coronation of the Archduke Joachim which was to take place that day in the townhall; how the new Archduke came of one of the best families, was married to the Emperor Napoleon's sister, was a perfect gentleman, wore his black hair in long ringlets, and how he would soon enter the town in state, and was certain to gain every woman's heart. Meanwhile I heard the beating of the drums in the street. I went to the front door and saw the French entering the town—this nation rejoicing in their glory, marching through the world to the sound of lute and tabor, the grave-gay faces of the grenadiers, the bear-skin caps, the tri-color cockades, the glittering bayonets, the merry knights full of *point d'honneur* and the great powerful drum major dressed in silver lace who could throw his gold-knobbed stick up to the first story of a house and his eyes as high as the second story, where pretty girls were sitting at the windows. I was glad at the thought of having soldiers quartered upon us—much more so than my mother—and I rushed to the market-place. There all was changed; the world looked as if freshly painted; a new coat of arms hung over the town-hall, the iron balcony was covered with embroidered velvet, French grenadiers were on guard, the old town councillors had put on fresh faces as well as their Sunday suits, and looked at each other as though they were Frenchmen and said *bon jour*. Ladies peered out of all the windows, inquisitive townsmen and gay soldiers filled the square, and I with other boys climbed up on to the great archducal horse, and looked at the motley crowd assembled in the market-place beneath us. . . .

The world appeared all right again next day, school went on as before, and we again prepared our lessons. Roman history, dates, nouns ending in *im*, irregular verbs, Greek, Hebrew, geography, German, mental arithmetic—heavens! the thought of it all makes me giddy—everything had to be learned by heart. . . . Dates are essential; I know people who have nothing in their heads but a few dates, but were thus able to find the right houses in Berlin and are now full professors. But at school these numbers caused me endless anguish. But arithmetic proper was worse still. I understood subtraction best, and there we have a very useful rule: "Four won't go from three, and so we must borrow one"—but I advise everybody in such cases to borrow a few pennies more: one can never know—.

But as to Latin, fair lady, you have no idea how complicated that is. The Romans would certainly not have had time to conquer the world if they had first had to learn Latin. These happy people knew while yet in their cradles which nouns take *im* in the accusative. But I had to learn this by heart in the sweat of my brow. . . . Of Greek I shall not even speak, or I shall grow too angry. The monks of the Middle Ages were not altogether mistaken when they declared Greek to be an invention of the devil. God knows the sufferings to which it subjected me. With Hebrew I fared better, for I always had a great predilection for the Jews, although they crucify my good name down to this hour. But I could not get on in Hebrew as well as my watch did, which was on intimate terms with moneylenders and thus learned many a Jewish habit—for example, not to go on a Saturday, and to speak the sacred language which it afterwards studied grammatically, as I often heard to my astonishment in sleepless nights when it ticked to itself in these words: katal, katalta, katalti; kittel, kittalta, kittalti; pokat, pokadeti; pikat; pik; pik.

However, I understood German better, and that is not so very easy. . . . A good part of the German language I learned from old Rector Schallmeyer, a good clergyman who had been interested in me from childhood. But I also learned some of it from Professor Schramm, who had written a book on everlasting peace, and in whose class my school fellows used to quarrel more than in any other class. . . . I will avail myself of this opportunity to show you, fair lady, that it was not my fault that I learned so little geography as not to be afterwards able to find my way about the world. At that time the French had altered all frontiers. Every day some country or other was newly tinted; those formerly blue suddenly became green, many even became red as blood; the definite facts of our school books grew so confused and mixed up that not even a devil could longer recognize them. Natural products also changed; chicory and beet-root grew where formerly there had been only hares and sportive young noblemen. Even the characters of people changed; the Germans became agile, the French ceased paying compliments, the English left off throwing their money out the window, and the Venetians were no longer sly enough. Among princes there was much promotion: old kings received new uniforms, new kingdoms were baked and sold off like hot cakes, whilst many potentates were sent about their business and had to earn their bread some other way. . . .

In this respect natural history is better, for here there cannot be so many changes, and we get distinct engravings of monkeys, kangaroos, zebras, rhinoceroses, and the like. As these pictures were firmly impressed upon my memory, it afterwards often happened that many people at first sight seemed to me like old friends.

In mythology, also, things went well. My chief delight was in that crew of gods who ruled the world in their frank nudity. I do not think that any school boy in old Rome ever got his chief articles of faith, for example, the loves of Venus, better by heart than I did. Honestly speaking, as we had to learn all the gods off by heart, we ought to have remembered them, and perhaps we are not much better off with our modern doctrine of the Romish Trinity or even of the Jewish Unity. . . .

But I fared best of all in the French class of the Abbé d'Aulnoi, a French émigré who had written many grammars, wore a red wig, and jumped about merrily when he recited his *Art Poétique* and his *Histoire Allemande*. He was the only person in the whole school who taught German history. However, French, too, has its difficulties, and in order to learn it we have to have soldiers quartered upon us and much drumming through the streets; there must be much *apprendre par coeur*, and above all one must not be a *bête allemande*. There was many a sour word. I remember well, as though it had only happened yesterday, that I experienced much discomfort owing to the word *la religion*. Full six times I was asked, "Henri, what is 'faith' in French?" And six times, each more tearful, I replied "le crédit." And the seventh time the furious examiner cried out, with a face red as a cherry, "It is *la religion*"; there was a rain of blows, and all my school-mates laughed.

—Ideas: The Book LeGrand

I was most vexed with French poetry, which was an affliction to me from my youth onwards.

The prime fault is probably the accursed Abbé Daunoi's, who

taught the French language at the Lyceum in Duesseldorf and brought every pressure to bear upon me to compose French verses. It wanted but little for him to make me abhor, not only French poetry, but poetry in general. . . .

Even now I can imagine nothing more insipid than the metrical system of French poetry, the *art de peindre par les images*, as the French themselves define it; this perverted notion perhaps contributes to their habit of always falling into pictorial circumlocutions.

Their meter was surely invented by Procrustes. It is a veritable straitjacket for thought, which is surely too spiritless to require one. That the beauty of a poem consists in overcoming metrical difficulties is a ridiculous principle which derives from the same silly source. . . .

So I think now, and so I felt even as a boy; and it is easy to imagine that differences between me and the old brown wig must break out into open hostility when I explained to him that it was utterly impossible for me to compose French verses. He declared that I had no sense for poetry, and called me a barbarian of the Teutoburg Forest. . . .

I could die for France, but compose French verses—never!

—Memoirs

It was Catholic priests to whom I owed my earliest instruction as a child and who guided my initial spiritual progress. In the higher educational institution at Duesseldorf, called the Lyceum under the French regime, the teachers were also almost all Catholic clergy, and all of them were concerned, with their grave kindliness, for my religious education. After the Prussian invasion, when the school adopted the Prussian-Greek name "Gymnasium," the priests were gradually displaced by secular teachers.

—Confessions

It is surely significant that as early as my thirteenth year all systems of free thinkers were presented to me, and indeed by a worthy cleric who did not in the least neglect his sacerdotal duties; I early saw how religion and doubt could walk calmly side by side without hypocrisy, and in consequence acquired not only unbelief but the most tolerant indifference.

—Memoirs

The favorable judgment with which Heine repeatedly testified his gratitude as a former pupil of the Duesseldorf Lyceum was not shared by the higher educational administration and historians of pedagogy. It is indeed generally acknowledged that Professor Aegidius Jacob Schallmeyer (1750-1818), whom Heine always characterizes with particular warmth, was a learned theologian and philosopher and a well-meaning teacher; but as director and administrator of the school he failed. As Heine aptly notices, Schallmeyer drew a sharp distinction in his philosophical lectures between the faith of the Church and the presentation of philosophical doctrines. Heine's distaste for Aulnoi, the French teacher, was apparently accentuated by the fact that Aulnoi was an ardent opponent of Napoleon. Heine entered the preparatory school of the Lyceum on August 1, 1804, after he had attended an evangelical school, which he describes in Citronia (p. 51-52), and for a short while, a private Jewish school run by a relative of the Heine family called Rintelsohn. The preparatory school used a former Franciscan cloister, but was not a monastery school. Its teachers, like those at the Lyceum, were former Catholic priests, of whom many were quite unsuited for teaching. In 1811, Heine entered the Lyceum, and from 1812 onwards attended Schallmeyer's classes in philosophy. For other school subjects Heine showed no particular gifts. His name does not occur in honors lists. Even years after Heine left school his letters betray uncertainty and errors in the use of prepositions. It was only about 1820, and after hard study, that Heine began to master the German language.

"The Life and Adventures of the Ingenious Knight Don Quixote de la Mancha set down by Miguel de Cervantes Saavedra," was the first book that I read after I arrived at boyhood's years of discretion and had tolerably mastered my letters. I have a very clear recollection of that time when, a very small boy, I stole from the house in the early morning and hurried away to

the Palace gardens, there to read *Don Quixote* in peace. It was
a fine May day: Spring in bloom lay listening in the still morning light and her praises sung by the nightingale, her sweet flatterer, who sang her song of praise with such soft caress, such
melting sounds, that the most timid buds burst open, and the
amorous grass and the scented sunbeams made haste to kiss, and
trees and flowers shivered in sheer delight. But I sat upon a mossy
old bench of stone in the Avenue of Sighs, as they call it, not far
from the waterfall, and charmed my little heart with the brave
adventures of the bold knight. In my childish heart I took it all
in earnest and however laughably the poor hero might be the
sport of Fate, I thought that it must be so, that it must be the
way of heroes to bear ridicule as well as the wounds of the body,
and I was brought to suffering by it, I shared it in my soul. I was
a child and knew not the irony which God has begotten in his
world, and the great poet in his little world of print imitates—
and I was able to shed the most bitter tears when the noble
knight for all his magnanimity only came by ingratitude and
blows. . . . Dulcinea's knight rose higher and higher in my esteem
and won my love ever more the longer I read the wonderful
book, and this I did every day in the garden, so that by the
autumn I had come to an end of the history—and never shall I
forget the day when I read of the sorrowful encounter in which
the knight was so shamefully laid low!

—Introduction to Don Quixote

The first book from which I learned to read French was the
Fables of La Fontaine; its naïve, sensible manner of speech impressed itself on my recollection ineffaceably, and as I now came
to Paris and heard French spoken everywhere, I was constantly
reminded of La Fontaine's *Fables*, I constantly imagined I was
hearing the well-known animal voices; now the lion spoke, then
the wolf, then the lamb, or the stork, or the dove; not seldom I
thought, I caught the voice of the fox.

—Florentine Nights: Second Night

Next to mother, her brother, my uncle Simon van Geldern,
was most concerned with my cultural development. He was a

queer fish, of unprepossessing and even foolish appearance. . . .
He dressed in old-fashioned clothes—short breeches, white silk
stockings, buckle shoes, and, after the old style, a longish pigtail. . . .

Often, when my uncle was sitting lost in thought or reading
the newspapers, a naughty longing would creep over me by
stealth to seize hold of his pigtail and tug at it like a bell-pull. . . .

However, if the man's exterior was not of a sort to inspire
respect, the inner man, the heart of him, was the more worthy of
regard, and he was the most honest and generous fellow that I
have ever met upon this earth. There was an honesty of purpose
in the man which called to mind the stern sense of honor of the
old Spanish drama; and for loyalty he was like one of their heroes.
. . . He was by no means an ascetic enemy of the senses; he doted
on fairs and the wine tavern of mine host Rasia, where he loved
to eat fieldfares and juniper-berries—but he would sacrifice
proudly and firmly all the fieldfares of this world and all the
pleasures of life if it were a question of an idea which he knew
to be good and true. And he would make his sacrifice so unpre-
tentiously and with such bashfulness that it was never remarked
what a martyr lay concealed beneath this facetious exterior.

From the material standpoint his life was a failure. Simon van
Geldern had pursued the so-called humanist studies—*humaniora*
—at the college of the Jesuits, but when the death of his parents
gave him free and full choice of a career he made none, renounced every practical study in foreign universities and preferred to remain at home in Duesseldorf in the "Noah's Ark," as
the little house was called that his father left him and that had
over its door a Noah's Ark quite charmingly carved and gaily
colored.

A man of untiring industry, he gave himself up to all his
learned hobbies and cranks, to his bibliomania, and especially to
his passion for writing, which had its chief outlet in political
news-sheets and obscure periodicals. It should be mentioned that
not only writing but also thinking was the greatest effort for
him. . . .

This uncle had a great influence on my mental development,

and for that I can never cease to thank him. However different
our points of view, and however laborious his literary efforts may
have been, it was perhaps they that roused in me the desire to
attempt to write.

My uncle wrote in a stiff formal style, such as is taught at the
Jesuit schools, where Latin is the chief subject, and could not
bring himself to look with a friendly eye upon my mode of
expression, which seemed to him too light, too frivolous and too
irreverent. But the zeal with which he pointed out for me the
means of intellectual development was of the greatest use to me.

When I was quite a boy he presented me with the finest and
most costly works, he placed his library at my disposal—it was
very rich in classical books and weighty tracts for the times—and
he even allowed me to burrow in the chests in the attic of Noah's
Ark which contained the old books and manuscripts of my
grandfather.

What sweet glee leaped in my boyish heart as I passed whole
days in that attic, a real garret of a place. . . .

Among the antiquities of the attic were globes, the most wonderful pictures of the planets, and soldering irons and retorts,
calling to mind astrological and alchemistic studies.

In the chests among my grandfather's books were also many
writings relating to such secret sciences. Most of the volumes
were trashy old medical books. There was no lack of philosophical tomes, but along with the arch-reasonable Descartes were
phantasts like Paracelsus, van Helmont, and even Agrippa von
Nettesheim, whose Philosophia Occulta I here came upon for
the first time. Boy though I was, I was amused by the epistle
dedicatory to the Abbot Trithem, and the accompanying reply,
in which one initiate repaid the bombastic compliments of his
fellow charlatan with interest.

Many of the writings which pertained to his grandfather's
interests Heine studied also later with great application, and he
used them for his books on German philosophy and religion
as well as for his work on the elemental spirits and his preparatory studies for his Faust ballet.

But the greatest and most precious find that I made in the dusty chests was a notebook written by a brother of my grandfather, who was known as "the Chevalier" or "the Oriental," and of whom my old aunts had many marvels to tell. This great-uncle, whose name was also Simon van Geldern, must have been a strange fellow. He was nicknamed "the Oriental" because he had travelled much in the east, and when he returned always wore Oriental clothes. . . .

A puzzling phenomenon, difficult to grasp, was this great-uncle. He led one of those wonderful lives which were only possible at the beginning or in the middle of the eighteenth century. He was half fanatic, making propaganda for cosmopolitan Utopias to bring blessing upon the world, half knight-errant, who, in the consciousness of his own strength breaks through or overleaps the rotten confines of a rotten society. In any case he was quite a man.

His quackery, which we do not cloak, was of no common order. He was no ordinary charlatan to draw the teeth of the peasants in the market place, but he thrust his way into the palaces of the great and plucked out their very back teeth for them, as once upon a time Sir Huon of Bordeaux did for the Sultan of Babylon. Puff is part of the trade, says the proverb, and life is a trade like any other.

And what man of any consequence is not a bit of a charlatan? The quacks of modesty are the worst of all with their conceit of their humble doing! If any man wishes to work upon the mob he must have quack ingredients. . . .

However that may be, my great-uncle busied his young relative's imagination to an extraordinary degree. Everything that was told of him made an ineradicable impression on my young intelligence, and I was so steeped in his wanderings and fortunes that often in the clear light of the sun I was seized by an uncanny feeling, and it seemed to me that I myself might be my deceased great-uncle, and was living only a continuation of a life long laid down.

In the night the same idea was reflected in my dreams. My life at that time was like a large newspaper of which the upper half contained the present, each day with its news and debates, while in the lower half, in a succession of dreams, the poetic past was recorded fantastically like a series of *feuilletons*. In these dreams I identified myself completely with my great-uncle, and it was a horror for me to feel that I was someone else and belonged to a different time. There were in that region relationships which I had never before suspected, and yet I wandered there sure of foot and bearing.

There I met men strangely garbed in bright-hot colors, men with wild adventurous faces, whom I nevertheless took by the hand like old acquaintances; I understood their barbarous, unfamiliar language, and answered them to my own astonishment in the same, while I gesticulated with a vehemence not my own and said things violently opposed to my habitual mode of thought.

This wonderful state of things lasted for about a year, and though I altogether recovered my singleness of being, yet there remained secret traces of it in my soul. Many idiosyncrasies, many extremely annoying sympathies and antipathies not at all in accordance with my nature, and many practices contrary to my habit of mind I explain to myself as after-effects of that time of dreams when I was my own great-uncle.

When I make mistakes the origin of which seems inexplicable to me, I lay them to the account of my oriental double. When I mooted such an hypothesis to my father by way of extenuation of some small misdeed, he observed waggishly that he hoped my great-uncle had not put his name to a bill of exchange which might be presented to me for payment.

No such oriental bill of exchange has been presented to me and I have had a long enough account with my own occidental obligations.

—Memoirs

The travel journal of the elder Simon van Geldern has been preserved and in part printed long after Heinrich Heine's death. The publication confirms Heine's judgment concerning his great-uncle. He was born in 1720 and began his travels shortly after

1747. He toured European and Asiatic Turkey, lingered in Jerusalem, and visited Egypt as well as almost all the principal cities
of Europe. He died on the road, in Alsace, near Colmar, in 1774.

Heine's remarks on the influence of this personality on his
imagination and his emotional life constitute one of his most
revealing confessions and self-analyses. Modern psychology designates the phenomena which Heine describes as depersonalization, schizophrenia, day-dreaming. The tendency towards
depersonalization of which Heine first becomes aware in his recollections of "the Oriental" remained a significant element in his
poetic constitution. Myths and legends penetrated his spirit irre-
sistibly and fused with impressions of the present. A related
aspect is Heine's frequent inclination to the dead, to marble
statues and to ghosts.

The allusion to Huon of Bordeaux refers to Wieland's Oberon.

Napoleon in Duesseldorf

When I think of the great Emperor, then all is summer green
and golden in my thoughts; a long avenue of limes blooms forth
into my vision, and in the bowers of their branches sit singing
nightingales: a waterfall roars, flowers stand in round beds and
dreamily nod their lovely heads—and I was in wonderful near-
ness to it all. The painted tulips greeted me with beggarly pride
and condescension; the nerve-sick lilies nodded tender and woe-
begone; the drunken red roses greeted me laughing from afar, the
night-violets sighed—I was not yet acquainted with the myrtles
and laurels, for they lured not with glowing blossoms, but I was
on particularly good terms with the mignonette, with whom I
now stand so ill—I am speaking of the palace garden at Duesseldorf, where often I lay on the turf and listened eagerly while
Monsieur LeGrand told me of the warlike deeds of the great
Emperor, and beat out the marches that had been drummed
during the doing of those deeds, so that I saw and heard everything vividly. I saw the march over the Simplon, the Emperor in
the van and the brave grenadiers climbing behind, while the
startled birds raised their clamor and the glaciers thundered in

the distance; I saw the Emperor, banner in hand, on the bridge of Lodi; I saw the Emperor in a gray coat at Marengo; I saw the Emperor ahorse in the battle at the pyramids, a blur of powder-smoke and mamelukes; I saw the Emperor at the battle of Austerlitz—ah, how the shots whistled over the icy, slippery road! I saw, I heard, the battle at Jena—dum, dum, dum; I heard the battle at Eylau, Wagram—nay, I could hardly bear it. Monsieur LeGrand drummed so that he well-nigh broke the drum of my ear.

But how did I feel when I saw him, I myself, with thrice-blessed eyes, his very self? Hosannah! The Emperor!

It was in the very avenue of the palace garden at Duesseldorf. As I thrust my way through the throng, I thought of the deeds and the battles which Monsieur LeGrand had drummed to me, and my heart beat the march of the General—and yet, at the same time, I thought of the police order prohibiting riding through the avenue, penalty five taler—and the Emperor with his suite rode down the middle of the avenue, and the scared trees bowed as he passed, and the sunbeams trembled in fear and curiosity through the green leaves, and in the blue heavens there swam visibly a golden star. The Emperor was wearing his modest green uniform and his little cocked hat known the world over. He was riding a little white horse that paced so calmly, so proudly, so securely, and with such an air—if I had been Crown Prince of Prussia at the time I should have envied that little horse. Listlessly sat the Emperor, almost loosely, and one hand held the rein high, and the other tapped gently on the neck of the little horse—it was a sunny, marble hand, a mighty hand, one of the two hands which had subdued the hydra-headed monster of anarchy and had brought order to the duel between nations—and it good-naturedly tapped the neck of the horse. The visage, too, had the color we find on marble heads of Greeks and Romans, and its lineaments were noble and restrained, like an ancient portrait, and upon this visage was inscribed: Thou shalt have no other gods besides me. A smile which warmed and calmed every heart hovered over the lips; and yet everyone knew that those lips needed but to whistle *et la Prusse n'existait plus;*

those lips needed but to whistle and all the clergy would have ceased to exist; those lips needed but to whistle and the whole Holy Roman Empire would dance. But those lips smiled, and the eye smiled too. It was an eye clear as heaven, it could read the hearts of men, it comprehended at a glance everything in the world, while we others saw them only gradually, saw only their painted shadows. The brow was not so clear; upon it nested the spirits of future battles. Ever and anon that brow twitched— and that was the creative thoughts, the great seven-league-boot thoughts with which the Emperor's spirit strode invisibly over the world; I think each of these thoughts might have provided a German writer material for all his life long.

The Emperor rode calmly down the middle of the avenue. No agent of the police opposed him; behind him proudly rode his followers on foaming steeds, and they were laden with gold and adornments; the drums rattled, the trumpets blared; near me Aloysius the Fool threaded his way and babbled the names of the Generals; not far off sottish Gumpertz bellowed, and with a thousand thousand voices the people cried, "Long live the Emperor!"

—Ideas. The Book LeGrand, 7-8

Napoleon's visit to Duesseldorf which Heine describes took place in the summer of 1811. The clergy of all faiths had also assembled to greet the Emperor and had chosen as their spokesman the Rabbi Abraham Scheuer who had refused Samson Heine the right to settle in Duesseldorf and with whom the poet's mother had had several other quarrels. Scheuer's address, in which he celebrated Napoleon as "the new Cyrus," was highly regarded generally and very graciously received by the Emperor. He responded to the rabbi with the words: "Before God all men are brothers. They should love and help one another without regard to differences of religion." This reply aroused great enthusiasm among the Jews of Duesseldorf. Undoubtedly it was joyfully discussed in Heine's household also. We may assume with equal assurance that the thirteen-year-old Harry, although he was distant from the Jewish religion, was deeply impressed. Hence-

forth he was convinced that the Jewish question would have been brought to a satisfactory solution if Napoleon's regime had endured. But because Rabbi Scheuer was on bad terms with his mother, the poet never mentioned this event.

Youthful Passion—Redhaired Sefchen

This woman was known as the Woman of Goch, because she was born at Goch, where her late husband lived and plied the infamous trade of executioner and was called in from near and far to exercise his office. It was known that he left his widow many *arcana*, and she knew well how to exploit her reputation. . . .

But indeed it was not witchcraft that took me to the house of the Woman of Goch. I continued my acquaintance with her, and I was about sixteen years old when I took to going more frequently than before to her house, attracted by a spell more potent than all her bombastic Latin philtres. She had a niece who was barely sixteen, but, having suddenly shot up and grown very tall, seemed to be much older, and because of her sudden growth she was very thin. She had that slimness of figure which is to be found in the quadroons of the West Indies, and, as she wore no corsets and very few undergarments her close-fitting gown was like wet cloth on a statue. No marble statue could vie with her in beauty, for she revealed life itself, and every movement showed forth the rhythm of her body and, I fain would say, the music of her soul. Not one of the daughters of Niobe had a face more nobly moulded: its color, like that of all her skin, was of a changing white. Her great, deep, dark eyes looked as though they had asked a riddle and were waiting tranquilly for the answer to it; while her mouth with its thin, arching lips and chalk-white teeth, rather long, seemed to say, "You are stupid, and will guess in vain."

Her hair was red, red as blood, and hung in long tresses below her shoulders, so that she could bind them together under her chin. When she did that, she looked as if her throat had been cut and the red blood were bubbling forth in red streams.

Josepha's voice—the pretty niece of the Woman of Goch was

called Red Sefchen—was not particularly sweet of sound, and sometimes her organs of speech were so muffled as to make her voice almost toneless; but suddenly, when passion came into it, there would break forth the most ringing sound, which particularly enraptured me, because Josepha's voice so much resembled my own.

When she spoke I was sometimes afraid and thought that I had heard myself speaking, and when she sang I was reminded of dreams in which I had heard myself sing after the same fashion.

She knew many old folk-songs and perhaps she called into being my taste for such songs, as she certainly had the greatest influence on the poet awaking within me, so that my first poems of the *Dream Pictures*, written soon after this time, have a grim and gloomy tinge like the relationship which at that time cast its bloody shadow on my young mind and life.

Among the songs which Josepha sang was a folk-song which . . . had often been sung to me in my childhood, so that I recollect two stanzas. . . . This is how they run—first wicked Tragig speaks:

> "Ottilia mine, Ottilia dear,
> You will not be the last I fear—
> Say, will you hang from yon high tree?
> Or will you swim the ocean blue?
> Or will you kiss the naked sword
> That is given by the Lord?"

Whereupon Ottilia answers:

> "I will not hang from yon high tree,
> I will not swim the ocean blue;
> But I will kiss the naked sword
> That is given by the Lord."

Once when Red Sefchen was singing the song and came to the end of this stanza, and I saw the emotion that was in her, I was so moved that I suddenly burst into tears, and we fell into each other's arms sobbing, uttering no word for perhaps an hour, while the tears ran from our eyes and we saw each other through a veil of tears.

I asked Sefchen to write the verses down for me and she did so; but she wrote them not in ink, but in her own blood. I lost the red autograph, but the verses remained indelibly imprinted on my memory.

The husband of the Woman of Goch was the brother of Sefchen's father, and was also an executioner, and as he died young the Woman of Goch adopted the child. But when her husband died soon afterwards and she settled in Duesseldorf, she gave the child to its grandfather, who was also an executioner and lived in Westphalia.

Here in the Free House, as they used to call the executioner's house, Sefchen stayed until she was fourteen and then her grandfather died, and the Woman of Goch once more gave a home to the orphan.

Owing to the disgrace of her birth Sefchen had to lead a lonely life from her childhood until adolescence, and in her grandfather's house she was cut off from all company. Hence came her shyness, her sensitive drawing away from contact with strangers, her mysterious day-dreams, together with the most obstinate truculence, the most insolent stubbornness and wildness. . . .

Once, when the woman of Goch was not at home, I asked Sefchen to show me her grandfather's executioner's sword. I had not long to ask and she went to the room and came back with a monstrous sword which she swung mightily in spite of the weakness of her arms, whilst she sang, half in menace and half in roguery,

> "Wilt thou kiss the naked sword
> That is given by the Lord?"

And in the same tone of voice I replied, "I will not kiss the bright, bright sword, I will kiss Red Sefchen!" And as she could not withstand me for fear of hurting me with the deadly steel, she had to let me kiss her, and very warmly I laid hands on her slender hips and kissed her defiant lips. Yes, in spite of the executioner's sword with which a hundred poor rascals had been beheaded, and in spite of the infamy which taints those who come in contact with any of that disgraceful trade, I kissed the lovely daughter of the executioner.

I kissed her not only because of my own tender feeling for her, but in scorn of society and all its dark prejudices; and in that moment there flared up in me one of the first flames of those two passions to which my later life has been devoted: the love of fair women, and the love of the French Revolution, the modern *furor francese* with which I, too, was seized in the struggle with medieval feudalism.

I shall not go into my love for Josepha in greater detail. But so much I will confess, that it was the prelude to the great tragedies of my riper period.

—Memoirs

Student in Frankfort

After Duesseldorf became Prussian in 1814, Heine left the Lyceum to prepare for a merchant's career at a business school. In 1815, his father apprenticed him to the banker Rindskopf in Frankfort. He left the banking business very soon and entered a colonial goods business as apprentice. Here too he stood it for only a few weeks, and returned to Duesseldorf.

It was in the year 1815 after the birth of Christ that I first heard the name of Boerne. I was with my father in the market in Frankfort, whither he had taken me with him in order that I might look about me and see what was to be seen: to improve my mind, as he said. It was a great spectacle. In the so-called booths above the Zeil, I saw the wax-works—wild animals and freaks of art and nature. My father also showed me the large shops, Christian as well as Jewish, in which one could buy goods at ten percent under wholesale—and still be cheated. He pointed out the Rathaus and the Guild Hall, where German emperors were bought, at ten percent under wholesale. Eventually this merchandise was completely exhausted. One day my father took me to the reading-room of one of the △ or □ lodges, where he often used to sup, drink coffee, play cards, and perform other such duties of freemasonry. While I was deep in reading a newspaper, a young man sitting near me whispered, "That is Dr. Boerne, who writes against the play-actors."

Looking up I saw a man who passed up and down the room several times seeking a newspaper, and soon went out again. Little time though he stayed, yet the whole being of the man lingered in my memory, and even now I could present him like a copyist's facsimile. He wore a black dress-coat, quite splendidly new, and gleaming white linen, but he wore them not like a fop but with a certain careless indifference which showed clearly enough that he had not long dallied before the mirror tying the knot of his white cravat and that he had pulled his coat on immediately the tailor brought it, without taking time to try whether it was tight or loose.

He was neither short nor tall in stature, neither thin nor stout; his face was neither ruddy nor pale, but of a reddish paleness or palish redness, and its predominant expression was one of exclusiveness and distinction, of a certain disdain such as one finds in men who feel themselves to be superior to their station, but have doubts of public acknowledgement of this. It was not that inner majesty which one sees in the countenance of a king or genius hiding under an incognito in the throng, but rather that revolutionary and more or less titanic discontent which one finds in the faces of pretenders of all sorts. His bearing, his movement, his gait, had a quality of sureness, definiteness, character. Are extraordinary men secretly surrounded by the rays of their spirit? Do our minds tell us of such glory as we cannot see with our physical eyes? The moral storm in such an extraordinary man has perhaps an electric effect on young unformed minds coming into contact with him, much as a material storm has an effect on cats. A flash from the eyes of this man touched me, I know not how, and I never forgot the touch nor the Doctor Boerne who wrote against the play-actors.

—Ludwig Boerne

Zeil is the principal street in Frankfort-on-the-Main. In the Guild Hall, the Council House of Frankfort, the Emperors of the Holy Roman Empire were elected and crowned. The last Emperor was Francis II, who was elected in 1792 and laid the crown of Germany down in 1806. Aside from Napoleon, Ludwig Boerne (1786-1837) was the first famous man whom Heine encountered personally. We cannot be sure whether he knew anything of Boerne's writings at that time. But Heine had already begun to write poetry and had already resolved to become a writer, though he could as yet see no way to realize his life-plan. Hence he must have been deeply moved by the sight of the critic who had so quickly become famous and who was, like himself, of Jewish origin.

First Hamburg Sojourn

Although, during his brief apprenticeship in Frankfort, Heine had shown no interest in, or capacity for, the career of merchant, his mother was still determined to force him to similar attempts in the same direction. In 1816, Salomon Heine, the younger brother of Samson, came to visit Duesseldorf, accompanied by his daughter Amalie. At a family council which took place on this occasion, Salomon Heine declared himself ready to set his nephew Harry up in his banking business. Shortly thereafter Harry proceeded to Hamburg and entered the firm of M. Heckscher & Company, which had been founded in 1797 and whose principal shareholder was Salomon Heine, until, in 1819, he opened a bank under his own name.

His rapid rise made Salomon Heine one of the largest bankers in Europe. His fortune was estimated at thirty millions. With no higher education and no personal participation in cultural life, Salomon Heine was nevertheless extremely well informed not only on economic but also on political matters, and understood how to make shrewd use of his knowledge. Baron Nathan Rothschild said of him, "When I tell him to buy for me, he buys the double for himself." He gave generously for humanitarian purposes, and supported Jewish and non-Jewish charitable institutions with a free hand; even the Orthodox-Evangelical domestic mission received contributions from him. But he remained a very precise, even petty calculator, and the slightest error could provoke his vehement anger. His speech and his private correspondence were shot through with Hebrew and Judaeo-German expressions. He also sponsored the Jewish Reform movement in Hamburg. But he was indifferent to religion and acknowledged Judaism chiefly in protest against the German government's discriminatory measures against the Jews. His daughters he married off to converted Jews.

Samson Heine and his family had long been dependent upon Salomon Heine. With Harry Heine's arrival in Hamburg began the poet's dependence upon his rich uncle which was to continue even after the latter's death. In view of the characters of uncle and nephew and of their opposing attitudes to life, conflicts were inevitable. There would surely have been conflict even if the nephew had led a life more suitable to the uncle's exclusive devotion to business, even if he were more prudent in his personal relations and more correct in balancing accounts with his uncle. Moreover, their relationship was darkened by malignant third parties who exploited every opportunity to prejudice the uncle against his nephew. Especially did Salomon's sons-in-law, who were frequently offended by the poet's sharp tongue, constantly endeavor to make Heine distasteful to his uncle. Even in his latest poems Heine avenged himself upon his kinsmen for these and other injuries to his dignity. He believed his claim to Salomon Heine's support was equal to that of his more immediate family, and always tried to convince his uncle that he was obligated to provide him support, whereas Salomon Heine expected and demanded to be celebrated as a benefactor and was unwilling to acknowledge any obligation. It was precisely because the poet could never forego his uncle's material support that he was especially concerned to preserve his own dignity vis-à-vis the head of the family. He could not even resist the temptation to irritate the man upon whom he was dependent by puckish jests. Many times his ready wit succeeded in dissipating his uncle's annoyance at his financial demands. But his wit also often militated against him. In any case, Heine eventually brought it about that his uncle respected the poet in him and was even proud of him—but not, as became a prudent merchant, before first obtaining a professional opinion from Hamburg's literary authority, Professor Zimmermann. On the other hand, Heine felt for his uncle not only the decent affection of a kinsman; the coarse and primitive nature of the man who had risen by force of his energy impressed him scarcely less than his weaknesses amused him. All the more was he pained by the harshness and disappointments to which he was exposed. He must often have felt that Salomon Heine and his immediate family despised him as a poor relation. Salomon Heine's house to him was "Affront Castle," and he never forgave the annoyances he suffered there. They early gave a grim tone to his poetic sensibility and his outlook; they tinted his concept of human nature with scepticism and even cynicism, and they sharpened his social criticism.

In this milieu of "Affront Castle," Heine experienced his first great and unhappy love. This was the unrequited love of Amalie Heine, whom he had met briefly in his parents' home in Duesseldorf. Apparently the object of his love never discovered what a turmoil she aroused in her cousin's emotions. Her father, Salomon Heine, surely had no inkling of it. For ten years Heine himself kept the name of his beloved silent, and then he communicated it only to trusted friends.

The obvious incongruity between the vehemence of the young poet's passion and the spirit and character of the girl who was its object has caused many of Heine's judges, even many of his admirers, to believe that he overestimated his emotion or exaggerated its expression. But in Heine's loves, according to his oft repeated avowals, sensual beauty was always of decisive importance. No one can appreciate how deeply and intensely another may be moved by the lineaments of a woman's face or the form of her figure. There is no need to doubt that Amalie's beauty, or what Heine regarded as her beauty, moved the poet of Youthful Passion as vehemently as his verses indicate. The only gauge of the intensity of the actual feeling which dominated Heine is the lyric worth of his poems, not knowledge—uncertain at best

—of Amalie's personality. It is very probable that the loving poet endowed his beloved with qualities she did not in fact possess; but this does not alter his immediate emotion, and subsequent recognition of the illusion intensified his disappointment. But for judging Heine's Youthful Passion, we must not leave out of account the fact that his love experience—like its prelude, the love of Josepha (see pp. 67 ff., above)—ran its course in the untrammeled region of his emotion and thought. It made him more acutely conscious of his own peculiar spirit, it permitted him to appreciate the full fury of emotional excitement, and it filled him with contempt of the conventional reactions of his environment which seemed to him a caricature of true feeling. His erotic failure showed him that brutal reality had a very different aspect than the world of his dreams and aspirations, and this experience brought him to the conclusion that in social life generally realization of aspirations for the happiness of the individual must encounter equally great hindrances. Thus Heine felt his disappointed love not only as a misfortune but as a grave injustice for which the general state of society and the imperfection of civilization were to be made responsible. Thence he proceeded to the further conclusion that all imperfections, cleavages and contradictions in his own inner life were caused by the shortcomings, disharmonies and unresolved problems of the civilization of his time. This view, which is given expression in Youthful Passion, Heine held until his death.

His experiences in "Affront Castle" and his disappointment over Amalie influenced Heine's view of life in Hamburg and of its people. His sojourn in Hamburg lasted from 1816 to 1819. For two years he was a minor functionary in Salomon Heine's bank. He seems to have done better there than in Frankfort, for in 1818 his uncle set him up in a commission business dealing in manufactured articles under the name of Harry Heine & Co. But the uncle was gravely disappointed. The new businessman was seldom to be seen in his office, but spent most of his business hours in the café; and a year later the firm was liquidated. The only documents of Heine's activity as a businessman which are preserved are three protests on bills of exchange. In the summer

of *1819, Heine returned to Duesseldorf, after his uncle had promised him means for studying law.*

*Amalie Heine married John Friedlaender, a property owner in
Koenigsberg, in 1821. During his Hamburg sojourn, Heine composed the greater part of the "Dream Pictures," songs and romances of the Youthful Passion. Some of these poems appeared
under the pseudonym Sy Freudhold Riesenharf (an anagram of
Harry Heine, Duesseldorf) in the antisemitic journal Hamburgs
Waechter in 1817.*

The city of Hamburg is a good city, full of solid houses. Shameful Macbeth is not ruler here, but Banquo. The ghost of Banquo
rules everywhere in this little free state, whose visible chief is a
wise and noble Senate. Indeed, it is a free state, and the greatest
political freedom exists in it. The citizens can do as they will,
and the noble and wise Senate can do as it will; every man is here
the free lord of his affairs. It is a republic. If Lafayette had not
had the fortune of finding Louis Phillippe, he would certainly
have recommended to the notice of his Frenchmen the Senators
and Aldermen of Hamburg. Hamburg is the best republic. Its
customs are English and its food is heavenly. Indeed, there are
dishes between Wandrahmen and Dreckwall of which our philosophers know nothing. The people of Hamburg are good fellows and they eat well. Their opinions on religion, science, and
politics are very varied, but there is a most beautiful concord in
the matter of eating. Dispute as its local Christian theologians
may concerning the importance of The Supper, on the importance of lunch they are quite unanimous. If there is a party
among the local Jews which says grace after meat in German
while another chants it in Hebrew, both parties eat well and
have a proper appreciation of food. . . .

The population of Hamburg may approach 100,000. I do not
know exactly, although I spent a whole day in parading the
streets in order to observe the men and women in them. And I
have most certainly overlooked many a man, for the ladies called
for so much of my particular attention. The ladies I found not
thin, but for the most part plump, but for all that charmingly

pretty. . . . As for the men, I saw for the most part stunted figures, clever cold eyes, low foreheads, pendulous red cheeks, jaws particularly well developed, hats that seemed to be nailed on to their heads, and their hands in their breeches pocket, as one who is about so say, "What do I have to pay?" . . .

For readers who do not know Hamburg—there are such, I suppose, in China or Upper Bavaria—I must remark that the most beautiful promenade of the sons and daughters of Hammonia bears the appropriate name of Jungfernsteeg, and that it consists of an avenue of lime trees, which is bounded on one side by a row of houses, and on the other by the Alster Basin, and that before the latter, and built out into the water, are two tent-like pleasant cafés, called pavilions. It is nice to sit there, especially in front of one called the Swiss Pavilion, of a summer's day, when the afternoon sun is not too hot, but only smiles gaily and pours its rays as in a fairy dream over the lindens, the houses, the people, the Alster, and the swans who cradle themselves in it. Yes, it is nice to sit there; and so I sat on many a summer afternoon and thought, as a young man generally does, that is to say, about nothing at all, and looked at what a young man generally looks at, that is, the girls as they passed. . . .

The banks of the Elbe are wonderfully charming, particularly back of Altona, near Rainville. Not far away Klopstock lies buried. I know of no locality where a dead poet can be so well buried as there. To live there as a living poet is much harder.

—Memoirs of Herr von Schnabelowopski, chs. 3, 4, 6

Dreckwall and Wandrahmen: streets in Hamburg, the former inhabited principally by Jews.

True enough, we have a debauched merchants' warren here. Harlots enough, but never a Muse. Many a German singer has sung himself into consumption on the Jalse. I must tell you something:

> Towards Ottensen when I turned my face,
> I came on Klopstock's burial place,

All bedecked; dignitaries stood around
The tomb with wreathed garlands bound,
And smiled, and to themselves they thought
'Twas a wondrous thing that they had wrought.
But I—I stood on that sacred ground,
Stood silent, uttered not a sound,
My soul to the earth below fixed hard
Where slept the sacred German bard.

Do you see? Even at Klopstock's grave my Muse falls mute. I can find only a wretched rhyme for "miserable."

But above all, dear Christian, I must ask you to look out for poor Levy. It is the voice of humanity that you hear. I adjure you by all you hold sacred, help him. He is in the direst need. My heart bleeds.

—To Christian Sethe
Hamburg, July 6, 1816

Christian Sethe (1798-1857), later a high Prussian finance official, was a friend of Heine's youth. The Fresco Sonnets are addressed to him. Heine met him often; he last visited him in 1843 on his journey to Hamburg. Joseph Levy was a fellow student of Heine's at the Duesseldorf Lyceum. He was the son of a grain merchant who was reputed to be a usurer, and was shunned by his fellows. Heine read philosophical works with him, though his parents had forbidden Heine to associate with Levy. Levy, before his death, burned the letters which Heine had addressed to him.

She loves me not! This last word, my dear Christian, you must pronounce very, very gently. The first little word contains everlasting heaven, the last little word everlasting hell. . . .

Although I have undeniable and irrefutable proofs that none could love me less than she—proofs which even Rector Schallmeyer would accept as logical and not hesitate to place at the head of his own system—nevertheless, the poor loving heart will never yield its *concedo* but will always say, "What care I for your logic? I have my own logic." . . . I have erected a marvelously beautiful house of cards, and upon it I stand and hold *her* in my arms. . . . But you can scarcely imagine, my dear Christian, the glory and amiability of my destruction. *Aut Caesar aut nihil* was always my motto, everything in everything.

I am a mad chess player. At the first move I have lost my queen, and yet I continue to play, and I play—for the queen. Should I go on playing? . . .

To be separated from her, to endure long years of ardent yearning in my heart, is infernal torment and extorts infernal cries of anguish. But to be in her proximity and to languish for eternally long weeks, often in vain, for the glance which brings bliss—ah, my Christian and O, my Christian, that can make the purest and most devout nature flare up unto wild godlessness. . . .

It is a heart-sickening thing too that she has so vilely humiliated my pretty songs, which I wrote only for her. In this respect she has played me a scurvy game. But you must believe me, in spite of it all the Muse is dearer to me than ever. . . .

I am writing a great deal, for I have time enough, and my enormous financial speculations do not give me much to do. Whether my current poems are better than my previous I do not know. Only this much I know: they are much gentler and sweeter, like pain dipped in honey. I am also minded to commit them to print soon—but that may take many months. But here is the rub: since they are pure minstrel songs they may do me great injury as a merchant. I cannot explain that to you precisely, for you do not know the spirit that reigns here. But I can honestly avow to you that, aside from the fact that not the slightest feeling for poetry is to be found in this huckster town—there are only specially ordered, cash-on-delivery marriage, burial and baptismal pasquinades—there has, for some time, been in addition a stifling tension between the baptized and unbaptized Jews. (I call all Hamburgers Jews; those I call baptized, to differentiate them from the circumcised, are what are commonly called Christians.) Under these circumstances it is easy to foresee that Christian love will not leave the love-songs of a Jew unassailed.

Hence good advice is dear. In any case, I do not know how one goes about publishing a book. . . .

My life here is quite isolated, as you could easily surmise from the indications I have given above. My uncle lives in the country. There everything is prim and curled, and the free and unpretentious bard very frequently sins against etiquette. Plumed diplomats, millionaires, sage senators and the like are not the people for me. But the magnificent and divinely Homeric Bluecher was here not long ago, and I had the good fortune to dine in his company at my uncle's. A fellow like that is fun.

The nephew of the great (???) Heine is, to be sure, everywhere well liked and well received. Pretty girls squint at him, their breast-coverings mount upwards, and their mothers calculate—but-but-keep to yourself; there is no one left to me but myself. . . .

In the matter of religion, perhaps I will soon have something astonishing to communicate to you. "Has Heine gone mad?" you will cry. But I must have my madonna. Will the heavenly one be a substitute for an earthly one? I want to intoxicate my senses. Only in the endless depths of mysticism can I shake off my endless pain. How beggarly knowledge now seems to me in its pauper rags. What once seemed perceptive clarity now reveals itself to me as bare nakedness. "Become as little children"—I long imagined I understood. What a simple fool I am. Children have faith.

—To Christian Sethe
Hamburg, October 27, 1816

Adolf Muellner's tragedy, *The Guilt* was my favorite little book, and I loved it so that I honored it by making it a lover's gift to my beloved. "Do you write something like that too," the fair one said in a mocking tone. Naturally I assured her, with high solemnity, that I would write something even better.

—To Adolf Muellner
Berlin, December 30, 1821

Heine presented Amalie with a copy of The Guilt, *and in-*

scribed it: *"I wish you much happiness for the New Year. Amen. Ottensen, January 1, 1818."*

Once upon a bright summer's afternoon, he went walking, the young fop . . . with a sixteen-year-old beauty, who kept teasing him about his preciosity. The sun had not yet set, it still glowed in its most golden splendor; but in the sky above, the moon, puny and wan, had already appeared, like a little white cloud. "Do you see," the young poet said to his love, "do you see yonder small and pale pane? This river in which it is reflected seems to carry its beggarly image upon its proud waves only out of pity, and now and again the curled billows cast it upon the bank in mockery. But only let the old day sink! As soon as darkness breaks, that pale pane above will glow ever more majestic, the whole river will be lighted by the rays of its light, and the waves now so proudly scornful will shudder at the sight of the heavenly body and voluptuously billow upwards to meet it."

—Introduction to Don Quixote

Departure from Hamburg

Fair cradle of my sorrow,
    Fair tomb of peace for me,
Fair town, my last good-morrow,
    Farewell, I say to thee!

Farewell, thou threshold holy,
    Where my lady's footsteps stir,
And that spot, still worshipped lowly,
    Where mine eyes first looked on her!

Had I beheld thee never,
    My bosom's beauteous queen,
Wretched now, and wretched ever,
    I should not thus have been!

Touch thy heart—I would not dare.
    Ne'er did I thy love implore;

Might I only breathe the air
　Thou didst breathe, I asked no more.

Yet I could not brook thy spurning,
　Nor thy cruel words of scorn;
Madness in my brain is burning,
　And my heart is sick and torn.

So I go, downcast and dreary,
　With my pilgrim staff to stray,
Till I lay my head aweary,
　In some cool grave far away.

　　　　　　　　　　　　　—Book of Songs

Perhaps I am unfair to the good city of Hamburg. The mood which dominated me when I lived there for a while was not calculated to make me an unprejudiced observer. My inner life was a brooding, sinking into the pit of the dream-world, illuminated only by bolts of fantastic light. My outer life was mad, desolate, cynical, repulsive; in a word, I made it a stark contrast to my inner life, so that the latter should not destroy me by its preponderance.

　　　　　　　　　　　　　—To Immanuel Wohlwill
　　　　　　　　　　　　　　Berlin, April 7, 1823

As this remark and numerous others show, his unhappy love for Amalie did not prevent the young poet from rushing into numerous other love affairs—indeed, in his own view, it was an additional incentive. These experiences give even his youthful lyrics a cynical tone, suggesting easy success with women and no very great depression at infidelity, because the poet expected nothing else than disillusionment from his conquests. Nevertheless, the sting of his hopeless love for Amalie continued to rankle in Heine's memory. Her complete indifference humbled him more than open rejection or infidelity would have done.

I'm black and blue from their worrying,
　They've tortured me early and late,

Some with their love—God help me!
The others with their hate.

They've poisoned the wine on my table,
They've poisoned the bread on my plate,
Some with their love—God help me!
The others with their hate.

But she who most has worried,
And tortured and troubled—she
Has never either loved me,
Or even hated me.

—Book of Songs
Lyrical Intermezzo, 17

This morning I am minded to visit a lady whom I have not seen for eleven years, and of whom they say that I was once in love with her. She is Madame Friedlaender of Koenigsberg, a cousin of mine, so to speak. The husband of her choice I saw yesterday, as a foretaste. The good lady has made great haste and arrived yesterday, precisely the day the new edition of my *Youthful Sorrows* was issued by Hoffmann and Campe. The world is stupid, and smells of dried violets.

—To Varnhagen von Ense
Hamburg, October 19, 1827

At last, dear cousin, I am no longer a windbag, and can send you herewith the book I have long promised. I beg you to receive it as a return for the pretty marzipan gravestone with which you once honored me.

This morning I have frightful headaches and a pain in my heart (really; I am not showing off); if it does not grow worse I shall see you this noon with your father, my dear uncle. I am, Amalie,

Your devoted
H. Heine
—To Amalie Friedlaender, née Heine
Hamburg, November 29, 1829

To the Daughter of His Beloved

I can scarce believe as I look on thee—
'Twas a pretty rose-studded tree—
Its alluring fragrance started a train
Which whilom confounded my poor brain;
Again sweet blooms to memory throng.
Ah, but then I was foolish and young;
I'm old and foolish now, and in my eyes
A smarting sting, and I must devise
Rhymed speech, which hard I find,
For my heart is full, but empty my mind.

Little bud of a cousin, at sight of thee,
Melancholy encompasses me,
Singular sadness, passing deep,
Images awaken from their long sleep,
Siren images, and open wide
Laughing eyes, and on sportive tide
Swim joyous; the fairest of the fair
Is thy very image, to a hair.

'Twas this dream of youth that visited me—
I can scarce believe as I look on thee.
Such was the Siren who did entrance,
Such were her tones, such her glance;
Like a dulcet tinkle her voice did fall,
Charming all hearts, both great and small;
Her laughing eyes frolicked green,
Like dolphins in an ocean scene.

Somewhat faint the eye-brows' mould,
Yet curved and lofty to behold,
An arch triumphal, bold and proud;
And darling dimples closely crowd
Under the eye, in the rosy cheek.
But alas, nor angels nor mortals meek

Are perfect wholly; the loveliest creature
Hath its fault, as well will teach you
Tales of yore. Herr Lusignan,
Who once the fairest mermaid won,
Discovered, when with her he'd dawdle,
Her secret of an appendage caudal.

—For Elisabeth Friedlaender's album
Hamburg, September 5, 1844

When Heine visited Hamburg from his exile for the second time, he met Amalie and her little daughter Elisabeth Friedlaender, then six years old; Elisabeth later married the Shakespearean scholar Friedrich August Leo. The last verses of the poem allude to the legend of Melusina.

II

STUDENT YEARS

Bonn

After Heine had finally convinced his family that he was not suited to a merchant's career and when his desire to become a student had prevailed, it was proposed that he begin his studies at the University of Bonn, which was not far from Duesseldorf. This university was founded by the Prussian government in 1818 with a view to influencing the youth of the Rhineland, who had hitherto received a French education, and inculcating in them Prussian sentiments and national German patriotism. To this end a number of outstanding scholars and German patriots were called to the faculty; chief among these was Ernst Moritz Arndt, for many decades the principal spokesman of German nationalism, an ardent foe of the French and a vigorous opponent of democracy, and also August Wilhelm Schlegel, the spokesman of German Romanticism, who, like Arndt, had taken an active part in anti-French propaganda during the war against Napoleon. Whereas Arndt was no scholar but a powerful propagandist by the written and spoken word, Schlegel had achieved a scholarly reputation as an authority on literary history and linguistics and was highly regarded as an expert in versification.

Since Heine had left the Lyceum before the final examinations, he was required to take an examination before the matriculation committee of the University of Bonn for admission. After a brief preparation in Duesseldorf, he reported for his examinations in December 1819. He was found to have little Latin, no Greek and no mathematics, but he was well founded in his history, and in German composition he demonstrated "curious

86

understanding but good effort." On December 11, 1819, he was
registered as a student.

*Doubtless the German national spirit which prevailed among
the majority of students and professors at Bonn caught young
Heine also. He joined a fraternity and was soon required to undergo a stringent examination before the University judicial body
for his participation in a patriotic celebration. Although Salomon
Heine and the poet's parents insisted on a rapid completion of
his juristic studies, Heine attended at Bonn more lectures in history and linguistics than in jurisprudence. He was a devoted pupil
of Arndt and formed a personal attachment with Schlegel in
particular. All the instructors with whom Heine studied at Bonn
recognized his extraordinary diligence.*

To A. W. von Schlegel

I

In hooped petticoats with flowers brocaded,
With beauty-spots upon her cheeks be-painted,
On high-heeled, sharp-toed shoes "enskied and sainted,"
With wasp-like waist, and hair in towers thick-braided,
Even so the Pseudo-Muse her charms paraded
What time she lured thee to her bosom tainted;
But, led by instincts dim, thou grew'st acquainted
With ways that drew thee from her alleys faded.

There, in the ancient wilderness, thou foundest
A bower; where lay in charmed sleep profoundest
The sweetest Maid, like some fair marble Attic;
Soon broken the spell; for, at thy kiss awaking,
Rose the true German Muse, her smiles out-breaking,
And sank upon thy breast in love ecstatic.

II

A viper most malignant is doubt's baneful dagger,
A venom most malignant one's own self to doubt,
My life's inward marrow well nigh did it rout;

A puny bough was I which with no support doth stagger.
Then didst thou pity that poor bough, with spirit stout
And kindly words didst stay the laggard,
And thine the thanks if buds that twig yet augur.
O mayst still abide, attend with care
Till it as tree will grace the garden rare
Of that fair fée who snared thee with her spell.
And of that garden doth my guardian tell:
There do wondrous sweet tones dulcet ring,
The flowers utter speech and the trees do sing.

III

Not content with thine own bounteous wealth,
From the Niblung's Rhine didst refreshment suck,
From the banks of Thames its gifts didst pluck,
And boldly didst clip Tagus' flowery pelf,
Tiber yielded thee treasures from its ruck,
Seine to thy glory did tribute pay,
Even Brahma's sanctuary thou didst essay,
And pearls wouldst draw from Ganges' muck.
Be thou content, thou man of greed,
With boons to mankind but seldom decreed;
Think not of getting now but aye of giving,
And what, with no toil, thou hast amassed of worth,
Haled together from Sweden and the North,
On disciples now bestow for thy legatees' glad living.
—Gesellschafter, 1821

I have alas (for fair bosoms' sake) neglected the Muses. My
punishment you yourself have seen, to wit, my poetic sterility of
the previous winter, which so much vexed me that I imagined I
was forsaken by the Muses forever and could not even produce
a poetic dirge on the subject. But old Schlegel, who is a very
clever man with the ladies, has reconciled the scornful fair to
me. . . .

Of my relationship with Schlegel I could write you much that
is pleasant. He is very well pleased with my poetry, and in some

astonishment at its originality. I am too vain to be surprised. I felt very set up when I was lately formally invited by Schlegel and chatted with him for an hour over a steaming cup of coffee. The more I visit him the more I realize what a great intellect he is, so that one might say

> Invisible graces about him flutter
> Greedy to hear whatever he utter.

His first question is always about the publication of my poems, and he seems eager to see them published. You too, dear Fritz, seem to ask me about the same thing. Unfortunately I have yet to make many new transcripts because of the many changes I have made upon Schlegel's advice, and I have to add many new poems and metrical translations from the English. The latter are going very well, and will foster my poetic deftness. Enough of self-praise.

—To Friedrich von Beughem
Bonn, July 15, 1820

Postscript

Exceptions taken to the great master have moved the author to print the above sonnets. They were written last summer in Bonn, where the author saw their hero in his full strength, majesty and vigor. His spirit has truly not aged. He has no leisure to sit in comfort upon the world-elephant! Whether the author of the bitter attacks is right or wrong in his indignation at the political tendency of Schlegel's present efforts need not be decided here; but Schlegel's undeniable merits as the reformer of literature should not have been overlooked.

—Gesellschafter
Berlin, May 14, 1821

To this statement Heine added the reprint of the three sonnets (see pp. 87 ff.) to defend Schlegel against satirical attacks in various periodicals. It demonstrates that Heine had as yet not found

the political standpoint which he later adopted, and in particular
with reference to romanticism, when his judgment became in-
creasingly critical, until he "pummeled his own school-teacher."
He was brought to this not only by a change in his own general
views, but also because he had discovered through Varnhagen
von Ense that Schlegel had had hateful things to say about the
Book of Songs and the Travel Pictures. Heine felt that he had
been betrayed by Schlegel and stabbed in the back. As always in
such cases, Heine attempted to outbid the man who insulted
him.

In 1819, I was following four courses in one and the same
semester at Bonn, where for the most part German antiquities
out of the bluest period were dealt with, to wit, (1) history of the
German language under Schlegel, who for almost three intermi-
nable months developed remote baroque hypotheses concerning
the origin of the Germans; (2) the *Germania* under Arndt, who
sought in the ancient forests of Germany the virtues which he
missed in the salons of the present; (3) Germanic state law under
Huellmann, whose historical views are at least vague; and (4)
primitive German history under Radloff, who had not gotten
further at the end of the semester than the age of Sesostris—then
the legend of ancient Hertha would probably have interested me
more than it does now. . . . But I could in no case have then
believed that I would one day find myself on the shores of the
North Sea without thinking of the ancient goddess with patriotic
enthusiasm. But it is in fact not the case, and I am thinking here
of quite other and younger goddesses.

—Travel Pictures 2, The North Sea 3

A. W. Schlegel's case later was virtually the same. His poetic
inadequacy became apparent when the languages were further
developed, so that even those who once regarded the singer of
Arion as a peer of Arion now see in him only a worthy school-
master.

—The Baths of Lucca, ch. 11

With the exception of Napoleon, A. W. Schlegel was the first great man I had ever seen and I shall never forget that sublime moment. Even today I feel the sacred tremor which ran through my soul when I stood facing his lectern and heard him speak. At that time I wore a coarse white coat, a red cap, my blond hair long, and no gloves. But Mr. Schlegel wore kid gloves and was dressed quite after the latest Parisian fashion, still fragrant with the perfume of good society and *eau de mille fleurs*. He was propriety and elegance personified, and when he spoke of the Prime Minister of England, he used the expression "my friend." By him stood his servant dressed in the livery of the knightly house of Schlegel, and trimmed the wax tapers which burned in silver candelabra standing near a glass of sugared water upon the lectern in front of the miracle man. Liveried servants! Wax tapers! Silver candelabra! My friend the Prime Minister of England! Kid gloves! Sugared water! We youngsters were not a little dazzled by this brilliance, and I in particular; and I composed three odes to Mr. Schlegel, each of which began with the words "O thou who dost etc." But only in poetry could I have dared to address that distinguished man with the familiar "thou." His outward appearance did, in fact, lend him a certain distinction. Only a few little silver hairs shone upon his thin little head; and his body was so thin, so meager, so transparent, that he seemed to consist wholly of spirit, that he almost looked like the symbol of spirituality.

—The Romantic School, 2

Journey from Bonn to Goettingen

In September 1820, Heine left Bonn to continue his studies in Goettingen. The larger part of the journey he made on foot. On his way he visited Duesseldorf, which his parents had left in March 1820. They had gone to Oldesloe in Holstein, where Samson Heine received sun treatments. When it appeared that his mental health would not improve, Salomon Heine brought his brother to Lueneburg, where he lived until shortly before his death.

One clear frosty Autumn day a young man, apparently a student, wandered slowly through the avenue of the Palace gardens at Duesseldorf, now merrily kicking the rustling leaves which covered the ground, now looking sadly up into the bare trees with their spare covering of yellow leaves. As he looked up, he thought of the words of Glaukos:

E'en as the leaves of the forest, so pass the races of mortals,
Leaves by the autumn blast are scattered abroad and perish,
Leaves bud again when spring recovers the forest with verdure;
So are the races of men; some coming and others departing.

In days gone by the young man had looked up at these self-same trees with quite different thoughts: then he was a boy looking for birds'-nests or for cockchafers which delighted him as they buzzed past, contented with this lovely world, with the juicy green leaves full of dew-drops, with warm sunbeams and with sweet-smelling herbs. At that time the boy's heart was as merry as the fluttering creatures about him. But now his heart had grown older, the few sunbeams in it had disappeared, the flowers in it were dead, even its beautiful love-dream had faded away, nothing but bravado and wretchedness filled that poor heart, and to tell the worst of it—it was my own heart.

That same day I had returned to my old native town, but I did not mean to spend the night there and longed to get back to Godesberg in order to sit at my friend's feet, and to tell her of little Veronica. I had visited the tombs of my loved ones. Of all my living friends and relations I had only found one uncle and one cousin. Although I recognized some well-known faces in the streets, nobody knew me, and even the town looked at me with surprise; many of the houses had been freshly painted, strange faces peered from the windows, weary sparrows fluttered about old chimneys, everything looked as dead and yet as fresh as salad growing in a churchyard. Where they formerly spoke French they now spoke Prussian; even a small Prussian Court had collected there, and the people bore Court-titles; my mother's for-

mer hairdresser had become Court hairdresser, and there were
now Court tailors, Court shoemakers, Court bug-destroyers,
Court whiskey-shops—the whole town appeared to be one Court
asylum for Court-lunatics. . . . I seemed to be as in a dream, and
thought of the legend of the bewitched town, and I hurried out
of its gates, in order not to awake from it too soon. I missed many
a tree in the Palace gardens, and many were crippled with age;
the four tall poplars, which formerly appeared to me like green
giants, had become pygmies. Some pretty, gaily-dressed girls
walked by like wandering tulips. And these tulips I had known
when they were only small bulbs. For, ah me! they were some of
my playmates with whom once upon a time I had played at pris-
oner's base. But the lovely damsels whom I had once known as
blooming roses now looked like faded ones, and across many a
high proud forehead which had once charmed me Saturn had
cut deep furrows with his scythe. Only now, but alas! too late, I
discovered the meaning of that look she had once cast on me, as
a youth, for since then I had encountered abroad many like
glances in fair eyes. I was much moved by the humble salutation
of one I had once known as a wealthy and respected man, but
who had since then become a beggar; for we see everywhere,
according to Newton's law, that people who are going down-hill
in life rush into misery with ever-increasing velocity. . . .

I was not tired, but I wished to rest once more on the wooden
bench on which I had formerly carved the name of my beloved.
I could hardly find it again: so many new names had been
scratched across it. Ah! once I had fallen asleep on this bench,
dreaming of love and happiness. "Dreams are bubbles." . . .

But whilst I was sitting on the old seat in the Palace gardens,
dreaming of days gone by, I heard a confused sound of voices
behind me—people pitying the fate of the unfortunate French,
who had been dragged as prisoners to Siberia during the Russian
War, and had been kept there many years in spite of the peace,
and were only now on their way home. Looking up, I actually
beheld these prisoners orphaned of their glory; dire misery lurked
in the tatters of their uniforms; hollow mournful eyes looked

forth from their weather-beaten faces, and although crippled, weary and mostly lame, they still seemed to keep a kind of military step.

—Ideas: The Book LeGrand

The sight of the returning French prisoners of war was the inspiration for Heine's famous poem, The Grenadiers.

I spent several days in Hamm, and there finally made the personal acquaintance of Dr. Schultz. I also became quite friendly with his associate, through many delightful walks which we took together. I was well received by both. But my wonderfully sweet little bride, Miss Romanticism, née Poetry, found the visit very tedious.

—To Friedrich Steinmann and Johann
Baptist Rousseau
Goettingen, October 29, 1820

Steinmann later injured Heine by the publication of forgeries; Rousseau became an opponent of Heine. Dr. Heinrich Schultz, partner in the Wundermann publishing firm, issued the Rheinisch-Westfaelischen Anzeiger, for whose magazine page Heine wrote his first prose essays and his Letters from Berlin.

As far as Soest I travelled on foot. There I stayed the night and the following day, for I expected that the Councillor would arrive towards evening. Nor were my expectations disappointed. My old heart was happy again. It was as if Christian had fallen from heaven. But I took the post only to the next city. There I stopped the rest of the night, and the following morning set out for Goettingen. I arrived here without particular annoyance. Think of it, I have even brought a whole *louis* with me.

—To Friedrich von Beughem
Goettingen, November 9, 1820

"Councillor" was Christian Sethe's nickname.

September of 1821 is limned all too clearly in my memory. The beautiful valleys around Hagen, friendly Overweg in Unna, pleasant days in Hamm, good old Fritz von Beughem, your good self, Wundermann, antiquities in Soest, even the Paderborn moor—everything is still vividly before me. I can still hear the old oak forests rustling about me, each leaf whispering in my ear: "Here dwelt the ancient Saxons, the last to surrender faith and Germanism." I can still hear an ancient stone calling to me: "Wanderer, stay! 'Twas here Arminius smote Varus!" One must traverse Westphalia on foot, and indeed, as I did, by Austrian infantry stages, if one wishes to know the grave strength, the stalwart honesty, and the unpretentious industry of its inhabitants.

—Letters from Berlin (to Dr. Schultz)
January 26, 1822

How I loved those honest Westphalian lads
   In the good old times that fled fast—
They were free of all vain ostentation and show,
   And always so true and so steadfast!

How squarely and proudly they stood when they fenced!
   How gallant their gay defiance!
How fairly they dealt their tierces and quartes,
   As they fought with heart of lions!

They can fight, they can drink, and, when hand-clasps seal
   Love's bond, their spirit mellows
And they weep; they are sentimental oaks,
   And the rarest of all good fellows!

May heaven guard you, gallant race,
   And bless your seed! May your story
Be untroubled alike by war and fame,
   By heroes and heroes' glory!

May your sons have luck and always be set
  An easy examination!
May your daughters be suitably married betimes!
  Amen to my supplication!

                     —Germany, Caput 10

One must have travelled on foot as a poor student through North Germany in order to know how much virtue, and, to qualify the word virtue by a really beautiful epithet, how much evangelical virtue is frequently to be found in an unassuming parsonage. How often of a winter's evening have I found therein a hospitable welcome—I, a stranger, whose only recommendations were hunger and weariness! When I had eaten well and slept soundly, and was preparing on the morrow morning to set forth again, the old pastor was sure to appear in his dressing-gown to bestow his blessing on my journey—a good act that never brought me misfortune. His kindly and loquacious wife would thrust into my pocket several slices of buttered bread, which proved not less comforting. Behind the mother stood in modest silence the fair daughters of the pastor, with their ruddy cheeks and violet eyes, and the recollection of their timid glances kept my heart warm throughout the whole winter day.

          —Religion and Philosophy in Germany, 1

First Sojourn in Goettingen

Much as I blame myself for so doing, I must honestly confess that I am frightfully bored here. The tone is stiff, priggish, disdainful. Everyone must live here like a recluse. Here one can only be a good ox; and that is in fact what brought me here.

          —To Steinmann and Rousseau
          Goettingen, October 29, 1820

My first fortnight here I did nothing else than write the third act of my tragedy. That was the biggest; the remaining two acts I will write next January, because for the present I must play the ox horribly, and so I do, for it was only for the ox's sake that I came here.

—To Friedrich von Beughem
Goettingen, November 9, 1820

The tragedy is Almansor; Heine had begun to work on it in Bonn.

Wonder of wonders! I have received the *consilium abeundi!* For the last month I have been living in great uneasiness through all sorts of dissensions and have been pursued by all sorts of misfortunes, and finally last week I was rusticated for six months "for infringing the laws against duelling." I have been allowed to stay here for a few days under pretext of being too ill to leave my room. . . . Imagine my vexation: eagerly expecting supplies from home, setting my papers in order, compelled to keep to my room. I sit the whole morning through and write, like anybody, in my album:

> In his love's arms, sorrow free
> Dreaming, happy as can be:
> Suddenly, his awful fate,
> Comes command to rusticate,
> And far away from his dear love
> Must the student then remove.

. . . First, since you urge me to do so, I shall speak of my own tragedy.

I have worked with all my power [at *Almansor*] and have spared neither my heart's blood nor the sweat of my brow, and have finished it all but half an act, and I find to my horror that the astounding and divine masterpiece is not only not a good tragedy, but is not even worthy of the name of tragedy. Yes; there are charming and fine moments and scenes in it, originality is shown in every word of it, and surprisingly poetic images and thoughts sparkle all through it, so that it shines and glitters as though it were covered with a film of diamonds. Thus speaks the

vain author, the poetic enthusiast. But the stern critic, the inexorable dramaturgist wears quite a different pair of spectacles
altogether, shakes his head, and pronounces it to be—a pretty
puppet-show. "A tragedy must be drastic," he murmurs, and that
is the death sentence of mine. . . . I have attempted to unite in
the drama the romantic spirit and stern plastic form. Therefore,
my tragedy will share the fate of Schlegel's *Ion*. That failed of
course because it was written as a polemic.

—To Friedrich Steinmann
Goettingen, February 4, 1821

Supplies (*Spiesse*): student expression for money.

Heine challenged a student, named Wiebel, to a duel with pis-
tols in a quarrel concerning fraternity matters. The penalty
seemed very severe because the law forbidding duels was applied
for the first time. In the trial, Wiebel was severely reproved,
whereas Heine's attitude was judged favorably.

A. W. Schlegel's Ion had as little success on the stage as did
Heine's Almansor. The combination of romantic spirit with plas-
tic form was the literary program of the youthful Heine, which
he formulated in his essay on romanticism, written at Bonn in
1820.

Visit to Hamburg

Before Heine went to Berlin, he visited his parents in Oldesloe
and thence made a side-trip to Hamburg. Amalie was a bride at
the time.

I knew it in advance and I told you in advance. I had scarcely
entered the suburbs of Hamburg when I suddenly felt as if I had
never left this warren, and everything I had thought and felt and
experienced in the two years of my absence was extinguished out
of my memory. I sat for an hour silent, thinking of nothing at
all. That hour is an insignificant and yet eloquent stretch of
memory in the book of my life. How will that book end? Does
the divine author intend to write a tragedy or a comedy? Thank
heaven, I still have a word to say in the matter, the catastrophe

depends upon my will, and it will cost me only a bit of powder to blast the fool's cap from the head of the hero of the play. What do I care whether the gallery hiss or applaud? Even the parterre may whisper. I laugh. All of the heavenly hosts may rage. I laugh!—

> I laugh at the coxcombs with dandified air
> Whose glazed philistine eyes but glare at me,
> I laugh at the wooden faces that stare at me,
> Goat-faces that stupidly sniff and stupidly stare.
>
> I laugh at the apes of artistry rare,
> Self-inflated connoisseurs to a hair,
> I laugh at the poltroon hurling a dare at me,
> Threatening secure from poisonous lair.
>
> For when fortune's gifts in which we're entrenched
> From us by destiny's hands are wrenched,
> At our feet hurled down and shattered
>
> So that our very hearts are bruised and battered,
> Crushed and torn, with life's blood drenched,
> Yet can my laughter ring out unstanched.

Aye, even if the gaping mortal wound of my heart could speak, it would say, I laugh.

But in the loge above there sits a smartly-turned-out Sunday doll at whose making the heavenly Carver has outdone himself. This adorable mask must not laugh, and I should even like it if divers drops of crystal should spring from its two aquatophana eyelets. Yes, that is the rock on which my reason has foundered, and which I would nevertheless cling to with deathly yearning. It is an old story. . . .

It was towards midnight when I betook myself to the house of my Dulcinea del Toboso to enact the role of my Almansor under her windows in the flesh. But unfortunately I had no cloak like my Almansor, and had to freeze like a tailor. Also, instead of a star-studded Andalusian summer night, I had only an ash-gray heaven, the damp Hamburg national wind, and freezing drops of rain. . . . All madhouses have released their lunatics and thrown them about my neck. This crazy company is celebrating its *Walpurgisnacht* in my brain; my teeth are chattering their dance-music, and red, red streams of heart's blood gush hotly from my breast. These spectral waves of blood rustled about me, the fragrance of her proximity enveloped and deafened me, and she herself, she herself appeared at the window above and nodded down and smiled in all the luminous glory of her beauty, so that I thought I should perish of infinite yearning and intensity and bliss.

Nevertheless, it was a two-edged pain which wrenched my inner emotions when I observed that my fantasy had sent me forth into the April air again. The little head with its shudderingly sweet curls which nodded down to me so amiably was only the old governess who was closing her venetian blinds. . . .

I found my family in a very sad state. My father is still suffering from his distemper, my mother is subject to severe headache, my sister has the catarrh, and both my brothers write bad verses. This last tears at my heart. For the younger I have not yet lost all hope. He does not like my poems. That is a good sign. But my sister judges my poetic merits more favorably. When I lately read one of my best things to her, she remarked, "Oh, that'll do." That girl sings like an angel.

—To Heinrich Straube
Oldesloe, Spring 1821

Heinrich Straube (1794-1847) was publisher of the periodical Die Wuenschelrute, to which many poets and scholars, like the brothers Grimm, Arnim, and Schwab contributed. Later he became a high official.

Berlin

In April 1821, Heine arrived at Berlin, where he remained for two years. This sojourn was of the greatest significance for Heine's spiritual development. Here he came into contact with

Hegel and his pupils, with Rahel and her husband Varnhagen von Ense, with Leopold Zunz, the founder of the science of Judaism, and with numerous other outstanding scholars and poets, like F. A. Wolf, whose criticism of the Homeric poems was of epochal importance; Franz Bopp, the pioneer of comparative linguistics; the poets Achim von Arnim and Adalbert Chamisso. As an active member of the Verein fuer Kultur und Wissenschaft der Juden, he began the great preoccupation with the Jewish problem which he continued to the last day of his life. His attitude to Judaism went through several phases. But from this Berlin period and his work in the Jewish Kulturverein onwards, consciousness of his Jewish origin became a basic trait of his being and dominated his thought and writing, despite the frequent and sharply divergent judgments which appear in Heine's remarks on Jews and Judaism.

Berlin is in truth not a town. Berlin is merely a place whither a crowd of men—and many of them men of intellect—foregather, to whom the place is a matter of indifference: these men make the spiritual Berlin. The stranger, passing through, sees only the terraces of houses, one like unto another, and the long wide streets which are built in regular order, and for the most part to suit the caprice of one man, and give no sort of indication of the disposition of the masses. Only a Sunday's child gazing at the long rows of houses can guess the private feelings of the inhabitants; and the houses try to keep each other at a distance, glaring at each other in mutual distrust. Only once on a moonlight night, as I was returning late from Luther and Wegner, did I see that hard temper resolve itself into gentleness and tender melancholy, and the houses standing opposite each other so inimically, look at each other in true Christian fashion, touched by their dilapidation, and try to throw themselves into each other's arms in reconciliation: so that I, poor man, walked in the middle of the street, fearing to be squashed. There are many who will laugh at this fear of mine, and indeed I laughed at it myself when I walked through the same street the next morning and saw it in the cold light of day, and the houses gaping at each other again so stupidly. Indeed, you need several bottles of poetry to make you see anything in Berlin but dead houses and Berliners. It is very difficult to see ghosts in Berlin. The town contains so little of old days, and it is so new; and yet its newness is already old, so decayed and withered. For, as I have said, it has arisen not from the consciousness of the masses but from that of individuals. Frederick the Great is the best of them: he found only solid foundations, and the town received from him its individual character; and even if nothing had been built after his death, it would remain an historical monument of the spirit of that strange dull hero who typified in himself, with true German valor, the extraordinary Philistinism and the freedom of understanding, the shallowness and the uprightness of his age. Take Potsdam for instance: that is such a monument to the philosopher of *Sans Souci:* it belongs to his posthumous works and, although it is now only a stony waste and contains enough of the ludicrous, yet we look at it with grave interest and suppress the desire to laugh which crops up now and then, as if we were afraid of being struck suddenly on the back by the Spanish cane of old Fritz. But such fear no longer strikes us in Berlin, where we feel that old Fritz and his Spanish cane have no power over us. Otherwise, so many sickly obscurantist faces would not glare down upon us from the old windows of that wholesome city of reason, and so many stupid and superstitious structures would not have made their way among the old skeptical, philosophical houses.

—Journey from Munich to Genoa, Ch. 2

Hegel's Disciples

A greater thinker now steps on the scene, one who rounds into a completed system the philosophy of nature, explains from this synthesis the whole world of phenomena, supplements the great ideas of his predecessors by yet greater ideas, subjects their philosophy to every form of discipline, and thus establishes it on a scientific basis. He is the pupil of Schelling, a pupil however, who, making himself by degrees possessor of all his master's might in the realm of philosophy, outgrows his master, and finally thrusts him into obscurity. This is the great Hegel, greatest of philosophers begotten by Germany since Leibnitz. There can be no doubt that he far outranks Kant and Fichte. To the penetration of the former and to the vigor of the latter he adds the tranquillity of a mind that works by constitutional methods, a harmony of thought not to be found in either Kant or Fichte, in both of whom the revolutionary spirit is predominant. No comparison is possible between this man and Joseph Schelling; for Hegel was a man of character. And though, like Schelling, he may have given support by certain suspicious vindications to the existing order of affairs in church and state, he did so in favor of a state that, in theory at least, rendered homage to the principle of progress, and in favor of a church that regarded the principle of unrestrained inquiry as its vital element; and he made no secret of this. He avowed all his intentions.

—Religion and Philosophy in Germany, 3

Pique at such oblivion finally drove A. W. Schlegel, after an absence of many years, back to Berlin, the former capital of his literary splendor, and there he again delivered a number of lectures on aesthetics. But he had learned nothing new in the meanwhile and now he addressed an audience which had received a philosophy of art and a science of aesthetics from Hegel. People jeered and shrugged their shoulders.

—The Romantic School, 2

To speak candidly, I seldom understand Hegel, and it was only by later reflection that I came to any understanding of his words. I think he wished not to be understood—hence the complicated structure of his discourse, hence perhaps his preference for persons of whom he knew that they would not understand him, and whom he was the more ready to grant the honor of his closer association. Thus everyone in Berlin was surprised at the intimacy of the profound Hegel with the late Heinrich Beer, a brother of Giacomo Meyerbeer, who is widely known by reputation and has been celebrated by the most critical journalists. That other Beer, Heinrich, was simply an unintelligent fellow who was actually later declared incompetent and put under guardianship by his family, because instead of making a name for himself, by reason of his great wealth, in art or science, he squandered his riches on silly baubles; one day, for example, he bought walking sticks for six thousand *taler*. This poor fellow, who had no desire to be regarded either as a great tragedian, nor a great stargazer, nor a laurelled musical genius, a rival of Mozart and Rossini, and preferred to spend his money on walking-sticks—this singular Beer enjoyed the most confidential relationship with Hegel, became the philosopher's intimate, his very Pylades, and accompanied him everywhere like a shadow. Felix Mendelssohn, who was as witty as he was talented, once tried to explain this phenomenon by suggesting that Hegel did not understand Heinrich Beer. But now I believe that the real ground of that intimate association consisted in the fact that Hegel was convinced that Heinrich Beer understood nothing at all of what he heard him say, so that he could pour out in his presence anything that came to utterance at the moment without constraint. In any case, Hegel's conversation was always a kind of monologue, uttered in periodic sobs in a dull voice; the baroque character of his expressions often struck me, and of the latter many stuck in my memory. One beautiful, star-studded evening we were standing by the window side by side, and I, being a youngster of twenty-two, had eaten well and had taken coffee—I spoke romantically of the stars and called them the abode of the blessed. But the master mumbled: "The stars, hum! hum! The stars are only a luminating eruption in the sky." "For heaven's sake," I cried, "is there then no blessed dwelling place above to reward virtue after death?" But he looked at me with his pale eyes fixedly and said cuttingly: "So you want a tip for having taken care of your sick mother and not having poisoned your dear brother." At these words he looked about him anxiously, but recovered his calm when he saw that it was only Heinrich Beer who had come to invite him to a party of bridge.

—Confessions

My ancestors were of the Jewish faith. I have never boasted of this origin, for I had always felt humiliated enough to be taken simply as a specimen of the genus *homo*—and Hegel made me believe I was a god!

—To Saint-René Taillandier
Paris, November 3, 1851

Meyerbeer's younger brothers were the dramatist Michael Beer (1800-1833), author of Paria and Struensee, and the banker Wilhelm Beer (1797-1850), whose observations of Mars and the moon were of service to astronomy.

The Publication of the Poems

Four weeks ago my friend Rousseau wrote me that your honor requested biographical details concerning me for your poets' gallery. I earnestly forbade him to give any, and for the simple reason that I do not now merit being called a poet; my works must prove that I am to be taken seriously in matters of poetry. . . .

If your honor desires to add some personal detail to the listing of my name, I beg you to use only the following note:

"H. Heine, age 24 (?), born in Duesseldorf, educated at the Gymnasium there, studied jurisprudence at Goettingen, Bonn and Berlin, and resides at present in the latter city."

Concerning my literary productions there is scarcely anything to say.

—To Friedrich Rassmann
Berlin, October 20, 1821

Rassmann published the Rheinisch-Westfaelischer Musenalmanach, to which Heine contributed poems. In the beginning of December 1821, Heine's Gedichte appeared. His fee consisted of forty free copies. One of these he sent to Goethe with the following accompanying letter.

I might have a hundred reasons for sending Your Excellency my poems, I will only give one: I love you. I believe that it is a

comprehensive reason. My efforts in poetry are, I know, of little
worth; only it may be that here and there there are passages to
show what I may in time be capable of putting forth. For a long
time my mind was divided as to what is poetry. I was told: "Ask
Schlegel." He said to me: "Read Goethe." That I have done in
all reverence. And if in the course of time there shall come from
me the Real Thing, then I shall know to whom I am indebted
for it. I kiss your blessed hand which has shown me and the
whole German people the way to Heaven.
                        —To Goethe, Berlin, December 29, 1821

Heine received no reply to this letter and the volume of poems
which accompanied it. But in the literary world of Germany the
poems immediately aroused great attention and were enthusiastically praised as well as vehemently attacked. One of the first to
acclaim him was Varnhagen von Ense, who hailed him as a true
poet of great originality. Karl Immermann, the greatest German
storyteller of Heine's generation, compared him with Byron. An
anonymous critic who is conjectured to have been the theologian
Schleiermacher declared: "Never before in our literature has a
poet set forth his entire subjectivity, his individuality, his inward
life, with such boldness and such astonishing ruthlessness as Mr.
Heine has done in his poems. Inasmuch as the strictly objective
representation of this singularly grandiose subjectivity bears the
stamp of truth, and since truth possesses a wonderful and irresistible power, we have another explanation for the fact that
Heine's poems exert an overwhelming fascination upon the
reader."
In January 1822, Heine began to function as regular contributor to the Rheinisch-Westfaelischer Anzeiger with his Letters
from Berlin. These reports, too, aroused general attention by
reason of their boldness. As Varnhagen von Ense remarks in his
notes, Heine was to have been banished from Berlin because of
them. The officials were prevailed upon to ignore the injunction,
but Heine had numerous disputes with persons who felt themselves injured by his reports. In these letters his criticism is directed against social conditions. In political matters he exercised

great restraint, and even has words of praise for the royal house of Prussia and the Prussian officer corps.

Vehement partisan conflicts between liberals and ultras, such as we see in other capitals, cannot break out among us because the royal power, mediating powerfully and impartially, stands at the center. But in Berlin we do often see instead a different and entertaining kind of partisanship, that in music. . . . It is the nobility in particular which is claimed by Spontini's music and which bestows upon him extraordinary marks of its favor. Attached to these noble patrons is an actual Spontini party, composed, naturally, of a crowd of people who pay blind homage to distinguished and legitimate taste, of a crowd who are enthusiastic about anything foreign, of certain composers eager to have their own works performed, and, finally, of a handful of actual admirers.

The composition of the opposing party is easy to surmise. Many are impatient with the good knight because he is a "dago." Others because they envy him. Others, again, because his music is not German. But the greatest part see in his music only a spectacle of drums and trumpets, resounding bombast and swaggering monstrosity.

—Letters from Berlin, 2
March 16, 1822

Other sentences were suppressed by the censorship, which did not permit free expression of opinion concerning Spontini, who was a favorite of the king. The opposing party exalted Karl Maria von Weber, whose Freischuetz was a colossal current success.

I do not wish to be unjust and make no mention of the honor which is paid to the name of Goethe, the poet who is most spoken of here. But, my hand upon my heart, perhaps it is Goethe's *savoir faire* which has contributed most to the fact that his outward standing is so brilliant here and that he enjoys the affection of our great to so high a degree. Far be it from me to

attribute a petty character to the old gentleman. Goethe is a
great man in a silk coat. Quite recently he proved himself magnificently to his artistically-minded countrymen, who wished to
set up a monument to him in a noble suburb of Frankfort and
canvassed all of Germany for contributions. There was an astonishing amount of discussion on the subject here, and I humbly
composed the following sonnet, which received the honor of
approbation:

> Hearken, ye Germans, man, wife, and maid,
> Collect subscriptions with right good will;
> Frankfort's citizens are determined still
> Goethe's monument to build and parade.

> "At the fair, foreign merchants will gape kindly,
> Thinking: 'Twas we, Goethe's townsmen-throng,
> From our manure hath this blossom sprung,
> And in trade they'll trust us blindly."

> O leave to Goethe the poet's own bays;
> Tradesmen, your money back in the till!
> Goethe's own memorial is his eternal praise.

> He was indeed your fellow—in his diaper days;
> But a whole world separates you still—
> As a brooklet parts you from Saxon ways.

The great man put an end to all discussion, as is well known,
by telling his countrymen that "he was no Frankforter" and
sending back the Frankforter civic privileges.

Ever since, to use the language of Frankfort, those privileges
have depreciated in value ninety-nine percent, and the Frankfort
Jews have a better prospect of acquiring that fine property. But,
to revert to the language of Frankfort, are not the Rothschilds
and the Baethmanns at par? Merchants have the same religion
the world over. Their counting house is their church, their desk
a prayer stool, memoranda their bible, warehouses their sanctu-

ary, their exchange clock tells their hours of prayer, gold is their god, and credit their faith.

—Letters from Berlin, 2

The focus of the Goethe cult in Berlin was Rahel Varnhagen, at whose salon Heine was a frequent visitor, though he did not share the unqualified admiration of Goethe and often disagreed with the Varnhagen couple. The sonnet gives renewed expression to Heine's distaste for the mercantile career and for the spirit of the mercantile cities. In this connection he repeats his endeavor, set forth in his letter to Sethe of October 27, 1816 and frequently reiterated thereafter, to discard the customary classification of people according to their official religious adherence and descent, and to adopt another classification according to psychology, profession and views of life. Such a classification would make all merchants Jews, and all thinkers poets, and heroes non-Jews. It is a prelude to Heine's later classification of people as Nazarenes or Hellenes. Even to a greater extent than this latter differentiation, the earlier sprang from a need to separate himself from the mass of mercantile Jews and to be exempted from their social disabilities.

But at the same time Heine felt himself strongly at odds with Germanism.

I move about in a very peculiar mood. . . . Everything German is repulsive to me, and you are, unfortunately, a German. Everything German raises my gorge. The German language shatters my ears. My own poems nauseate me at times, when I realize that they are written in German. Even the writing of this note sours my stomach, because the German script irritates my nerves. I had never believed that these beasts, styled Germans, could be a race at once so tedious and so malicious. As soon as my health is restored, I shall quit Germany and pass my time in Arabia.

—To Christian Sethe
Berlin, April 14, 1822

I have an opportunity to speak of two novelties here, first of

the new mercantile exchange, furnished after the manner of that
at Hamburg, which was opened a few days ago, and secondly of
the warmed-over project of converting the Jews. But I shall pass
over both, for I have not yet been in the new hall, and the Jews
are too sad a spectacle. I shall eventually return to them, when
I speak of their new ritual, which has been promulgated especially from Berlin. But I cannot do so now, for I have neglected
to attend the new Mosaic service. Nor will I write of the new
liturgy which was introduced in the cathedral church some time
ago and has become the chief topic of conversation in the city,
because my letter might swell to the proportions of a book. The
ritual has a crowd of opponents, of whom Schleiermacher is called
the most excellent. I attended one of his sermons lately; he
spoke with the power of a Luther, and there was no lack of
flowery exceptions to the new liturgy. I must confess that no
particularly devout feelings were aroused in me by his preaching;
but I find myself edified in the better sense, strengthened and
scourged from the soft downy bed of slack indifference as by
stinging words. This man need only cast off his black clerical
garb to stand forth as a priest of truth.

—Letters from Berlin, 2

*Friedrich Daniel Schleiermacher (1768-1834), one of the great-
est of German pulpit orators, author of the book* On Religion:
To the Educated among its Contemners, *one of the most
effective speakers on German patriotism during the rule of
Napoleon, was later celebrated as "the reformer of Protestant
theology." He opposed the union of Lutheran and Reformed
churches introduced by the Prussian King, Friedrich Wilhelm
III, and in 1822 attacked the liturgy proposed by the king. In his
sermons also, which were well attended, he gave utterance to
politically liberal demands and in consequence came under police
surveillance. In the Preface to his* French Affairs, *Heine protested that pressure was exerted by the Prussian government
upon Schleiermacher to compel him "to enjoin Christian surrender to the will of the authorities."*

There is an inordinate deal of social life here, but it is fragmented into scraps. There are many disparate small circles, rather reducing than enlarging their perimeters. If one would glance at the various balls here, he would think that Berlin consisted wholly of social groups. . . . Masquerades always delight me hugely. When the drums thunder and the trumpets blare and the charming tones of flute and fiddle intrude their alluring notes, I hurl myself like a mad swimmer into the tossing and gaily lighted flood of humanity and dance and skip and jest and chaff everyone and laugh and chatter—anything that pops into my head. At the last masquerade I was especially gay and could have walked on my head; a bacchanal spirit had seized upon my whole being, and if I had encountered my deadliest enemy I should have said to him, "Tomorrow we will shoot at one another, but today I will kiss you right heartily." The most unadulterated pleasure is love. God is love, *ergo* God is the most unadulterated pleasure. *Tu es beau! tu es charmant! tu es l'objet de ma flamme! je t'adore, ma belle!*—these were the words my uninstructed lips repeated a hundred times. And I pressed everyone's hand, and courteously doffed my hat to everyone; and everyone was as courteous to me. There was only one German lad who was coarse and upbraided my aping of dago mincing; he thundered in a primitive Teuton beer-bass: "At German mummeries Germans should talk German!" Ah, German lad, how sinful and shabby I find your words at moments when my soul would embrace the whole world with love, when I would exultantly throw my arms around Russians and Turks, when I would melt into tears upon the fraternal bosom of a fettered African!

—Letters from Berlin, 4

The Rhinelanders are begrudged their Rhenish judicial procedures; there is a move to redeem them from those "fetters of French tyranny," as the unforgettable Justus Gruner—God rest his soul—once called the French law. May our beloved Rhineland long bear these fetters, and be loaded with yet others like them! May that genuine love of freedom long flourish on

the Rhine, freedom not based on national egotism and hatred
of France, that genuine vigor and youthfulness, not swilled out
of a brandy-flask, and that genuine love of Christ, which has
naught in common with heresy-hunting bigotry and hypocritical
proselytization!

—Letters from Berlin
June 7, 1822

*In the Prussian Rhine province the Napoleonic code remained
in force until the introduction of the German civic law code in
1900, though reactionaries and nationalists constantly pressed for
its abolition. Justus Gruner was the first Prussian governor in
Duesseldorf; in 1814, he took the city into possession for Prussia
and introduced the Prussian system of obligatory military service.
Heine also loathed him for his activity in the secret patriotic
societies which prepared for the war against Napoleon. Fear of
censorship and the police prevented Heine from attacking the
society for converting Jews more explicitly than he does here.
This society enjoyed the protection of the king and the court.
Its activity became an open scandal, for almost all the "converts"
were discovered to be adventurers or cheats after they had received, upon baptism, gifts of houses in Berlin and its vicinity or
large sums of money.*

Polish Intermezzo

*At the university of Berlin, Heine very soon became acquainted
with a Polish student, Eugen von Breza (1802-1860), and formed
a friendship with him which lasted to the poet's death. In the
beginning of February 1822, Breza was dismissed from Berlin,
for the Duchess of Cumberland fell in love with him and the
king thought that scandal could be avoided only by removing
the young Pole from the scene. Heine deplored Breza's departure
openly:*

My most delightful friend, the most amiable of all mortals,
Eugen von B. departed day before yesterday. That was the only

man in whose company I was never bored, the only one whose original wit could gladden me and give me joy in life, and in the lineaments of whose sweet and noble countenance I could clearly discern how my soul once looked, when I still led a pure and beautiful life of flowers and had not yet tainted myself with hatred and lies.

—Letters from Berlin
March 16, 1822

Breza went to the estates of his father, who had been Polish minister under Napoleon, but also enjoyed the favor of King Frederick William III, who rewarded his services with large landed properties. Heine was invited there in August 1822. Since his friend's mother came of the Radolinski family, Heine became acquainted with large numbers of the most distinguished Polish nobility. He was invited to neighboring estates and visited the cities of Gnesen and Posen. Heine's first impressions of this new and strange world are set forth in his letter to Ernst Christian August Keller (1797-1869), who was then writing liberal articles under the pseudonym "Hartmann von Rhein" and later occupied a high position in the Prussian ministry of religion.

I was to travel to Dresden and Teplitz to recover my health, but my unruly nature drove me to the forests of Poland. I wanted to know the country and meet certain Polish friends. The country is repulsive; the Polish villages, where men live like cattle, afford a melancholy spectacle. Yes, my dear doctrinaire, I was deeply distressed when I reflected on the wretched state of the Polish peasants, that result of a developed aristocracy. That a similar state shall never recur in our beloved Germany, that we shall never retrogress to the Middle Ages, I find a pledge in the many warriors for right and truth whose iron voices still echo abroad, a pledge in men like the doctrinaire of the red earth, who, a strict usher of God in the great hall of nature, shows everyone to his appropriate place, helps the Ikey, downtrodden like a worm, to a seat among humans, and scourges the

laughing clubman from his lazy arm-chair upholstered with soft
privilege.

But the people in Poland are good. The noble is lively and
gallant, and deserves respect. Germans who have travelled
through Poland and brought home a contrary opinion have
usually looked at the Poles through German spectacles, or have
carried their national prejudices in their bosoms.

—To Ernst Christian August Keller
Gnesen, September 1, 1822

In the "Memoir on Poland," which Heine published in the
Berlin periodical Der Gesellschafter *in January 1823, he speaks as*
a political critic for the first time.

For some months past I have been wandering about, up and
down the Prussian part of Poland. I did not go far in the Russian
part, and not at all into the Austrian. I have made the acquaintance of many, and from all parts of Poland. These were indeed
nobles for the most part, and very aristocratic. But while in the
flesh I moved only in the circles of the higher society and in the
confines of the castles of the Polish nobility, my spirit often
strayed to the huts of the lower orders. . . .

Anyone who wishes to see obedience personified need only
look at a Polish peasant standing before his lord; only the wag-
ging dog-tail is missing. At such a spectacle I involuntarily
remember "And God created man in his image"—and am
afflicted with infinite pain to see a man so degraded before
another. Men should bow only before royalty; except for this
last article of faith I quite accept the North American catechism.
I do not deny that I love the trees of the field better than family
trees, that I esteem human rights higher than canon rights, and
value the commands of reason above the abstractions of myopic
historians. But if you ask me whether the Polish peasant is really
unhappy, if his lot would be improved if oppressed tenants were
turned into freeholders, I should be lying if I answered with an
unqualified affirmative. . . .

Between the peasant and the nobleman in Poland stand the

Jews. These amount to somewhat more than a fourth of the population, follow all trades, and might appropriately be called Poland's third estate. . . . I was told that the Jews of the Arch-duchy stand at a lower level of humanity than their more easterly coreligionists, and so I shall say nothing definite about Polish Jews in general but rather refer you to David Friedlaender's *On the Improvement of the Israelites in the Kingdom of Poland* (Berlin, 1819). Since the appearance of this work, written with singular truth and humanity, except for the unfair neglect of the merits and moral significance of the rabbis, the condition of the Polish Jews has probably not altered appreciably. It is said that they once monopolized all skilled trades in the grand duchy, as they still do in the rest of Poland; but now one sees many Christian artisans migrating from Germany, and the Polish peasants also seem to find more taste for handicrafts and other trades. But it is rare for a common Pole to become an ordinary cobbler or brewer or distiller. In Walischei, a suburb of Posen, I found every second house decorated with a cobbler's sign, and I thought of the city of Bradford in Shakespeare's *Pinner of Wakefield*. In Prussian Poland the Jews obtained no state office without submitting to baptism; in Russian Poland even Jews are admitted to all state offices, because such a policy is considered useful there. In general, the arsenic in the local mines has not yet been sublimated to a hyper-pious philosophy, and the wolves in the ancient forests of Poland have not yet been instructed to howl with historical citations.

It is to be desired that our government seek by appropriate means to inspire the Jews of the arch-duchy to love of agriculture, for there are said to be very few Jewish farmers here. In Russian Poland they are numerous. The distaste of the Polish Jews for farming probably came from their having observed the extremely wretched state of peasants held in serfdom. If the peasantry is now raised from its degradation, Jews too will turn to farming. With few exceptions all the inns of Poland are in the hands of Jews, and their numerous distilleries are injurious to the country, for they incite the peasants to drunkenness. But I have already shown above that drinking is the peasants' path to happiness.

Every nobleman has a Jew in the village or city whom he calls
his factor; this Jew carries out all his commissions, purchases,
sales, inquiries and the like. This is a singular institution, which
demonstrates the love of comfort of the Polish nobility. The
external aspect of the Polish Jews is horrible. A shudder runs
over me when I think of the first Polish village I saw, back of
Meseritz, inhabited mostly by Jews. . . . But loathing was soon
replaced by sympathy when I examined the condition of these
people more closely and saw the pigsty holes in which they lived,
jabbered, prayed, haggled—and were miserable. Their speech is a
German interlarded with Hebrew and trimmed with Polish.
Long ago they had immigrated to Poland from Germany because
of religious persecution; in such cases the Poles have always
distinguished themselves by their tolerance. . . . The Jews first
brought handicrafts and trade to Poland and, under Casimir the
Great, they were favored with significant privileges. They appear
to have stood much closer to the nobility than to the peasants,
for according to an ancient law, upon conversion to Christianity
the Jew was *ipso facto* raised to the noble estate. I do not know
whether or why this law fell into abeyance and whose value it
was that declined. But in those early days the Jews were surely
far superior in intellect and culture to the nobility, whose only
trade was crude warfare and who even lacked their French polish.
But the Jews at least were always preoccupied with their Hebrew
scholarly and religious books, for the sake of which they had
forsaken their country and their comfort. But they obviously
did not keep step with European culture, and their intellectual
outlook degenerated into a quagmire of crude superstitions
which a hair-splitting scholasticism squeezed into a myriad remarkable forms. And yet, in spite of the barbaric fur cap which
covers his head and the even more barbaric ideas which fill it,
I esteem the Polish Jew far higher than so many a German Jew
who wears a beaver upon his head and carries his Jean Paul in it.
By reason of its rigid isolation, the character of the Polish Jew
attained a oneness; and by breathing a tolerant atmosphere, this
character acquired the stamp of freedom. The inner man did
not become a *quodlibet* compound of heterogeneous feelings,

and was not stunted by the constraint of the walls of the Frankfort Judengass, sage city ordinances and loving limitations of the law. With his dirty fur, his well-populated beard, his bouquet of garlic and his jabber, the Polish Jew is still much dearer to me than many another who is a nabob with government bonds.

A characterization of the Polish nobility would produce a colorful mosaic of adjectives: hospitable, proud, spirited, flexible, false (this little yellow stone must not be omitted), sensitive, enthusiastic, frolicsome, voluptuous, gallant and overweening. But I have myself been too often indignant with our scribblers of brochures who, when they see a Parisian dancing master skip about, immediately write it down as a characterization of the whole people, and who, when they see a fat Liverpool cotton merchant yawn, forthwith pontificate on the whole nation. These generalizations are the source of all evil. It takes more than a generation to comprehend the character of a single individual, and a nation is comprised of millions of individuals. Only if we study the history of a man, the history of his education and his life, is it possible for us to grasp a few outstanding traits of his character. Yet among classes whose individual members acquire similar tendencies through their upbringing and their manner of life, certain prominent traits can be noticed; this is the case with the Polish nobility, and it is only from this standpoint that certain generalizations on their character may be hazarded. Education itself is everywhere and always conditioned by circumstances of place and time, by the soil and by political history. In Poland the circumstances of place are more important than elsewhere. Poland is situated between Russia and France. . . . Barbarism attacks from the east, through hostile contacts with Russia, and hyper-culture invades from the west, through friendly contacts with France: hence that singular mixture of culture and barbarism in the character and in the domestic life of the Poles. . . .

Of the arrogance of the nobility vis-à-vis the bourgeoisie, the Poles know nothing; such arrogance can arise only in the countries where a strong bourgeoisie arises and proffers its claims. Only when the Polish peasant will buy land and the Polish Jew no longer display servility to the nobleman, will the arrogance of nobility burgeon—and thus betoken the advance of the country. Because the Jews here are superior to the peasants, they must be the first to collide with the pride of the nobility; but then the thing will surely be given a religious name. . . .

Even the heart of the non-Pole is wrung with sympathy upon enumerating the political sufferings which have afflicted the Poles in a brief span of years. Many of our journalists deftly remove this feeling from their necks by saying lightly that the Poles have drawn their fate down upon themselves by their disunity and are therefore not to be pitied. This is a silly consolation. No people, regarded as a whole, can be guilty of anything; its action springs from inner necessity, of which its fate is always the result. The investigator has a revelation of divine thoughts, to wit, that history (Nature, God, Providence, and the like) designs its own large purposes with whole peoples as with individual men, and that many peoples must suffer so that the whole may be preserved and flourish. The Poles, a Slavic border people at the gate of the German world, seem destined by their very situation to fulfil certain purposes in world events. Their moral struggle against the suppression of their nationality has always evoked manifestations which impress a different character upon the entire people, and which must also affect the character of neighboring peoples.

—On Poland

Heine's remarks on Poland provoked a literary uproar which eventually caused the Prussian government to investigate their author. The Poles for their part protested against the designation of the Jews as a third estate. German journalists were indignant at Heine's favorable judgment of Polish nationality. Heine's figures on the proportion of Jews in the general Polish population were rightly condemned as being too high. He was also in error in speaking of the corporal bondage of Polish peasants. Peonage had been abolished by Napoleon, and indeed earlier than in Prussia. The drama The Constable of Wakefield was falsely ascribed to Shakespeare in Heine's day; The Pinner of Awakefield

was written by Robert Greene. *The last section of Heine's conclusions concerning Poland presented here, clearly shows the
influence of Hegel's philosophy of history.*

I am sending you, by the next post, my essay on Poland, which
I wrote for Breza while I was under the shower bath. Professor
Gubitz has shamefully disfigured it with his substitute jests and
the censor has thoroughly maltreated it. The essay has won me
the enmity of the barons and the dukes, and in higher places
too my name has been blackened.

—To Christian Sethe
January 21, 1823

It is very decent of you to be pleased by my memoir on
Poland. Great praise has been bestowed on my sharp treatment
of Poland from all sides, but I cannot myself agree to this praise.
During the winter and even now I have been in too wretched
a state to produce anything good. The essay has agitated the
entire Archduchy of Posen. Posen periodicals have abused it to
thrice the extent of the essay itself. The Posen Germans in particular cannot forgive me for describing them so accurately and
for raising the Jews to be Poland's third estate.

—To Immanuel Wohlwill
Berlin, April 7, 1823

*The periodical which attacked Heine because of the Jews was
a Polish organ published in German.*

The Verein fuer Kultur und Wissenschaft der Juden

*On August 4, 1822, Heine was accepted as a member in the
Verein fuer Kultur und Wissenschaft der Juden at the instance
of Eduard Gans, whom he had met shortly before his journey to
Poland. On September 29 he participated in the meetings of the
Verein for the first time and was greeted with an address by the
president, Eduard Gans. For some weeks he was secretary of the
Verein meetings, and for a considerable period gave instruction*

in history and French thrice weekly in the educational institution
established by the Verein, without receiving compensation. He
undertook the organization of an association of Jewish women,
but was prevented from carrying this work forward by the state
of his health. Heine was also interested in the Verein's project
of issuing a new textbook in Jewish religion. In this connection
he remarked that "Judaism must not be treated after the fashion
of modern Protestantism." He acquired several members for the
Verein, among them Michael Beer and Simon van Geldern.

The Verein had already been in existence for three years when
Heine joined it. The grounds for its establishment were the attacks of antisemitic publicists, especially those of the philosopher
Friedrich Jacob Fries and the historian Friedrich Ruehs, who
accused the Jews of spiritual and moral shortcomings and denied
their claim to justice; the measures of the German government,
which withdrew the concessions it had made during the war
against Napoleon; and, finally, the outbreak of pogroms which
in 1818 threatened the life and property of Jews in a number of
German cities, particularly in Hamburg and Frankfort. To a
number of Berlin Jews these events brought the conviction that
nothing could be achieved by individual and ad hoc defense
measures. They set their hope rather on an internal reform of
Judaism, which must embrace all departments of life—economic
activity, education, morality, religion, ritual, relationship to state
and society. As a result of such reform they hoped to acquire
recognition of the personal rights of individual Jews and also
higher regard for Judaism on the part of non-Jews. To most of
the members of the Verein maintenance of the Jewish people,
once these reforms had been achieved, was a matter of slight
importance. Many, particularly the president Eduard Gans, were
not interested in the survival of Judaism.

In his addresses Gans repeatedly expressed the thought that a
time would come when distinctions between Jews and non-Jews
would entirely disappear and that it was the task of the Verein
to facilitate the advent of such a state. Obviously Gans' position
represented the sense of the preponderant majority of Verein
members. They were unwilling to accept Christianity as the

state religion, and they combated the attitude of governments which made membership in or conversion to the religion of the state a condition for access to public employment. But they counted upon a progressive de-Christianization of general education and culture, and saw the precursors of this movement in the philosophy of the enlightenment, in the classical poets—Lessing, Goethe, Schiller—and in the philosophical development pioneered by Kant. Insofar as they were interested in politics (as Gans in particular was), they believed in a rapid victory of liberal ideas, of which one of the chief goals was the separation of church and state. Political progress, they thought, would introduce a state in which membership in a community determined by religion or descent would become meaningless. From the spread of leading ideas of culture they expected that the dogmas of the Christian state would be transcended and, hence, that all partitions between Jews and non-Jews would be abolished. In the meantime they were determined to cling to Judaism, convinced that the principles of the Jewish religion presented fewer difficulties than did Christianity in acknowledging the truths of philosophical rationality. In this concept the older members of the Verein, like David Friedlaender, the pupil and friend of Moses Mendelssohn, and the Kantian Lazarus Bendavid, were at one with the younger members who had been brought up in the school of Hegel. All strove for as abstract and ideal a concept of Judaism as was possible, without interest in its historical coloring. Only Leopold Zunz remained at a distance from philosophic speculation. Insofar as he gave expression to philosophic concepts in his historical researches at this time, they show a surprising similarity to the positivism of Comte and Mill, which he could not as yet have known.

When Heine joined the Verein and became one of its most zealous members, it was already certain that he would go over to Christianity, at latest upon the conclusion of his studies. Of this necessity Heine's mother, at whose desire the son studied jurisprudence, as well as Salomon Heine, who provided means for his studies, were quite convinced, and he himself was equally clear on the point that, as long as the juridical position in Germany remained basically unchanged, he could only obtain legal work there—at that time even the career of lawyer was not free but had an official character—if he would undergo baptism. But recognition of this constraint wounded Heine's self-esteem greatly. He had grown up without any knowledge of Judaism. His parents had been at odds with the rabbinate of the Duessel-dorf community, and in all probability they had no high regard for rabbis in general. The historical studies which Heine pursued before his arrival in Berlin brought him no nearer to Judaism. In Hegel's philosophy he saw the pantheistic tendency dominate, and was inclined to place pantheism and atheism in a common front against the personal God of the Bible. In any case, his thought on the subject was not entirely consistent. In his family letters the notion of a personal God is very evident. When he thinks of the welfare of his mother and sisters, he invokes the personal God whose existence he questions, often in a tone of mockery, in his letters to his friends and in the writings of his youth. Insofar as he occupied himself with Jewish religion before his entry into the Kulturverein, it was to him one of the "positive religions," to which he felt himself opposed. The little that he knew of Judaism he drew from Voltaire's Dictionnaire Philo-sophique, in which the Jewish religion is presented with even greater hostility than is the Christian. Traces of Voltaire's influ-ence had not fully vanished even in the last years of Heine's life. But the fact that he and his family differed from their non-Jewish environment as Jews in manner of thought and style of life, and that other Jews who were even more sharply distinguished from non-Jews by their physiognomies and physical characteristics than was Heine, shared the same fate with him, was present to Heine's consciousness from his childhood onwards. As a schoolboy he was teased because of his Jewish origin, and as an apprentice mer-chant in Frankfort and then in Hamburg, and also as a student in Goettingen, even if not in Bonn as well, he discovered in his own person that as a Jew he was discriminated against by officials and by parts of the population quite as other Jews were. He found compensation in his pride in his mother's family and in the position which Salomon Heine had reached, but this family

pride was only lightly tinted with pride in the Jewish people.
Since it was precisely in Salomon Heine's household that he had
had to endure the worst humiliation, his self-esteem searched
for other supports. The more he grew conscious of his poetic
gifts, the higher claims did he make to being an exceptional case.
Because as a poet he felt superior to the average, he thought it
behooved him to resist energetically being despised by the average—among whom he counted the nobility of birth and office—
because of his Jewish origin. For this reason he felt entitled and
obligated to set himself apart from other Jews, the preponderant
majority of whom were merchants. For this reason also he called
Christian merchants "Jews," and insisted on classifying people
according to gauges which had nothing to do with religion and
descent. But for this reason also Christianity was particularly
repulsive to him, the "despiser of all positive religions," great as
was his sympathy with the founder of that religion. His hostility
to the state religion Heine never gave up. To be forced to
acknowledge such a religion by the act of baptism seemed to
Heine the basest degradation. Even before Jewish consciousness
was awakened in him, he gave expression to this feeling in his
drama Almansor, which he had begun to write in Bonn. In this
drama, Moors who had gone over to Christianity out of self-
seeking or fear of death are treated with scorn; the hero persists
in his old faith and carries off his beloved, whose father had
caused her to be baptized, immediately before her wedding with
a Christian knight. In the words and deeds of Almansor, Heine
unmistakably expresses his own personal feelings and wishes,
whereas the representation of the house of the beloved, is a
caricature of Salomon Heine's "Affront Castle." This unsuccess-
ful tragedy, of whose dramatic inadequacy Heine himself was
perfectly aware, reveals, along with his passionate resistance to
baptism, his own inward helplessness with respect to a solution
of his dilemma.

For rejection of "positive religions" and hostility to any state
religion could not suffice the emotional needs of Heine, who had
steeped himself in romanticism and had never surrendered his
inclination towards the romantic. Hegel, Heine's teacher and

mentor, was far from underestimating the religious. It was rather precisely in Hegel's lectures that Heine conceived an interest in questions of religious history. On the occasion of a sermon of Schleiermacher, Heine expressed his displeasure with "slack indifference." At the same time he asserts that this impressive preacher had not touched him in respect to religion (see p. 110). If Schleiermacher could not succeed in reconciling Heine to baptism, there was no prospect that anyone could make a believing Christian of him.

Almost at the same time, upon the occasion of a quarrel with most of his Rhenish-Westphalian comrades, on whose loyalty he could previously place unqualified reliance, Heine uttered a vigorous rejection of Germanism (p. 109). Some weeks later, Heine became acquainted with Eduard Gans. The result of their first conversations was that Gans, doubtless with Heine's consent, proposed Heine as a member of the Kulturverein. Conversations between Heine and Gans must therefore have frequently dealt with Jewish problems, and there must have been a certain unanimity of opinions and points of view. Agreement between them must have been easy, since Gans, and with him all the younger members of the Verein, were not far behind Heine in their derogatory criticism of Jews. Their zeal for a radical reform of Jewish life implied the conviction that the spiritual constitution, intellectual attitude and manner of living of Jews at the time merited the most vigorous condemnation. Harsh reproach of their coreligionists was a prevailing motif in the conversations of the Verein. In this respect Heine needed to withdraw none of his earlier expressions concerning Jews. At the same time, the task of cooperating in the reforming transformation of Jewish life attracted him, though he was on the point of dissolving his formal connection with the Jewish community. Perhaps he was even more moved by his desire to learn Jewish history with the help of Jewish authorities, and thus to attain clarity concerning his own origin and the conditions of his personal involvement in it. This need grew out of the awareness that the criticism of his recently published poems had been influenced by knowledge of his Jewish origin. The earliest criticisms took no account of this

fact, or had been written without knowledge of it. But very soon
the fact was bruited abroad that the author of these striking and
provoking poems was a Jew, and Heine had grounds for assuming
that freedom of judgment of his work was vitiated by knowledge
of that fact. To confront this menace Heine needed some stronger
spiritual resource than opposition to the state church and the
challenging truculence of his Almansor drama. He needed proof
that he not only belonged to a family which had won the esteem
of non-Jews but also to a race which during its history had produced as great martyrs and heroes of the spirit as the greatest
among the nations of Europe. His earliest contacts with the men
of the Kulturverein promised that such proof could be produced,
and Heine set himself to cooperate with his Jewish contemporaries in an "intensification of energy," and to study the history
of the Jews in the German Middle Ages, which was drenched
with blood of martyrs, and the even more magnificently developed history of the Spanish Jews. The fruit of these studies, not
fully matured to be sure, is Heine's fragment, The Rabbi of
Bacherach.

The need for concrete facts of history which arose out of his
own situation, and the general requirements of his poetic nature
which was directed towards actual phenomena, brought it about
that he followed Zunz, rather than the other friends who sought
to make Judaism acceptable to contemporary culture by some
general formula. Yet, although Heine felt himself attracted by
the historical individuality of Judaism, he required for its understanding a general orientation also, such as his friends more
interested in philosophy could supply. But it was precisely these
discussions which distracted him from a true knowledge of the
Jewish religion. Friedlaender, Bendavid and the Hegelians were
at one in conceiving Judaism as a "deism," as the Enlightenment
had defined it; they assumed an abstract intelligence which had
created the universe but then no longer interfered in historical
life, leaving natural development to its own course. Later, in his
Saint-Simonist period, this concept led Heine to grave misappre-
hension of the Jewish idea of God.

In his contacts with the members of the Verein, Heine did

more than receive information concerning Jewish history and religion which deeply influenced his thinking. To Eduard Gans, the philosopher of law, he owed instruction concerning tendencies in the development of world history and even more in the actual politics of the day. The greatest profit came to Heine from his friendship with Moses Moser, a merchant of purest character and comprehensive education, who read Greek and Indian poetry in the original, and had penetrated deeply into Hegel's philosophy. He was Heine's most patient and most sacrificing friend until the quarrel with Platen resulted in their separation (p. 253). Moser also taught Heine to recognize Jewish traits in the personality of the founder of the Christian religion and to appreciate the historical Jesus of Nazareth as a purely human figure as against its theological transformation by the dogma of the Church. Next after Moser, Heine attached himself to Immanuel Wohlwill, who later became known as the director of the Jacobson school in Seesen, and to Joseph Lehmann, the founder of the Magazin fuer Literatur, a periodical which retained its importance in the literary life of Germany for more than half a century. Lehmann even visited Heine in his "mattress crypt." Heine's friendship with Zunz similarly survived changes of time and place. Heine was frequently in Zunz's house, and on terms of friendship with Zunz's wife Adelheid. Heine saw the Zunz couple six months before his death. On this occasion, Zunz had to give the poet information concerning the Kabbalah. Never before in his life and never afterwards did Heine enjoy so lively an exchange of ideas, never again did he so long and earnestly discuss the weightiest questions with his friends, as in the days of the Verein fuer Kultur und Wissenschaft der Juden.

The Verein was destined to only a short life, for its direction was not able to raise material means necessary for carrying out its program. The futility of repeated appeals to wealthy Jews to make contributions discouraged not only the volatile Gans but also the calmer Moser. Gans laid down the presidency and caused the Verein to dissolve. After he had endeavored in vain to find a position in France, England and even in America, he was converted and became associate professor at the university of

*Berlin. The only survival was the branch Verein in Hamburg,
which concentrated wholly upon reform of ritual.*

The little man's [Ludwig Marcus'] outward appearance, which
not infrequently excited laughter, did not prevent his being one
of the most honored members of that society which published
the above-mentioned periodical, and under the name of the
"Jewish Union of Culture and Science," pursued great ambi-
tions, but impracticable ideas. Intellectual and great-hearted men
endeavored in this way to procure the salvation of a lost cause,
and at best they succeeded in discovering the bodies of the old
combatants on the battlefields of the past. The whole output
of the society consists of a few historical works and research,
among which the treatises of Dr. Zunz on the Spanish Jews in
the Middle Ages must be counted one of the marvels of higher
criticism.

How can I speak of that *Verein* without mentioning the admirable Zunz, who showed unshakable steadfastness in a time
of transition, and in spite of his own acuteness, scepticism and
erudition, remained faithful to everything that he had said
and to the generous impulses of his soul; a man of words and
of action, he created and wrought while others were dreaming
and succumbing to despair.

I cannot leave the subject without mentioning my dear
Bendavid, in whom great spirit and strength of character were
united with large-minded and urbane refinement, and, although
he was very old, he shared all the youthful wild ideas of the
Verein. He was a philosopher of the old style, steeped in the sun-
light of Greek serenity, a pattern of the purest virtue, and by
discipline as hard as the marble of the Categorical Imperative
of his master, Immanuel Kant. All his life Bendavid was the
most zealous disciple of the Kantian philosophy, and in his
youth he suffered the utmost persecution for it; and yet he
would not sever himself from the old community of the Mosaic
creed, and he would never change the cockade of his beliefs.
Even the semblance of such a renunciation filled him with anger
and disgust. Lazarus Bendavid, as I have said, was a thorough-

going Kantian, and in saying that I have indicated his intellectual limitations. When we spoke of Hegelian philosophy, he used to shake his bald head and say that it was superstition. He wrote well, but spoke better. He submitted an extraordinary article for the periodical of the *Verein*, about the messianic idea in Judaism, in which he tried to prove with critical penetration that the belief in a Messiah is not part of its fundamental principles, but is rather to be considered as an incidental accessory to the Jewish religion.

The most active member of the Union, the life and soul of it, was M. Moser, who died a few years ago. Even as quite a young man he was not only profoundly learned, but also fired with a great pity for mankind, and the desire to put his knowledge into practice for the healing of their woes. He was untiring in his philanthropic endeavors. He was very practical, and toiled unostentatiously at his labors of love. The great public knew nothing of his activity. He fought and bled incognito. His name is unknown, and is not written on the role of self-sacrifice. Our generation is not so poor as we think: it has produced an extraordinary number of such nameless martyrs.

Writing the obituary of Marcus led me naturally to writing the obituary of the *Verein* of which he was one of the most honored members. Eduard Gans, who died the other day, was its worthy president. This gifted man cannot be accounted great for his unassuming self-sacrifice or his nameless martyrdom. Indeed, though his soul might be fired with the resolve to procure the salvation of mankind, yet even in moments of exaltation he never lost sight of his personal interests. A witty lady, at whose house Gans often used to take tea of an evening, once observed aptly that even in the fiercest discussion and in spite of his great distraction of mind, when he reached out his hand to the plate of sandwiches, he always took those that were made of fresh salmon and not those made of cheese.

Gans' services to German science are common knowledge. He was one of the most active apostles of the Hegelian philosophy, and in jurisprudence he waged war upon the lackeys of the old Roman Law, who, without any concern for the spirit which

once lived in the old legislation, are only concerned with dusting
the wardrobe that it has left behind, and with cleaning it of
moths, or botching it up for modern use. Gans chastised such
servility even in its most elegant livery. How the wretched soul
of Herr von Savigny whimpered under his kicks! But Gans
furthered the development of the idea of liberty in Germany
more by the spoken than by the written word. He set free the
most closely bound ideas and tore the mask from lies. His was
a nimble spirit of fire, the sparks of which blazed bravely, or
at least glowed finely. But the melancholy expression of the poet
(in the second part of *Faust*):

> Old the word, but ever does its high truth abide,
> Never shall shame and beauty side by side
> Pursue over the green earth their way.
> Always in each deep hatred holds sway,
> And when one encounters the other's track,
> Each upon her enemy turns her back—

must be applied equally to the relationship between genius and
virtue. Both are similarly in constant feud, and frequently turn
their backs upon one another in pique.

I have to say, though I say it with sorrow, that Gans fell very
far short of uprightness in his dealings with the Jewish Union
of Culture and Science, and exposed himself to an accusation
of the most unpardonable felony. His downfall was all the more
calamitous inasmuch as he had played the role of moving spirit
and had undertaken presidential duties. There is a traditional
obligation on the captain of a ship to be the last to leave it when
it sinks. But Gans saved himself first. Little Marcus was morally
superior to the great Gans, and he could justly complain that
Gans was not more equal to his task. . . . Only this much shall I
say here, that the esoteric purpose of the *Verein* was nothing
other than to be an intermediary between historical Judaism
and modern knowledge, of which it was assumed that it would
in the course of time obtain universal dominion. In similar circumstances, in the age of Philo, when Greek philosophy declared

war against all old dogmas, a like attempt was made in Alexandria, with more or less failure. It was not a matter of schismatic doctrinaire enlightenment, and even less of that emancipation which is thrashed about in our day with such disgusting lack of spirit that one may well lose all interest in it. Specifically, the Israelitish friends of this movement have succeeded in enveloping it in a watery gray cloud of tedium which is more injurious to it than the malignant poison of its opponents.

—Ludwig Marcus Memorial

Ludwig Marcus (1798-1843), an orientalist, was a member of the Kulturverein. In 1825, he went to France. Before Heine became acquainted with him, he suffered a nervous breakdown of which the consequences were long noticeable. He died in mental darkness. Despite his illness, he was untiringly active in his studies. He was particularly concerned with research concerning the Falashas in Abyssinia. Heine met him in Paris a number of times.

Early in 1823, Heine's sister Charlotte became engaged to Moritz Embden in Hamburg.

Dear Embden: Your letter of the 23rd ult. filled me with great joy. I congratulate you upon your betrothal to my sister. Although the news moved me deeply, surely more than I am credited, it did not strike me as an "odd quirk of fate." Rather it appeared like something I had long known, known for many years, something I had gradually forgotten in the course of a life stormy within and without. I hope that you and my sister will make a happy pair, for Lottchen is capable of appreciating the worth of your character, and you understand the worth of my sister's character. You surely do not, as does our distorted world of fashion, esteem a woman exclusively for some outstanding excellence of mind or heart or person; surely, as I judge you, you recognize true culture in a seemly balance of all spiritual powers and true amiability in the harmony of soul and body. Dear Lottchen is music, perfect balance and harmony—a brother need not refrain from such expressions in the presence of the bridegroom.

The political part of your letter pleased me greatly; I am glad that my sister's future husband is no revolutionary. I find it quite proper that a man who is comfortable and a happy bridegroom should not desire the overthrow of existing forms, but be concerned for his own and Europe's tranquillity. In my case different conditions obtain, and besides I have a strange feeling when I happen to read in the newspapers that a number of people have frozen to death in the streets of London, or starved to death in the streets of Naples. Though I may be a Radical in England and a Carbonari in Italy, in Germany I do not belong to the demagogues, for the quite incidental and simple reason that a victory of the demagogues would mean that some thousands of Jewish throats—and those precisely the best— would be slit.

—To Moritz Embden
Berlin, February 2, 1823

Heine's misgivings concerning the German radicals is here given expression for the first time. For an understanding of his political attitude it is essential that we take these misgivings into consideration. Heine was a bitter foe of the reactionary governments in Germany and the conservative parties which supported them. But in the German left he saw a much greater danger for the peace of Europe, for European civilization, and not least for the fate of the Jews. He was always convinced that any uprising of the masses in Germany must be accompanied by pogroms. This view determined his political position in the period following, regardless of the deep sympathy which he felt for every revolutionary movement. Despite his numerous charges against political reaction in Germany, he shared their hostility to the nationalist tendencies which were at the time inextricably involved with liberal and democratic tendencies. Only the group of German liberals whose goal was a renewal of the Rhine Union (see p. 236) were at one with Heine in this view. The others opposed him as inconsequential, or even silly. The extreme

*nationalist tendency in German efforts for unity and constitu-
tion has not been noticed by many modern historians. In point of
fact, the German left of this period was far more inclined to
ruthless power politics than were the reactionary governments.
It was Bismarck who first allied conservative-reactionary and
nationalist tendencies.*

I am very fond of Zunz and painfully distressed at seeing that
excellent man go unrecognized because of his harsh and repellent
exterior. I have high expectations of his sermons which are soon
to appear—surely no mere edification and mild soul-salve, but
something much better, a quickening of power. That is what is
lacking in Israel. Certain chiropodists (Friedlaender and Company) have sought to cure the body of Judaism of its fatal
inflammations by blood-letting, and Israel must bleed to death
because of their clumsiness and their spidery bandages of reason.
Would that the blindness which regards all excellence as con-
sisting in powerlessness, in the alienation of all strength, in uni-
lateral negation, in idealized Auerbachism, soon come to an end!
We no longer have the strength to wear a beard, to fast, to hate,
and by hate to tolerate: that is the motive of our Reform. Some
who have received their education and enlightenment from
comedians would give Judaism new decorations and new back-
drops, with a prompter who is to wear white clerical bands
instead of a beard; they would pour all the sea into a puny basin
of papier-mâché, and would clothe the Hercules of the Wilhelms-
hoehe in Kassel with little Marcus' brown jacket. Others desire
a bit of evangelical Christianity under the name of a Jewish
firm, and make themselves a *talles* out of the wool of the lamb
of God, a jerkin out of the feathers of the dove of the Holy
Ghost, and drawers out of Christian love; and they go bankrupt,
and their successors style themselves: "God, Christ, and Company." Happily this house will not long endure; its drafts upon
philosophy come back protested, and it is bankrupt in Europe
even though the agencies established by its missionaries in Africa
and Asia may continue for some centuries. This eventual fall of
Chr. becomes clearer to me daily. Long enough has the vile

notion been maintained. I call Chr. an idea; but what an idea! There are dirty families of ideas which have nested in the crannies of this old world, the forsaken bedstead of the Holy Ghost, even as bed-bug families nest in the bedstead of a Polish Jew. If one steps on one of these bed-bug ideas, it leaves a stench which is pervasive for a millennium. Such is Chr., which was trodden upon eighteen hundred years ago and which still makes the air pestilential even for us poor Jews today.

Forgive me this bitterness; the blow of the rescinded edict has not struck you. Nor is it all to be taken very seriously, not even the earlier portion. I, too, have no strength to wear a beard, to have people cry "kike" after me, to fast, and the like. I have not even the strength to eat *matzes* decently. I am living with a Jew (across from Moser and Gans), and now get *matzes* instead of bread, and break my teeth on it. But I comfort myself and think, "Ah, but we are in *Goles!*" Nor is the sting at Friedlaender meant so ill; not long ago I ate an excellent pudding at his house. He lives across from me, and is now standing at his window and trimming a pen, and will soon write to Elise von der Recke, and, looking at his face, one can already read: "Noble lady, I am really not so incorrigible as Professor Voigt says, for—."

—To Immanuel Wohlwill
Berlin, April 1, 1823

In 1799, in agreement with the heads of a number of Jewish families, David Friedlaender addressed a published a Letter to the Provost Teller, a leader of the Protestant Enlightenment. This brochure proposed that the Berlin Jews go over to Protestantism, but that they be exempted from all churchly ritual and not required to recognize the divinity of Jesus Christ. As Friedlaender was soon forced to realize, his proposal rested upon a complete misunderstanding of the Protestant religion, for which the dogma of the divinity of its founder was of central importance. Teller rejected Friedlaender's proposal. The majority of Berlin Jews protested vehemently against the suggestion that the Jewish community be dissolved. Thereupon Friedlaender

concentrated his efforts upon the support of the Jewish Reform
movement and the defense of the civic rights of the Jews. To
refute antisemitic authors, he published, in 1820, a Letter addressed to the authoress Elise von der Recke, entitled: Contribution to the History of the Persecution of the Jews in the
Nineteenth Century by Writers. With all his personal friendship
for Friedlaender, Heine regarded his position as untenable. But
Heine himself shared Friedlaender's initial error. Heine, too,
assumed that it was possible to be a Protestant without believing
in the divinity of Jesus. Heine not only condemned the Jewish
Reform preacher Isaac Levin Auerbach (1791-1853) as superficial
and nerveless, but repeatedly treated him with personal disdain.
The edict of March 11, 1812, which guaranteed civic rights to the
Jews in Prussia was rescinded in 1820. Thereupon the Jews of
Prussia were excluded from access to public employment. In
consequence, Heine expressed an intention to emigrate either to
Russian Poland or to France; but he abandoned these plans when
his uncle Salomon promised funds for him to continue his
studies for two additional years.

Lyrical Intermezzo

In April 1823, Heine's second book, entitled Tragedies, with a
Lyrical Intermezzo, appeared. It contained both tragedies,
Almansor and William Ratcliff, and sixty-six lyric poems.
Almansor is a protest against conversion; its scorn of the Moors
who were converted to Christianity is only a slight disguise for
an attack against the German Jews who underwent baptism.
William Ratcliff celebrates the protest against the bourgeois
order of society. Even more than Almansor, it is influenced by
the "tragedy of fate" which had become fashionable in German
drama; it sought to transfer the ancient Greek concept of fate
to modern conditions, and the superficial and awkward imitation
made the dramatic treatment extremely ineffective. For a long
while Heine was a devout admirer of Adolf Muellner, the chief
exponent of this perverse movement (see p. 184). Almansor had a

single presentation which was a stunning failure; William Ratcliff was never presented. Even at a later period, Heine had an affection, which no one shared, for William Ratcliff. The poems of the Lyrical Intermezzo, on the other hand, raised Heine's reputation as a poet considerably. They became popular at once. With several new poems they were included in the Buch der Lieder, of which they are the best portion. The success of the Lyrical Intermezzo was based, not on the artistic merit of the individual poems, but upon their arrangement in sequence, which made of them a kind of a romance. The principal heroes of this lyrical romance are the poet Heine and a lady whose identity is disguised, though her personal character is plainly marked. In biographical details concerning the objects of his love poems, Heine was always extremely discreet. Only rarely did he permit it to be recognized what actual person he referred to. This practice corresponded to his repeatedly stated requirement that biographical considerations must not enter into the enjoyment of a poem. In a poet who gives such open expression to his own subjectivity, this requirement seems to be a contradiction. But it was consistently maintained by Heine, until he liberated himself from it in the poems From the Mattress Crypt. Doubtless the poems of the Lyrical Intermezzo are based on actual experiences, but these have been freely transformed by the poet. Despite the prudence he enjoined upon himself, the course of these experiences may be surmised. Heine's love for Amalie, whose memory is echoed in the Intermezzo, had gone unrequited; but here he is heeded and enjoys the love of the girl, whom he then has to leave to another man; but even after the marriage of his beloved, he finds himself in her company again. These events probably took place in 1821, for the last poem of the Intermezzo ("The Song so Old and Bitter") was originally intended as a New Year's song for that year. The following selection from the Lyrical Intermezzo presents the principal points in the love romance which Heine tells; its joy in psychologic complications is at the opposite pole from the melancholy of the Youthful Sorrows.

The world is dull, the world is blind.
 Each day more of a mad one!
It says, my dear, that, to its mind,
 Your character's a bad one.

The world is dull, the world is blind.
 Its dullness is really distressing;
It does not know how clinging and kind
 Are your kisses that burn with their blessing.
      —Lyrical Intermezzo, 15

 Say, love, art thou not a vision,—
  Speak, for I to know am fain,—
 Such as summer hours Elysian
  Breed within the poet's brain?

 Nay, a mouth of such completeness,
  Eyes of such bewitching flame,
 Girl so garner'd round with sweetness,
  Never did a poet frame.

 Vampires, basilisks, chimaeras,
  Dragons, monsters, all the dire
 Creatures of the fable eras,
  Quicken in the poet's fire.

 But thyself, so artful-artless,
  Thy sweet face, thy tender eyes,
 With their looks so fond, so heartless,
  Never poet could devise.
      —Lyrical Intermezzo, 16

 Like the foam-born of the waters,
  Gleams my love in beauty's pride;
 But that fairest of earth's daughters
  Is a stranger's chosen bride.

Heart, keep patience; never lose it;
  Murmur not that thou'rt betrayed;
Bear it, bear it, and excuse it
  To the lovely, stupid maid.
                    —Lyrical Intermezzo, 17

I blame thee not, a broken heart my lot,
O Love for ever lost! I blame thee not.
Though thou art splendid with the diamonds bright,
There falls no gleam within thy heart's deep night.

I've known this long. I saw thee in clear dream,
And saw black night within thy soul supreme,
And saw the worm still fretting at thy heart,
I saw how wretched, O my Love, thou art.
                    —Lyrical Intermezzo, 18

Yes, thou art wretched, and I do not mourn;
  Wretched, my love, it seems we both must be!
Until in death the weary heart is torn,
  Wretched, my love, it seems we both must be!

I see the scorn that on thy lips doth ride,
  I see the courage in thy flashing eye;
I see thy bosom heave with quenchless pride—
  Yet thou are wretched, wretched even as I.

Thy lips contract with unseen wounds and pain,
  And secret tears bedim the eyes I see;
Thy haughty bosom bears the hidden bane—
  Wretched, my love, it seems we both must be.
                    —Lyrical Intermezzo, 19

So now you have forgotten wholly
How once your heart was mine, mine solely;
Your heart had so sweet and so false a glow,
Naught could be sweeter or falser, I know.

So the love and the pain is forgotten wholly
That tortured my heart and made it lowly.
But whether the pain was as great as my love,
I know not. I know they were both great enough.
—Lyrical Intermezzo, 20

They have told you many stories
  And made a great to-do;
But why my spirit worries
  Has not been told to you.

They made a stir and pother,
  Complaining and shaking the head,
"A devil!" they said to each other;
  And you believed all they said.

And yet the very worst thing
  They never even have guessed;
For the worst and most accurst thing,
  I carry hid in my breast.
—Lyrical Intermezzo, 24

When the lime-trees bloomed, and the sun shone bright,
And the nightingale sang in the morning light,
You kissed me then, and your soft arm pressed
And clasped me close to your throbbing breast.

When the sun shone pale, and the leaves were dead,
And the raven croaked in the trees o'erhead,
We wished one another a cold "Good-day,"
You made me a courtesy, and went your way.
—Lyrical Intermezzo, 25

We have felt for each other a deal through life,
  And yet behaved ourselves as we ought;
We often have played at husband and wife,
  And yet we never have wrangled and fought.

We have shared together, in mirth and bliss,
The fondest embrace and the sweetest kiss;
And to end the matter, from childish pique
We have played with each other hide and seek:
And have hidden so well, that at last 'tis plain
We never shall find one another again.

—Lyrical Intermezzo, 26

You were steadfast and true the longest;
   Your care you always gave me,
   Your thought would cheer and save me
When fear and need were strongest.

A gift of gold would not grieve you,
   And food you ne'er denied me;
   With linen you supplied me,
My passport I owe to you.

And for this great amount, He,
   The Lord, I pray will be tender
   To you and reward the splendor
Of your everlasting bounty.

—Lyrical Intermezzo, 27

Although Heine was a Prussian subject, he always travelled with the passport of the free city of Hamburg. According to the preceding poem, he obtained this passport, not by the intercession of Salomon Heine, but through his beloved, who upon other occasions also had used her influence with the Hamburg senators in the poet's interest.

From my great grief, I fashion
   The little songs I utter;
   They lift bright wings and flutter
Off to her heart with passion.

Over her bosom they hover—
　　But soon they fly homeward complaining;
　　Complaining but never explaining
What, in her heart, they discover.
—Lyrical Intermezzo, 36

I loved thee once—and I love thee now.
　　Though the stars, in a golden shower,
Should fall . . . above the chaos and glow
　　The flame of my love would tower!
—Lyrical Intermezzo, 44

　When two that are dear must part,
　　In sorrow the hands are pressed;
　Their tears begin to flow,
　　Their sighing knows no rest.

　With us there was no weeping,
　　Nor had we aught to say—
　Our sighing and our weeping
　　Came on an after-day.
—Lyrical Intermezzo, 49

For the romance narrated in the Lyrical Intermezzo Heine composed an epilogue which he did not himself publish. It is improbable that the Bertha mentioned in it is the real name of his beloved.

　She seemed so sweet and good, my heart
　　Among the angels set her;
　She could not even hurt a flower,
　　And she wrote a charming letter.

　The wedding was near, her kinsfolk heard,
　　And they all began to scold her.
　Oh, Bertha was a stupid thing:
　　Did as aunts and cousins told her.

She broke her pledge, she broke her vow,
   Yet with right good-will I acquit her,
For had we been married I'm sure she'd have made
   My love and life both bitter.

And now when I think on a woman false,
   I think on Bertha faithless;
But I honestly hope, when her child is born,
   She herself may come off scatheless.

*This poem was communicated by E. Schmidt-Weissenfels,
from a copy which he received in 1850, in his book* On Heinrich
Heine *(1857)*.

Departure from Berlin

I am going away soon and I beg you not altogether to throw
away my image into the lumber room of oblivion. I could make
no reprisals, and though I were to say to myself a hundred times
a day, "You will forget Frau von Varnhagen!" it could not be.
Forget me not! You cannot excuse yourself on the score of bad
memory, your spirit has made a contract with time, and if after
some hundreds of years I have the pleasure of seeing you as the
fairest and most beautiful of all the flowers in the fairest and
most beautiful of all the valleys of heaven, then you will have
the kindness to greet me as a holly tree (or shall I be something
worse?), as an old acquaintance, with your friendly glance and
your soft-breathing sweetness. It is certain that you will do so.
You have done so in the years 1822 and 1823 when you treated
me, a sick, bitter, morose, poetic and insufferable human being,
with a kindliness and goodness which I have certainly not deserved in *this* life, and must owe alone to tender recollections of
an earlier acquaintance.

              —To Rahel Varnhagen von Ense
              Berlin, April 12, 1823

*This was written in a copy of the Tragedies.
In his letters to Rahel and to her sister-in-law Friederike Rob-*

ert, Heine often plays with thoughts of metempsychosis. Friederike Robert is the "Madame" or "Fair Lady" to whom the stories
of The Book LeGrand (Reisebilder, 2) are told. Rahel was a convert to Christianity, but retained a lively interest in Jewish problems and personalities. In the last years of her life, she turned
nearer to Judaism again. She never made a secret of her Jewish
origin. Among her friends and admirers were Goethe, princes of
the Prussian royal house, poets of German Romanticism, and
numerous foreign nobles and diplomats. Like Heine, Gans and
Moser were also frequently in her house. Rahel had great experience in handling unruly and untamed poetic characters. The
relationships between her and Heine were not always free of
misunderstandings and quarrels, and the fault was not always
Heine's. But Rahel's enthusiasm for ideas and works of art, to
which she reacted as to living people, and her wit, her keen perception and her predilection for complicated natures, struck
kindred chords in Heine.

My attachment to Jewishness stems solely from a deep antipathy to Christianity. Yes, I the contemner of all positive religions, may some day go over to the crassest rabbinism, and simply
because I consider it a proven counter-poison.

—To Moritz Embden
Berlin, May 3, 1823

A few days later Heine left Berlin. The remainder of the year
he spent at his parents' house in Lueneburg. Only in January
1824, did he resume his studies in Goettingen.

In the "Abode of Tedium"

His sojourn in Lueneburg affected Heine's nerves seriously.
The condition of his mentally ailing father, which he observed
daily, was a torment to him. The quiet provincial city at first
offered him few incentives. Only later did he come to know
people who interested him, and in particular the lawyer Rudolph
Christiani.

On my arrival in Lueneburg I noticed that great *rishes* prevailed here, and determined to lead an isolated life. My brother's library consists wholly of Latin and Greek classics, and it is these that boredom will make me read. I should very much like you to send me some parts of Gibbon, the two volumes of Basnage, which contain simple history, a short Italian grammar, and an Italian reading book. . . .

Truly, you are the man of most beautiful feeling in Israel. I can only give expression to the beautiful feelings of others with difficulty. Your feelings are massive gold ingots; mine light paper currency. Paper is valuable only because of people's trust; but paper remains paper even if the banker credits it, and gold remains gold even if it lies in some corner as an unnoticed lump.

Have you not observed from the above picture that I am a Jewish poet? But why should I stand on ceremony? We are among friends, and I like to speak in our own national symbols. When a Ganstown will come to be built, and a happier generation blesses the *lulef* and crunches *matzes* on the Mississippi, and a new Jewish literature burgeons forth, then our current mercantile-exchange expressions will belong to the language of poetry, and a poetic great-grandson of little Marcus, swathed in *talles* and *tefillim* will chant before the entire Ganstown *kille:* "By the waters of the Spree they sat, and counted treasury notes. Then came their enemies and spake, Give us London bills; high is the exchange."

—To Moses Moser
Lueneburg, May 1823

Edward Gibbon's History of the Decline and Fall of the Roman Empire *interested Heine because of its outspokenly unfavorable views of the victory of Christianity over ancient paganism. Byron, too, acclaimed its author for "sapping a solemn creed with a solemn sneer." Jacques Basnage de Beauval published in 1707 a* History of the Religion of the Jews from Jesus Christ to the Present, *in which he diligently strove for objectivity. Heine studied this work intensively for his* Rabbi of Bacherach, *and made extracts of it for use in the text of his novel. Heine often re-*

read the book in later periods. The jest at "Ganstown" alludes to
the efforts of Mordecai Manuel Noah (1785-1851) to establish a
Jewish colony called Ararat on Grand Island near Niagara. He selected Gans and Zunz as his trusted agents to publicize his
scheme among the Jews of Germany.

I was deeply and bitterly vexed yesterday when I saw from a
letter of an acquaintance that he would construe my entire poetic
being out of bits of history swept together, and let fall unpleasant
expressions about "impressions of life," "political attitudes," "religion," and the like. Such things openly uttered would have
infuriated me, and I am heartily glad that such is not the case.
Readily as a poet's history may lead to conclusions concerning
his poem, readily as it may be demonstrated that political attitudes, religion, private enmity, prejudice and prudence, have
affected his work, these things must nevertheless not be mentioned, and especially not during the lifetime of a poet. One
deflowers the poem, one tears the mysterious veil from its face,
if the influence of the history which is suggested is actually present, and one disfigures the poem if such influence is falsely
attributed. And how seldom does the outer garb of our history
correspond to our actual inner story! With me, at least, it never
corresponds.

—To Karl Immermann
Lueneburg, June 10, 1823

In his Paris period, Heine gave a sharper formulation to his
demand that a poem must be judged solely by its artistic merit,
without regard for the biography of the author and his attitude
to questions of the day, on the basis of the principle "art for
art's sake."

My life at this moment is entirely isolated, cut off from all
actual human intercourse, and still, because of my illness, quite
without occupation; and it is therefore quite natural that I should
think of you and your wife the greater part of the day. I have a
lively memory of the many kindnesses and the love which you
have shown me, of how you cheered and strengthened and en-

couraged the morose and sick man, and supported him by word and deed, and refreshed him with macaroni and food of the spirit. I have found so little genuine kindliness in life and have been so much mystified; it was from you and your magnanimous wife that I first experienced thoroughly humane treatment. I must impress your dear images the more firmly in my mind because again so much that is unclean, evil and confused presses upon me, and my head is still sick and my heart not yet well.

—To Varnhagen von Ense

Lueneburg, June 17, 1823

Karl August Varnhagen von Ense (1785-1858), diplomat and historian, husband of Rahel, was a loyal friend to Heine, after initial frictions, until the end, took his part in all quarrels and rendered him much valuable service. Heine's political views were very close to those of Varnhagen. Because of his advocacy of liberal ideas, Varnhagen was in great disfavor with the King of Prussia, but because of his experience and skill he was employed in difficult confidential missions. He was also on terms of confidence with Metternich, who came to know Heine's poems through him; Metternich loved the poems, though he caused their author to be prosecuted. As a decided opponent of antisemitism, Varnhagen was in close touch with almost all significant Jewish personalities of his day.

> My heart is full of sorrow
>   Though May is full of cheer;
> I stand beside the linden,
>   High on the bastion here.
>
> I watch the blue moat idly;
>   Gently it flows along.
> A boy in a drifting rowboat
> Angles and whistles a song.
>
> Beyond, like a quaint toy village,
>   Tiny and many-hued,

Are houses, gardens, and people,
  Oxen and meadow and wood.

To bleach their piles of linen
  The laughing maidens come;
The millwheel spatters diamonds;
  I hear its distant hum.

Upon the old gray tower
  A sentry box stands low;
And there a chap in scarlet
  Is pacing to and fro.

He practises with his rifle
  That catches the sunset's red;
He shoulders it and presents it—
  Would that he shot me dead!
            —Book of Songs: Home-Coming
                      Louis Untermeyer

*The description of the Lueneburg wall corresponds to its state
in Heine's day.*

Jews here as everywhere are insufferable hagglers and draggle-
tails, the Christian middle class unamiable, with extraordinary
rishes, the higher classes the same and in higher degree. . . . I
am impelled to express the great *Judenschmerz* (as Boerne calls
it) in a newspaper article, and I shall as soon as my head will
tolerate it. . . .
    I shall visit Cohen in Hamburg. Of you I expect that you will
write me (but briefly) how I should behave there with respect to
the *Verein*, whom I am to visit, and the like. . . .
    From Rousseau I have as yet received no letter; partly your hint
about the magazine, by whose anti-Jewish position I was struck,
and partly other things provide me sure indications that my
Almansor is very displeasing to the Catholics on the Rhine, that
they would gladly ignore it, but discuss it everywhere, and have

incited Rousseau against me. . . . I shall observe without bitterness that the people who have raised me to heaven will spatter me with mud for a change. . . .

Fouqué recently sent me a cordial letter and dedicated a pretty poem to me; I will show it to you when occasion offers. He too will some day wish the poem unwritten, when he investigates my family tree more closely.

—To Moses Moser
Lueneburg, June 18, 1823

Gustav Gerson Cohen was a sugar-broker in Hamburg, friend of Salomon Heine and zealous advocate of Jewish Reform. For Rousseau see page 94. Friedrich de la Motte Fouqué (1771-1843), Prussian officer, romantic poet, passionate devotee of the middle ages and defender of the privileges of the nobility, was Heine's earliest model. The poem which Fouqué dedicated to Heine shows warm sympathy and deep understanding of Heine's nature.

On June, 22, 1823, the marriage of Moritz Embden and Charlotte Heine took place near Hamburg.

On the 22nd I stayed with my family, on the occasion of the marriage of my sister. It was a fine day of feasting and concord. The food was good, the beds were bad, and my uncle Salomon was very pleased. I think I shall stand well with him in future: outwardly we are on the best of terms and he makes up to me in public. I have also entered into good relations with my uncle Henry.

—To Moses Moser
Lueneburg, June 24, 1823

How is Mlle. Sobernheim? I deeply regret that I am not in Berlin at this moment, and I bid you to give the amiable young lady my most cordial greetings. She is among the most beautiful, that is, the happiest, acquaintances that I made in Poland. You know, my dear Lehmann, I went hunting there after pure and healthy human nature, which I understood well how to find, for the impure and the sick is so well known to me. I have always

found the healthiest natures among Jewesses, and I cannot blame
God the Father for getting Bethlehemite Mary with child.

What you suggest with reference to Rousseau seems justified.
I have been three months and longer without a letter from him,
and have evidence that he is collecting mud to throw at me. I
have long known that he is again allied with my angry old enemies, the Old Germans; and the displeasure which the tendentiousness of my *Almansor* has aroused on the Rhine, a
tendentiousness which he can now himself realize, must have
contributed to the eruption of his anger against me. . . .

You were almost the first man in Berlin to show me friendship,
and in my helplessness in many things you proved yourself un-
selfishly ready to serve me. It is inherent in my character, or, more
accurately, in my illness, that at moments of discouragement I
never spare my best friends and even chaff and maltreat them
most offensively. You too must have learned this amiable trait of
mine, and I hope you will learn it even better in future. Yet you
must never forget that poisonous plants grow where a lush soil
produces the gayest and strongest vegetation, and that barren
moors which are spared such poisonous plants remain only barren moors. . . .

I also expect that, since you read all papers, you will inform
me if any exception is taken to me, particularly in respect of
religion. You know how much that interests me.

—To Joseph Lehmann
Lueneburg, June 26, 1823

I was in Hamburg at a bad time. My pains made me dull, and
because of the death of a cousin and the resulting shock to my
family, I found little gaiety in others. At the same time the magic
of the place is working fearfully upon my soul, in which a quite
new principle is emerging. This principle will probably direct me
through a series of years and determine my acts of commission
and omission. If I were a German—but I am no German: see
Ruehs, Fries *loc. cit.*—I would write you long letters on this
theme, lavish accounts of my mood. But I do long to uncover

my heart to you at some intimate hour and to show you "how
the new folly is grafted on to the old."

—To Moses Moser
Ritzebuettel, August 23, 1823

The "new principle" is love of Therese Heine, Amalie's
younger sister. This love was as hopeless as the other. Ruehs,
Fries: see above, p. 120.

By chance I met on my journey
    My dear one's family;
Sister and mother and father;
    Smiling, they greeted me.

How was my health—and spirits?
    They? . . . Oh, the same old tale,
I hadn't changed much, they told me.
    Only a trifle pale.

I asked about aunts and cousins
    With interest (save the mark!)
And other such pleasing people,
    And the dog, with his gentle bark.

How was my married sweetheart
    Whom they had left behind?
And smilingly they told me
    That she soon would be confined.

I coughed congratulations,
    And, stammering wretchedly,
I asked them all to greet her
    A thousand times for me.

Then spoke the little sister:
    "That puppy pet of mine

Grew up so big and horrid,
    We drowned him in the Rhine."

The child resembles her sister,
    Sometimes remarkably so—
Those eyes and that way of laughing
    That brought me so much woe.
                    —Book of Songs: The Home-Coming

Little girl with big, big eyes,
I have told you over and over:
Words for my love I cannot devise,
But it gnaws at my heart-strings ever.

But only in my room alone
Dared I in such wise speak;
But in your presence never a tone,
In your presence silent and meek.

Sure, they were bad, bad angels
Who kept my lips shut tight;
And now those bad, bad angels
Have made me wretched for spite.
                    —Book of Songs: The Home-Coming

Heine dedicated the second part of his Reisebilder, *entitled*
Ideen: Das Buch LeGrand, *to his cousin Therese, under the*
pseudonym Evelina.

She was amiable and he loved her;
but he was not amiable, and she did
not love him.

                    —Old Play

Fair lady, do you know the old play? It is a very remarkable
one, only rather too melancholy. Once upon a time I acted the
chief part, making all the ladies weep; only one remained ob-

durate, not dropping a single tear; and this was just the point of the play, the real catastrophe. . . .

The old play is a tragedy, though the hero does not fall by the hand of another or of himself. The eyes of the heroine are beautiful—fair lady, do you not smell violets?—most beautiful, and yet so piercing that they penetrated my heart like crystal daggers and surely peered out at my back—and yet I did not die by those lethal eyes.

—Ideas: The Book LeGrand, 1-2

Therese Heine married the Hamburg lawyer Adolphe Halle, a converted Jew, whom Heine regarded as one of his most danger-ous enemies in the circle of his uncle Salomon. In the summer of 1853, in company of her brother Carl Heine, she visited the poet, now on his death-bed, and unconsciously recalled the memory of his disillusionment.

> Thou wert a blonde-hair'd maid without a stain,
> So neat, so prim, so cool! I stay'd in vain
> To see thy bosom's guarded gates unroll,
> And Inspiration breathe upon thy soul.
>
> A zeal and ardor for those lofty themes,
> By chilly Reason scorn'd for airy dreams,
> But wringing from the noble and the good
> The toil of hand and heart, and brain and blood.
>
> On hills with vineyards' clambering leafage gay,
> Glass'd in the Rhine we roamed one summer day;
> Bright was the sun, and from the shining cup
> Of every flower a giddy scent flew up.
>
> A kiss of fire, a deep voluptuous blush,
> Burn'd on each pink and every rosy bush,
> Ideal flames in dandelions glow'd,
> And lit each sorriest weed that edged our road.

But thou went'st on with even-stepping feet,
Clad in white satin, elegant and neat;
No child of Netcher's brush more trim and nice,
And in thy stays a little heart of ice.

—Lazarus, 6

My cause at Reason's bar was heard:
  "Your fame is clear as noon-day's sun,"—
The sentence ran,—"by deed or word
  The fair Accused no ill has done."

Yes! while my soul was passion-torn,
  She dumb and motionless stood by;
She did not scoff, she did not scorn,
  Yet "guilty, guilty," still I cry.

For an accusing Voice is heard,
  When night is still and thought is dim,
Saying, "It was not deed or word,
  But her bad heart, that ruined him."

Then came the witnesses and proofs,
  And documents of priceless cost;
But when the dawn has touched the roofs,
  All vanish, and my cause is lost:

And in my being's darkest deep
  The plaintiff seeks the shame to hide:
One sense—one memory—will not sleep—
  That I am utterly destroyed.

—Lazarus, 7

The sight of the ailing poet, on the occasion of this visit, so shocked Therese that she wrote him from Hamburg after her return as follows: "My dear Harry: After the visit I paid you when we were last in Paris, your image stands before me constantly, and I think with great distress of your physical sufferings, which you endure with very very great moral strength, a strength which fills me with such esteem that I feel constrained to make it known to you. I hope, my dear Harry, that you will receive these lines with your earlier friendly attachment and understand that they are addressed to you by a warm and sympathetic heart. May dear God stand by you—that is my most earnest wish for you—and alleviate this severe trial for you, give you greater and greater strength, and preserve your spiritual vigor so that you may remain master of your torment and of your will . . ."

This letter called forth the following poem:

Suddenly, a levin bolt illuminating
Abysmal night, your letter descended;
Its blinding light showed all was ended,
Showed how deep my woe, how devastating.

You, even you, must sympathy unfold,
You who in my life's sad carnage
Stood silent, as you were an image,
Like marble beautiful, like marble cold.

God! Wherefore must I wretched wait!
She, even she, must utter speech,
From her eyes flow tears to heal the breach,
The very stone proves compassionate.

What I beheld fair shattered me;
Pity me Thou, and on me bestow
Tranquillity, O God, and with one blow
End, O end my tragedy.

Cohen was a very dear friend to me in Hamburg, and I grew very fond of him. The Jews there are a miserable pack; if one wishes to do something for them it is better not to see them, and I find it more tolerable to keep my distance. I visited Dr. Salomon, and he did not wholly displease me, but he is still an Auerbachian. Kley I did not visit; you know he was always repulsive to me, and he is really loathsome. Monas is still the same old woman; I love him and would cheerfully cure him of the sentimentality into which he has deceived himself and which now spoils him. Bernays I have heard preach; he is a charlatan, and none of the Jews understands him. He wants nothing and will never play a role; but he is a gifted man and has more spirit in him than Dr. Kley, Salomon, or Auerbach I or II. I have not visited him, though I have long had opportunity to do so. I honor him insofar as he hoodwinks the Hamburg dunces; but I honor the lamented cartouche more. . . . What they think of me cannot be anything extraordinary, but to me that is a matter of indifference. I have disabused them of the illusion that I am an enthusiast for the Jewish religion. But I confess that I shall be an enthusiast for the rights of the Jews and their civic equality; and in the bad times which must inevitably come, the German populace will hear my voice, and it will echo in beer-taverns and in palaces. But the born enemy of all positive religions will never rise as champion of that religion which first nurtured that censoriousness which has cost us so much anguish in the present. If it happen that I somehow should, there will be special reasons —complaisance, obstinacy, desire to preserve an antidote. But I shall never tell Steinweg in advance, if I wish to do anything for him; he must never expect anything from me, and must never be able to say that I have disappointed his expectations. . . .

At this moment I am like a beaten man. All night I sailed about on the North Sea, wishing to go to Helgoland, but when we were near that island the captain had to turn back because the storm was too severe. What people say of the savagery of the sea is entirely justified. It is supposed to have been one of the wildest storms; the sea was a mountain range in motion, the watery peaks crashed into one another, the waves broke over the ship and hurled it upwards and downwards; there was the music of sea-sick passengers in the cabin, the cries of the sailors, the gloomy howling of the winds, roaring, buzzing, whistling; it was a murderous spectacle, the rain pouring down as if the heavenly hosts were emptying their chamber pots—and I lay upon the deck, with nothing further from my thoughts than pious reflections. I tell you, though I could hear the trumpets of the last judgment in the wind and see Abraham's bosom opened wide in the waves, I found myself far better pleased than in the company of the Jew-jabbering Hamburgers and Hamburgeresses. Hamburg!! At once my Elysium and my Tartarus! Spot that I detest and love, where I am tortured by the most disgusting feelings, and yet where I wish to be, and where I will doubtless frequently find myself in the future.

—To Moses Moser
Ritzebuettel, August 23, 1823

Gotthold Salomon (1784-1862), preacher of the Hamburg Reform congregation after 1818, was an impressive orator, and defended the Jews against Ruehs, Fries, and later Bruno Bauer. Eduard (Israel) Kley (1789-1867) was director of the Jewish school and Reform preacher in Hamburg. Monas: nickname for Wohlwill. Isaac Bernays (1792-1848): Haham of the orthodox congregation in Hamburg. Auerbach II: Baruch Auerbach, director of the Jewish communal school in Berlin, on bad terms with Zunz. His brother, Isaac L. Auerbach, an influential advocate of Reform, is referred to as Auerbach, I. Steinweg: street in Hamburg, inhabited chiefly by Jews in Heine's day.

His experience at sea, which Heine relates in this letter, he treats of in a poem also:

> The storm tunes up for dancing,
>   With whistle and sough and roar,
> Hurrah! how the good ship capers,
>   Night lustily takes the floor.
>
> Live ranges of water-mountains
>   Are shaped by the raging sea,
> Here yawning in black abysses,
>   There towering white on our lee.
>
> What cursing, puking, and praying
>   In reeks from the cabin come;

I hug the mast like a lover,
And wish myself safe at home.
—Book of Songs: The Home-Coming

I am once more in Lueneburg, the Abode of Boredom. My health is the same: nerves stronger, but the headaches lasting longer. This brings me to despair, for I am working again at my Law. . . .

Do not think that I am bitter against Cohen, however bitter he may be against me. You would surely have laughed if you heard that my quarrel with him was about the Temple. I gave him my honest opinion about it when I was first in Hamburg, but in the mildest possible terms. On my second visit to Hamburg he accused me (and on my honor, unjustly) of speaking to Salomon Heine about Kley and Bernays quite differently than I had spoken to him. The result was that when I met him at my uncle's I repeated what I had said as outspokenly as possible. . . . I am irritated and sickened, and at present very bitter against those dull fellows who gain their livelihood from a thing for which I have made the greatest sacrifices and all my life long must bleed in spirit. *I* must be made bitter. I! Just at a time when I was reconciled to letting the waves of Jew-hatred break upon me. Truly, it is not the Kleys and Auerbachs who are hated in dear Germany. On all sides I feel the workings of that hatred, which yet is scarcely out of the germ. Friends with whom I have passed the greater part of my life now turn from me. Admirers become traitors, those whom I most love hate me most, and all seek to injure me.

Meanwhile, my family affairs and my financial condition are in the worst possible case. You say that I was lacking in prudence in my behavior towards my uncle. You do me wrong. I know not why I should not maintain towards my uncle that dignity which I show towards all other men. You know that I am no delicate, sensitive youth, who blushes when he has to borrow money and stammers when he asks help of his best friend. Indeed, I do not need to avow that to you, for it is your own experience that I have a very thick hide in such matters; but I am also singular in this, that I will not extort by the intercession of my friends any money from my uncle, who possesses some two millions but will not willingly part with a farthing. . . . I have agreed with my uncle that I should receive from him only 100 *louis d'or* for my studies, from January 1824 to 1825, because I counted on it, and I assured him that so far as I was concerned I would never again trouble him for more. For such complaisance, my uncle, at whose country house in Hamburg I spent many days, has rewarded me by treating me with respectful attention and graciousness. But in the last analysis I am a man who cannot behave otherwise and whom no monetary consideration can move to part with his self-respect. Hence you see that despite my headaches I continue my study of the Law, which is to earn me bread.

As you can surmise, my conversion is involved. None of my family is opposed except me. But *me* is an obstinate character. From the nature of my thinking you can deduce that baptism is a matter of indifference to me, that I do not regard it as important even symbolically, and that in the circumstances in which it will be carried out in my case it will have little significance for others likewise. For me perhaps its significance will be that I can better devote myself to championing the rights of my unfortunate brethren. And yet I hold it beneath my dignity and a stain on my honor to undergo conversion in order to obtain a position in Prussia. Dear old Prussia! I really do not know what course to take in this bad situation. I'll turn Catholic yet for spite, and hang myself. . . . We are living in sad times. Scoundrels become our "best," and the best must turn scoundrel. I understand well the words of the Psalmist: "Lord, give us our daily bread, that we blaspheme not Thy name."

—To Moses Moser
Lueneburg, September 27, 1823

The six weeks at Cuxhaven cost me thirty *louis d'or.* (My uncle bestowed ten *louis* on me before my departure for the baths.) Here I live with my parents and am at no expense. It is fatal that in my case the whole man is governed by the budget. Want or excess of money has not the least influence on my principles, but all the more influence on my conduct. Yes, great Moser, Heinrich Heine is very small. Verily, tiny Marcus is bigger than I. It is no joke, but grim earnest. I cannot repeat it to you often enough, so that you should not measure me by the gauge of your own great soul. Mine is of elastic rubber, and may stretch to infinity or shrink to puniness. But a soul I do have; as Sterne put it, "I am positive I have a soul." Let that suffice you. Love me for the sake of the remarkable kind of feelings which in me are expressed in folly and wisdom, in kindliness and meanness. Love me simply because it occurs to you to do so, not because I am worth it. I do not love you because you are a storehouse of virtue and understand Adelungish, Spanish, Syrian, Hegelian, English, Arabic and Calcuttish, and have lent me your cloak, and have lent me money, and have troubled your head for my sake, and the like: I love you perhaps only because of certain funny faces I have caught you making, and of certain ridiculously silly expressions which fell from your lips and remained stuck in my memory, and they peep knowingly at me if I am in a jolly mood or with Cassa or sentimental. . . .

For heaven's sake, do not think that I dislike that good man Gans or that I depreciate his merits. It is true that him too I do not love because of the fat books he writes or the noble way in which he acts, but simply because of the comical way he stumps about when he tells a story, and because of the kindly, childish face he makes when something disagreeable or bad happens to him. The only thing I have against him is that his garrulity has provoked much unpleasantness for me, and in particular that despite my well-grounded request that he refrain, he has spoken about me to that blackguard Dr. Gustorf. That blackguard is a Jew, and has tried to ingratiate himself with certain paltry persons of the uncircumcised by picking at me; he is not the only one of his stripe, for I have to put up with much of the same sort and shrug my shoulders. But I take it ill of my friends when they have time for such scoundrels despite my request. This fellow is a bosom friend of a certain Koechy, who has also shown himself most hostile to me, out of envy of my poetry. . . . I am convinced that that fellow either directed the hissing at my *Almansor* in

Braunschweig or at least instigated it. I know how these things are done, I appreciate the baseness of men, and now you will realize sufficiently the importance of the few measures I had to take at the appearance of *Almansor*. I hear the piece has been stamped down; have you heard any particulars? The market Jews of Braunschweig have spread the report throughout Israel, and in Hamburg I received formal condolences. For me the story is catastrophic and it harms my position; I do not know how to repair it.

How is poor Marcus? Has Cohen done anything for him? He promised me he would. I asked him to most urgently. During my first stay in Hamburg he behaved generously to me in the matter of money. He asked whether I was embarrassed for money, and offered to help; to make the thing business-like, he informed me that my credit with him was good to the sum of 150 *taler*. I thanked him, saying that at most my embarrassment was for an occasional *louis d'or* or two, and then I was always in the habit of turning to you. But Cohen's gesture was very decent, and therefore I took the opportunity to speak to him about Marcus and with good auspices. I am vexed that I myself am now too poor to help the good man. I shall try to become as rich as the Hamburg vagabond, ass, hedgehog, and other men of honor. . . . Convey my cordial greetings to Zunz and also to Lehmann. Do not imagine that I never think of the *Verein* at all; I am now only too concerned about it. Find out from the treasurer when and how much I have to pay. Do you need Basnage for your article in the paper? It is your copy and at your service; shall I send it to you?

I have one more request. My brother, who studied practical farming for several years and can head some inspecting service, is now without a position. The blame is partly, he says, the circumstance that he is circumcised, and partly the circumstance that all farmers are now in depression and are dismissing their people; but most of all, it is the Jew that stands in his path when he looks for a post. Since I know from Berlin that Jacobsohn has estates in Mecklenburg, I believe it may be possible that my brother, whose wants are very modest, may find some sort of employment on those estates if some one in Berlin would say a word to Jacobsohn in his behalf.

—To Moses Moser
Lueneburg, September 30, 1823

Johann Christof Adelung: German linguist of the eighteenth century. Ludwig Gustorf, M.D., did in fact spread many reports unfavorable to Heine and say hateful things about him. He belonged to a round table whose chief was the dramatist Christian Dietrich Grabbe. Grabbe was highly esteemed by Heine and in return Grabbe felt obligated to procure recognition of Heine's efforts; but by reason of his frequent intoxication he insulted Heine with antisemitic abuse and with overt acts, and Gustorf joyfully spread these incidents abroad. Karl Koechy was likewise a member of Grabbe's round table, and later dramaturgist at the court theater in Braunschweig. There Heine's Almansor could not be performed to the end at the only presentation the piece had, because of a tumult in the theater. A rumor was started in the audience that a Jewish banker resident in Braunschweig was the author, whereupon confusion and noise arose which prevented the actors from continuing. Koechy was innocent in this incident. Heine's brother Gustav wished to become a farmer.

Donna Clara

In the evening through her garden
Wanders the Alcalde's daughter;
Festal sounds of drums and trumpets
Ring out hither from the castle.

"I am weary of the dances,
Honeyed words of adulation
From the knights who still compare me
To the sun with dainty phrases.

"Yes, of all things I am weary,
Since I first beheld by moonlight

Him, my cavalier, whose zither
Nightly draws me to my casement.

"As he stands so slim and daring,
With his flaming eyes that sparkle
From his noble pallid features,
Truly, he St. George resembles."

Thus went Donna Clara dreaming,
On the ground her eyes were fastened;
When she raised them, lo! before her
Stood the handsome knightly stranger.

Pressing hands and whispering passion,
These twain wander in the moonlight.
Gently doth the breeze caress them,
The enchanted roses greet them.

The enchanted roses greet them,
And they glow like love's own heralds;
"Tell me, tell me, my Belovèd,
Wherefore all at once thou blushest."

"Gnats were stinging me, my darling,
And I hate these gnats in summer,
E'en as though they were a rabble
Of vile Jews with long hooked noses."

"Heed not gnats or Jews, Belovèd,"
Spake the knight with fond endearments.
From the almond-tree dropped downward
Myriad snowy flakes and blossoms.

Myriad snowy flakes and blossoms
Shed around them fragrant odors:
"Tell me, tell me, my Belovèd,
Looks thy heart on me with favor?"

"Yes, I love thee, O my darling,
And I swear it by our Savior,
Whom the accursèd Jews did murder
Long ago with wicked malice."

"Heed thou neither Jews nor Savior,"
Spake the knight with fond endearments;
Far off waved as in a vision
Gleaming lilies bathed in moonlight.

Gleaming lilies bathed in moonlight
Seemed to watch the stars above them:—
"Tell me, tell me, my Belovèd,
Didst thou not erewhile swear falsely?"

"Nought is false in me, my darling,
E'en as in my bosom floweth
Not a drop of blood that's Moorish,
Neither of foul Jewish current."

"Heed not Moors nor Jews, Belovèd,"
Spake the knight with fond endearments;
Then towards a grove of myrtles
Leads he the Alcalde's daughter.

And with love's slight subtle meshes,
He hath trapped her and entangled;
Brief their words, but long their kisses,
For their hearts are overflowing.

What a melting bridal carol
Sings the nightingale, the pure one!
How the fire-flies in the grasses
Trip their sparkling, torchlight dances!

In the grove the silence deepens;
Nought is heard save furtive rustling

Of the swaying myrtle branches,
And the breathing of the flowers.

But the sound of drum and trumpet
Burst forth sudden from the castle;
Rudely they awaken Clara,
Pillowed on her lover's bosom.

"Hark, they summon me, my darling,
But before I go, oh tell me,
Tell me what thy precious name is,
Which so closely thou hast hidden."

And the knight, with gentle laughter,
Kissed the fingers of his Donna,
Kissed her lips and kissed her forehead,
And at last these words he uttered:

"I, Señora, your belovèd,
Am the son of the respected
Worthy, erudite Grand Rabbi
Israel of Saragossa!"
                        —Book of Songs: The Home-Coming

In the romance which I have sent you, you must change the
second verse of the fifth strophe to read "As he sang the words
of love." There was an Abraham of Saragossa, but I found Israel
more significant. The whole romance is a theme from my own
life, except that the zoo has been transformed into the garden
of the Alcalde, a baroness into a señora, and I myself into a St.
George or even an Apollo. It is only the first piece of a trilogy, of
which the second will show the hero mocked by his own child
who does not recognize him, and the third, this same child grown
up to be a Dominican who causes his Jewish brethren to be tortured to death. The refrain of both these pieces corresponds to
the refrain of the first piece—but it may be very long before I
write them down. In any case, I will include this romance in my

next collection of poems. But I have very important reasons for wishing that it does not fall into Christian hands before publication.

Truly, I did not behave like an egoist in Hamburg. Despite all accessory considerations, I could not bring myself to approve of offensive faithlessness and to rail against strength. I allude to my expressions concerning Kley and Bernays which have been so calumniated. If you know me, you must understand that the former with his satellites must be repulsive to my nature and that the energetic Bernays, although he lacks the negative Temple virtues, must strike me as worthy of respect. My predilection for the consistency and rigor of rabbinism I have had for many years as the result of historical studies, not as an *a priori* assumption or as a calculation *a là* G. G. Cohen. If I were not a big man, I would give myself the pleasure, after the good student fashion, of throwing stones at "the gentleman's window." But precisely because I am a big man, or at least a man, or, if you will not yield even that, a whole man, I cannot give satisfaction in Hamburg. That I noticed at once, and I kept away from the Jewish crowd. And will that crew still insist on speaking of me? People of whose existence I am ignorant have told my brother that I have spoken with them and have said heaven knows what. Such are the Jewish pests, or, more accurately, pests only possible in Israel, which assail me.

—To Moses Moser
Lueneburg, November 5, 1823

Not to be petty is a thing that pleases me better than all the spiritual qualities which are so highly praised in our moral handbooks . . . I am very, very concerned for the recognition of the masses, and yet there is no one who so despises popular approval and conceals his personality from the expression of such approval.

I have not forgotten my promise with reference to the *Rhine Blossoms*. I am pleased that you wish to have a poem which you saw at Moser's for the *Rhine Blossoms*. I intend it for that use, therefore, and wish that it be signed merely with the symbol —e, and that the superscription be *The Daughter of the Alcalde*. Perhaps I must polish it a little more, for I wrote it quickly and sent it without reading it over. I am glad that you were not displeased with it, for I had some doubts of its value; the poem does not well express what I wish to say, and perhaps even says something quite different. It is not really meant to provoke laughter, much less to show a tendency to mockery. I simply wished to render in a poem, without ulterior motive and with epic objectivity, something which is at once an individual and a general happening, something which belongs to world history and is clearly reflected in me; I conceived of the whole thing quite seriously and without jesting, and it was even to be the first play in a tragic trilogy. . . .

You can scarcely believe how courteous my deportment to Frau von Varnhagen is: I have read all of Goethe except for a little scrap! I am no longer a blind pagan, but a seeing one. Goethe pleases me very much. I should gladly write to Frau von Varnhagen, but it would cause me too much pain; without dissembling I could not leave Herr von Varnhagen unmentioned. That man has shown me much kindness and love, more than I could ever thank him for, and I shall surely be grateful to him my life long; but a pain compared to which toothache (do you know what toothache is?)—the toothache which I have this moment is true bliss—wrenches at my soul when I think of Varnhagen. He himself is little to blame; he merely had the idea of playing the Antonio towards me and telling me how much superior a well-turned diplomat, who everywhere practises the art of deciphering, is to a poor candidate of the Hospital of St. Anne, who speaks against his friends without prejudice and without measuring his words, in whatever mood he happens to be. I can endure a great deal and would have shaken this off also, as usual, but it happened precisely at the hour when I could not tolerate anything, and when any ungentleness, be it only a word, a glance, or a motion, inflicted an incurable wound upon me.

—To Ludwig Robert
Lueneburg, November 27, 1823

Ludwig Robert (1778-1832), an author, was the brother of Rahel. He was married to the authoress Friederike Robert, who published the almanac Rhine Blossoms. The romantic poem, Donna Clara, which Heine sent to Moser and Moser to Robert, was originally to be entitled The Daughter of the Alcalde. Heine's quarrel with Varnhagen arose when Varnhagen accused the poet of having shown the poem which Fouqué had dedicated to him (see p. 147) without the author's permission. Fouqué produced written evidence that Heine's conduct was correct. On this occasion, Varnhagen wished "to play the Antonio" against Heine, that is, to emulate the statesman Antonio in Goethe's drama Torquato Tasso who corrects the exalted Tasso and desires to teach him prudence, sagacity and a feeling of civic order. This took place with Rahel's consent, for she wished to use an apparent error of Heine's in order to "keep him in discipline."

I have received your letter of October 8, with which mine crossed. That is a mercantile expression which I recall from the days when I was bent on becoming a merchant. Hoho! I know many other such expressions and could write a work of Israelitish edification. . . .

I have received a letter from my uncle van Geldern. He writes me that I am as much hated along the whole Rhine stream as I was previously beloved, because it is said there that I concern myself for the Jews. Truly, I laughed. How I despise the human pack, the uncircumcised as well as the circumcised! . . . I also laughed at Jacobsohn's reply. If I were in Berlin, I should propose to the Verein that Dr. Jacobsohn be elected president of the agricultural society. Truly, I shall take care of ever coming into a situation where I should desire to claim the favor of a rich Jew for myself.

—To Moses Moser
Lueneburg, November 28, 1823

Good heavens! How much must I be misunderstood by other men when Moser, a pupil of Friedlaender and a contemporary of Gans—Moser, Moses Moser—my friend of friends, the philosophical part of myself, the correct deluxe edition of a real human being, "the man of liberty and of virtue," the permanent secretary of the *Verein*, the epilogue to *Nathan the Wise*, the reviewer of Bernays, the iron chest of Cohen, the normal-humanist—where shall I stop?—I will only say how black the outlook is for me if even Moser misunderstands me. . . . You write me very little about the *Verein*. Do you think that the cause of our brothers is not so near my heart as it was? You are mightily mistaken. Even if my headaches now lay me low, I have not given up working. "May my right hand wither if I forget thee, Jerusalem," are approximately the words of the Psalmist, and they are mine too, always. I wish I could talk with you for a single hour about what I have thought, largely through my own situation, concerning Israel, and you would see how the race of asses flourishes in the Steinweg, and how Heine is and must always remain Heine. . . .

Apropos of that, how was the *Paria* received? Surely well, for it is no worse than the tragedies of most other poets of the day, and the axiom that a tragedy must of necessity be bad if a Jew wrote it need no longer be brought upon the carpet. For that, Michael Beer can no longer thank me enough. If the poor and rejected *Paria* was actually rejected by the bespectacled Brahmins, and the epaulette-decorated Sutras of the parterre, I comfort him with the fate of Ben Abdullah and advise the poor Paria to forget the pressures of the caste system in the arms of a Bajadere.

—To Moses Moser
Lueneburg, January 9, 1824

Michael Beer's tragedy, The Paria, *enjoyed a great success upon its presentation in Berlin. Ben Abdullah: Almansor.*

Actually I am no German, as you well know (see Ruehs, Fries, *loc. cit.*). I would not be too proud if I were a German. "Oh, they are barbarians." There are only three educated and civilized peoples: the French, the Chinese and the Persians. I am very proud of being a Persian. That I write German verses is as circumstances require. . . . But although I am a Persian, I acknowledge that the greatest poet art thou, O great prophet of Mecca; and thy Koran, although I know it only from Boysen's translation, will not easily slip from my memory.

I heard yesterday at Celle that Michael Beer's *Paria* met with great success in Berlin, and indeed, remarkably enough, from an old Jew with whom I exchanged a few ducats. He had had it from a chiropodist who had come directly from Berlin, where he had been convinced that *Paria* was on a par with the works of Schiller and Goethe. I am half curious, dear Moser, to hear your judgment of the piece; you must have had a large part in it, for Beer as well as Frankel are among your representatives. I have known the piece for a long while, for its author read it to me. I was much pleased with it, and would have been better pleased if I had not at that time had too exact a knowledge of India and the Indian spirit.

The chief point of the poem, namely that the Paria is a disguised Jew, was to me utterly fatal. Every effort must be made that no one should imagine that the Jew has any resemblance to the Indian Paria; and it is very stupid deliberately to insist upon a resemblance. But most stupid of all and most injurious and worthiest of cudgelling is the odd idea which the Paria proposes: his ancestors were themselves to blame for their sad condition because of some bloody misdeed.

This allusion to Christ will probably please many people, particularly since it is a Jew, a water poet, who utters it (be careful to interpret the expression correctly: a Jew, a water poet, does not mean a Jew who is a water poet, but a Jew who is not yet baptized, a water-proof Jew). I wish Michael Beer had been baptized, and had spoken bluntly in the true *Almansor* fashion, with regard to Christianity, instead of so carefully sparing it, and even, as is shown above, flirting with it.

—To Moses Moser
Hanover, January 21, 1824

In Goettingen Again

I arrived in Goettingen asleep; what can that mean? As I stood at my inn window the following morning, I saw my old bootblack pass, and I called him up. The comical fellow came up, without uttering a word, cleaned my clothes and boots, without uttering a word; and marched out without showing the least surprise at my having been away from Goettingen for three years. He had never forgotten my injunction never to speak in my presence.

I have only few acquaintances here, and the professors are not particularly friendly, because when I was given my marching orders I sent frivolous farewell cards to the members of the academic senate.

—To Charlotte Embden
Goettingen, January 31, 1824

I have been here for nine days and am already consumed with tedium. My life is devoted to my jurisprudence. If you think that I am not going to become a great jurist you are mistaken. You can dismiss me as a lawyer, but don't say so to other people, else I must starve. I shall eat my dinners out of the balances of Themis, and no more from my uncle's charity bowl. . . .

—To Moses Moser
Goettingen, February 2, 1824

I know that I am one of the most beastly of German beasts, I know only too well that German is to me what water is to a fish, that I cannot live outside that element, and, to keep my fishy figure, must wither to a stock-fish, if—to keep to my watery metaphor—I should ever leap out of the sea of Germanism. At bottom, I love what is German more than anything else in the world; it is my joy and delight, and my bosom is an archive of German sentiment, as my two books are an archive of German song. My first book is quite German even outwardly, for love of what is German had not yet been dimmed in me. My second book is German only inwardly; its outer aspect is alien. Probably my Muse cut her German dress somewhat after a foreign fashion out of a displeasure with things German, occasioned by valid reasons of righteous *ennui*.

—To Rudolph Christiani
Goettingen, March 7, 1824

Rudolph Christiani, a jurist and the son of a Lueneburg clergyman high in the Protestant Church, became friendly with Heine during the later part of the latter's sojourn in Lueneburg, introduced him to society, and so put an end to the "isolation" of which he so frequently complains in his Lueneburg letters. Christiani was also zealous in proclaiming Heine's fame as a poet. He became a leader of the liberal party in the Kingdom of Hanover, whereupon Heine dubbed him "the Mirabeau of the Lueneburg heath." Heine similarly made fun of Christiani's enthusiasm for Goethe. Christiani married a daughter of Isaak Heine of Bordeaux. Heine made him executor of his will; he died in 1859.

As I write this I hear that my cousin, Lord Byron, died at Missolonghi. So that great heart, too, has ceased to throb! It was great and a heart, no puny ovary of feelings. Yes, that man was great; he discovered new worlds in anguish; Prometheus-like, he defied miserable men and their more miserable gods, and the fame of his name penetrated the icebergs of Thule and the burning deserts of the east—"take him all in all, he was a man." We shall not soon look upon his like again.

I have proclaimed general mourning. English literature now rests upon only two eyes, Scott and Moore. Our literature is stone blind.

—To Rudolph Christiani
Goettingen, May 24, 1824

My life here is in the same old rut, which is to say, I have headaches eight days in the week; I rise about four-thirty and think what I should start doing; meanwhile, nine o'clock comes

gradually creeping on, and I take my brief-case and hurry to
the divine Meister. The fellow *is* divine. He is ideal in his
woodenness, and because he is the most perfect antithesis to
everything poetical, he himself becomes a figure of poetry;
indeed, when the material he treats of is particularly dry and
leathery, he regularly becomes inspired. In point of fact, I am
perfectly satisfied with Meister, and with his and God's help I
shall be rid of the pandects.

Aside from that, I am giving much study to the chronicles,
and a very great deal to *historia judaica*—the latter in connection with my *Rabbi*, and perhaps also to satisfy an inward need.
I am stirred by very strange emotions when I turn the pages of
those sad annals so full of instruction and of pain. The spirit of
Jewish history becomes clearer and clearer to me, and this
spiritual armory will surely stand me in good stead one day. I
have completed only a third of my *Rabbi*; I have been interrupted by racking pains, and heaven knows whether I can finish
it at all.

I notice, in this connection, that I have no talent at all for
narrative; but perhaps I am being unjust to myself and it is
the material which is intractable. The Passover part is successful,
and I am grateful to you for your information on the Haggadah;
please send me in addition a literal translation of the *Caholach
Manga* and of the little legend *Maasse be Rabbi Leser*, and also
of the passage from the Psalms in the evening prayers—"Ten
thousand armed men stand before Solomon's bed." Perhaps I
shall subjoin several pages of illustrations as a supplement, in
the English style, and also some original extracts concerning
Jews and their history. Benjamin of Tudela, who is doing his
travelling on my writing-table, sends you hearty greetings, and
desires that Zunz edit him and publish him, with translation.
The edition and translation of the French Dr. Witte, which I
have before me, is just a schoolboy's job, and bad from every
point of view. On the Jews of Frankfurt, Schudt was very
useful to me. I read both quarto volumes carefully, and cannot
say whether I was more exasperated by the *rishes* which he

spread over every page, or more amused by the bovine clumsiness with which he introduced his *rishes*. Ah, how we Germans have improved! I still lack some notes on the Spanish Jews of the fifteenth century, and especially on their academies at that time. Where can I find something? Or rather fifty years before their expulsion. It is interesting that in the very year of their expulsion the new land of freedom of religion, America, to wit, was discovered.

Little poetic harvest will this year yield; I write hardly any poems, and my time is preempted by my headaches and studies. God knows whether I shall finish this year, and God help me if I don't! I will in no case start a new public-relations campaign on my uncle; I have not written him for nine months. Truly, I am not really the swine the Hamburgers believe I am. . . .

How do things stand (or lie) with the *Verein*? Don't forget this point. Have you broken with Hamburg? What's new there? I worried about Gans for four weeks here, not having had time to do so in Berlin. And is it not annoying that one of the greatest thinkers of our time thinks so little about himself and his outward aspect? It was really unfair of me to tease him, but nothing was further from my mind than to hurt him, and he unconsciously so invites teasing. It would have been better if I had told him the unvarnished truth each time he made a display of his weakness and became a public joke. That is what his friends ought always to do. . . .

The death of Byron has moved me much. He was the only man with whom I felt kinship, and we were probably alike in a great many ways. Jest about it as much as you will. For some years I have read him rarely; we prefer to associate with people whose characters are different from our own. But with Byron my association was always comfortable, as with a completely equal mess-mate. With Shakespeare I cannot feel comfortable because I am too much aware that I am not his equal. He is the most powerful minister, and I only a courtier, and I feel as if he might dismiss me at any moment.

—To Moses Moser
Goettingen, June 24, 1824

Haggadah: *Collection of prayers, interpretations, legends and songs read at the celebration of the Passover festival in the home.* Caholach Manga: *a transcription (which proves that Heine knew the words only from having heard them) of k'ho lahma anya ("This is the bread of affliction," the opening words of a declaration in Aramaic with which the Seder proper begins).* Maasse be Rabbi Leser: *properly ma'ase b'Rabbi Eliezer; the familiar story, from the Haggadah, of how Rabbi Eliezer and other sages at Bene Berak spoke of the exodus throughout Passover night, until their disciples came to inform them that it was time for morning prayer, is recounted by Heine in the first chapter of his* Rabbi of Bacherach. *"Ten thousand armed men stand before Solomon's bed": Heine used this line (cf. Song of Songs 3.6) to close the first chapter of his* Rabbi, *and later made it into a poem in the* Lamentations. Benjamin of Tudela *was a Jewish merchant who, between 1160 and 1173, travelled from Saragossa in Spain through France, Italy and Greece to Palestine, and thence through Persia and Central Asia, returning by way of the Indian Ocean and Egypt. He was probably the first medieval traveller to journey from Europe to Asia. The Hebrew account of his travels,* Massa'ot Rabbi Benjamin, *was first published in Constantinople in 1543, was subsequently translated into many languages, and was edited by Zunz in 1840. A modern critical edition was prepared by Marcus Nathan Adler (Oxford, 1907). All that is known of Benjamin personally is that his father was Jonah of Tudela (in the Kingdom of Navarre).* The French Dr. Witte: *A French translation of Benjamin's Travels with critical appendices was printed at Amsterdam in 1734, when its editor was not yet fourteen years old. A similar prodigy in Heine's day was Karl Witte (1800-1883), later known as a Dante scholar and a jurist, who matriculated at the university at the age of nine and a half years, obtained his doctorate of philosophy at fourteen, and became Privatdozent in jurisprudence at the University of Berlin at seventeen. His appointment evoked stormy protest, and Eduard Gans publicly defended Witte.* Schudt: *Johann Jakob Schudt (1664-1722) endeavored to convert Jews to Chris-*

tianity, and to this end studied their language, religion, history and habits. He was in close contact with the Jews of Frankfort, from whom he learned a great deal concerning Jewish usages. Of his writings Heine used and made excerpts from the Juedische Merkwuerdigkeiten ("Noteworthy Matters Pertaining to Jews"), published in 1714.

Even this night I dreamt of you. In old Spanish garb and upon an Andalusian steed, you rode in the midst of a great swarm of Jews going to Jerusalem. Little Marcus, with his big maps and travel-books, walked in front as guide. Zunz, marching on the flank, carried the periodical bound in red morocco. Doctoress Zunz ran alongside as a market wife carrying a jug of holiday brandy on her back. It was a large Jewish host, and Gans ran from one to the other to keep order. Lehmann and Wohlwill carried banners upon which were inscribed the shield of David and Bendavidic doctrines. Sugar-Cohn led the temple gate-keepers. Former Verein youth carried the skeleton of Saul Ascher. All converted Jews followed as a supply train, and the rear guard of the train was composed of a crowd of carriages. In one sat the Tr. . . . Doctor Oppert as field-surgeon and Jost as historian of the deeds which were to transpire; in another coach sat Friedlaender and Mrs. von der Recke; and in one of the most elegant of state coaches sat Michael Beer as chief-of-staff, and with him Wolff and Mme. Stich, who were to present the Paria in Jerusalem without fail and to reap their merited praise. Apparently I fell asleep last night reading Basnage.

Speaking of Basnage, I cannot sufficiently express my admiration for that author. He is a man of much spirit, acute historical perception, noble heart, pure impartiality—a man of incalculable merit. . . .

I am up to my neck in jurisprudence and, thank heaven, I am gradually getting the trash into my head. I exert myself greatly, overcome my pain, and permit myself to write no poetry. . . . I am very anxious just now regarding the forthcoming accouchement of my sister. I am very busy with student affairs. At most of the duels I am either second, or witness, or non-partisan, or at least a spectator. That is my amusement, for I have none better.

—To Moses Moser
Goettingen, July 20, 1824

Wolff and Mme. Stich: Berlin actors.

Dear Father Moritz: I cannot tell you how much Mother's line and your postscript delighted me. With what anxiety did I await the news! I congratulate you on the sweet little daughter and wish that she may be like her sweet mother. I had to think of our dear Lottchen day and night. . . .

Now a new bond has joined you in harmony and happiness. The sweet creature to whom you both have given life shall be a new source of new happiness and love to you.

I too, my dear Moritz, am now more closely allied to you by the new family bond: your daughter is my niece.

Heaven grant that these two beings whom we so dearly love, mother and daughter, be preserved in health. . . .

I beg you, please do not give the child any fancy name; give it some simple, pure German name.

—To Moritz Embden
Goettingen, August 9, 1824

Heine's first niece received the name of Marie.

I have spent a gloomy summer—jurisprudence and headaches. My only relaxation were bad student pranks, duels and some trials which I conducted and lost. Since I am a jurist, I am imposed upon more than ever. I have tormented myself with the law like a desperate man and yet heaven knows whether anything is wrong with me. If Meister loses his deanship this time, I am a lost man. For then Hugo, the friend of my bitterest enemies, will become dean. You must realize that even here I have acquired a number of enemies; that is in the nature of things. . . .

I have written precious little this summer. A couple of sheaves of memoirs, no poems at all, little on the *Rabbi*, so that scarcely a third of it is done. That will run to some length, quite a thick volume, and I cherish the whole thing in my heart with ineffable love. For it is out of love that it grows, not vainglory. On the contrary, if I should hearken to the voice of practical prudence I would never write it at all. I can foresee how much mischief I shall be doing myself and how much enmity I shall call down of my head. But precisely because it grows out of love it will become an immortal book, an eternal lamp in God's cathedral and not a sputtering theater candle. Much that I wrote for this book I have extinguished, and only now have I succeeded in grasping the whole, and I pray God to grant me enough hours to write it down in tranquillity. Don't laugh at this cackling before laying. And don't laugh at the long brooding; an ordinary goose egg (I don't mean Dr. Gans ["Goose"]) is more quickly hatched than the dove's egg of the Holy Ghost. You have forgotten to send me the few notes for the *Rabbi* which I requested in my last letter. A thousand thanks to Dr. Zunz for his communication on the Spanish Jews. Although it is very sparse, Zunz' single acute suggestion has been more useful than a number of quarto volumes I have ransacked in vain; he will unknowingly have influenced my *Rabbi*. . . .

My painful reading of Basnage was finally completed towards the middle of last month. What I was particularly searching for I did not find, but I did discover much that was new, and many new ideas and emotions were aroused in me. Taken as a whole the book is magnificent; a part of the impression it made upon me I jotted down September 11 in the following reflections:

To Edom

With each other, brother fashion,
Have we borne this many an age.
Thou hast borne with my existence,
And I borne have with thy rage.

Many a time, in days of darkness,
Wonder-strange hath been thy mood,
And thy dear and pious talons
Hast thou reddened in my blood.

Now our friendship groweth closer;
Nay, it waxeth daily now:
I myself begin to bluster
And am nigh as mad as thou.

But just as one word leads to another, so does one verse
suggest another, and I will write down for you some insignificant
verses which I made last evening as I was walking in the rain
and storm and was thinking of you and the pleasure I should
take when I could send you my *Rabbi*. I even composed the
verses which I would inscribe as a dedication to you on the
clean over-leaf of your copy; since I keep no secrets from you
I shall write you those verses now:

Burst out in wailing riot,
    Thou darkling martyr-lay,
That in my soul, flame-quiet,
    I've borne this many a day!

It thrills through every hearing
    And so the heart doth gain.
I've conjured up, unfearing,
    The thousand-year-old pain.

Great, little, weep and even
    Cold hearts do tearful grow:
The small stars weep in heaven,
    The maids and flowers below.

The tears, still southward fleeting,
    To the still conclave go;

And all, each other meeting,
Into the Jordan flow.

I don't have to inform you that the verses which I am now writing are of little worth and are being made solely for my own pleasure. But consider my situation: I never leave the forum the live-long day, and hear talk of nothing but *stillicidium*, wills, *emphytheusis*, and the like. And if I take ship for Thessaly in a free hour and climb Parnassus, I meet only Jews who raise vegetables there (see Basnage), and I speak with them of the sorrows of Israel. . . .

I am sorry to miss news of the *Verein* in your letter. You could tell me its state in a few words. Has the *Verein* already sent cards of leave-taking around? Will it survive? Will God be strong in the weak, in Auerbach and company?

—To Moses Moser
Goettingen, October 25, 1824

Heine's apprehensions in regard to his examiners were realized insofar that Professor Meister, whose lectures were the most important Heine attended, was supplanted as Dean of the Law Faculty by Professor Hugo. Hugo was a determined opponent of Gans, and knew that Heine was on friendly terms with Gans; but he did not allow himself to be prejudiced against Heine by this fact at the examination.

Stillicidium: Roof-drippings, a moot point in the Pandects concerning the use of rain water, specifically, the right of drawing such water off to neighboring property. Emphytheusis: The right of legacy.

A Tour in the Harz

Before Heine reported for his examination in jurisprudence, he undertook an extensive walking tour, upon the advice of his physician, for the benefit of his health. This tour took him through the Harz to Thueringen and then back to Goettingen by way of Kassel. The first part of this tour is described in the Tour in the Harz. Immediately upon publication, it met with much greater approval than Heine had expected. This humorous and sentimental account, spiced with factual allusion and digressing from present-day impressions to fantastic dreams in the realm of fairy-story and legend, gave Heine wide popularity as an artist in German prose.

The town of Goettingen, so celebrated for its sausages and university, belongs to the King of Hanover, and contains 999 inhabited houses, various churches, a lying-in hospital, an observatory, a university prison, a library, and a small town-hall tavern where the beer is excellent. The stream that flows past the town is the Leine, and serves in summer for bathing. The water is very cold, and in some places it is so broad that Lueder had to take a really good run to clear it. The town itself is pretty, and presents the most agreeable aspect—when we have turned our backs upon it. Of its antiquity there can be no doubt, for I remember when I matriculated there five years ago (just before I was requested to take my name off the books), it had the same gray, knowing look about it that it has now and was as fully provided as now with Charleys, beadles, dissertations, thés dansants, washerwomen, cram-books, pigeon-pies, Guelfic orders, graduates' visiting coaches, pipe-bowls, court-councillors, law-councillors, rustication councillors, bulldogs and other sad dogs. Some authorities actually maintain that the town dates from the days of the barbarian invasions, and according to them each German tribe dropped on its way a rough copy of itself, which accounts for all the Vandals, Frisians, Swabians, Teutons, Saxons, Thuringians, etc., who may be found in Goettingen even to the present day. Our young barbarians still go in hordes, and you may distinguish them by the colors of their caps and pipe-tassels. They lounge along the Weenderstrasse on their way to the sanguinary battlefields of Rasenmuehle, Ritchenkrug, and Boveden, where they are always pitching into one another. Their manners and customs are survivals from the age of the barbarian invasions, and they are governed partly by their Duces (prize cocks they style them), partly by their primitive code, styled the Comment. It well deserves a place among the leges barbarorum.

The inhabitants of Goettingen may be roughly classified under
the heads of student, professor, philistine, and brute; but between these four estates there is no clearly marked distinction.
The most important class are the brutes. To commemorate by
name all the students and all the regular and irregular professors, would exceed my limits, and at the present moment I
cannot call to mind the names of all the students, while of the
professors many have, as yet, no name. . . .

The children, thought I, are younger than we, and may still
remember when they were once trees or birds, and are consequently still able to understand them. We ourselves are, alas!
too old for that, and carry about in our heads too much legal
lore, and too many sorrows and bad verses. But the time when
it was otherwise recurred vividly to me as I entered Clausthal.
In this pretty little mountain town, which the traveller does not
behold until he stands directly before it, I arrived just as the
clock was striking twelve and the children came tumbling merrily out of school. The little rogues, nearly all red-cheeked, blue-
eyed, flaxen-haired, sprang and shouted, and awoke in me melancholy and cheerful memories—how I once myself, as a little
boy, sat all the forenoon long in a gloomy Catholic cloister school
in Duesseldorf, without so much as daring to stand up, enduring
meanwhile such a terrible amount of Latin, whipping, and
geography, and how I too hurrahed and rejoiced beyond all
measure when the old Franciscan clock at last struck twelve.
The children saw by my knapsack that I was a stranger, and
greeted me in the most hospitable manner. One of the boys
told me that they had just had a lesson in religion, and showed
me the Royal Hanoverian Catechism, from which they were
questioned on Christianity. This little book was very badly
printed, so that I greatly feared that the doctrines of faith made
thereby but an unpleasant blotting-paper sort of impression upon
the children's minds. I was also shocked at observing that the
multiplication table contrasted with the Holy Trinity on the
last page of the catechism, as it at once occurred to me that
by this means the minds of the children might, even in their
earliest years, be led to the most sinful scepticism. We Prussians

are more intelligent, and, in our zeal for converting those heathens who are familiar with arithmetic, take good care not to print the multiplication table behind the catechism. . . . After dinner I went forth to visit the mines, the silver refineries and the mint.

In the silver refinery, as has frequently been my luck in life, I could get no glimpse of the precious metal. In the mint I succeeded better, and saw how money was made. Beyond this I have never been able to advance. On such occasions mine has invariably been the spectator's part, and I verily believe that if it should rain dollars from heaven, the coins would only knock holes in my head, while the children of Israel would merrily gather up the silver manna. . . .

A visit to the two principal Klausthaler mines is very interesting. . . .

The affair is entirely devoid of danger, though it at first appears quite otherwise to those unacquainted with the mysteries of mining. . . . I did not descend to those deepest depths where it is reported that the people on the other side of the world, in America, may be heard crying, "Hurrah for Lafayette!" Where I went seemed to me, however, deep enough in all conscience. . . .

> Now the fir-tree's long, green fingers
>   Tap against the window-pane,
> And the moon, that quiet listener,
>   Sheds a flood of golden rain.
>
> Father, mother, sleeping soundly,
>   Snore for hours without a break;
> But we two, with lively chatter,
>   Keep each other wide awake.
>
> "That you spend much time in praying
>   I've my doubt; for always there
> Is a sneer about your features
>   That was never caused by prayer.

"Oh that sneer, so cold and evil,
　　Frightens me and terrifies—
But my terror seems to vanish
　　When I see your gentle eyes.

"And I doubt that you believe in
　　The inspired Faith of most.
Don't you worship God the Father,
　　And the Son and Holy Ghost?" . . .

"Ah, my child, while still an infant,
　　While at mother's knee I stood,
I believed in God the Father,
　　He whose rule is great and good.

"He who made the earth we dwell on,
　　And the people here below;
He who made sun, mood and planets,
　　Teaching them the way to go.

"Then, my child, as I grew older,
　　My belief had but begun,
And I mastered many new things,
　　And I worshiped God—and Son;

"The Belovèd Son, who, loving,
　　Gave us love to bless and guide;
And for his reward, as usual,
　　He was scorned and crucified.

"Now that I've matured and learned much,
　　Read and roamed from coast to coast,
Now my heart, with deep conviction,
　　Bows before the Holy Ghost.

"He has worked the greatest wonders,
　　And he works them still; he broke,

Once for all, the tyrant's power,
    And he broke the bondman's yoke.

"All the ancient scars have vanished,
    Justice takes its rightful place;
Now all men are free and equal
    In a pure and noble race.

"Mists and every evil fancy
    That had filled each night and day,
Cares that crowded out our gladness—
    These have all been swept away!

"And a thousand armored champions
    He has sanctified and sent
To fulfill his sacred mission,
    Fired with their high intent.

"Lo, their splendid swords are shining
    And their tossing flags are bright!—
What, my child, you long to look on
    Such a proud and holy knight?

"Well, my child, come here and kiss me;
    Look at me and you can boast
You have known just such a doughty
    Champion of the Holy Ghost."
                                    —A Tour in the Harz

Wilhelm Lueder: *a student known for his strength and skill,
and a play-fellow of Heine. Charleys, beadles, etc.: Student slang.
Vandals, Frisians, Swabians: Names of student organizations at
Goettingen, called, as in German universities generally, after
ancient Germanic tribes.*
    *From the Harz, Heine travelled by way of Halle to Weissen-
fels, where he visited Adolf Muellner, whom he had previously
admired (see p. 134). Heine's drama, William Ratcliff, shows how*

long he continued under Muellner's influence. In the interval, Muellner had become a journalistic power as the publisher of a periodical, and he used his power unscrupulously. Although Heine had already altered his views of the value of Muellner's literary productions, he wished to remain on good terms with the influential man. But his visit did not have the desired results. The Tour in the Harz was unfavorably reviewed in Muellner's periodical. Heine took his vengeance by declaring Muellner "morally annihilated," and added that "loathing of Muellner filled every decent heart."

Aside from Muellner, Heine also visited Goethe on this tour. Though Goethe had made no response to Heine's tenders, Heine did not give up hope of obtaining Goethe's recognition. On October 1, 1824, Heine came to Weimar and immediately requested Goethe to receive him in his house.

Your Excellency: I beg you to grant me the good fortune to appear before you for a few moments. I shall not trouble you, but only kiss your hand and depart. My name is H. Heine, I am a Rhinelander, I now reside at Goettingen, and previously I lived for some years in Berlin, where I associated with a number of your old acquaintances and admirers (the late Wolf, the Varnhagens, etc.), and grew to love you more and more daily. I am also a poet, and three years ago took the liberty of sending you my *Poems*, and a year and a half ago, my *Tragedies with a Lyrical Intermezzo (Ratcliff and Almansor)*. Furthermore, I am ill, and for that reason took a tour to the Harz for my health's sake three weeks ago; on the Brocken, I was seized by a desire to make a pilgrimage to Weimar to pay homage to Goethe. It is truly as a pilgrim that I have come, that is, on foot and in weather-beaten clothing, and I await your acknowledgment of my petition, and remain

With enthusiasm and devotion,
H. Heine
—To Goethe
Weimar, October 1, 1824

On the following day Heine was received by Goethe. The visit plainly gave satisfaction to neither. In his journal, Goethe entered the simple notice, "Heine of Goettingen." On his return to Goettingen, Heine, according to the report of his student-friend, Philipp Spitta, "gave in the presence of his comrades who fetched him home free and undisguised rein to his indignation at the fact that his excellency had really received him with unseemly frigidity. He felt his honor as a poet was affronted, and had expected more." Apparently Goethe had read none of Heine's books, and this lack of interest vexed the younger poet. The oft-repeated account which Heine's brother Maximilian spread abroad is incredible. According to this report the conversation at first touched on indifferent matters, and then Goethe asked his visitor what he was then engaged upon. Upon Heine's answer "on a Faust," Goethe asked in a barbed voice, "Have you no other business in Weimar, Mr. Heine?" Heine replied quickly, "One foot over the threshold, your excellency, will complete all my business in Weimar," and took his leave. Such conduct on Heine's part is in keeping neither with his tact nor with the tactics which he customarily employed. At Goettingen, Heine did indeed entertain a plan to write a poem on Faust, but this very fact would have kept him silent on the subject in Goethe's presence. He habitually refrained from speaking of unfinished works and had not the slightest cause prematurely to reveal himself to Goethe as a competitor. Furthermore, he knew that Goethe was working at the completion of the second part of his Faust and regarded this work as the "chief business" of his life, which had claimed his thoughts for six decades. Heine's purpose in visiting Weimar was to influence Goethe in his behalf by enthusiastic adulation. It is more likely that he exaggerated and assumed a tone of veneration which Goethe found displeasing. His letters to Goethe show that Heine did not yet comprehend Goethe's idiosyncrasies and did not know Goethe's manner of affecting others. But even then Heine possessed sufficient general experience and tact to understand that he would only bring about the opposite of his intention to win Goethe's sympathy if he spoke of his own plans for writing on Faust.

The late Wolf: The Homeric critic Friedrich August Wolf whose lectures Heine had attended in Berlin.

Heine was reluctant to inform his closer friends about his visit in Weimar.

I forgot to tell you that six weeks ago I took a long tour, returning only a fortnight ago, so that I was on the road for four weeks. It was a wholesome thing, and I feel much improved by the journey. I covered the entire Harz on foot and mostly alone. I wandered through beautiful mountains and charming forests and valleys, and breathed freely again. I returned by way of Eisleben, Halle, Jena, Weimar, Erfurt, Gotha, Eisenach and Kassel, again always on foot. I had many grand and lovely experiences, and if the specter of jurisprudence had not stuck close I should have found the world very fair. . . .

I was in Weimar; the beer there is very good. . . .

I was in Weimar; the roast goose there is good too. I was also in Halle, Jena, Erfurt, Gotha, Eisenach and in Kassel. Long walks, always on foot, and in my shabby old brown overcoat. The beer in Weimar is really good; I'll tell you more when I see you.

—To Moses Moser
Goettingen, October 25, 1824

The best thing I have written in the interval is an account of a tour in the Harz which I took last autumn, a mixture of description of nature, humor, poetry and observations, after the manner of Washington Irving.

—To Ludwig Robert
Goettingen, March 4, 1825

Washington Irving was in Germany during 1822-1823; his Tales of a Traveller appeared in a German translation in 1825.

In the fall I took a walking tour in the Harz, during which I traversed its length and breadth, and on my return through Weimar visited the Brocken and Goethe himself, for my return journey took me through Eisleben, Halle, Jena, Weimar, Erfurt, Gotha, Eisenach and Kassel. I saw much that was beautiful on this trip; the valleys of the Bode and Selke are unforgettable. With some economy I could staff my poems for the rest of my life with trees from the Harz.

I was utterly appalled by Goethe's appearance. His face is yellow and mummy-like, his toothless mouth has an anxious twitch, and his whole figure is the picture of human decrepitude —perhaps the result of his latest illness. Only his eye is clear and shining. That eye is the only thing in Weimar worth notice. I was touched by Goethe's deeply human concern for my health; the late Wolf had spoken to him of it. In many features I recognized the Goethe for whom life, its beautification and preservation as well as its more practical concerns, is of supreme importance. For the first time I felt the contrast between that nature and my own, to which anything practical is abhorrent, which basically holds life light and would defiantly immolate it for the sake of an idea. That is precisely the cleavage in me: my reason is at constant war with my native predilection for enthusiasms. Now I understand clearly why Goethe's writings have been basically repulsive to me, much as I revered him as a poet, and much as my ordinary view of life agreed with his. I am really at war with Goethe and his writings, just as my own views of life are at war with my inherent inclinations and secret emotions. Yet . . . these wars will not be revealed outwardly. I shall always belong to the Goethean free corps, and whatever I write will proceed from artistic discretion, not crazy enthusiasm.

—To Rudolph Christiani
Goettingen, May 26, 1825

You have suffered small loss by my not writing you about Goethe, how I talked to him in Weimar, and the friendly and condescending things he said to me. He is only the shell in which magnificence once blossomed, and that is what interested me in him. He aroused a feeling of melancholy in me, and he has become dearer to me since I began to pity him. But basically Goethe and I are disparate natures which must, by

reason of their polarity, repel one another. He is at bottom a
frivolous man devoted to life and conceiving of pleasure as the
highest good; at times he feels and senses life in an idea and
expresses it in his poems, but he has never possessed an idea
deeply, and even less has he lived it. I, on the other hand, am at
bottom an enthusiast, that is, I am inspired by an idea to the
point of sacrifice and always feel a compulsion to submerge
myself in it; yet I have also grasped pleasure and found satisfaction in it. Now I am the battleground in a struggle between lucid
reason, which accepts pleasure and rejects self-sacrificing devotion as folly, and my inclination to enthusiasm which often casts
its darts unexpectedly and seizes me with violence and will perhaps some day again draw me down to its ancient realm—
perhaps I had better say, draw me up; for it is still a great
question whether the enthusiast who devotes his very life to an
idea does not live a more abundant and happier life in a single
moment than does Mr. Goethe during the entire seventy-six years
of his self-centered and comfortable existence.

But more of this another time. Today my head is dull with
unspeakable weariness. You will find that theme again in the
Rabbi.

—To Moses Moser
Goettingen, July 1, 1825

*The characterization of Goethe which Heine here presents is
obviously influenced by his personal disaffection at the visit in
Weimar. But Heine's judgment of Goethe is also affected by
views which were widely prevalent in Germany at this time.
Goethe's indifference to the patriotic uprising of 1813 and his
opposition to the national and liberal tendencies of the period
following had created general opposition to him, to which only
individual circles like that of the Varnhagen house and other
Berlin salons, certain small groups in university cities in Northern Germany, and persons living in isolation like Christiani,
formed an exception. The romanticists who had initially revered
Goethe as the greatest poet after Shakespeare had now come
to the view that Goethe could not, indeed, be surpassed in form*

but could in intellectual and spiritual content, and they desiderated some "intellectual center of gravity" in his work. Their derogatory statements concerning Goethe—who for his part adopted a decided attitude against Romanticism and designated it as "sick"—were seized upon by orthodox Protestants and Catholics and employed for vigorous agitation against Goethe's treatment of the erotic. They charged him with immorality and indifferentism. This denigration was accentuated by tactless glorifications which celebrated Goethe as "an artist of life," and by indiscreet communications concerning Goethe's private life which spread the conviction that he was more concerned for the maintenance of his own tranquillity than for anything else. Diverse as were the political, church and social groups to which these opponents of Goethe belonged, all saw in him an "egotistical self-deifier," who was only concerned for the refinements of pleasure in his own life, and to this end sacrificed the loftiest ideas of humanity. Of the contemporary spokesmen of German liberalism, Ludwig Boerne and Wolfgang Menzel in particular were most vigorous in raising such charges against Goethe. Menzel later altered his political viewpoint, but not his opposition to Goethe. Boerne remained a bitter opponent of Goethe to the end. A large proportion of "young Germany" also adhered closely to Boerne's views. Only after the break-through of Naturalism, which rediscovered Goethe's youthful revolutionary poetry, was the modern concept of Goethe confirmed, and the writer of Werther defended against the charge that he had no heart for human concerns. On the other hand, of late a Goethe criticism has come to the fore which does not reject the validity of the positions of the opponents of Goethe even though it greatly modifies them.

After Heine had expressed himself so scornfully against fusion with an idea (see p. 187), it is surprising that he now describes himself to Christiani and Moser as one who, in contrast to Goethe, lives for an idea and in an idea and is ready to give his life for an idea. By "idea" Heine means striving for political, social, economic and cultural reforms which he regards as the challenge of the age, as a necessity of dialectical development.

This Hegelian view is alien to Goethe, and he rejected political change even more sharply than did the Archduke of Weimar in whose service he was. It was known to Heine that Goethe in particular regretted the concessions which his Archduke was prepared to make to the Jews with respect to political rights. That accentuated Heine's bitterness against Goethe. Yet he soon realized that the criticism of Goethe's opponents aimed similar charges, and with even greater indignation, at his own writings; Heine's personal development, particularly in his first Paris period, brought him nearer to Goethe. But even here, in formulating his opposition to Goethe, Heine became aware of a significant conflict in his own personality. He described it as the conflict between his native inclination to enthusiasm and his reason which recognized enthusiasm as foolish, as a conflict of tendencies to self-sacrifice on behalf of an idea and to pleasure. This conflict between reason and urge remained effective in Heine until the end. But he soon found another formula which enabled him to combine his poetic feelings and his political attitudes into a greater unity (see p. 221).

And in truth one finds to perfection in Goethe that union of personality with genius such as we wish remarkable men to have. His exterior was as deeply impressive and significant as the word which lived in his works, and his form was harmonious, clear, cheerful, nobly proportioned; and one could study Greek art in him as in an antique. This dignified body was never bent by Christian worm-like humility, the features of his face never distorted by Christian wretchedness, his eyes were never shy, like those of a Christian sinner, never inspired cantingly, rantingly, or with celestial gleams. No; his eyes were calm as those of a god; and it is the sign by which the gods are known—that their glance is steady and that their eyes never vacillate. Therefore, when Agni, Varuna, Yama and Indra assume the form of Nala at the wedding of Damayanti, the bride recognizes her beloved by the winking of his eyes, since, as I have said, the eyes of the gods are always immovable. The eyes of Napoleon had this peculiarity; therefore I am persuaded that he was a god. Goethe's eyes were as divine in old age as in his youth. Time could cover his head with snow, but never bend it. He also held it proudly and high; and when he spoke, he became greater, and when he put forth his hand, it was as though he would show unto the stars in heaven their appointed course. It was thought that there played about his mouth a cold expression of egoism; but this trait is peculiar to the eternal gods, and even to the great Jupiter, the father of the gods, with whom I have never before compared Goethe. In truth, when I visited him at Weimar, and stood before him, I glanced involuntarily to one side to see whether there was not the eagle holding the lightning in his beak. I was about to address him in Greek, but observing that he understood German, I remarked to him in the latter that the plums on the road between Jena and Weimar tasted delicious. During many a winter night had I reflected what sublime and profound things I would say to Goethe, should I ever meet him; and when at last I saw him, I told him that the Saxon plums were good. And Goethe smiled—smiled with the same lips which had kissed the beautiful Leda, Europa, Danae, Semele, and so many other princesses, or even common nymphs.

—The Romantic School, 1

This latest account of his visit to Weimar Heine wrote in 1833, one year after Goethe's death. The ancient Indian heroic poem Nala and Damayanti *forms a portion of the great epic,* Mahabharata.

It is six years since, on a walking tour through the Fatherland, I arrived at Wartburg and visited the cell where Dr. Luther had been housed. . . . At Wartburg, I visited the armory where the ancient armor and weapons hang, the old pikes, targets, halberds, broadswords—the iron wardrobe of the medievals. I wandered about the hall reflectively with a university friend, a noble young gentleman whose father was one of the most powerful quarter-princes in our homeland at the time and ruled the whole trembling little country. His ancestors, too, had been mighty barons, and the young man revelled in heraldic reminiscences as he

viewed the armor and weapons which declared, on an attached
label, that they had belonged to some knight of his line. When
he reached his ancestor's claymore down from its hook and tried
out of curiosity whether he could wield it, he had to confess that
it was a bit heavy for him, and dropped his arm discouraged.
When I saw this, when I saw that the arm of the grandson was
too weak for the sword of his fathers, I thought to myself, "Germany might be free."

—Ludwig Boerne, 2

(written 1830)

Examination and Baptism

I have made a discovery: Everyone in Germany is a genius,
and I, even I, am the only one who is not a genius. I am not jesting; I am in earnest. Things the most ordinary people can comprehend are difficult for me. I wonder how people can retain
in their heads things half understood, things wrenched out of
the context of knowledge, and then retell them, with an air of
complete fidelity, in their books or from their university lecterns.
A man who can do this I regard as a genius. Meanwhile, because
of their rarity, the name of genius is also applied to men who
cannot do it. That is the great irony. That is the ultimate basis
of my being a genius. That also is the ultimate basis for my
tormenting myself to death with my jurisprudence, for my not
yet being done with it, my not being done with it till Easter.

Genius in poetry is a similarly equivocal thing. Talent is more
valuable. For perfection talent is required. To be a poetic genius
one must first have talent for it. That is the ultimate basis of
Goethe's greatness. That is the ultimate reason for so many poets
coming to grief, for example, I. . . .

I work strenuously at my Law, and otherwise live like a recluse.
I am not liked here, and do not yet know whether it is advisable
for me to take my doctorate here at Easter. Three days ago I
wrote my uncle Salomon Heine that I wished to remain here
another semester. I wrote concisely and without beating about
the bush. I am eager to see his answer. . . . I write little, read
much. Still chronicles and source writers. Before I realized it, I

got into the history of the Reformation, and at this moment the second folio volume of von der Hardt's *Historia Literaria Reformationis* is lying upon my table. Last evening I read in it Reuchlin's piece against burning the Hebrew books. For your study of the history of religion I can recommend Schroeckh's *Church History* warmly because of its thoroughness. Since the holidays I have run through two dozen volumes of it. . . . I cannot at this moment proceed further with my *Rabbi*.

—To Moses Moser
Goettingen, January 11, 1825

Johannes Reuchlin (1455-1522), outstanding philologist, with a thorough knowledge of Greek and Hebrew, defended the Talmud and the Jews against the attacks of the apostate Pfefferkorn who, in 1509, had received a commission from the German emperor to confiscate all Hebrew books and to burn them at his discretion. Reuchlin was involved in a lengthy trial by the Dominicans at Koeln, who used Pfefferkorn as their tool, and was condemned for heresy by Pope Leo X. But the sympathy of humanists generally for Reuchlin prevented penalties from being actually carried out. The fundamental significance of Reuchlin's campaign against Pfefferkorn was recognized even by contemporaries, and is generally and correctly taken as a prelude to the struggle for intellectual freedom. Hermann von der Hardt (1661-1746): Christian talmudic scholar; the work mentioned by Heine appeared in 1717. Johann Matthias Schroeckh (1733-1818) wrote his Christian Church History in forty-five volumes (1768-1811).

On April 16, Heine applied to the faculty for his examination. On May 3, he took the examination, and on July 20, 1825, after he had defended his thesis in a public disputation in Latin, he was awarded the degree of Doctor of Both Laws by the Dean. Previously, on June 28, Heine had gone over to Protestantism in the small town in Heiligenstadt.

All the past winter I worked at jurisprudence incessantly and hence was in position to take my doctoral examination last week;

I passed it quite creditably. For the purpose of obtaining my degree, that is the principal thing; everything else, for example, the public disputation, is mere formality and hardly worth mention. Actually then I am now Doctor, and the effect will no longer be ironical when you give me this title in your letters. . . . That is the best news that I can give you; everything else is gloomy. You can easily imagine why I spare you accounts of my external situation which, as with everyone, is involved in economics. I may be charged with folly and confusion, but I know that my thought and action beseem my inward dignity. There is a jury appointed, dear Moritz, for everything that I do, but this jury has not yet assembled to pass judgment upon me. It will hardly include merchants. . . .

On the question of my settling in Hamburg—only the gods who create hunger know. I shall not settle there without being provided with bread for a couple of years. In the meanwhile, everything on my part is done: converted, fitted with a J.D. degree, and hopefully also well, I will soon come to Hamburg. I shouldn't be writing you these things if you had not frequently inquired about them.

—To Moritz Embden
Goettingen, May 11, 1825

I have rented a house with a garden, go walking in the evenings amid rose bushes, and am awakened every morning at 5:45 by nightingales. Anyhow, it is better to be awakened by nightingales than by bootblacks knocking at the door.

Then I work as strenuously as I can—jurisprudence, history, the *Rabbi*, etc. The latter proceeds very slowly, every line being a struggle, but it does go forward, for I carry within me the consciousness that only I can write this book, and that the writing of it is a useful business pleasing to God. But I will break off from this theme, for it may easily bring me to the point of advertising my own greatness of soul.

Zunz, indeed, has already written me through you where the outstanding school of the Spanish Jews in the fifteenth century was, namely in Toledo; but I should like to know if this is to be understood as applying to the end of the fifteenth century also. He also named Seville and Granada to me, but I think I read in Basnage that the Jews had already been expelled from Granada. Also, as I remarked to you, I should like to find something about the Abarbanels that I cannot find from Christian sources. The latter are all cited by Wolf in his *Bibliothek*. Bagl is scanty. Schudt has similarly swept a few things together. Bartolocci I have not yet read. The Spanish historians have little, incredibly little, about the Jews. In general, it is an Egyptian darkness. At the end of this year I think the *Rabbi* will be finished. It will be a book that the Zunzes of all centuries will call "a source."

—To Moses Moser
Goettingen, July 1, 1825

Wolf: Johann Christoph Wolf (1683-1739), non-Jewish Hebraist. His four-volume Bibliotheca Hebraica appeared 1715-1733 and was regarded as the most valuable reference work for the history of Jewish literature, before the work of Steinschneider. Wolf used the large collection of David Oppenheimer, which is now in the Bodleian at Oxford.

I defended my fourth and fifth theses, oaths and *confarreatio*, like a truck horse. It all went very well, and Dean Hugo made me a panegyric on this festive occasion, expressing his astonishment that a great poet should also be a great jurist. If the last had not made me a little sceptical of such praise, I should have preened myself no little upon the fact that a long Latin oration delivered from the chancel compared me to Goethe and declared that by general judgment my verses are to be set beside Goethe's. These things the great Hugo said out of the fullness of his heart; privately he said many other nice things to me when we went driving together, and he invited me to dinner. I think Gans is wrong to speak of Hugo disparagingly. Hugo is one of the greatest men of the century. . . .

My cordial greetings to Zunz, and tell him that I thank him kindly for his notes. Jews actually lived in Granada in 1492, for they are expressly mentioned in the capitulation of that city. On

Abarbanel I have looked up Majus' dissertation *Vita Abarbanelis* and compared all the Christian sources; but there is very little.
—To Moses Moser
Goettingen, July 22, 1825

Heine's five theses were: (1) The husband is owner of the dowry; (2) The creditor must furnish a receipt; (3) Legal procedures must be public; (4) No obligations arise from an oath; (5) Confarreatio was the oldest form of legal wedlock among the Romans. The fourth and fifth theses required spirited defense against the objections of Heine's opponents; the defense, according to auditors, was carried on "in a Latin not particularly classical," and frequently provoked laughter. Goethe, too, studied jurisprudence, and for a time practised law in Frankfurt.

My cordial greetings to Moritz, and if you are sure he is no gossip, tell him that I am not only Dr. *Juris* but something else too. It rained yesterday, as it did six weeks ago.
—To Charlotte Embden
Goettingen, July 31, 1825

This is Heine's first communication concerning his conversion.

The baptismal certificate is the ticket of admission to European culture.

The Jews alone maintained their freedom of religion at the Christianization of Europe.

My becoming a Christian is the fault of those Saxons who suddenly changed saddles at Leipzig, or of Napoleon, who really did not have to go to Russia, or of his teacher of geography at Brienne, who did not tell him that Moscow winters are very cold.
—Thoughts and Reflections

At the battle of Leipzig (October 16-18, 1813), the Saxon troops went over from Napoleon to the Allies, and thus ensured the defeat of the French army.

In Cordova's old cathedral
Thirteen hundred columns tower;
Thirteen hundred giant columns
Bear the cupola stupendous.

And on walls and dome and pillars,
Run in quaint design and tracery,
From the roof unto the basement
Passages from out the Koran.

Moorish monarch whilom builded
This cathedral unto Allah
And his praise, but much has altered
In the vortex dark of ages.

On the tower where the warder
Called to prayer the Moslem Faithful,
Now the melancholy droning
Hum of Christian bells is ringing.

On the steps where the Believers
Sung the praises of the Prophet,
Now sleek tonsured priests are showing
Their stale Mass' mawkish marvel.

. . . .

And he dreams: again he's standing
With bowed head all wet and dripping,
In Cordova's old cathedral,
And he hears dark voices many.

All the lofty giant columns
He hears muttering, grimly wrathful,
That they will not bear it longer,
And they tremble and they totter;—

And they fiercely crack and crumble,
Pale as death grow priest and people,
With wild crash the dome o'erwhelmeth,
And the Christian Gods moan wailing.
—The Home-Coming: Almansor

To an Apostate

Ah, sacred spirit of youth pulsating!
Alas, how quickly tamed and penned!
And now how coolly calculating
To the gentlemen's wish dost yielding bend.

To the cross thou crawledst meekly bending,
To the cross once boldly contemned,
To worship in a week perpending
What to trample didst once pretend.

'Tis books too many have brought you low,
Schlegel, Haller, Burke, and all—
But yesterday still a stout hero,
Vile today, a poltroon thrall.

This poem is not as has hitherto been generally assumed, directed at Eduard Gans, who went over to Christianity the same time as Heine, but is rather the poet's reproach to himself.

I advise everyone who stands on the peak of Ilse rock to think neither of the Emperor nor the Empire nor even of the beautiful Ilse, but of his feet. For as I stood there lost in thought, I suddenly heard the subterranean music of the magic castle and saw the mountains round about stand on their heads, and the red tiles of Ilsenburg begin to dance, and the green trees fly about in the air, so that my sight turned blue and green; and I am certain that, seized with giddiness, I should have toppled to the abyss if

in my desperate need I had not clung fast to the iron cross. That
I did so in so distressing a situation surely no one will blame me.
—Tour in the Harz

In their first printing, those symbolic allusions to his baptism
are followed by the phrase, "and I have not regretted it to this
hour." Heine eliminated the phrase in the book edition.

III

THE NON-VALID TICKET OF ADMISSION

Heine's hope that his conversion to Protestantism would give him access to a position in Germany was not realized. The years between his baptism and his emigration to France were a period of constant and futile search for some secure position in civic life. At first he cherished a plan to lecture on history at the University of Berlin as a Privatdozent, but soon realized that there was not the slightest prospect of his doing so. For some time he entertained the hope of receiving a professorship in Munich. The disappointment of this hope was all the more acute. Repeated attempts to settle in Hamburg as a lawyer were also futile, and the possibility, very uncertain from the start, of being employed by the Hamburg senate as a syndic collapsed before he could take any serious steps towards its realization. Only for a few months did Heine have regular paid employment as the editor of a political periodical. But this did not satisfy his ambition.

In this period of futile efforts to find a civic career, Heine published the works to which he owed his world reputation, the Book of Songs and the Travel Pictures, which transported his contemporaries and many succeeding generations to a state of enthusiasm and enchantment. But with public recognition, the hostility of literary opponents and the suspicions of the government grew. The last two years which Heine spent on German soil in Hamburg were particularly embittered for him by the fact that not only his odious relatives but also malignant and ruthless opponents of the poet were received with friendship in Salomon Heine's house. So Heine felt that not only was his security as a political writer threatened, but also that he was surrounded by enemies in his social existence.

Failure in the Law: Poetry of the Sea

Heine's desire to recover from the exertions of his examinations by sea-bathing was fulfilled by his uncle Salomon. His uncle provided means for a considerable sojourn upon the island of Norderney, where Heine spent pleasant days in the company of beautiful ladies. He flirted with the Princess von Hohensolms-Lich, and spent two days with Christian Sethe, the friend of his youth, who came to Norderney on his honeymoon. At Norderney, Heine was inspired to write his North Sea Pictures, poems in free rhythms in which a description of the sea with mythological fantasies is combined with acute expression of the poet's own moods. Heine's North Sea Pictures discovered the sea for German poetry. But in world literature also Heine's skill in comprehending variations in color of water and atmosphere in suggestive words has held its own peculiar place.

I am still the old fool who, when he has concluded peace with the outer world, is immediately plagued anew by inward war. There is a dreary storm and I hear nothing but the roar of the sea. Would that I lay buried under the white dunes. I have become very moderate in my desires. Once, I wished to be buried under the palms of the Jordan.

—To Christian Sethe
Norderney, September 1, 1825

Since we are speaking of books, I recommend to you Golownin's *Journey to Japan*. From it you will see that the Japanese are the most civilized and urbane people on earth. I might have said the most Christian people, if I had not read, to my astonishment, that nothing is so loathed by this people as Christianity. Nothing is so hated as the cross. I shall become a Japanese.

Perhaps I will send you today a poem out of the *Rabbi*, which I have again unfortunately interrupted. I urgently request you not to communicate this poem, or anything else that I may say to you of my private circumstances, to anyone. A young Spanish Jew, a Jew at heart but one who has undergone conversion out of pride and luxury, corresponds with the youthful Judah Abar-banel and sends him that poem translated from the Moorish. Perhaps he is a little embarrassed to write his friend unreservedly of an action which is not very noble. But he sends him that poem. —Don't reflect on it.—

As soon as I settle down in Hamburg or Berlin I will continue working on the *Rabbi*. . . .

I am looking forward to Gans' return with eagerness. I believe that Gans is coming back actually as Eli-Gans. I also believe that although the first portion of the law of inheritance can justly be regarded, according to Zunz's library division, as a source of Jewish history, yet the portion of the law of inheritance which will appear after Gans' return from Paris will be no source of Jewish history—as little as the words of Savigny and other *Goyim* and *Reshoim* ("wicked Gentiles"). In brief, Gans will return from Paris as a Christian, in the most watery sense of the word. I fear that Sugar-Cohn will be Carl Sand.

—To Moses Moser
Lueneburg, beginning October 1825

I am glad to hear, dear lady, that you have met my uncle, Salomon Heine. How did he please you? Tell me, tell me! He is a considerable man, one who has the most excellent qualities, allied with great defects of character. We are continually at odds, but I have an extraordinary love for him; I love him almost more than I know myself. We are very similar, too, in character: we have the same obstinate boldness, unfathomable softness, and unreliable crankiness. But fortune has made him a millionaire and myself a poet, and has therefore fashioned us altogether differently in ways of living and thought.

—To Friederike Robert
Lueneburg, October 12, 1825

A short while ago I read *Werther*. That was a real happiness for me. A short while ago I also read Heinrich von Kleist's *Kohlhaas*. I am filled with admiration for that author, and cannot sufficiently deplore his having shot himself; but I can understand well enough why he did so.

As for my material life, it is not worth the trouble of talking about. You are seeing Cohen these days, and he can tell you how I came to Hamburg to become a lawyer and failed. Probably Cohen will not be able to give you the reason for it; but neither can I. . . .

I don't know what to say: Cohen assures me that Gans is preaching Christianity and trying to convert the children of Israel. If he is doing so out of conviction, he is a fool; if out of hypocrisy, he is a scoundrel. I will not cease to love Gans, but I confess I would much rather have heard that Gans had been stealing silver spoons.

That you, my dear Moser, should think as Gans does I cannot believe, although Cohen assures me that it is the case, and insists that he has it directly from you. It would distress me much if my own conversion would appear to you in a favorable light. I assure you that if the laws permitted the stealing of silver spoons, I would not have undergone baptism. More of this orally.

Last Saturday I was in the Temple and had the pleasure of hearing with my own ears how Dr. Salomon assailed baptized Jews, and particularly excoriated them for "being seduced to faithlessness to the religion of their fathers by the mere hope of obtaining *a position*" (his very words).

I assure you the sermon was good and I intend to call on the man one of these days. Cohen is magnanimous to me. I eat at his house on *Shabbes*; he heaps glowing *kugel* on my head, and I crunch this sacred national dish, which has been more effective for the preservation of Judaism than all three numbers of our paper. Furthermore, it has been in greater demand.

—To Moses Moser
Hamburg, December 14, 1825

Heine was one of the first to appreciate the long neglected but great dramatist Heinrich von Kleist, who was born in 1777 and took his life in 1811. Kleist's romance, Michael Kohlhaas, *tells the story of a man who creates his own right by violence and insur-*

rection against his feudal lord after the court had denied it to him.

I hope that the *Sea Pictures*, the manuscript of which you will receive through Cohen, will please you somewhat better. . . . Tieck and Robert, if they did not create this form, have at least made it better known; but its contents are among the most individual things that I have written. You see, I come out of the larva each summer and a new butterfly flutters forth. So I am not limited to a mere lyric-malicious two-strophe manner.

—To Moses Moser
Hamburg, December 15, 1825

If I had time I would write a nice Jewish letter to Doctoress Zunz. I am now become a proper Christian. I am toadying to rich Jews.

—To Moses Moser
Hamburg, December 18, 1825

Life here is bad. Rain, snow, and too much food. And I, very gloomy. By day Hamburg is a large counting-house, and by night a large brothel. Everyone looks at me as if they wish to parody the *Lyrical Intermezzo*. And I myself am full of irony and sentimentality. I visited your friend Dr. Halle. He is very amiable, very obliging, and a true Jew. He showed his Jewish complaisance at the first moment with the question, "You are to become my colleague?" Vexed as I was (Kleistian expression), I said: "Yes; everyone believes that I shall remain here to be a lawyer." But I do not know at all what I shall do here. Only do not believe that I shall be idle. On the contrary, wherever I may be, I make verses. I wrote the following famous song last evening. Is it not exquisite?

> They loved one another, yet neither
> Would tell the other so;
> With love they were almost heartbroken,
> Yet looked on each as a foe.

They parted at last—and sometimes,
Though only in dreams, they met;
They had long been dead, those lovers,
But themselves scarce knew it yet.

Do you know a better song in all German literature?

But really, Christiani, after you have read this song, do you actually believe that I shall be a lawyer here?

—To Rudolph Christiani
Hamburg, December 1825

On Halle, see p. 151.

The good reception of my first productions has not—as unfortunately is usually the case—lulled me into the sweet belief that I am now a genius, once and for all, and need do nothing but let the dear clear stream of poetry flow peacefully from me to the admiration of the world. No one knows better than I how difficult it is to put forth in literature anything that does not already exist, and how unsatisfying it must be for any profound spirit to write merely for the pleasure of the idle herd.

—To Karl Simrock
Hamburg, December 30, 1825

Karl Simrock (1802-1876), poet and literary scholar, was a longtime friend of Heine.

I am happy at Cohen's return. He has shown me much affection and has procured my uncle's favor for me, which is the more meritorious to the degree that my uncle is surrounded wholly by people who are hostile to me. I am now hated by Christian and Jew. I am very sorry that I was baptized. I do not see that I have prospered better; on the contrary, I have had nothing but bad luck since. . . . Isn't it ridiculous that I am no sooner baptized than I am upbraided as a Jew. But I tell you, there have been nothing but contradictions since then, for example, I am even cheated of the fame of 1825.

—To Moses Moser
Hamburg, January 9, 1826

I got into two fist-fights at the university because of contemptuous looks, and once into a duel with pistols because of an indecent expression. These were attacks on my personality, without whose integrity I should not like to live. . . . My sister's husband, provoked by the well-earned contempt which I showed him, sought to exact vengeance by calumniating me and my manner of life before the whole world; among others he instigated even Cohen to depict my bad manner of life to my uncle, for my own best interests, in order to incite him to remove me from this place. Cohen is said to have remarked in my uncle's house that I was a playboy, an idler, in bad hands, characterless, and, in a word, much more of the same; whether because he wished to make himself important, or out of a clumsiness which led him to think such talk useful. . . . But what irks me most is that I am myself to blame because of my open and childish devotion to friends or friends of friends. It shan't happen again; at need, I shall show so determinedly serious an exterior as you others. . . . This day I have lost my sister.

—To Moses Moser
Hamburg, February 24, 1826

Heine was soon reconciled with his sister; his relations with his brother-in-law continued strained.

It was much warmer at that time. If I am not mistaken, Gans was then not yet baptized, and wrote long discourses for the *Verein,* and paraded the quotation: "The victorious cause was pleasing to the gods, the vanquished to Cato."

I remember that the Psalm "By the rivers of Babylon" was at that time your *forte* and you recited it so beautifully, so majestically, so movingly that my tears flow even now, and not merely for the Psalm.

At that time you had some very good ideas about Judaism, the baseness of Christian proselytization, the baseness of the Jews who not only intended to be rid of difficulties by baptism but sought some profit by it, wished to use it in bargaining—and other such good ideas which you must some day write down. You are an independent enough person not to refrain from venturing it for Gans' sake; and as for me, you do not need to dissemble at all for my sake.

Solon says that no man can be called happy before his death; we might add that no man should be called brave before his death.

I am glad that old Friedlaender and Bendavid are old and will soon die; we shall then be sure of them, and our age will not be liable to the charge that it could show no single man without reproach.

Forgive me this depression; it is directed mostly against myself. Often I rise in the night and stand before the mirror and upbraid myself. . . . So I thought last night with what a face Gans would appear before Moses, if Moses should suddenly appear on earth. And Moses is surely the greatest jurist who ever lived, for his legislation endures to this day.

I also dreamed that Gans and Mordecai Noah met at Stralau, and Gans—wonderful to relate—was as mute as a fish. Zunz stood by smiling sarcastically and said to his wife, "Do you see, little mouse?" I think Lehmann delivered a long discourse in full voice and trimmed out with "enlightenment," "change of conditions," "progress of the world-spirit"—a long discourse at which I did not fall asleep, but on the contrary, woke up.

I have not yet succeeded in finding myself a nest anywhere here; I am entirely lacking in that talent which insects and certain local doctors of the law possess in such high degree. I have therefore had to give up my plan to be a lawyer here, but do not think that I will leave this place so soon. I am singularly well pleased here. It is the classic soil of my love. . . . I have alienated many helpful friends, some with and some without my fault, and have thereby acquired a wealth of opponents. . . . Because of the un-

appetizing character of my brother-in-law, I have had to give up
my sister entirely.

—To Varnhagen von Ense
Hamburg, May 14, 1826

To Dr. Zunz, judge designate over Israel, vice-president of the
Verein fuer Kultur und Wissenschaft der Juden, president of the
Scientific Institute, editor of the *Zeitschrift fuer die Wissenschaft des Judentums*, member of the Agricultural Commission,
librarian—

At this last title I will pause, for I send you herewith a copy of
my latest book for the *Verein* library, with the request that, in
case the library has now removed to Ararat, you kindly deliver
the said copy to Mme. Doctor Zunz for use in the kitchen.

The largest portion of this book is *Source*, and hence indis-
pensable for the history of our Jews.

But with all love and friendship, I remain

Your friend,
H. Heine
Dr. jur., and member of the *Verein fuer
Kultur und Wissenschaft der Juden*
in the eighteenth century.

P.S. In the second portion of the *Travel Pictures* there appears
the *Rabbi*, and indeed much circumcised; nevertheless, there are
many other curiosities in that same portion.

—To Leopold Zunz
Hamburg, May, 1826

Inscription in the first portion of Travel Pictures.

Times are bad, and I must care for my reputation, for I must
half live on it. . . . In the second volume, my *Rabbi* also is to
appear, and I am prepared to be quite generally despised for it
in the Christian world. . . . The anti-Christian tone in the first
part of the *Travel Pictures* will also meet with disapproval.

—To Joseph Lehmann
Hamburg, May 26, 1826

Ye deities! Never have I adored you!
To me the Greeks are always repugnant,
To me the Romans more hateful are;
Yet sacred compassion and shuddering pity
Stream through my heart
When I see you above me walking,
Forsaken deities,
Death-like, night-wandering shadows,
Weak as mists that the breezes drive,
And when I bethink me what windy cowards
The new gods are who overcame you,
The new rulers, the doleful deities,
Who joy in pain, in humility's sheepskin,
O then grips me a bitter regret,
And fain I'd shatter the new-made temples
And fight for you, ye ancient deities,
For you and your good, your ambrosial right,
And fronting your loftiest altars,
Rebuilded again with their smoking sacrifice,
I myself might kneel and implore you
And raise up these arms as in prayer—

For after all, ye ancient deities,
Always you joined in the battling of peoples,
Always of old, on the side of the victors;
So it is that man is greater than ye,
And I hold with you in the strife of the gods,
And with the side of the conquered deities.

Thus I spoke and visibly blushing,
Over me the pallid, mist-moulded figures
Like perishing men looked down on me,
Pain-transfigured, and vanished sharply.
The moon was wholly hidden
Under the clouds that darklier gathered,
High up-billowed the sea.

And then, victorious, shone in heaven
The starlight eternal.

—The North Sea, Second Cycle, 6

I shall spend this winter, or at least part of it, in Berlin; my
thoughts on the subject are not yet definitely fixed. But what is
fixed is that I feel the urgent need of saying farewell to my German fatherland. It is less the desire to travel than the torment of
my personal situation (for example, the never-to-be-effaced Jew)
which drives me hence.

My health is improved, but not entirely, and now I refrain
from definitely reckoning upon the cooperation of my *physis*.
Now I am afloat once more on the North Sea. I love salt water,
and I am well and happy when my boat is tossed hither and
thither by the waves, and there is comfort for me in the idea of
drowning, the only comfort which the horrible priest of Heliopolis has left me—he has not planked over the sea.

How deeply rooted is the myth of the Wandering Jew! In the
still forests of the valley the mother tells her children the terrible
story, and the little ones fearfully close round the hearth. Outside is the night—the post-horn sounds—haggling Jews are jour-
neying to Leipzig for the Fair. We who are the heroes of the
story, we do not know it. No barber can shave the white beard,
the ends of which Time is for ever blackening with new youth.

Your *Verein* picture, "the Gigantic Christ with Crown of
Thorns who Strides Through the Centuries," often recurs to my
memory. You are gentler and better than I, and hence your pictures are more beautiful, milder and more conciliatory.

My "*Christ Upon the Water*," 12th *Sea Picture*, has roused
much displeasure against me. So have my *Travel Pictures* in
general made me many enmities. . . . My financial situation has
been improved by the book. The second portion is to be printed
at the end of the year. It will contain many remarkable things,
for example, the *Rabbi*. "Thee hath the goddess of wisdom,
Pallas Athene, never protected by her counsel."

—To Moses Moser
Norderney, July 8, 1826

The myth of the Eternal Jew is of Christian, not Jewish origin. *Heliopolis: City of Egypt called On in the Bible, principal seat of the cult of the sun.* Heine is here following Voltaire, who conceives of the Jewish religion as a borrowing from the teachings of Egyptian priests. Moser's picture of "the gigantic Christ" inspired Heine to the sea-picture Peace. It continued to influence Heine's thoughts on Judaism and Christianity later also. The Jesus of Nazareth of the Synoptic Gospels was regarded by Moser and other members of the Kulturverein as a Jewish prophet and social revolutionary. The completion of the Rabbi of Bacherach and its publication in the Reisebildern, which Heine so frequently announces in his letters, never came to pass. Before his conversion Heine had completed only two chapters. It was only in 1840 and in a quite different mood that he wrote a third chapter, without bringing the work to its completion. "Thee hath the goddess of wisdom etc.": citation from Heine's North Sea picture Poseidon, where the poet represents himself as being ridiculed by the god. Moser repeatedly advised against premature publication of the Rabbi.

Peace

The sun stood high in the heavens
Swathed in white clouds;
The sea was still.
I lay in the helm of the vessel,
Dreamily musing . . . When, half awake
And half asleep, I saw the Christ,
The Savior of the world.
In a white, waving garment
He walked, tall as a giant,
Over land and sea.
His head rose into the heavens,
His hands were stretched in blessing
Over land and sea;
And like a heart in his breast,
He carried the sun,
The great, red, burning sun.

And that flaming heart, that fiery splendor,
Poured all its hallowed sunbeams,
And all its tender, compassionate light,
Wide-spread and warming,
Over land and sea.

Clear and happy bells were ringing,
Drawing on the gliding vessel;
Drew, like swans with ropes of roses,
Lightly to a fair, green harbor
Where men lived in a lofty, towering
Sky-scraping city.
Wonder of peace! How quiet the town!
The cries and the clamor were hushed;
The clatter of trade was over.
And, through the clean-swept, echoing streets,
Men in white raiment wandered
Carrying palm-branches.
And where two met in that city,
They gazed at each other with understanding,
And, thrilling with love and a sweet abnegation,
Kissed each other on the brow.
And both looked up
At the glowing heart of the Savior
That joyfully sacrificed its red blood
In streams of ruddy light.
And they, thrice-blest, would cry,
"Praise be to Jesus Christ!"

If such a conception would have been granted you,
What would you have given,
Dearly belovèd brother!
You who are so weak in the head and the loins
And so strong in the faith!
You who worship the Trinity so religiously
And kiss the cross and the pup and the paw

Of your noble protectress daily.
You who talked yourself into the council
And a place on the bench
And, at last, to a part in the governing
Of that virtuous city,
Where dust and Faith arise,
And the long-suffering Spree, with its holy waters,
Washes the souls and dilutes the tea of the faithful—
Had you but conceived this vision,
Dearly belovèd,
You would have taken it to market
And offered it in high places.
Your white, simpering features
Would melt with devotion;
And the high and mighty lady,
Enraptured and trembling with bliss,
Would sink, praying, on her knees beside you.
And her eyes, beaming with happiness,
Would promise you an increase of salary
Of a hundred sterling Prussian dollars.
And you would fold your hands and stammer,
"Praise be to Jesus Christ!"

Only the first portion of this poem is contained in the Book
of Songs and in the text of the collected editions of Heine's
works. In the editions of the Reisebildern prepared by Heine it is
printed in its complete form as given here.

I stayed at Norderney until the middle of September; from the
beginning of that month until my departure I was virtually the
only remaining bathing-visitor. I hired a wherry and two boatmen
and spent whole days rowing about the North Sea. The Sea was
my only companion, and I have never had a better. Nights by the
sea—magnificent, grand. I thought of you often. Indeed, it occurred to me that I was just beginning to comprehend you. Our
souls must be enlarged by great impressions of nature before we

are capable of comprehending great men wholly. Only remain well disposed to me and do not be annoyed. I will gladly confess all my transgressions and bow down before you.

The only thing that offends me is that you are so large and yet so abstemiously humble, whereas I am so much smaller and yet demand so much recognition. . . .

In January, I shall probably be in Hamburg for a short while, and by Easter the second portion of my *Travel Pictures* is to be printed. This portion is to be an extraordinary book and create a furore. I must produce something powerful. The second section of the *North Sea*, which will open the second volume, is far more original and acute than the first section and will surely please you. In it I have pioneered a new path, at the peril of my life. I have also attempted free humor in an autobiographical fragment. Hitherto I have displayed only wit, irony, whim, but never pure and unadulterated humor. . . .

I cannot believe that Gans, who is hardly a sophomore in Christianity, has already begun to Christianize. No, our G. G. Plumper has deceived me. But if he should ever do so, your brand of Christianity, crucified as Savior, will cry out in anguish: Doctor Eli! Doctor Eli! *lama asabhtani!*

You must have heard a stinking Jew in Hamburg has lied everywhere about giving me a beating. The swine only attacked me on the street, a fellow I have never spoken to in my life. That attack (he barely grabbed the skirt of my coat, and the mob in the Burstah immediately pulled him away); that *attentat*, that assault, the fellow even denied when I made a complaint to the police. That was all that I wanted. He said that I had attacked him because of an 1815 grudge (at that time I was not yet in Hamburg) in my writings, and then on the street. The story has been exploited by infamous rogues.

—To Moses Moser
Lueneburg, October 14, 1826

The "autobiographical fragment" alludes to the Book LeGrand, *which comprises the principal portion of the second volume of the* Travel Pictures. *G. G. Plumper: Gustav Gerson Cohen, see* page 147. By "your brand of Christianity" Moser and Heine understood Judaism, whose sufferings they paralleled to those of the founder of the Christian religion. Eli, Eli, lama asabhtani: Jesus of Nazareth's cry in Aramaic at Golgotha before his crucifixion, according to the tradition of the New Testament; the words are untranslated in the Greek text. Joseph Friedlaender, a Hamburg merchant of manufactured articles, felt personally offended by a passage at the close of the Tour in the Harz which speaks of a "black, unhanged huckster and his cloddish hardware phiz," and called Heine to account on the Burstah, a street in Hamburg. The quarrel continued for some time further, for Heine's and Friedlaender's accounts of the police action are contradictory. In this action, Heine was effectively supported by his publisher Julius Campe, his friend Friedrich Merckel, and the administrator of the Hamburg police.

In the spring of 1827, there appeared the second volume of the Travel Pictures, whose principal content is the third section of the North Sea, in prose, and Ideas: The Book LeGrand. Here Heine expresses himself on political and social conditions with far greater boldness than ever before. He enters into unequivocal opposition to the dominant forces, utters sharp criticism of nobility and church, both of which he regarded as the principal representatives of the medieval spirit and the strongest bulwarks against the ideas of the French Revolution, but does not criticize the monarchical constitution in itself. He combats the monarchy only insofar as it is supported by nobility and church. He combats all hereditary privileges. He combats all discrimination on the grounds of birth, family and religion. He does not desire to abolish inequality in distribution of property, but demands that the "have-nots" be protected against ruthless exploitation by the "haves," and that among the latter the spirit of social responsibility be aroused or strengthened. His program envisages a strong monarchy in a democratic society, whose representatives should control the measures of the crown. His political ideas are largely identical with those of Mirabeau, who similarly rejected a republic. To this political program Heine adhered throughout his life, although he felt human sympathy at times with the French republicans and the English radicals, and agreed more nearly with their attitude on religious questions. Heine's glorification of Napoleon was designed as a strong provocation to the dominant powers and their adherents, but also to German patriots of the left, and was so received. Heine's judgment of Napoleon made a distinction between the personality of the man and his deeds. The personality was unqualifiedly glorified; the deeds frequently sharply criticized (see pp. 249, 304). Heine regarded Napoleon as the consummator of the French Revolution, who subsequently proved unfaithful to his mission, but who achieved more for the democratization of society than did the republicans, and whose fall again delivered the unprivileged classes into the hands of their oppressors. With the second volume of the Travel Pictures, in which descriptions of travel are secondary to political polemic, Heine became a spokesman whose voice was heard and regarded everywhere in Germany and far beyond its borders. The book was immediately banned in Prussia, Austria, Hanover and several other German states; but Heine's publisher, Julius Campe, was shrewd enough to spread the book abroad notwithstanding. Heine remained grateful to him and later refused attractive offers of larger publishers, though he frequently had occasion to complain of Campe's conduct towards him.

In the challenging posture which Heine assumed as political writer, he believed he would be able to draw great advantage from his current adherence to Protestantism. He had grounds enough to fear that in the state of Germany of that day his political opponents would employ his Jewish origin as an effective weapon against him and would be able to nullify his arguments in the eyes of many readers merely by pointing at Heine's Jewish descent. It is primarily for tactical reasons, therefore, that from the third section of the North Sea onward, he emphasizes his Protestant viewpoint, or at least his adherence to Protestantism. But it was not solely tactics, or at least not solely the effort to place himself ouside of Judaism, that occasioned his more favorable judgment of Protestantism. Here Heine adopted without criticism the concept, then—and long afterwards—prevalent in lib-

eral circles, which saw in Luther's Reformation the first act of the
European revolution and in Protestantism the embodiment of
the principal of the intellect. Hence Protestantism for Heine, because of its maintenance of the Bible as authority against the
authority of the Pope, was an approach to Judaism. His view overlooked the importance of the anti-Jewish Pauline-Augustinian
element in Luther's reform.

The days of spiritual bondage are passed; weak with hoary age,
the old spider sits among the broken columns of its coliseum and
still continues to spin its old web; but the web is weak and de-
crepit and only butterflies and bats are caught in it, no longer the
golden eagles of the north.

It is truly laughable: while my intention is to expand with
right good will concerning the purposes of the Roman clergy, I
am suddenly seized by the wonted Protestant zeal which is at the
opposite pole. Precisely this dichotomy of opinion within me fur-
nishes me a picture of the fragmentation of thought in our era.
What we admired yesterday we hate today, and tomorrow we
may mock at it with indifference.

—The North Sea, 3

The Lord knows I am a good Christian, and even often get so
far as to intend to make a call at His house, but by some mishap
I am invariably hindered in my good intentions. Generally this
is done by some long-winded gentleman who holds me by the
button in the street, and even if I get to the gate of the temple,
some jesting, irreverent thought comes over me, and then I regard it as sinful to enter. Last Sunday something of the sort happened, when just before the door of the church there came into
my head an extract from Goethe's *Faust*, where the hero passing
with Mephistopheles by a cross, asks the latter—

> "Mephisto, art in haste?
> Why cast'st thou at the cross adown thy glances?"

To which Mephistopheles replies—

"I know right well it shows a wretched taste,
   But crosses never ranked among my fancies."
                                  —The North Sea, 3

Shooting on this beach is also said to present many very great attractions. As far as I am concerned, I am not particularly qualified to appreciate its charms. A love for the sublime, the beautiful and the good is often inspired in men by education, but a love for hunting lies in one's *blood*. When ancestors in ages beyond recollection killed stags, the descendant still finds pleasure in this legitimate occupation. But my ancestors did not belong to the hunters so much as to the hunted, and the idea of attacking the descendants of those who were our comrades in misery goes against my grain.

                                  —The North Sea, 3

I truly realize at this instant that I am no worshipper, or at least no bigoted admirer of Byron. My blood is not so splenetically black; my bitterness comes only from the gall-apples of my ink; and if there be poison in me, it is only an anti-poison for those snakes which lurk so threateningly amid the shelter of old cathedrals and castles. Of all great writers, Byron is just the one whose writings excite in me the least passion, while Scott, on the contrary, in his every book gladdens, tranquillizes and strengthens my heart.

                                  —The North Sea, 3

Rejection of the Byron cult: see pp. 220-221. Heine polemicized against Scott's biography of Napoleon in the Annalen.

As once in Granada men and women ran with the wail of desperation from their houses, when the song of the departure of the Moorish king rang in the streets, so that it was prohibited, on pain of death, to sing it, so hath the tone which rings through Scott's romance thrilled with pain a whole world. This tone re-echoes in the hearts of our nobles, who see their castles and armorial bearings in ruins; it rings again in the hearts of our burghers who have been crowded from the comfortable narrow way of their ancestors by wide-spreading cathedrals, whence faith has fled; in rabbinic synagogues, from which even the faithful flee. It sounds over the whole world, even into the Banyan groves of Hindustan, where the sighing Brahmin sees before him the destruction of his gods, the demolition of their primeval cosmogony and the total victory of the Briton.

But this tone—the mightiest which the Scottish bard can strike upon his giant harp—accords not with the imperial song of Napoleon, the new man—the man of modern times—the man in whom this new age mirrors itself so gloriously that we are well-nigh dazzled thereby, and never think meanwhile of the vanished past, nor of its faded splendor.

—North Sea, 3

My bowels have little appetite for immortality. I have reflected upon the matter and have determined to be only half immortal and wholly satiated. If Voltaire was willing to surrender three hundred years of his immortal fame for a good digestion, I offer twice that amount for food to digest.

—Ideas: The Book LeGrand

I certainly am not one of the wise, but I side with that party, and we have waged war against fools for the last five thousand five hundred and eighty-eight years. The fools fancy themselves wronged by us, because they declare that there exists in this world only a limited quantity of wisdom, and that the wise—heaven knows how—have appropriated the whole of it; and it is scandalous to perceive how frequently a single person has got hold of so much wisdom that he puts his fellow-citizens and all the country round completely into the shade. This is the secret cause of the war, and it is a veritable war of extermination. . . . But poor me they specially hate, for they declare that I come originally of their stock, that I am unfaithful and a pervert who have broken the holiest bonds, have even become a spy, trying to find out what the fools are doing in order to make fun of them afterwards with my new companions, and that I am so stupid as not to see that these latter are laughing at me all the while and would never dream of putting me on an equality with themselves—and here the fools are perfectly right.

It is quite true, they do not consider me their equal, and their titterings behind my back are often meant for me. I know it well, but I give no sign. My heart bleeds in silence, and when I am alone my tears flow. I know it full well, my position is abnormal. Whatever I do is foolishness to the wise and an abomination to the fools. They hate me . . . and they are right in hating me. It is quite true that I have broken the holiest bonds. In the name of God and justice I ought to have lived and died amongst the fools. Ah me! how well they would have looked after me! Even now, were I to turn back, they would receive me with open arms. . . . I should be the very man to fill almost any post, seeing that I can distinguish in Latin the declensions from the conjugations, and do not, like some people, take a Prussian postillion's boot for an Etruscan vase. My sentiment, my faith, my inspiration might be of use during religious exercises, that is, to myself; and my remarkable poetical talent would stand me in good stead at birthdays and weddings. Nor would it be amiss were I to sing in some great national epos of all those heroes of whom we know for certain that worms from their putrified bodies have given themselves out as their descendants.

Many people not born fools, and who once were wise, have gone over to the fools on account of benefits such as I have described. They live there in a perfect fool's paradise; the foolish pranks which at first went against the grain have now become their second nature; in fact, they can no longer be regarded as hypocrites, but as true believers. One of these, whose mind is not yet in total darkness, loves me dearly, and when I was alone with him the other day he locked his door and said to me solemnly: "O thou fool who pretendest to wisdom and yet hast less sense than a child unborn, knowest thou not that the great of the land show honor to him alone who humbles himself and praises their blood as superior to his own? And even now thou art spoiling thy case with the pious of the land! Is it so hard then to turn thine eyes piously to heaven, to hide thy hands clasped in prayer in the sleeves of thy cloak, to hang thy head in meekness like a lamb of God, and to mumble texts learned off by heart? Believe me, the great will not reward thee for thy heresy, the godly will hate thee, curse thee and persecute thee, and there will be no career for thee either in heaven or on earth."

Ah, all that is true enough! But it happens to be my misfortune to be enamored of wisdom! I love her, though my love is not returned. I sacrifice all to her, though I receive nothing. I cannot part with her. And as once the Jewish King Solomon sang of the Christian Church in his Song of Songs, comparing it to a black-eyed maiden throbbing with passionate love, so as to throw dust in the eyes of his Jews—so have I sung in countless songs of the very opposite, namely of wisdom, comparing her to a pure, cold maiden who by turns attracts and repels me, now smiles and now frowns, and ends by turning her back on me.

—Ideas: The Book LeGrand, ch. 15

Here Heine conceives of the contrast between Romantic and modern attitudes to life and of their religious and political consequences as that contrast between reason and energy which, after his visit to Weimar, he formulated as opposition between pleasure and sacrifice on behalf of an idea. He feels himself as naturally a Romantic, but one who rejects Romanticism's hostility to modern reason, and who, for the sake of the highest general good, wages war against his own nature. In humorous guise, Heine here presents us with one of his most profound self-analyses. Until the end he was preoccupied with the problem of the contradiction between the Romantic and modern traits in his poetry and his personality, but, disregarding persiflage and caricature, he has never set the problem forth so clearly. No other German poet who derived from Romanticism has so sharply differentiated the Romantic attitude to life from predilection for medieval conditions and advocacy of political and religious reaction. Heine employed this self-analysis to deride his opposite, the "rationalist" who put himself at the service of reaction. Such turn-coats were by no means lacking in Germany in Heine's day; many of reaction's spokesmen had begun as radicals. They suc-

cumbed to enticements which were doubtless tried on Heine also. Even during his efforts to settle in Hamburg as lawyer, he was informed that the Senate's consent to his petition depended upon his political moderation. That political and religious dissidents who exhibited their "repentance" advanced rapidly in Berlin and Vienna, Heine could observe out of his own circle of acquaintances.

The allusion to the Song of Songs is a jest at the expense of the Christological interpretation of the Old Testament, according to which the prophets and psalmists of Israel foretold the advent of Jesus in veiled language. The conflict concerning Christological interpretation raged all through the Middle Ages and was waged by Luther with even greater vehemence against the rabbis, who did not accept it. Modern Protestant theology has acknowledged that it is untenable.

England and the English

Warned by various friends, Heine found it advisable to await the first effects of his new book abroad. He went to England, because a journey to France at this time would have increased the suspicion of the government. As an admirer of Napoleon, he was prejudiced against the English.

It is snowing outside and there is no fire in my chimney. . . . I have seen and heard much, but have not had a clear view of anything. London has surpassed all my expectations as to its magnificence, but I have lost myself. Up to now the theater has been my principal resource. . . . Living is terribly dear here. So far I have spent more than a guinea a day. I had to pay thirty shillings in landing fee and tips on the steamer, and I had to pay almost a pound in duty on my few books and so forth. Books are terrifically dear here. Nothing but fog, coal smoke, Porter and Canning. I have not yet visited my friends in Westminster Abbey. . . .

I have not yet seen Dr. Lieber, an acquaintance of Campe and Buek, whom I was to find here; but I hear that he is going to America next Saturday. The poor Germans! I wonder how things will go with me in this world! I shall never again, in spite of my better intelligence, let it play stupid tricks, that is, speak candidly. I am eager to find out from you whether any government has taken exception to my book. All that a man wants is to sit quietly at his hearth at home and read the *Deutsche Anzeiger* or the *Hallische Literaturzeitung* and eat German bread and butter. It is so fearfully damp and uncomfortable here, and no one understands me, and no one understands German.

—To Friedrich Merckel
London, April 23, 1827

Franz Lieber (1800-1872) became professor of history and political science in America. George Canning (1770-1827) succeeded Castlereagh in the foreign office, in 1822, and crossed Metternich's plans by his policy of nonintervention. The hopes of Europe's liberals centered on him. On April 10, 1827, he became Prime Minister, after a conflict with Peel and Wellington, and required the support of the Whigs. The dates of Canning's ministry coincide with Heine's sojourn in England.

Your *Bluecher* pleased me uncommonly. I read it twice, and admired the treatment of this crude material by the subtle diplomat without use of violence. . . .

It is remarkable how two like-minded people, at the same time, present to the public the hostile leaders, Napoleon and Bluecher, and each with enthusiasm. And yet I think our desires have been the same and we are still like-minded. Nevertheless— I must confess it—I cannot read your *Bluecher* with love. Perhaps the echoes of the LeGrand march still resound in me. I am vexed when I reflect that the man of the idea, the man transformed into idea, Napoleon to wit, was destroyed by two men of whom the one was a Hussar playing Pharaoh, and the other a dull English ne'er-do-well; I might put it better by saying that you could scarcely imagine how lamentable he looked last week when I saw him coming out of St. James'. Perhaps his gracious king notified him of Canning's complete victory with a shrug of the shoulders, and he saw that victory upon the smiling faces of passing Englishmen. This time the idea conquered without cannons, and the victor of Waterloo was forced to withdraw. . . .

It was not anxiety that drove me away, but rather the law of prudence, which advises everyone to take no risk where nothing is to be gained. . . . I left Hamburg on the very day that the book was to appear (great self-control), and hence have as yet no word of its fate. But I know it in advance. I know my Germans. They will be frightened, think the matter over, and do nothing. I even doubt whether the book will be prohibited. But it needed to be written. In this rotten, servile age something must be done.

—To Varnhagen von Ense
London, May 1, 1827

I see much and am learning much. . . . Everything is too dear and too distant. There are many attractive things too—the houses of Parliament, Westminster Abbey, English tragedy, and pretty women. . . . English literature is at present pitiful, more pitiful even than ours.

—To Moses Moser
London, June 9, 1827

Send a *philosopher* to London, but, never in your life, a poet! Send a philosopher there, and place him at a corner of Cheapside, where he will learn more than from all the books of the last Leipzig fair; and as the billows of human life roar around him, so will a sea of new thoughts rise before him, and the Eternal Spirit which moves upon the face of the waters will breathe upon him; the most hidden secrets of social harmony will be suddenly revealed to him; he will hear the pulse of the world beat audibly, and see it visibly; for if London is the right hand of the world—its active mighty right hand—then we may regard that route which leads from the Exchange to Downing Street as the world's pyloric glory.

But never send a poet to London! This downright earnestness of all things, this colossal uniformity, this machine-like movement, this troubled spirit of pleasure itself, this exaggerated

London, smothers the imagination and rends the heart. And should you ever send a German poet hither—a dreamer, who stares at everything, even a ragged beggar-woman, or the shining wares of a goldsmith's shop—why, then, at least he will find things going right badly with him, and he will be hustled about on every side, or perhaps be knocked over with a mild "God damn!" God damn!—damn the knocking about and pushing! I see at a glance that these people have enough to do. They live on a grand scale; and though food and clothes are dearer with them than with us, they must still be better fed and clothed than we are—as gentility requires. Moreover, they have enormous debts; yet occasionally, in a vainglorious mood, they make ducks and drakes of their guineas, pay other nations to box about for their pleasure, give their kings a handsome *douceur* into the bargain; and, therefore, John Bull must work to get the money for such expenditure. By day and by night he must tax his brain to discover new machines, and he sits and reckons in the sweat of his brow, and runs and rushes, without much looking around, from the Docks to the Exchange, and from the Exchange to the Strand; and therefore it is quite pardonable if he, when a poor German poet, gazing into a print-shop window, stands bolt in his way on the corner of Cheapside, should knock the latter sideways with a rather rough "God damn!"

But the picture at which I was gazing as I stood at the Cheapside corner was that of the French crossing the Beresina.

And when I, jolted out of my gazing, looked again on the raging street, where a parti-colored coil of men, women and children, horses, stage-coaches, and with them a funeral, whirled groaning and creeking along, it seemed to me as though all London were such a Beresina Bridge, where every one presses on in mad haste to save his scrap of life; where the daring rider stamps down the poor pedestrian; where every one who falls is lost for ever; where the best friends rush, without feeling, over each other's corpses; and where thousands in the weakness of death, and bleeding, grasp in vain at the planks of the bridge, and are shot down into the icy grave of death.

—English Fragments, 2

Shakespeare was indeed as a spiritual sun for that country where the real sun is wanting twelve months in the year, for that island of damnation, that Botany Bay without a southern climate, that coal-stinking, machinery-buzzing, church-going, and vilely drunken England! Benevolent nature never quite disinherits her creatures, and while she denied the English all which is beautiful or worthy of love, and gave them neither voice for song nor sense of enjoyment—and perhaps endowed them with leathern porter-bottles or jacks, instead of human souls—bestowed on them in recompense a large portion of civic freedom, the talent to make themselves comfortably at home, and William Shakespeare.

Yes, this is the sun which glorifies that land with its loveliest light, with its gracious beams. Everything there reminds us of Shakespeare, and by this memory the most ordinary objects appear transfigured and idealized. Everywhere the wings of his genius rustle round us, his clear eye gleams on us from every significant occurrence, and in great events we often seem to see him nod—nod gently—softly and smiling.

This unceasing memory of and through Shakespeare became significantly clear to me during my residence in London, while I, an inquisitive traveller, ran about from early morn till deep into the night, to see the so-called noteworthy objects. Every lion recalled the greater lion Shakespeare. All the places which I visited live an immortal life in his historical dramas and were known to me from my earliest youth. But these dramas are known in England, not only by the cultivated, but by the people, and even the stout beef-eater who, with his red coat and red face, acts as guide to the Tower and shows you behind the middle gate the dungeon where Richard caused the young princes, his nephews, to be murdered, refers you to Shakespeare, who has described minutely the details of this harrowing story. Also the verger, who leads you round through Westminster Abbey, always speaks of Shakespeare, in whose tragedies those dead kings and queens whose stony counterfeits here lie stretched out on their sarcophagi—and whom he shows to you for eighteen-pence—play such a wild or lamentable part.

He himself, or the image of the great poet, stands there the size of life, a noble form with a thoughtful head, holding in his hand a roll of parchment. There may be magic words inscribed on it, and when he moves his white lips at midnight, and calls the dead who rest in the vaults below, they rise with rusted armor and antiquated court dress—those knights of the white and red rose; even the ladies come forth sighing from their resting-place, and a clatter of swords, laughter and curses, rings around, just as at Drury Lane, where I so often saw Shakespeare's historical dramas played, and where Kean moved my soul so mightily when he rushed desperately across the stage crying—

"A horse, a horse, my kingdom for a horse!"

But I must copy the guide-book of London if I would mention every place where Shakespeare was brought to my mind. This happened most significantly in Parliament; not so much because its place is the Westminster Hall, so often spoken of in the Shakesperean dramas, but because while I there listened to the debates, Shakespeare was alluded to several times, and his verses were quoted, not with reference to the poetical, but to their historical importance. To my amazement, I remarked that Shakespeare is not only celebrated in England as a poet, but recognized as a writer of history by the highest state or parliament officials.

—Shakespeare's Maidens and Women. Introduction

Botany Bay in Australia was then a penal colony.

The life of England after the execution of Charles I is pale and dun; outraged poetry fled the soil which she had once ornamented with her brightest hues. How deeply I felt this when, upon a midnight, I passed the fateful windows of Whitehall and the cold and damp prose of England today shivered through me!

—French Painters: Delaroche

I had made up my mind not to be astonished at the magnificence of London of which I had heard so much. But it happened to me as to the poor schoolboy who had made up his mind
not to feel the whipping he was to receive. . . . I anticipated
great palaces, and saw nothing but mere small houses. But their
very uniformity and their multiplicity are wonderfully impressive. . . .

In the principal streets of the city . . . this characteristic uniformity is less striking—the less so, indeed, because the eye of
the stranger is incessantly caught by the new and brilliant articles
exposed for sale in the windows. And these articles do not merely
produce an effect because the Englishman completes so perfectly
everything which he manufactures, but also because of the art of
arrangement. Through the contrast of colors and in the variety
of the English shops, even the most commonplace necessaries
of life appear in a startling magic light. Ordinary articles of food
attract us by the new light in which they are placed, even un-
cooked fish lie so delightfully dressed that the rainbow gleam
of their scales attracts us; raw meat lies, as if painted, on neat
and many-colored porcelain plates, garlanded about with parsley
—yes, everything seems painted, reminding us of the brilliant,
yet modest, pictures of Franz Mieris. Only the people are not
so cheerful as in the Dutch painting; they sell the most delightful
playthings with the most serious faces.

—English Fragments, 2. London

Talk to the stupidest Englishman about politics, and he will
always have something intelligent to say; but turn the conversation to religion, and even the cleverest Englishman will produce
nothing but foolishness.

—English Fragments, 9. The Opposition Parties

I . . . saw a man hung in London for stealing a sheep, and
from that time forth lost all relish for roast mutton. . . . With
him was hanged an Irishman, who had imitated the writing of
a rich banker; and I think I can still see the naïve deathly agony
of poor Paddy, who before the assizes could not understand why

he was so severely punished for imitating other men's signatures, when he was quite willing to let any mortal man imitate his own! And these people talk always about Christianity, and go to church every Sunday, and flood the world with Bibles!

. . . If nothing was to my taste in England, neither men nor meat, the fault lay partly in myself. I had brought a good stock of ill-temper and discontent with me from home, and I sought to be cheered up by a race which can only subdue its own ennui in the whirlpool of political and mercantile action. The perfection of machinery, which is there everywhere applied to some purpose, and which executes so many human tasks, had for me something mysterious and terrible; the artificial headlong action of wheels, shafts, cylinders, with a thousand small hooks, cogs and teeth, which whirl so madly, filled me with dread. The definiteness, the exactness, the meted out and measured punctuality of life tormented me quite as much, for as the machines in England seem like men, so the men seem to me like mere machines.

—Florentine Nights. Second Night

I laughed at many things while I was in England, but most heartily at the Lord Mayor, the real master of the precincts or limits of London, who has maintained himself as a ruin of medieval communality, in all his majesty of full peruke and broad-spreading dignity of guilds and companies. I saw him in the society of his aldermen, who are the grave chiefs and elders of the bourgeoisie, daddy tailors, and uncle glovemakers, mostly plump tradesmen, with red beefsteak faces, living pots of porters, but sober and very rich through industry and economy, so that I was assured that many of them had more than a million pounds sterling lying in the Bank of England. This is a great building in Threadneedle Street, and if a revolution were to break out in England, the Bank might be in danger, and the rich citizens of London lose their property and become beggars in an hour. Nevertheless, when King William broke his word, and the freedom of England was in danger, the Lord Mayor of London put on his mighty wig, and set forth on his way with the fat aldermen, and they all seemed as serene and secure and officially calm as if they were going to a glorious banquet in Guildhall; but they went to the House of Commons, and there protested most vigorously against the new government and the King in case he did not dismiss it, and would rather set life and property at stake by a revolution than permit the overthrow of English freedom. Strange fellows, truly, are these Englishmen!

I shall never forget a man whom I saw sitting at the left side of the Speaker in the English House of Commons, for never did a man displease me more. . . . There is in his whole being a something niggardly, sordid and shabby—in short, he is the true son of Scotland, Mr. Joseph Hume. One should place an engraving of this head in the beginning of every account-book. He always belonged to the Opposition, and the Ministers all have sore dread of him when sums of money are in question. Even when Canning was Minister, he continued to sit on the Opposition bench, and if Canning had to cite a figure in his speech, he asked in a low voice from Huskisson who sat near, "How much?" and when it was whispered, he repeated it aloud, whilst looking almost laughingly at Hume. Truly, no man ever displeased me as did this one. But when King William broke his word, Joseph Hume rose high and heroic as a god of freedom, and spoke words which hang as powerfully and solemnly as the great bell of St. Paul's; although the question here too was of money, it was to say that the people should pay no more taxes—and Parliament adopted the proposal of its great citizen.

—French Affairs, 8

King William IV first adopted the proposal of Lord Grey, leader of the Whigs, to carry his Reform Bill by creating new peers, but then withdrew his promise and attempted to replace Grey as Prime Minister by Wellington. Joseph Hume (1777-1855): spokesman of the radicals in financial and labor questions. William Huskisson (1770-1830): generally respected expert in finance and economics.

At that time all was dark in Germany . . . and when the gleam of Canning's words shone from afar on us, the few hearts which still felt hope rejoiced. As for the writer of these words, he kissed farewell to his loving and most loved ones, embarked, and went to London to see and hear Canning. There I sat whole days in the gallery of the Chapel of St. Stephen, and lived in his sight and drank the words from his mouth, and my heart was intoxicated. He was of middle height, a handsome man, who had a nobly formed and open countenance, very high forehead and somewhat bald, lips curving in a good-natured expression, soft persuasive eyes, but a man vigorous enough in his movements when he now and then struck on the sheet-iron box which was before him on the table for documents. Yet, even in moments of excitement and passion, he was always well-mannered, dignified, *gentlemanlike.* . . .

I think that I still see the grinning faces which surrounded him, especially that of the ludicrous Sir Thomas Lethbridge, who asked him with much feeling if he had already selected the members for his Ministry. On which George Canning rose calmly, with the air of one who is about to deliver a grand oration, and exclaiming with equal pathos, "Yes," sat down, while the whole House rang with laughter. . . . Never can I forget the hour when I heard George Canning speak regarding the rights of nations, and listened to the words of liberation which rolled like sacred thunder over the whole earth and left behind them a consoling echo in the hut of the Mexican as well as of the Hindu. "That is my thunder!" Canning could well say in those days. His fine, full, deep voice came sadly, yet with energy, from his suffering breast in the clear, unveiled parting words of a dying man. His mother had died a few days before, and the mourning apparel which he wore increased the solemnity of his appearance. I can still recall him in his black overcoat and the black gloves, at which he often looked while he spoke, and when he seemed to regard them with special attention, then I reflected, "Now he is thinking of his dead mother, and her long misery and suffering, and on that of all the other poor who hunger in wealthy England, and these gloves are the guarantees that Canning knows how they suffer and will help them." In the excitement of debate he tore one of these gloves from his hand, and I believed at the instant that he would cast it at the feet of the whole high aristocracy of England as the black gauntlet of defiance to all foes of suffering humanity.

—French Affairs, 4

Thomas Lethbridge was an extreme Tory. Canning's mother had been an actress.

The London presses are fully busied with fashionable works, with romances which move in the glittering sphere of "high life," or mirror it; as, for instance, *Almacks,* or *Vivian Grey, Tremaine, The Guards,* and *Flirtation.* This last romance bears a name which would be most appropriate for the whole species, since it indicates that coquetry with foreign airs and phrases, that clumsy refinement, that heavy bumping lightness—in a word, the entire lifeless life of those wooden butterflies, who flutter in the salons of West London. . . .

If I have above remarked that the English of the present day are seeking to become light and frivolous . . . I must also add that the tendency in question proceeds rather from the nobility and gentry, or aristocratic world, than from the citizens. On the contrary, the trading and working portion of the people, especially the merchants in the manufacturing towns, and nearly all the Scotch, bear the external marks of pietism—yes, I might almost say of Puritanism, so that this blessed portion of the people contrast with the worldly-minded aristocrats, like the cavaliers and Roundheads so truthfully set forth by Scott in his novels. . . .

Despite these diametrically opposed tendencies of mind and of life, we still find in the English people a unity in their way of thinking, which comes from the very fact that they are always realizing that they are a people by themselves; the modern cavaliers and Roundheads may hate and despise one another mutually and as much as they please; they do not, for all that, cease to be English; as such they are at union and together, like plants which have grown out of the same soil and are strangely interwoven with it. Hence the secret unity of the entire life and activity and intercourse of England, which at the first glance seems to us but a theater of confusion and of contradiction. Excessive wealth and misery, orthodoxy and infidelity, freedom and serfdom, cruelty and mildness, honor and deceit—all of these incongruities in their maddest extremes; over all a grey misty heaven . . . —all this hangs together in such-wise that we can hardly think of the one without the other; and that which, singly, really ought to excite our astonishment or laughter appears to be, when taken as a part of the whole, quite commonplace and serious.

—English Fragments, 3. The English

   Almacks: A novel which appeared anonymously in 1827, named for the brilliant subscription balls which were given after 1765 at Almacks, a hotel in King's Street, St. James Square. Vivian Grey: A novel by Benjamin Disraeli, published in 1826. Tremaine; or The Man of Refinement: A novel by Robert Plumer Ward, 1825. The Guards: Anonymous novel, 1827. Flirtation: A novel by Lady Charlotte Bury, 1828. Heine's judgment of contemporary English literature is very one-sided. He ignores Wordsworth and Coleridge, who were still alive. Of the great lyric poets who had recently died, he had very slight knowledge of Shelley and none at all of Keats.

   When I saw The Merchant of Venice presented at Drury Lane, there was standing behind me in the loge a handsome English woman who wept bitterly at the end of the fourth act, and cried out repeatedly, "The poor man is wronged!" Her face was chiseled after the noblest Greek fashion and her eyes were large and black. I could never forget those large black eyes which shed tears for Shylock.

—Shakespeare's Maidens and Women. Jessica

   Edmund Kean . . . was no ordinary hero of the stage; and I confess that during my last journey to England I did not disdain to include in my journal, after a criticism of the most important

Parliamentary orators of the day and of the world, my fugitive observations on Kean's acting. Unfortunately this book was lost with many more of my best papers. But I think I can remember reading to you in Wandsbeck something of Kean's rendering of Shylock from it. The Jew of Venice was the first heroic part which I saw him play. I say heroic part, for he did not play it like a broken-down old man . . . but like a real hero. So he appears to me in memory, dressed in his black silk roquelaure, which is without sleeves and only reaches to the knee, so that the blood-red undergarment which falls to the feet seems more startling by contrast. A black broad-brimmed felt hat rolled up on both sides, its high conical crown wound round with a crimson ribbon covered his head, the hair of which, like that of his beard, hung down long and black as pitch, forming as it were a wild disordered frame to the healthy red face from which two white rolling eyeballs glare out as if in ambush, inspiring uncanny dread. He holds in his right hand a staff, which is a weapon rather than a support. He only leans the elbow of his left arm on it, and in the left hand rests, in treacherous meditation, his black head with still blacker thoughts, while he explains to Bassanio what is to be understood by the expression, which is to this day current, of "a good man." When he narrates the parable of the sheep of the patriarch Jacob and of Laban, he seems to find himself entangled in his own words, and breaks out suddenly with, "Ay! he was the third." And while, during a long pause, he seems to reflect on what he shall say, one feels how the tale is gradually shaping itself in his head, and when he suddenly breaks out with "No, not take interest!" as if he had found the clue, it did not seem as if one listened to a role learned by heart, but to a speech improvised with great difficulty. And at the end he smiled like an author who is very much pleased with his own conception. He begins slowly—

"Signior Antonio, many a time and oft,"

till he comes to the word "dog," which is thrown out with more force. His anger rises from "and spit upon my Jewish gabardine" till "own." Then he approaches, upright and proudly, and says with scornful bitterness, "Well then . . ." to "ducats." But all at once, bowing low, he takes off his hat, and with servile mien continues, "Or shall I bend low" unto "monies." Yes, his very voice becomes submissive; one only seems to hear in it a slight ring of intense wrath; gay little serpents twine round his complaisant lips—only his eyes cannot restrain themselves, and continue to shoot forth their poisoned arrows; and this contrast or combat between external humility and internal vindictiveness ends at the last word, "monies," with a terrible prolonged laugh, which suddenly breaks off, while the face, convulsively contracted or compelled to servility, remains for a time motionless as a mask, and only the eye—that evil eye—glared out threatening and deadly.

—Letters on the French Stage, 7

Kean was by no means a universal actor, for though he could play many parts, it was always himself whom he played. But in so doing he gave us a tremendous truthfulness; and though ten years have passed since I saw him, I still behold him before me as Shylock, Othello, Richard, or Macbeth. The full meaning of many a passage which had been dark to me was made clear by his acting.

—Letters on the French Stage, 6

On August 8, the day of Canning's death, I left London. Great mental profit. Life there is large and dear. I was sunk up to the neck in adventure, lost more than three hundred guineas through bad luck and stupidity, and am happy to be out of it again. The women there are pretty, the men large and magnanimous.

—To Varnhagen von Ense
Hamburg, October 19, 1827

Heine's London sojourn was interrupted by a trip to the sea, at Ramsgate. Allusions to adventures there are to be found in the Baths of Lucca, the Town of Lucca, Florentine Nights, and certain poems of the New Spring. The journey to England also occasioned a vigorous exchange with Salomon Heine. Besides travel money, Salomon had opened for Heine, at the latter's suggestion, a credit at the house of Rothschild, which, however, was to serve only as a token and by no means be drawn upon; but immediately upon his arrival in London, Heine withdrew the very considerable sum. When the firm of Rothschild reported this to Salomon Heine, the latter became furious. When, upon the poet's return, his uncle reproached him and charged him with malfeasance, he replied: "Uncle, the best thing about you is that you bear my name." This further enraged the uncle. Later, Salomon Heine was much amused by the incident. In 1843, he wrote "To the man who discovered that the best thing about me was that I bore his name," and requested him, alluding to the London incident, to assist him in irritating the banking house of Fould in Paris in a more innocent maneuver. Heine used the money which he had improperly withdrawn to pay debts in Germany and to set aside a reserve fund which he deposited with Varnhagen.

Rhine Union Politics

Shortly after his return from England, Heine accepted an invitation of the publisher Cotta to direct the periodical Neue Politische Annalen as joint editor. This was the only time in his life that Heine had regular employment after he forsook the mercantile career. As editor of the Annalen he gave the greatest satisfaction to the publisher, his fellow editor and all his colleagues, but was from the start determined not to continue long in this position, for he hoped to obtain a professorship in the University of Munich, in which city the periodical was published.

The Neue Politische Annalen was an organ of the German Triaspartei, whose spiritual headquarters was the publishing house of Cotta. This Triaspartei strove for a union of all the medium and small German states to form, with the support of France, a counterpoise to the two great German powers, Austria and Prussia. It sought to refurbish under another name the Con-

federation of the Rhine which France had repeatedly formed and
protected from the sixteenth century until Napoleon. The notion
of such a tripartite division of Germany was condemned by historians and statesmen of Prussian-unitarian convictions. But during the centuries of the history of Rhine Unions, not only many
far-seeing German princes, but also men of outstanding importance in the intellectual history of Germany had placed themselves at the service of this cause, which was to prevent the
hegemony, first of the house of Hapsburg, and then of the Hohen-
zollern dynasty. The last Rhine Union, the Confederation of
the Rhine, which had been founded by Napoleon in 1806 and
dissolved after his fall, still engaged lively sympathy in southern and western Germany in Heine's day. In the period 1820-
1830, efforts were made, especially in Bavaria and Wuerttemberg,
to resurrect the Union. Baron Cotta, the publisher of Goethe
and Schiller, assembled on the staff of his various periodicals all
German writers with Bonapartist tendencies. The undertaking
must have been very attractive to Heine. He championed the
cause of the Triaspartei, which was also called "the French
party," with zeal, and served it even after he had gone to Paris.
Nevertheless, he soon recognized that, in view of the growing
military and economic superiority of Prussia, its goal must inevitably be reduced year by year.

On his journey from Hamburg to Munich, Heine took the
opportunity to visit as many liberal German writers as he could,
in order to persuade them to contribute to the Annalen.

I am travelling to Munich where much has been promised me,
and, what is better, already guaranteed. My health, which is again
downgrade, permits me no great activity. It is horrible that I
must nevertheless undertake a journey at the bitter time of the
year. The outward manifestation of my life in Munich will be
the *Allgemeine Politische Annalen* which has been published
there since 1828 and is to appear in regenerated form under my
editorship. I wish that you too would support this important and
distinguished diplomatic journal with suitable essays. Choose

some continuing heading under which you can communicate remarks concerning events and books. Go to work at once, so that I can have something of yours, if only a page or two, for the January number. At last I hope that I can extract something printable from you. You can count on my discretion. Say nothing to Gans. That I displease that slave of the aristocrats, Goethe, is quite natural. Reproach from him is an honor, for he praises everything that is weak. He is afraid of the growing Titans. . . .

The *Book of Songs* is nothing but a collected edition of my familiar poems. . . . It is beautifully got out, and, like an innocent skiff, will quietly sail down the sea of oblivion under the protection of the second volume of the *Travel Pictures*. The fact that the latter is a man-of-war armed to the teeth with cannon has horribly displeased the world. The third volume will be even more fearfully armed, the caliber of the cannon will be larger, and I have invented a new kind of gunpowder. . . .

Thank heaven that my finances are now in a better state. It is only in the disposition of them that I am not yet expert.

—To Moses Moser
Lueneburg, October 30, 1827

Despite his disillusionment at his visit to Weimar, Heine sent Goethe a copy of his Tour in the Harz *as "a mark of the highest esteem and affection," and celebrated Goethe's merits in the second volume of his* Travel Pictures. *But, as Moser informed him in a letter, Goethe disparaged Heine in conversation. Heine's charge that Goethe "praised everything weak" is thoroughly justified. In the last two decades of his life, Goethe overlooked every vigorous talent in German literature which newly appeared, and recommended mediocrities or even dilettantes to the public. The* Book of Songs *appeared shortly before Heine's departure for Munich. Despite Heine's misgivings, it enjoyed singular success. Although it contained, almost exclusively, poems which had already been printed, the artful sequence produced the effect of a quite new work and afforded readers a new view into Heine's personality.*

When I . . . had occasion to pass through Frankfort in 1827, on my way to Munich, I determined to pay Dr. Boerne a visit at his residence.

I had difficulty in recognizing the man, whose earlier appearance was vividly present to my memory. There was no longer a trace of lofty dissatisfaction or proud disdain. I now saw a contented little man, very frail but not ill, a small head with fine and straight black hair, even a bit of color in the cheeks, light, very lively brown eyes, ease in every glance, in every movement, even in his voice. Furthermore, he wore a little knitted waistcoat of gray wool which fitted close like a corselet and gave him a droll, gnome-like look. He received me cordially and affectionately, and before three minutes had passed we were talking to one another confidentially. What did we talk of first? When cooks get together they talk of their employers, and when German writers get together they talk of their publishers. And so our conversation began with Cotta and Campe, and when I admitted, after the usual complaints, that Campe possessed good qualities, Boerne confided that he was with child with a complete edition of his writings and would consider Campe for this enterprise. . . .

After the publishers were disposed of there began the mutual compliments between two writers who speak to one another for the first time. I shall pass over Boerne's expressions concerning my merits and mention only the gentle reproach which he occasionally dropped into the foaming cup of praise. He had recently read the second portion of my *Travel Pictures*, and was of the opinion that I spoke of God, who had after all created heaven and earth and ruled the world so wisely, with too little reverence, and of Napoleon, on the other hand, who was merely a mortal despot, with exaggerated honor. It was already noticeable that it was a deist and liberal that faced me. . . .

With droll kindliness he extorted a promise that I would grant him three days of my life; he never let go of me, and I had to run about the city with him, visit all sorts of friends, including women friends also, for example, Madame Wohl auf dem Wollgraben. This Madame Wohl auf dem Wollgraben is the well-known goddess of liberty to whom the *Letters from Paris* were later addressed. . . .

After Boerne had shown me Madame Wohl auf dem Wollgraben, he wished to show me the other sights of Frankfort, and he delightedly ran at my side, at a comfortable jog-trot, as we wandered through the streets.

Whatever objects Boerne happened to come into contact with, not only gave his intellect present occupation, but immediately affected his mood also, and his good or bad humor was immediately involved in the alternation of such objects. Just as the sea receives its color from the clouds that pass over it, so did Boerne's soul take on the coloring of whatever object he encountered on his way. The sight of pretty gardens, or of a group of playful girls who smiled at us, at once cast a rosy glow over Boerne's soul, and its reflection found expression in a bubbling wit. But when we passed through the Jews' quarter, the black houses seemed to cast their dark shadows over his mood.

"Look at these alleys," he said with a sigh, "and then praise the Middle Ages! The people who lived and wept here are dead, and cannot answer back when our mad poets and madder historians print their transports over the antique grandeur; but where dead men are silent, the living stones speak all the louder."

And in fact the houses of those alleys looked at me as if they would tell me distressing stories, stories which we actually know but would rather not, would rather forget than recall to memory. Thus I remember a tall-gabled house whose coal-blackness was made more striking by a row of chalk-white tallow candles hanging under the windows. The entrance, half latticed with rusty iron bars, led into a dark cave where dampness seemed to drip from the walls, and from the interior there sounded a very singular nasal chant. The cracked voice seemed to be an old man's, and the melody swayed in gentle strains of lamentation which gradually swelled to terrifying anger. "What manner of song is that?" I asked my companion. "It is a good song," he answered with a sulky laugh, "a lyrical masterpiece whose peer will hardly be found in the year's *Muses' Almanac.* You may know it in the German translation: 'By the rivers of Babylon we sat down, upon the willows we hanged up our harps.' A magnificent piece! An old Rabbi Hayim sings it very well in his tremulous and worn-out voice; Mme. Sonntag might sing it with better modulation, but not with so much expression, not with so much feeling. That old man still hates the Babylonians and daily weeps for the fall of Jerusalem at the hands of Nebuchadnezzar. That misfortune he can never forget, though so many new things have happened since, and quite lately the Second Temple was destroyed by wicked Titus. I must inform you that old Rabbi Hayim by no means regards Titus as the *delicium generis humani*; he thinks him rather a wicked man, who was overtaken by the vengeance of God. For you must know that a tiny flea flew into his nostril, gradually grew, burrowed about in his brain with its claws, and caused him such infinite pain that he only obtained relief when several hundred smiths hammered away at their anvils in his close proximity. It is very remarkable that all the enemies of the children of Israel come to so bad an end. You know what happened to Nebuchadnezzar: in his old age he turned into an ox, and had to feed on grass. Look at the Persian minister Haman: in the end, was he not hanged in Susa the capital? And Antiochus king of Syria—did he not putrify from an affliction of lice while he was still alive? Wicked men of later times who are enemies to the Jews had better take care—. But what's the use? They are not deterred by horrible examples. . . ."

From the corner of Schnurgasse to the Bourse we had to press through the crowd; here flows the golden artery of the city, here the esteemed trading class foregather and haggle and jabber. The jabber we call "Jew-talk" in northern Germany is nothing else than the ordinary Frankfort vernacular, and it is spoken as well by the uncircumcised population as by the circumcised. Boerne spoke this jargon badly, though he, like Goethe, could not wholly deny his native dialect. I noticed that Frankforters who kept at a distance from all mercantile interests eventually quite unlearned that Frankfort accent which we in north Germany call, as I have said, "Jew-talk." . . .

When we walked through Judengasse again that same evening and our talk again turned to its denizens, the fountain of the Boerne spirit bubbled all the gayer, for even that street which by day kept its gloomy look was now most cheerfully lighted because the children of Israel, as my guide informed, were celebrating their jolly Feast of Lights. This was established for an eternal memorial of the victory which the Maccabees so heroically won over the King of Syria.

"Look you," said Boerne, "this is the Eighteenth October of the Jews, except that this Maccabee Eighteenth October is more than two thousand years old and is still celebrated, whereas the Leipzig Eighteenth October has not yet reached its fifteenth year and is already fallen into oblivion. The German should go to school to old Madame Rothschild to learn patriotism. Look here; in this little house lives that old lady Letitia who has given birth to many financial Bonapartes, the great mother of all loans, who, despite the world dominion of her royal sons would never forsake the little family castle in Judengasse, and today decks her windows with white curtains in honor of the great festival of joy. . . .

"For look you," said he, "the Rothschilds have so much money, so vast a quantity of it, that they inspire us with an almost gruesome respect. They are identified, so to speak, with the abstract concept of money, and one cannot despise money. But these people have employed the surest means of avoiding the ridicule to which so many other titled millionaire families of the Old Testament have become liable; they have refrained from Christian holy water. Baptism is now the order of the day for rich Jews, and the gospel which was preached in vain to the poor of Judaea is now flourishing among the rich. But since its acceptance is only self-deception if not complete falsehood, and the pretended Christianity is at times in stark contrast with the old Adam, these people expose themselves most dangerously to wit and ridicule. . . .

"In Berlin I have seen elderly daughters of Israel upon the

street, wearing long crucifixes from their necks, crucifixes longer
even than their noses and reaching to their navels; in their hands
they carried Protestant hymnals, and they spoke of the magnificent sermon they had just heard in the Church of the Trinity.
One asked the other, of whom she had taken holy communion,
and their breath smelled. More repulsive to me was the sight
of the dirty, bearded Jews who came from their Polish sewers,
won for heaven by the conversionist society in Berlin, and who
preached Christianity in their obscene dialect, stinking horribly
the while. It would be surely desirable to baptize such lice-
infected Polish gentry not with ordinary water but with *eau de
Cologne.*"

"In the house of one hanged," I interrupted, "one may not
speak of ropes; tell me rather, dear doctor, where are those great
oxen which, as my father once told me, run about in the Jewish
cemetery here in Frankfort and bellow so loudly at night as to
disturb the neighbors' rest?"

"Your father actually told you no lie," Boerne cried, laughing,
"it was once the practise that Jewish cattle dealers dedicated
the first-born male of their cows to God, according to the biblical prescription, and for that purpose brought them here to
Frankfort from all parts of Germany. The oxen were turned
out to graze in the Jewish cemetery; they ran loose until their
happy end, and really bellowed horribly sometimes. But the old
oxen are now dead, and modern cattle no longer have the true
faith, and their first-born stay quietly at home, if they do not
actually turn Christian. The old oxen are dead."

I cannot omit mentioning on this occasion that, during my
sojourn in Frankfort, Boerne invited me to dine with one of his
friends, and, indeed, because that friend, adhering faithfully to
Jewish usages, would serve the famous *shalet;* and in fact I enjoyed that dish, which may be of Egyptian origin and as old
as the pyramids. I wonder that, when Boerne later, in a seemingly humorous vein but actually with plebeian designs, incited
the populace by many inventions and insinuations against the
crowned head of a poet as against wearers of crowns in general—
I wonder that he never recounted in his writings with what

appetite, with what enthusiasm, with what devotion, with what conviction, I once devoured the ancient Jewish *shalet* dish at the house of Dr. St. But that dish is quite delicious, and it is to be deplored that the Christian church, which has borrowed so many good things from ancient Judaism, should not have adopted the *shalet* also. Perhaps it kept this borrowing for future use: when things should go badly, when its most sacred symbols, even the cross itself, should lose their force, then the Christian church would turn to *shalet*, and the people who had slipped away would press back into its bosom with renewed appetite. The Jews, at least, would then adhere to Christianity with conviction—for, as I clearly perceive, it is only the *shalet* which keeps them together in their old covenant. Boerne even assured me that the apostates who went over to the new covenant needed only to smell the *shalet* to feel a certain nostalgia for the synagogue, that the *shalet* is, so to speak, the homing-call of the Jews. . . .

In larger gatherings Boerne was taciturn and monosyllabic, and to the flow of conversation he would give himself only in a dialogue, if he thought he was next to someone like-minded. That Boerne regarded me as such was an error, which later resulted in much vexation for me. Even then, in Frankfort, we were at one only in the realm of politics, but not in philosophy, or art, or nature, all of which were closed doors to him. . . .

The three days which I spent at Frankfort in Boerne's company passed in almost idyllic peacefulness. He spared no pains to please me. He made the rockets of his wit flare as gaily as possible, and just as in Chinese fire-works the operator himself ascends in the air at the end with a spraying cackle of flames, so the man's humorous speeches always closed with a brilliant, mad flare in which he would boldly immolate himself. He was as gentle as a child. Up to the last moment of my stay in Frankfort he was perpetually with me, watching me to see if he could show me some further affectionate attention. He knew that I was going to Munich upon the inducement of old Baron Cotta to take up the editorship of the *Politische Annalen* and to devote my activities to certain projected literary institutions.

It was a question of founding for the liberal press those organs which have since exercised so wholesome an influence. It was a question of sowing for the future, sowing for which only enemies at present have eyes, so that the poor sower reaped only vexation and contempt. The venom and the meanness with which the ultramontane aristocratic propagandists attacked me and my friends are well known.

"Beware of coming into collision with the parsons of Munich," were the last words which Boerne whispered in my ear as I left. As I sat in the coupé of the post-coach, he remained looking after me for a long while.

—Ludwig Boerne, 1

Madame Wohl: Jeanette Wohl (1783-1861), a friend of Boerne of many years' standing, a highly educated and warm-hearted woman; Heine's strictures upon her, in the latter parts of his book on Boerne, brought him much ill-feeling. Sonntag: Henrietta Sonntag (1804-1854), famous coloratura singer. The great oxen: Concerning these "Jews' oxen" Heine found an account in Schudt's Juedische Merkwuerdigkeiten. They were slaughtered only if they broke a horn or suffered some serious injury; the meat was then distributed to the Levites and to the poor of the Jewish community. Dr. St.: Heine's memory here failed him. Heine had eaten shalet, not at the home of the newly baptized Dr. Stiebel, but in that of the Jewish painter Moritz Oppenheim, whose Pictures from Jewish Family Life became very well known. Oppenheim also painted Heine's portrait at the time.

I arrived here several days ago, half dead. I travelled slowly, stopping everywhere—in Kassel, Frankfort, Heidelberg and Stuttgart. I am so ill that I must now virtually keep to my room. I am much pleased with Cotta, who awaited me here and departed at once for Stuttgart, as also with Dr. Lindner and the others who are with me here. All conditions arranged to my satisfaction. I may take a position or not; my living requirements are provided for. I do not even have to write. I am editing the *Annals* with Dr. Lindner, and also some articles in the *Ausland*.

Do not be afraid. The third volume of the *Travel Pictures* will not suffer, and my best hours shall be given to it. If I had not to consider that, I might perhaps have been persuaded to take over the *Morgenblatt*, the editor of which is just dead, or the editorship-in-chief of the *Ausland* and so have earned very, very much money. But I want to be free, and if the climate is really as terrible as they have threatened, I must not be fettered. If my health is endangered, I shall pack my box and go to Italy. I shall not starve anywhere. I do not care about marks of honor; I want to continue to live. Everywhere in my travels I found the *Travel Pictures en vogue*, everywhere enthusiasm, complaint and admiration; and I should not have believed myself to be already so famous. I have two men to thank for it: H. Heine and Julius Campe. These two must hold together. I at least shall not change in order to better my position or my income.

—To Julius Campe
Munich, December 1, 1827

Friedrich Ludwig Lindner, the joint editor of Annalen, became known through his essay Manuscript from Southern Germany, in which he developed the political program of the Triaspartei. Metternich called him "Bonaparte's active agent in Germany." Lindner also provided for the spread of German translations of Napoleon's writings. He was a strong opponent of German nationalism. He also enjoyed high esteem among the liberals, for he uncovered the secret intelligence service which the Czar maintained in Germany. He enjoyed a long-standing friendship with Rahel. Heine continued on good terms with Lindner for many years after he left Munich, but never became intimate with him. Ausland and Morgenblatt fuer die gebildeten Staende were influential journals published by Cotta.

As the last fighter of the Bonapartists I have launched an attack against Scott. To be read in the next number. Here life is pleasant, cheap, and tranquil.

—To Johannes Witt von Doerring
Munich, January 23, 1828

Witt von Doerring was a political adventurer. Friendship with him injured Heine greatly. Rahel in particular was displeased. Heine's polemic review of Scott's Life of Napoleon Bonaparte forms the fourth chapter of his English Fragments.

Witt von Doerring, the ill-famed, is here; heaven knows what sort of scandal he will end up with. Personally I like him well enough, and he compromises me everywhere by calling me his friend; this results, firstly, in the revolutionaries' keeping away from me through mistrust, which pleases me, and, secondly, that the governments think I am not so bad and are convinced that my involvements are not bad. I only want to talk. In general, Witt is my Fouché. He cannot harm me, and if I liked, I could harm anyone I wished through him. Indeed, if I had the power, I would have him hanged.

—To Varnhagen von Ense
Munich, February 12, 1828

I live here as a *grand seigneur*, and the five and a half people here who can read let me know that they esteem me highly. . . .
Do you know the daughters of Count Bothmer in Stuttgart where you have often been? One of them no longer young but infinitely charming and secretly engaged to my dearest friend here, a young Russian diplomat by the name of Tutscheff, and her quite young and very beautiful sister, are the two ladies with whom I associate here most comfortably and agreeably. These two and my friend Tutscheff and I frequently have our midday meal together in a party of four, and in the evening, when I find still other beauties there, I chatter to my heart's content, chiefly ghost stories. Everywhere in the most desolate desert I am able to find some sort of fair oasis. . . .
I am becoming very serious here, almost German. I believe the beer does it. Frequently I yearn for the capital, to wit, Berlin. Here, in Bavaria, I have become a Prussian. . . .
Boerne, as I hear, is now with you. He loves me very much. He is much better than I, much greater—but not so grand.

—To Varnhagen von Ense
Munich, April 1, 1828

Fyodor Ivanovitch Tyutschev: Russian poet.

How tedious—aside from our essays—are the whole contents
of the *Annalen*. I am convinced that the Germans have no sense
for politics, for no good political writers are to be dug up.

—To Wolfgang Menzel
Munich, April 16, 1828

*Wolfgang Menzel (1798-1873), after Boerne the most vigorous
and influential opponent of Goethe, was at the time also Boerne's
political ally in the struggle for liberal principles. Heine visited
him in Stuttgart and procured his services as a contributor to the
Annalen.*

How can I thank Frau von Varnhagen for her kind and
lovely letter! I have felt it all through. She is quite right in what
she says about Napoleon. He should never have given himself
to the pleasures of society, for society's friendly smile draws
all strength out of the heart of a man—like a magnetic mountain draws all iron out of an approaching ship. But what would
Frau von Varnhagen have of me? I am no Napoleon. I do not
even dream of conquering Pankow, much less the world. My
entire desire for conquest is limited to perhaps ten or eleven
hearts. I am a man who lives for his pleasures. . . .

And yet Frau von Varnhagen is right. In my review of *The
Life of Napoleon* the whispers of Bonapartist friends are to be
heard.

—To Varnhagen von Ense
Munich, June 6, 1828

Pankow: suburb of Berlin.

Italy

In July 1828 publication of Annalen discontinued. Heine
entered on his Italian journey, which he described in the third
volume of the Travel Pictures. He travelled through the Tyrol, by
way of Innsbruck and Trieste to Verona, and thence by way of

*Milan to Genoa, and then to Livorno and Lucca where he made
a longer sojourn.*

"We are on the battlefield of Marengo!" How my heart leapt
with joy when the postillion uttered these words! I had quitted
Milan in the evening in company with a very agreeable Livonian
who rather aped the Russian, and the following morning I saw
the sun rise over the celebrated battlefield. Here it was that
General Bonaparte drank so deep a draught from the cup of
glory that through the fumes thereof he became Consul, Emperor, conqueror of the world, and could only be sobered therefrom at St. Helena. It did not fare much better with us; we shared
the intoxication and dreamed the same dreams; we were similarly
awakened, and in the desolation of sobriety we made all kinds
of wise reflections.

It has seemed to us from time to time as though the glory of
war were an antiquated pleasure, as though war were merely of
importance to nobles, and that Napoleon is perhaps the last
conqueror. Symptoms now point to the possibility that spiritual,
instead of material, interests may be fought over; that the history
of the world may no longer be a history of robbery, but a history
of the human spirit.

The chief lever, which ambitious and covetous princes knew
how to wield so efficaciously for their private aims, namely, nationality, with its vanities and its hatreds, is now rotten and worn
out; these foolish national prejudices dwindle daily away; all
rugged idiosyncrasies disappear under the levelling tendencies of
European civilization. Nations no longer exist in Europe, only
parties; and it is an instructive sight to see how these parties instantly recognize one another in spite of their manifold colorings,
and understand each other in spite of their difference of speech.
Just as there existed material state politics, so now also there
exists spiritual party politics. And it is with state politics as with
the most insignificant war, which, if it break out between two
unimportant powers, immediately grows to a general European
conflict wherein all the states of more or less ambition, or in any
case with interests, must join. So likewise, the slightest strife can-

not occur in the world without the general spiritual importance being immediately perceived by means of those party politics, or without the most remote and heterogeneous parties being constrained to take sides for or against.

By virtue of these politics, which I call spiritual politics on account of their spiritual interests, and because their *ultimae rationes* are not of metal, two great masses are constituting themselves, even in the very heart of state politics. They take up hostile positions opposite one another and fight with words and looks. The watchwords and representatives of these two great parties change daily; confusion is imminent. Often the direst misunderstandings arise, and are intensified rather than lessened by those diplomats of spiritual politics, the authors. Nevertheless, even if heads err, hearts feel none the less keenly what they desire, and Time marches steadily on in fulfilment of its great task.

And what is this great task of the day?

It is emancipation. Not simply that of the Irish, Greek, Frankfort Jews, West Indian blacks, and all such oppressed people, but the emancipation of the whole world, and especially of Europe, which is come of age and is tearing itself away from the iron leading-strings of the privileged class of the aristocracy.

—Travel Pictures, 3. Journey from
Munich to Genoa, 29

As editor of the Annalen also, Heine incessantly emphasized that there were "no more nations, only parties." In the realization that common ideologies united parties of various nations, Heine was in advance of his century. On the other hand, he underestimated the vitality of nationalism.

Want of knowledge of Italian bothers me greatly. I do not understand the people and cannot speak with them. I see Italy, but I do not hear it. Yet I am not quite without conversation. Here the stones speak, and their mute language I understand. . . . There is something spectral about coming to a country where one does not understand the living language and the living people, but instead has full knowledge of the language which flourished there a millennium ago.

—To Eduard von Schenk
Livorno, August 27, 1828

The dramatist Eduard von Schenk became Bavarian minister. Through him Heine hoped to obtain a professorship in Munich.

It is believed in Munich that I will no longer assail the gentry so vigorously, for I live in the vestibule of the nobility and love the most amiable aristocratic ladies, and am loved by them. But people are wrong. My love for human equality and my hatred against the clergy was never stronger than now.

—To Moses Moser
Lucca, September 6, 1828

I have thought of you so vividly these days, I have so often longed to kiss your hand, that it is quite natural for me to write you. If I should put it off until my spirits sink again and bitterness and vexation re-enter my heart, I should write something vexatiously bitter. But that shall not be; I will not think of the complaints that I might make against you and that are perhaps greater than you can imagine. I beg you then to reduce your complaints against me somewhat, for they can all be reduced to money terms, and if they were all reckoned up in farthings and pennies, they would only amount to a sum which a millionaire could quite easily throw away.—But my complaints against you are incalculable, infinite, for they are of a spiritual nature, rooted in the depths of offended sensibilities. If I had ever by a single word or a single look been wanting in respect for you, or have injured your house—I have loved it only too much!—then you would have the right to be angry. But not so now; if all that you allege against me were counted up, it would all go comfortably into a purse of no very great capacity. And I say, that if the gray bag were to be too small to hold all that Salomon Heine complains of in me, and were to break—do you think, my uncle, that it would matter as much as the breaking of a heart that has been choked with injuries?

But enough; the sun is shining so beautifully today and when I look out at the window I see nothing but smiling vine-clad hills. I will not complain: I will only love you as I have ever done, and I will only think of your soul and confess that it is more beautiful than all the splendor that I have yet seen in Italy.

Farewell, and give my greetings to your family, Hermann, Carl and dainty Therese. I take qualified joy in her betrothal. Next to myself, I would begrudge her to no one less than to Dr. Halle. . . . Greet Moritz Oppenheimer. . . . I do not love him, though as a Christian I ought to love my enemies; but I am still too young a beginner in Christian love. But Moritz Oppenheimer is an older Christian and should love me and not try to ridicule me out of people's esteem. . . . Adieu, dear, kind, generous, stingy, infinitely beloved uncle.

—To Salomon Heine
Lucca, September 15, 1828

Hermann: Son of Henry Heine. Carl: Salomon Heine's only son. Moritz Oppenheimer: Salomon Heine's eldest son-in-law.

The market place of Florence affords the loveliest and most interesting view that a man can find. The air of antiquity, the meaningful statues, the lofty arcades, the magnificence, and with it all, everywhere the breath of ancient Florentine grace, everywhere the bloom of the Medici, and far above in the Uffizi palace, the abode of the Greek gods! I will freely confess to you that in the boudoir of the Medici Venus I quite forgot Schenk and his letter. But it was not the patched ancient goddess of love which gave me so mighty a lift, but rather the eyes of a pretty Italian which worshipfully gazed at her.—I think that the old gods are still worshipped in Italy.

Ah, Schenk, my soul is so full, so overflowing, that I know not what to do other than write a few enthusiastic books. At the baths of Lucca, where I dallied for the longest and most divine time, I have already written half a book, a sort of sentimental journey.

—To Eduard von Schenk
Florence, October 1, 1828

The book mentioned is the Journey from Munich to Genoa. Heine remained in Florence until the middle of November and waited in vain for a letter from Schenk, who was to inform him of his appointment as professor. But upon the intervention of the Munich clergy, Schenk left Heine in the lurch. When Heine returned to Germany, he received news of the death of his father, which was a great shock to him. This disturbance and his bitterness at the frustration of his Munich plans were aggravated by the satirical attacks directed against Heine by Count August von Platen in his drama The Romantic Oedipus. Platen jeered at Heine as "the Petrarch of the Feast of Tabernacles," whose kiss breathes the savor of garlic. In this state of agitation, which caused friction with some of his close friends, Heine, in his Baths of Lucca, undertook a counter-attack against the offending Platen with a ruthlessness which almost lost him all sympathy in Germany. It ended his friendship with Moses Moser, who sharply condemned Heine's campaign of vengeance, and also his friendship with Gans. Varnhagen von Ense was one of Heine's few defenders on this occasion. Heine soon realized how much he had injured himself with his polemics against Platen and sought to pacify private and public disapproval of his writing by characterizing it as a "party matter," as a move in his campaign against aristocracy and clericalism. But Heine's vengeance was of a thoroughly private, not ideological, character. There is no doubt that he was gravely affronted and struck at a vulnerable point, his Jewish descent. But his counter-attack against those who insulted him failed to emphasize the ideological aspects—freedom, equality, the Jewish claim to rights—and to war against prejudices. Heine rather attempted to strike at the vulnerable points of his opponent's private character. To the mockery on Heine's Jewishness he replied by excoriating Platen's homosexual predilections, which are indubitably to be read out of Platen's poems. It is rather a man of abnormal sexuality than a champion of aristocratic privilege that Heine warred against. In point of fact, Platen's political ideas and expressions were not far removed from Heine's own. He was a decided liberal and a vigorous opponent of German nationalism. Furthermore, Heine's suspicion that Platen sheltered under the same blanket with the Munich clergy was unjustified, though quite understandable, for Ignaz von Doellinger, who subsequently altered his political convictions and his attitude to the Jews, but at that time headed the agitation of the Bavarian clergy against Heine with antisemitic slogans, was a friend of Platen's. But Platen had no part in the agitation against Heine. He was a solitary and unhappy man who struggled against his inclinations, and in his private life gave no occasion to any of the charges made against him by Heine. It was not antisemitism, which he rejected, but a morbidly exaggerated self-esteem which urged Platen to the vulgar affront to Heine, whose works he had scarcely read, but whom he wished to discredit as a poetic rival.

His vengeance on Platen cost Heine very dear. He had started a humorous novel which would doubtless have been numbered among his best creations if he had carried out its original plan. It is the story of the amorous adventures of Baron Gumpelino, a converted Jew, and his servant Hyacinth Hirsch, who remained loyal to Judaism. For both these figures Heine used Hamburg acquaintances as models. His scenes of overwhelming and hard-hitting humor are successful. But his desire to avenge himself upon Platen moved him to transform the Baths of Lucca from chapter nine onwards into a satire against Platen. The new point, that by reading Platen's poetry Gumpelino is consoled for his unhappy love for a beautiful Englishwoman and disgusted with the female sex, is extremely witty, but its indiscreet treatment aroused strong disapproval. Fragments of the continuation of the novel as originally planned are included in The Town of Lucca.

Alienation from Germany

"If I attach so much importance to it that I come to you, you would not even receive me." This is what you said to me yester-

day, at least in essence if not in the same words. When I reflected
on the matter this morning, I unfortunately had to confess that
I had been spoiled by my other friends who were always happy
when they could have me, under whatever conditions and however much I overrated myself. It will surely take some time before
I acquire better habits and sink so deep in my self-esteem that I
could be of use to you. Until such time, you must content yourself with scribblers who are so highly esteemed, who are able to
gabble so as to satisfy the demand, who fit in any desired birdcage.

You will declare me a vain man. Nay! The sequel may prove
that I am capable of sacrificing my private vanity and all external
appearances to a nobler interest.

—To Rahel von Varnhagen
Berlin, April 1, 1829

*Heine's friendship was restored the same month when Rahel
fell seriously ill of erysipelas and Heine sent her a large bouquet
of fresh roses. Rahel wrote in her diary:*

"*A bridge to life is roses; there is none finer.*

These roses wonders work—they come to me from Heine.
*In great illness, when continuous refreshment of face and hands
with moistened roses, which the above-named sent in great beauty
and abundance, gave me the first feeling of a change to health.*"

I am no longer an utterly lonely Crusoe here. A number of
officers have landed. Cannibals. Last evening, in the New Garden, I was even in the company of ladies and sat between some
Potsdam women, like Apollo amidst the cows of Admetus.

Day before yesterday I was in Sans Souci where everything
glows and blooms, but, by heaven, how! Everything is only a
warmed-over winter streaked with green, and on the terraces are
spruce saplings masquerading as orange trees. . . .

I have again laid my large humorous work aside and am now
returning to the *Italian Travels*, which are to fill out the third
part of the *Travel Pictures*, and in which I will come to a reckon-

ing with all of my enemies. I have made a list of all of those who have tried to annoy me, so that I should not forget any in my present gentle mood. Ah, sick and lonely as I am, I am now describing the most brilliant period in my life, a period in which, drunk with confidence and happy love, I exulted on the heights of the Appenines and dreamed of great wild deeds which would spread my glory over the whole world. . . . Now, how tame I have become after the death of my father.

—To Friederike Robert
Potsdam, May 30, 1829

Perhaps they are right, and I am only a Don Quixote. Perhaps the reading of all manner of wonderful books has turned my head, even as in the case of the Knight of La Mancha; and Jean Jacques Rousseau was my Amadis of Gaul, Mirabeau my Roldan or Agramanth; and I have studied too much the heroic deeds of the French Paladin and the Round Table of the National Convention. Certainly my madness and the fixed ideas which I created out of these books are of an opposite kind to the madness and fixed ideas of him of La Mancha. He wished to re-establish the waning knighthood; I, on the contrary, wish wholly to annihilate whatsoever has survived from that time; and thus we act from totally different motives. My colleague mistook windmills for giants; I, on the contrary, see only vociferous windmills in our modern giants. He mistook a leathern wine-skin for a crafty wizard, and I see only a leather wine-skin in our modern wizards. He mistook every beggar's inn for a castle, every donkey-driver for a knight, every stable wench for a court lady; I, on the contrary, look upon our castles as trumpery inns, our knights as donkeydrivers, our court ladies as stable wenches. Just as he mistook a puppet play for a state action, so do I hold our state action to be a pitiful puppet play. Nevertheless, as bravely as the brave knight do I strike in amongst the wooden company. Alas! such deeds of heroism often result as badly with me as with him, and like him I have to endure much for the honor of my lady. Were I to deny her only from paltry fear or from a base desire for gain, I could live comfortably in this existing reasonable world. I would lead a pretty Maritorne to the altar, allow myself to be blessed by a fattened magician, banquet with noble donkey-drivers, and beget innocuous novels and more little slaves.

Instead of that, decorated with the three colors of my lady, I must be always upon the defensive and fight my way through unspeakable oppression; and I gain no victory that has not cost me some of my heart's blood. Day and night I am in tribulation, for those enemies are so tough that many whom I have struck to death can nevertheless present themselves with an appearance of life, change themselves into all manner of forms, and molest me day and night. What agonies I have already been forced to endure from these cursed ghosts! Wherever love blossoms for me there they slink in, these malignant sprites, and nip off the guiltless bud. Everywhere, and where I least anticipate it, I discover their silvery, shiny track on the ground; and did I not take great care, I might slip disastrously even in the house of my next love.

—Travel Pictures, The Town of Lucca 17

Amadis of Gaul: *Typical romance of chivalry, which originated in Spain and influenced all European literature of the sixteenth century. Roldan: So Roland is called in Amadis. Agramanth: Malagys of Aigremont, a magician in the legend of the Children of Haymon. Maritorne: A disgusting stable wench in Don Quixote. Heine's comparison of his situation with that of Don Quixote constitutes a pendant to his characterization of himself as a "fool on the side of reason."*

I have nothing to tell you except what the whole world knows, namely that your tragedy, well acted, was received by a crowded theater with most deserved approval.

I went to the theater again for the first time in six months and was in the company of dear ladies whose lips looked most amiable as they uttered Immermann's praise.

Yesterday morning I trounced Count Platen, and yesterday evening I applauded Immermann. I had so long delayed the first business that I had to apply myself to it; it has only been done half-successfully, and I was just as curious as others to see what

I should do. . . . For the rest, the book is written very tamely, and is not in the least demagogic.

The death of my father left me gloomy for a long while, and only now am I being gradually restored to a better mood.

—To Karl Immermann
Hamburg, November 17, 1829

Immermann's Tragedy in Tyrol: Andreas Hofer was presented in Hamburg. Immermann's verses satirizing Platen, which were reprinted in the second part of Heine's Travel Pictures, *gave rise to Platen's polemic.*

Herewith I send you the third part of the *Travel Pictures*, which I received only yesterday from the printer and had bound at once so that you and Robert could read, hot off the stove, what I have written this month about Count Platen who, as you will remember, was so venomous in his play. I have now caused an antidote to be printed which should satisfy twenty more counts their life long.

—To Friederike Robert
Hamburg, end of December, 1829

Poor Platen! *c'est la guerre!* This is no playful game, but a war of annihilation, and with all prudence I cannot overlook the consequences of my book. I wrote it under bad circumstances, and the tone of indifference which it may have is the result of contrast.

—To Karl Immermann
Hamburg, end of December, 1829

I do much wish that the characters in my *Baths of Lucca* may please you. My Hyacinth is the first complete figure that I have created life-size. . . .

As for Platen, I am very curious to have your judgment. I ask no praise, and I know that blame would be unjust. I have done my duty; let the consequences be what they will. At first people were anxious to know what would happen to Platen. Now, as always after an execution, there is compassion for him: I should not have handled him so severely. But I do not see how a man can be overthrown with gentleness. People do not see that I only chastised him as the representative of his party; I did not wish merely to attack the impertinent play-boy of the aristocrats and the parsons on aesthetic grounds. It was a war of men against men, and the approach which is publicly made against me, that I, the humbly born, should have spared the noble estate, makes me laugh—for that was precisely my motive: I wished to make an example whatever the consequences, and now I have made one for the Germans. . . .

But my friend Campe is truly a rascal; to reduce my pecuniary claims, he even entered into secret plots against my book. Thus am I in distress on all sides. Do not misunderstand me: my distress is in part literary, in part for my personal safety, in part for my future, for I see that my water is being channeled off on all sides.

—To Varnhagen von Ense
Hamburg, January 3, 1830

No one feels more deeply than I that I have done myself untold injury with the Platen chapter, that I should have attacked the business differently, that I have offended the public, and indeed the better class; but at the same time I feel that, with all my talent, I could not have produced anything better, and that— *coûte que coûte*—I had to make an example. The national servility of the Germans and their night-cap habit will be most brilliantly revealed on this occasion. I doubt whether I have succeeded in divesting the word "Count" of its magic. . . . Then there is once more the complaint that I have done a thing unheard of in German literature—as if the times were always the same! The Schiller-Goethe-Xenien war was only a potato battle; it was the period of art; art—imitation of life, not life itself— was in question. Now the highest interests of life itself are at stake, the revolution enters into literature, and the war is in earnest.

I say this because I make no claim to a civic crown in the

Platen story. I was looking out for myself, but the reasons for doing so stemmed from the general combat of the age. When the parsons at Munich first attacked me and flung the Jew in my face, I laughed—I thought it mere stupidity. But when I scented a systematic attack, when I saw that the ridiculous bogey was gradually growing into a menacing vampire, when I perceived the aim of Platen's satire, when I heard through the booksellers that productions steeped in the same poison were crawling about in manuscript, then I girded my loins and struck as hard as I could and as quickly as I could. Robert, Gans, Michael Beer, and others have always borne it with Christian fortitude when they were attacked as I have been, and have always maintained a prudent silence; I am a different man, and that is well. It is well when the evil find a just man who avenges himself and others ruthlessly and mercilessly.

—To Varnhagen von Ense
February 4, 1830

I have no news from the South, but I know that in north Germany it is still not considered the thing to speak about my book; yet gradually it is eating its way along. . . . Very many free Protestants are enthusiastic on my behalf, and I perceive that I might easily create a party among such people. One cannot know what opposition might be evoked in Protestant Germany by revealing Jesuit plots, and thus it may well come about that I should obtain a following among evangelical people.

—To Varnhagen von Ense
Wandsbeck, April 5, 1830

At the end of July 1830, Heine journeyed to Helgoland, and there he heard of the outbreak of the Revolution in France.

Helgoland, July 1, 1830
I myself am weary of this guerrilla warfare and long for peace, at least for a condition of affairs in which I can give myself freely to my own natural inclinations, my dreamy way of life, my fan-

tastic thoughts and ruminations. What irony of fate that I who am so fain to bed down on the quiet and contemplative pillow of ease should be marked out to scourge my poor fellow Germans from their complacency and goad them to activity! I who most dearly love to occupy myself with watching trailing clouds, with solving the metrical magic of words, with overhearing the secrets of elemental spirits, with losing myself in the wonderland of old tales—I have to edit political annals, further the interests of the time, excite revolutionary desires, stir up passions, always pull at the nose of the poor honest German, and rouse him from his sound giant sleep. . . . I am weary and long for rest.

Helgoland, July 8

Since yesterday was Sunday and a leaden tedium covered the whole island and almost crushed my head, I reached for my Bible out of despair . . . and I confess that, though I am secretly a Hellene, the book not only entertained me well but even edified me heartily. What a book!—large and broad as the world, rooted in the abysses of creation and towering up to the blue secrets of heaven. . . . Sunrise and sunset, promise and fulfilment, birth and death, the whole drama of humanity—everything is in that book. . . . It is the book of books, *biblia*. The Jews may easily take comfort for having lost Jerusalem and the Temple and the Ark of the Covenant and the golden vessels and the treasures of Solomon: such loss is slight compared to the Bible, the indestructible treasure which they have saved. If I am not mistaken it was Mohammed who called the Jews "the People of the Book," a name which they have retained in the orient to this day and which is profoundly significant. A book is their country, their property, their ruler, their fortune, and their misfortune. They live in the peaceful marches of this book, here they enjoy their inalienable civic rights, here none can expel them, none despise them, here they are strong and admirable. Sunk in the reading of this book they observed little of the changes which have taken place in the actual world. Peoples have risen and vanished, states have flourished and suffered extinction, revolutions have raged over the earth; but they, the Jews, were bowed over their book and perceived nothing of the wild chase of time which swept over their heads.

Just as the prophet of the East called them "the People of the Book," so the prophet of the West, in his philosophy of history called them "the People of the Intellect." Even in their earliest beginnings, as we observe in the Pentateuch, the Jews exhibited their predilection for the abstract, and their entire religion is nothing other than a piece of dialectic, wherein matter and spirit are separated and the absolute is recognized solely in the form of spirit. How fearfully isolated their position must have been among the peoples of antiquity, who were devoted to the joyous service of nature and who conceived of spirit only in its manifestations in matter, in image and in symbol! How stark a contrast did they offer to colorful Egypt teeming with hieroglyphs, to the Phoenicians and their great pleasure-shrine of Astarte, or even to that beautiful sinner, Babylon, steaming with sweet passion, and finally even to Greece, the blooming homeland of art!

It is a remarkable spectacle how the people of the spirit gradually liberated itself from matter and wholly spiritualized itself. Moses provided the spirit with spiritual bulwarks against the actual pressure of neighboring peoples: round about the field where he sowed spirit, he planted his severe ceremonial law and an egotistical nationality as a protecting briar-hedge. But when the sacred plant of the spirit had struck root so deep and had sprung so high heavenward that it could no longer be extirpated, there came Jesus Christ and tore the ceremonial law down, which no longer had useful significance, and even uttered a capital sentence upon Jewish nationality. . . . He summoned all peoples of the earth to participate in the kingdom of God, which had previously belonged to only one chosen people of God, and he gave all humanity the Jewish civic right. . . . That was a great question of emancipation, but its solution was far more magnanimous than that of modern questions of emancipation in Saxony and Hanover. . . . To be sure, the redeemed who liberated his brethren from the ceremonial law and nationalism and established cosmopolitanism, became a victim of his humanity; the city magistrate of Jerusalem caused him to be crucified and the mob jeered at him. . . .

But only the body was mocked and crucified, the spirit was glorified, and the martyrdom of the triumphator who won world dominion for the spirit became the symbol of this victory; ever since, all humanity strives, in imitationem Christi, for the death of the body and for supersensual merging with absolute spirit. . . .

When will harmony be restored, when will the world recover its health from this one-sided striving for spiritualization, this mad error through which souls as well as bodies sicken! A great remedy lies in political movement and in art. Napoleon and Goethe have worked to good effect. The former by forcing people to observe all manner of wholesome physical movement; the latter by making us again receptive to Greek art and by creating solid works to which we may cleave as to marble images of the gods, in order not to be submerged in the mystic cloud of absolute spirit.

—Ludwig Boerne, 2

The Helgoland journal comprised a portion of Heine's Memoirs in their first form, which was destroyed. This portion was saved from destruction by the fact that, in 1839, Heine included it in his book on Ludwig Boerne. Apparently the notes in his journal were worked over for this purpose.

The "Prophet of the Orient," that is, Mohammed, applied the expression "People of the Book" to Jews and Christians. It was only later that the expression came to refer exclusively to Jews.

The "Prophet of the West" is Georg Wilhelm Friedrich Hegel (1770-1831) who said of "Judaea" in his lectures on the philosophy of history: "Nature which is first and basic in the Orient is now reduced to creature, and spirit is now first." This concept of Hegel's became paramount for Heine. It often misguided him to the wrong view that in the Old Testament nature "was degraded" and that in the course of Jewish history progressive spiritualization of the concept of God resulted in depreciation of actual life. In his Paris period, the influence of the Saint-Simonist school is amalgamated in Heine's concept of history with that of Hegel. This influence, too, prevented Heine from obtaining an unprejudiced view of Jewish history, religion, and evaluation of life. Heine's opinion, that the Jewish "ceremonial" law arose in opposition to the "actual pressure of neighboring peoples," is untenable, for the lives of these ancient peoples also were regulated by ritual. The difference between Israel and its neighbors is not comprised in the fact that it possessed ceremonial laws and its neighbors none, but rather in the Jewish concept of God and also in Jewish piety, that is, in the peculiar relationship of the Jewish individual to the personality of God. Heine is similarly in error in maintaining that Jesus of Nazareth pulled down the ceremonial law and departed from Jewish nationalism. There is no support for such a view in the Gospels. It was Paul who first took this step, after a vehement conflict with the disciples led by James, the brother of Jesus.

On the other hand, Heine's appreciation of the epic and pictorial beauties of the biblical narrative are perceptive. With the trained glance of the ballad-writer he recognizes in the account of the defilement of Dinah and the vengeance of her brothers (Genesis 30 and 34), the traces of heroic poetry, and his judgment is in consequence more just than that of modern Bible critics. But Heine was not aware that the poetry of the Old Testament, which he recognized, confuted his thesis of the predilection of the Jewish spirit for abstraction.

Helgoland, July 18

In the Old Testament, I have read the first book of Moses all through. Like long caravan trains, the sacred primitive world passed through my spirit. The camels range prominently. Upon their high backs sit the veiled roses of Canaan. Pious cowherds drive oxen and cows before them. The caravan passes over bare hills and hot sandy plains where only an occasional cluster of palms appears and provides a cool breeze. Slaves dig wells. Sweet, calm, sunny, east-land! How charming it is to rest under your tents! Ah, Laban, would that I could pasture your flocks; I would gladly serve seven years for Rachel and another seven for Leah, whom you give me in recompense! I hear them bleat, those sheep

of Jacob's, and I see him put the streaked staves before them
when they go to drink at breeding time. The speckled ones now
belong to us. Meanwhile Reuben comes home, and brings his
mother a posy of *dudaim* which he plucked in the field. Rachel
demands the *dudaim*, and Leah gives them to her on the condition that Jacob sleep the following night by her side. What are
dudaim? The commentators have broken their heads in vain over
the point. Luther has no better solution than to call familiar
flowers *dudaim*. Perhaps they are Swabian wallflowers. I found
the love story of Dinah and young Shechem very moving. Her
brothers Simeon and Levi did not take the matter so sentimen-
tally. It is horrible how they strangled the unhappy Shechem and
all his kinsmen with cruel cunning, although the poor lover undertook to marry their sister, to give them lands and estates, to
ally himself with them into a single family, and although, with
this end in view, he had caused himself and all his people to be
circumcised. The two lads should have been happy that their
sister was making so brilliant a match; the intermarriage agreed
upon was of the greatest advantage to their race and would bring
them, besides a most valuable dowry, a good stretch of land of
which they were in great need. . . . A man could not comport
himself more decently than this Shechem prince in love, who
only anticipated conjugal rights out of love. But there it is: he
had defiled their sister and for this transgression the brothers,
proud in their honor, knew no other requital than death. And
when their father chided them for their bloody deed and mentioned the advantages which marriage with Shechem would have
brought them, they replied, "Should we trade with the virginity of
our sister?" Headstrong and grim hearts, these brothers. But
beneath the hard stone there wafts a breath of the most delicate
feeling of morality. A curious thing—this feeling of morality, as
revealed also upon other occasions in the life of the Patriarchs,
is not the result of a positive religion or political legislation; nay,
the ancestors of the Jews had neither positive religion nor political legislation, for both arose at a later date. I believe that I
can therefore maintain that morality is independent of dogma
and legislation, it is a pure product of wholesome human feeling;

and true morality, the reason of the heart, will always survive though church and state perish.

I wish we had another word to designate the thing we now call morality. We would then be tempted to regard morality as a product of mores. . . . But true morality is as independent of the mores of a people as it is of dogma and legislation. Mores are the product of climate and history, and legislation and dogmatism arise from similar factors. Hence there are Indian mores, Chinese mores, Christian mores, but there is only one sole morality, to wit, a human morality. Perhaps this cannot even be conceived, and the law of morality which we call "morals" is only a dialectical play on words. Morality is revealed in actions; and only in their motives, not in their form and color, is moral significance implied.

As long as I have thought, I have reflected on this subject of morality. The problem of the nature of good and evil which has set all great spirits into troublesome commotion for a millennium and a half has been present to me only in the question of morality.

Out of the Old Testament, I frequently leap into the New, and here, too, the supreme power of the great book awes me. Upon what sacred soil does your foot here tread! For this reading you must take off your shoes, as in the vicinity of sanctuaries.

The most remarkable words of the New Testament for me is the passage in the Gospel of John, 16.12-13: "I have yet many things to say unto you, but ye cannot bear them now. Howbeit, when he, the Spirit of Truth, is come, he will guide you into all truth: for he shall not speak of himself; but whatsoever he shall hear, that shall he speak: and he will shew you things to come." Thus the last word has not yet been spoken, and here perhaps is the ring to which a new revelation may be linked. It begins with release from the word, puts an end to martyrdom, and establishes the kingdom of eternal joy—the millennium. All promises eventually find rich fulfilment.

A certain mystical ambivalence prevails in the New Testament. The words are a clever digression, not a system: Render unto Caesar the things that are Caesar's, and unto God the things that are God's. So also when Christ is asked, Art thou King of the Jews?, the answer is an evasion. So is the answer to the question whether he be son of God. Mohammed is far more open, more definite. When he was approached with a similar question, namely, whether he was the son of God, he answered, God has no children.

What a great drama is the Passion! And how deeply is it motivated by the prophecy of the Old Testament! It could not be circumvented, it was the red seal of authenticity. Just as did the miracles, so did the Passion serve as annunciation. If a savior should now arise, he no longer need suffer crucifixion to spread his doctrine impressively abroad: he can quietly have it printed and announce the pamphlet in the *Allgemeine Zeitung* at a cost of sixpence per line.

What a sweet character is this God-man! How narrow-minded seems the hero of the Old Testament in comparison! Moses loves his people with a touching devotion; he cares for the future of this people like a mother. Christ loves humanity, that son flames about the whole earth with the warming rays of his love. What a soothing balm for all of the sores of this world are his words! What a fountain of healing for all sufferers was the blood that flowed on Golgotha! The white marble gods of the Greeks were sprinkled with this blood, and sickened of inward horror, and could never regain their health! Most of them, indeed, had long borne within themselves the consuming pestilence, and now the fright hastened their death.

—Ludwig Boerne, 2

Dudaim: *Love apple, mandragora, aphrodisiac. Heine read the Old Testament in Luther's translation. In Luther's Bible and in all editions produced under his influence the "Christological" interpretation of the Old Testament is carried out in full, that is, the utterances of the prophets are construed to mean that they foretell the coming of Jesus of Nazareth, his passion, and resurrection. This Christological interpretation, which was adopted by the Medieval Church and even more vehemently defended by Luther, is today recognized as untenable even by Christian the-*

ologians and historians of the Old Testament and has been given up. Heine, who accepted it here, questions it in other works.

Helgoland, July 29

I have again been reading in the Old Testament. What a great book! More remarkable for me than the content is the manner, where the word is as much a natural product as is a tree, a flower, the sea, the stars, man himself. It shoots, it flows, it sparkles, it smiles, one knows not how, one knows not why; one finds everything quite natural. That is truly the word of God, whereas other books demonstrate only human wit. In Homer, that other great book, the manner is a product of art, and even if the material is always drawn from reality, as in the Bible, it is nevertheless fashioned into a poetic image as if it were transmuted in the crucible of the human spirit; it is refined by a spiritual process which we call art. In the Bible there is no trace of art: it is in the style of a notebook in which the absolute spirit, without any individual human assistance, notes down the events of the day, approximately with the same factual fidelity with which we write our laundry lists. Upon this style no judgment whatever can be made; we can only affirm its effect upon our spirit, and the Greek grammarians must have been no little embarrassed if they attempted to define many striking beauties in the Bible according to traditional notions of art. Longinus speaks of the sublime. More modern aestheticians speak of naïveté. Ah, as I have said, here all criteria fail—the Bible is the word of God.

Only in one single author do I find something reminiscent of that immediate style of the Bible. That is Shakespeare. With him too the word frequently steps forth in that terrifying nakedness which frightens and shocks us; in Shakespeare's works we frequently see the body of truth without the robe of artistry. But that happens only at individual moments; the genius of art, perhaps feeling its impotence, here left nature its office for several instants, and then claimed its sway in the plastic fashioning and the clever concatenation of the drama all the more jealously. Shakespeare is at once Jew and Greek; or rather, both elements, spiritualism and art, have penetrated him in conciliation with one another and produced a loftier whole.

Perhaps such harmonious intermingling of the two elements is the task of all European civilization. As yet, we are very far from such a result. Goethe the Greek, and with him the whole poetic party, has most recently expressed its antipathy to Jerusalem almost passionately. The opposing party, which has no great name at its head, but only a few squallers, as for example the Jew Pustkuchen, the Jew Wolfgang Menzel, the Jew Hengstenberg—these raise their Pharisaical outcries all the more sorrowfully against Athens and the great pagan.

—Ludwig Boerne, 2

Johannes Friedrich Wilhelm Pustkuchen: Orthodox Protestant clergyman, an opponent of Goethe. Ernst Wilhelm Hengstenberg (1802-1869): Orthodox Protestant professor of theology, opponent of modern literature. For the basis of Heine's calling these men Jews, see p. 370.

Helgoland, August 1

I have taken with me no book that deals with the interests of the day. My entire library consists of Paul Warnefried's *History of the Langobards*, the Bible, Homer, and certain pieces of trash on witchcraft.

Helgoland, August 6

I had just been reading Paul Warnefried, when my thick mail came from the mainland with the news, warm, glowing, hot. There were sunbeams wrapped up in printed paper and they kindled my soul so that it burned with a wild flame. . . . It is all as if it were still a dream; the name of Lafayette especially echoes like the legend out of my earliest childhood. Is he again actually on horseback, commanding the National Guard? . . . Lafayette, the tricolor, the *Marseillaise*—I am intoxicated.

Helgoland, August 10

Lafayette, the tricolor, the *Marseillaise*—
Gone is my longing for peace. Now I know again what I wish

to do, what I should do, what I must do. I am the son of the
Revolution, and again seize the magic weapon over which my
mother spoke her charms.

This morning another packet of newspapers arrived. I devoured them like manna. Child that I am, the moving details
occupied me far more than the meaningful whole. . . . I can no
longer sleep, and the most bizarre visions of the night hurtle
through my charged spirit.

—Ludwig Boerne, 2

*Paulus Diaconus, the son of Warnefried, wrote a Historia
Langobardum during the time of Charlemagne, at the end of the
eighth century. Under the earlier Bourbons the tricolor was abolished and the singing of the Marseillaise forbidden.*

As there are birds who have a presentiment of a physical revolution by storm, earthquake or flood, so there are men who feel
the coming of social revolutions, and are paralyzed, stunned and
dumbfounded by it. That has been my condition this year until
the end of July. I was sound and well, but I could do nothing
but read the history of the Revolution day and night. I was by
the sea in Helgoland for two months, and when the news of the
great war reached there, it was as though it were a matter of
course, as though it were only a continuation of my studies. On
the Continent I experienced the events of this country which
might well have put a less stout heart out of countenance with
the beautiful. Nevertheless, disturbed on all sides, I am undertaking to make out of old materials a little book for the times.
I shall call it "A Supplement to the Travel Pictures." . . . The
book is deliberately one-sided. I know very well that the Revolution embraces every social interest and that the aristocracy and
the Church are not its only enemies. But I have represented them
as the only allied enemies so as to consolidate the struggle. I myself hate the *aristocratie bourgeoise* even more. . . . If my book
contributes towards emancipating feelings in matters of religion
in Germany where people are unbendingly religious, I shall be

happy and willingly endure the outcry of the devout which confronts me. . . .

At heart I feel very free and vigorous and contemplate doing great things. But my external situation deteriorates daily and the studies which have so much preoccupied me, and, above all, world events, have unfortunately alienated me more from my own concern than I can justify to myself. Furthermore, I am occasionally smitten with a kind of blindness and suffer myself to be cheated on all sides; just now I have again let my book-dealer cheat me. . . . All of this is the fault of my uncle, who even last year promised me Holland and Brabant, so that I had no money difficulties and willingly sacrificed something on behalf of literary interests. In promoting the latter there is no better publisher than Julius Campe.

—To Varnhagen von Ense
Hamburg, November 19, 1830

The local events: After the July Revolution, persecution of Jews broke out in Hamburg. Salomon Heine's house was also attacked. The poet was so indignant that he expressed the wish that Prussia put an end to Hamburg's independence as a free city. These pogroms strengthened Heine's distrust of the German revolutionaries.

All of my efforts are devoted to obtaining a secure position à *tout prix*. Without one, I can contribute nothing. If I cannot find one shortly in Germany, I shall go to Paris, where I shall unfortunately have to play a role in which all of my artistic and poetic capacities will be destroyed and where the breach with the powers-that-be at home will be consummated. I am taking no steps, but should like to discover from you whether something can be found for me in Berlin or—Vienna (!!!). I will leave nothing untried and will determine upon extreme steps only in the extreme case.

—To Varnhagen von Ense
Hamburg, January 4, 1831

I am still under the most urgent pressure here. With the best will, I realize that, if I cannot employ the wisdom of the governments for myself, nothing is left but that I protect myself from their follies.

—To Varnhagen von Ense
Hamburg, April 1, 1831

IV

LIFE IN PARIS

First Impressions

At the end of April 1831, Heine left Hamburg to go to Paris. Since he could not foresee how long he would remain in France, he left far the greater part of his papers, among them all letters addressed to him and many manuscripts, at the home of his mother. They were destroyed in a great fire in 1833. Heine travelled by way of Hanover, Kassel, Frankfort (where he remained a week and was welcomed by the men of the liberal party), Heidelberg and Karlsruhe. On May 1, 1831, he entered French soil at Strasbourg, and on May 3 he arrived in Paris.

I crossed the Rhine, May 1, 1831. I did not see the old river-god, Father Rhine, so I contented myself with dropping my visiting card into the water. I am told that he was sitting down below, conning Meidinger's French Grammar, for during the Prussian rule his French had grown rusty from long disuse, and now he wished to refurbish it, to be prepared for contingencies. I thought I could hear him conjugating *j'aime, tu aimes, il aime, nous aimons*—but what does he love? Surely not the Prussians. I saw the Strasbourg cathedral only from the distance; it wagged its head like the faithful Eckart when it saw a young fop on his way to the Venusberg.

I awoke at St. Denis from a sweet morning sleep, and for the first time heard the shout of the coucou driver, "Paris! Paris!" as well as the bell of the coco seller. Here we already inhaled the atmosphere of the capital, now visible on the horizon. A rascally lackey tried to persuade me to visit the royal sepulcher at St. Denis; but I had not come to France to see dead kings. I contented myself with listening to the local legend as told by the guide, how the wicked pagan king struck St. Denis' head off, and St. Denis ran to Paris, his head in his hand, to have himself bur-

273

ied there. When one thinks of the distance, my informant remarked, one must be astonished at the miracle of a man going so far afoot without a head. But he added with a peculiar smile, "In such cases it is only the first step which counts." That was worth two francs, and I paid them to him, for the love of Voltaire. In twenty minutes, I was in Paris, entering through the triumphal arch of the Boulevard St. Denis, which was originally erected in honor of Louis XIV, but now served to grace my entry into Paris. I was surprised at meeting such multitudes of well-dressed people, tastefully arrayed like the pictures of a fashion journal. I was also impressed by the fact that they all spoke French, which, in Germany, is the distinguishing mark of the higher classes; the whole nation are as noble as the nobility with us. The men were all so polite, and the pretty women all smiled so graciously. If someone accidentally jostled me without immediately asking pardon, I could safely wager that it was a fellow-countryman. And if a pretty woman looked a little sour, she had either eaten sauerkraut or could read Klopstock in the original. I found everything quite charming. The skies were so blue, the air so balmy, and here the rays of the sun of July were still glimmering. The cheeks of the beauteous Lutetia were still flushed from the burning kisses of that sun, and the bridal flowers on her bosom were not yet wilted. But at the street corners the words, *liberté, égalité, fraternité*, had already been erased. Honeymoons fly so quickly!

I immediately visited the restaurants to which I had been recommended. The landlords assured me that they would have made me welcome even without letters of introduction, for I had an honest and distinguished appearance, which in itself was a sufficient recommendation. Never did a German landlord so address me, even if he thought it. Such a churlish fellow feels himself in duty bound to suppress all pleasant speeches and his German bluntness demands that he shall tell only the most disagreeable things to our faces. In the manner, and even in the language, of the French, there is so much delicious flattery, which costs so little, and is yet so gratifying. My poor sensitive soul, which had shrunk with shyness from the rudeness of the fatherland, again expanded under the genial influence of French urbanity. God has given us tongues that we may say something pleasant to our fellow-men.

My French had grown rusty since the battle of Waterloo, but after half an hour's conversation with a pretty flower-girl in the Passage de l'Opéra it soon flowed fluently again. I managed to stammer forth gallant phrases in broken French, and explained to the little charmer the Linnaean system, in which flowers are classified according to their stamens. The little one practised a different system, and divided flowers into those which smelled pleasantly and those which smelled unpleasantly. I believe that she applied a similar classification to men. She was surprised that, notwithstanding my youth, I was so learned and spread the fame of my erudition through the whole Passage de l'Opéra. I inhaled with rapturous delight the delicious aroma of flattery, and amused myself charmingly. I walked on flowers, and many a lark fell to me ready roasted. How much that was amusing did I see here upon my arrival! There were all the notables of public entertainment and official ridiculousness. The serious Frenchmen were the most amusing. I saw Arnal, Bouffé, Déjazet, Debureau, Odry, Mademoiselle Georges, and the great Pot in the Invalides. I saw the morgue, and the Académie Française where many unknown corpses were similarly on display, and, finally the Necropolis of the Luxembourg where all the mummies of perjury were present, along with their embalmed perjuries which they had sworn to all the dynasties of the French Pharaohs. In the Jardin des Plantes I saw the giraffe, the three-legged goat, and the kangaroo, which amused me particularly. I also saw M. de Lafayette and his white hair; of the latter I saw only a *parte*, for it was located in a medallion which a beautiful lady wore on her neck, whereas the man himself, the hero of two worlds, wore a brown wig, like all old Frenchmen. I visited the royal library and there saw the keeper of medals, which had just been stolen. I also saw in an obscure corridor there the zodiac of Dhontera, which had once aroused so much attention; and on the same day, I saw Madame Recamier, the most famous beauty of the Merovingian Age, as well as M. Ballanche, who was one of the *pièces justificatives* of her virtue and whom she dragged about with her from time immemorial. Unfortunately, I did not see M. de Chateaubriand, who would surely have amused me. To make up for it I saw in the Grande Chaumière, the père Lahire, at a moment when he was in a great passion; he had just seized two young Robespierres with spreading white vests of virtue by the collar, and set them before the door. A little Saint-Just, who was being very impertinent, he threw after them; the same fate almost befell a number of pretty *citoyennes* of the Latin Quarter, who complained of offenses against human rights. In another, similar, locality I saw the famous Chiccard, the famous hide-dealer and cancan dancer, a thick-set figure whose ruddy face contrasted prettily with his gleaming white cravat; stiff and sober, he was like a city-hall official on the point of crowning a pretty *rosière* with the flower of virtue. I admired his dance, and informed him that it bore great similarity to the ancient dance of the sileni, which was performed at the Dionysiac festival and received its name from Silenus, the worthy tutor of Bacchus. Mr. Chiccard said many flattering things to me about my scholarship and presented to me certain ladies of his acquaintance, who likewise took pains to spread word of my thorough knowledge abroad, so that my fame was soon broadcast all over Paris, and the directors of periodicals searched me out to obtain my services.

—Confessions

Meidinger's Practical Grammar of the French Language, distributed in many editions after 1783, was used by Heine himself. Coucou: A small carriage. Coco: Licorice water. Etienne Arnal (1794-1872); Maria Buffé (1800-1853), and Charles Jacques Odry were favorite comedians. Jean Gaspard Deburau (1796-1846); the greatest pantomime actor of the nineteenth century, was enthusiastically applauded in the Théâtre des Funambules by all classes of society, including the greatest poets and artists of the age, and was also admired by Heine. Mlle. Georges (Marguerite Josephine Weymar), the actress, was esteemed by Heine—who called her "the huge beaming sun of flesh in the Boulevards' theater-heaven"—as an artist, though virtually all serious French dramatic critics thought otherwise. Heine did not know that she had been a paramour of Napoleon I. The Luxembourg Palace was the seat of the senate under Napoleon and in the Third Republic; from 1815 to 1848 it was the House of Lords. Giraffes were unknown in Europe for centuries until a few were brought to London and Paris in 1827. Grande Chaumière: Pleasure resort in Boulevard Montparnasse: see Atta Troll, ch. 1. On the theft of the coins Heine has given a report in French Affairs, article 3. Dhontera: Ceiling images in the temple ruins of Dendrah in Upper Egypt. Julie de Récamier (1777-1849), wife of a great Paris banker, a famous beauty, assembled at her salon almost all the great men of her day. Heine, too, was introduced there. Pierre Simon Ballanche (1776-1847), a social philosopher of a mystical tendency, was underestimated by Heine. Rosière: a young woman who was crowned with a rose as the prize of virtue.

Heine's reputation was naturally not spread abroad in Paris by way of the pleasure resorts, as this satirical passage would suggest. He came with good recommendations from Varnhagen von Ense and other friends and immediately found a welcome in literary circles. His reputation as a poet had also preceded him to Paris. He at once formed a close attachment with Adolphe Loeve-Weimars, the son of Jewish parents who had lived in Hamburg and became Heine's first French translator. Loeve-Weimars was respected in Paris and had great influence with leading periodicals and publishers. Furthermore, Heine found in Paris his friend of the Berlin days, David Ferdinand Koreff. Koreff, who had similarly undergone baptism in order to obtain a post, played an important role in German Romanticism and, for a time, was personal physician to the Prussian chancellor Hardenberg, one of the most powerful men in Prussia. The hatred of his opponents who, despite his baptism, suspected him as a Jew, drove him to France. There he soon again acquired a great reputation by his hypnotic cures. He was a friend of Talleyrand, Balzac, and Stendhal-Beyle. He introduced Meyerbeer and Heine to Parisian society. In the beginning, he also treated Heine as physician. Koreff's rise was followed by a steep fall when, in

1837, he sent a patient a bill to the amount of 400,000 francs, and was gravely compromised in the ensuing litigation. Heine's relations to him had grown lax even before this.

Immediately after his arrival in Paris, Heine visited the Saint-Simonists Michel Chevalier and Emile Pereire. These introduced him to other members of the sect, and also to Saint-Amand Bazard, Lafayette's comrade in arms, from whom Heine received invitations. As early as 1831 also Heine became acquainted with the Princess Christine Belgiojoso, an Italian fighter for freedom, whose beauty, literary gifts and eccentric moods attracted him greatly. At her salon Heine become acquainted with the historian and minister Louis Adolphe Thiers, the poet Alfred de Musset, the composers Donizetti, Bellini, Franz Liszt, the painters Ary Scheffer and Chenavard, the philosopher Victor Cousin, and very friendly with the friend and protégé of the Princess, the seriously ailing historian, Augustin Thierry, whose sufferings and whose strength in enduring them had much in common with the poet of the Mattress Crypt. A faithful friend of Heine was Caroline Jaubert, whose husband Maxime Jaubert was one of the most influential jurists and parliamentarians of France. Heine's relations to the novelists George Sand, Honoré de Balzac, and Eugène Sue, to Alexandre Dumas, Théophile Gautier, and to the great composers Frédéric Chopin and Hector Berlioz became very cordial. With the exception of Alphonse de Lamartine, who rejected Heine sharply, and Sainte-Beuve, who kept his distance after a brief friendship, there were no significant personalities in the literary and artistic world after 1832 who were not ready to accommodate Heine.

It was Heine's conversation, his ready wit, which won him his social position. Heine spoke French with a heavy German accent which he never lost. He could never write a French letter correctly without help. But he had an extraordinary sense for French linguistic nuances which enabled him to perfect the work of his translators and to find the appropriate word in conversation. Thus his reputation spread as a sprightly and witty conversationalist who astonished Parisian society. He was very soon called le plus spiritual des Français; Sainte-Beuve, the famous critic,

who regarded Heine's success with disfavor, could not refute this,
but thought Heine would be more French if he were less
sprightly.

On the other hand, Heine had no glimpse into French family
life. He met his French friends in the great salons or in restaurants or walked with them on the boulevards or in the garden of
the Tuilleries; but he was never invited to small family circles, as
long as he was unmarried; and after his marriage, the character of
his wife made intimate intercourse with cultured families impossible. This fact is reflected in Heine's literary accounts of French
life. When he speaks of women, the family, or the relations between the sexes in France, his experience is limited to what he
could have observed either in the salons or in the demi monde.
He could have known little of the bourgeois manner of life from
his own experiences. This limitation in his observations also nar-
rowed his judgments on the state of political affairs in France.

Heine frequently received political information from Hippo-
lyte Carnot, son of Lazare Carnot, the "organizer of victory" in
the wars of the first French Republic, and also from Baron James
de Rothschild, who was a great admirer of Heine, as was his wife
also, and often rendered him financial assistance without ever
wounding the sensitive self-esteem of the poet, as Salomon Heine
had so often done. Heine's relations with Giacomo Meyerbeer
were very changeable. He rendered him important service in the
press, especially against Spontini's intrigues, but demanded considerable recompense for his service. Heine's most unselfish and
most helpful friend was the great historian François Mignet,
permanent secretary of the French Academy, whose intervention
helped the poet out of many embarrassments.

Even during the first days of my arrival at the capital of the
Revolution I observed that in actuality things bore quite a different color than the lighting effects of my enthusiasm had bestowed upon them from a distance. . . .

Not for itself had the people bled and suffered from time immemorial, not for itself but for others. In July 1830, it achieved
victory for that bourgeoisie which was as rotten as the nobility

which it supplanted, displaying the same egotism. By its victory the people won nothing but regret and greater distress.

—Ludwig Boerne, 2

"What did you do," Boerne once asked me, "on the first day of your arrival in Paris? What was your first walk?" He surely expected that I would name the Place Louis XVI or the Pantheon, the tombs of Rousseau and Voltaire, as my first excursion; and he pulled a wry face when I confessed to him the honest truth that immediately upon my arrival I went to the Royal Library and asked the keeper of manuscripts to fetch me the Manesse Codex of the Minnesinger. And that is the truth; for years I had longed to see with my own eyes those precious pages which have preserved for us, among others, the poems of Walther von der Vogelweide, the greatest German lyric poet.

—Ludwig Boerne, 4

The Manesse Manuscript, or "Great Heidelberg Song Manuscript," was brought to Paris in 1657, and in 1888 was returned to Heidelberg by exchange.

It was a little more than a year ago, shortly after my arrival in the capital. I was going to see the house in which Molière had dwelt, for I honor great poets and seek everywhere for traces of their earthly career: it is a *cultus*—a religion. On my way, not far from that sacred dwelling, I saw a being in whose played-out and worn-away features I saw some likeness to the former August Wilhelm Schlegel. I thought I saw his spirit, but it was only his body.

—The Romantic School, 2

La force des choses, the power of things! In truth I have not carried things to extremes, but things have carried me to a high extremity, to the top of the world, to Paris—yes, yesterday morning I stood on the topmost peak of this summit, on the Panthéon. *Aux grands hommes la patrie reconnaissante*—that I believe is the text of the golden inscription. What a mockery! Petty men erect such temples to great men after their death. They would do better to place such inscriptions on Véry's restaurant and to feed the great men well while they are still alive, instead of honoring them after they have died of starvation or other tortures. But Véry's is the pantheon of living little men; here they sit and eat and drink and invent ironic inscriptions.

Poor La Fontaine has a marble column in Chateau Thierry, his native town, which cost forty thousand francs. I laughed heartily when I saw it as I rode past. When he was alive the poor devil begged for a crust of bread, and after his death they give him forty thousand francs' worth of marble. Jean Jacques Rousseau and men like him, who could scarcely afford a garret in their lifetime, now have whole streets named after them. . . . I am surrounded by Prussian spies. Although I am keeping clear of political intrigue, they are all much afraid of me. Indeed, if they make war on me, then let them know that I shall let fly at them, and with all my strength.

Ah, I forsaw it all six months ago, and would fain have retired into poetry and left to others the rough and tumble of battle— but it could not be: *la force des choses*, we are pushed to an extremity.

At Frankfort, where I stayed for eight days and talked with several Congregationalists, I discovered the source of many of my own ills which had been inexplicable to me. I led a deadly life at Hamburg; I did not feel secure, and since the idea of going to Paris has long been stirring in my subconscious mind, I was easily persuaded when a great hand beckoned to me. However, it would be easy to flee if one did not drag the Fatherland along on the soles of his shoes! I parody Danton with pain. It is painful to walk in the Luxembourg and always to drag about with one a piece of Hamburg or a piece of Prussia or Bavaria on his soles. . . .

Things can go no worse with me here than at home, where I have nothing but struggling and necessity, and cannot sleep safely, and all resources of life are poisoned. Here, indeed, I am drowned in the vortex of events, the dayspring, the roaring revolution. I am made wholly of phosphorus, and while I drown in a wild sea of men, I also burn by the combustion of my own nature.

—To Varnhagen von Ense
Paris, June 27, 1831

Great hand: Metternich. Evidence of Metternich's intention to cause Heine's arrest has not been previously known. Nevertheless, Heine's fear of such a danger need not have been baseless. Even less must his statement be dismissed as an invention, as is done not only by the influential historian Heinrich von Treitschke, but also by favorably-disposed biographers of Heine. If Heine gives this information to Varnhagen, of all people, who had accurate information and had means of verifying the action, there can be no doubt that Heine had received some grave warning from some quarter, probably the Hamburg senator Sieveking, who was his friend. In point of fact, Metternich, who admired Heine's poetry greatly, rather exaggerated than underestimated the political danger of the poet. In Paris, Heine was always kept under surveillance by Austrian and frequently also by Prussian agents. Danton: When Danton, shortly before his arrest, was warned of Robespierre by a friend and admonished to immediate flight from France, he replied, "Does one carry his Fatherland on the soles of his shoes?" Heine knew this expression from Adolphe Thiers' History of the French Revolution, which he had already read in Germany with great interest.

My greatest sorrow for two years has been that I have had to leave behind my little family, particularly my sister's youngest child. And yet, duty and discretion counselled departure. I had the choice between laying down my arms completely or lifelong struggle, and I chose the latter, and indeed not lightheartedly. But I was constrained to take up arms in the first place by the mockery of others and by the omens of my birth: the line of march of my whole life was marked out in my cradle.

—To Varnhagen von Ense
Paris, July 16, 1833

The First Writings on France

Even during the first weeks of his sojourn in Paris, Heine began to acquaint himself, as a writer, with French culture. First he wrote reports on the Paris art exhibition, the Salon of 1831, which was published in Cotta's Morgenblatt fuer die gebildeten Staende. In December of the same year, Heine began his political reporting for the Allgemeine Zeitung; at the end of 1832, these reports appeared in book form under the title French Affairs. His work on the Allgemeine Zeitung gave Heine a new and very important circle of readers. The Allgemeine Zeitung, which was published by Cotta's establishment, served the Triaspartei. Its chief editor, Gustav Kolb, a reliable friend of Heine from the period of the Annalen to his death, was, like most other editors of the journal at the time, a consistent adherent of the Rheinbund. Nevertheless, this policy was very carefully veiled, for the newspaper served the large public as spokesman for the governments of almost all German states and European powers. No other contemporary paper in Europe was in a position to publish so much confidential information, correspondence and authentic interpretations of political events as was the Allgemeine Zeitung, which was supplied with material by almost all the cabinets and ministries in Europe. In any case, the editorial staff was more than once exposed to the pressure of a government, which threatened withholding further information if the paper persisted in some inconvenient campaign. In general, Kolb was shrewd enough to tack prudently and to maintain his paper at an unusually high level, until the Revolution of 1848 disturbed its relations with important cabinets, and the movement for German unity cut the ground from under the Triaspartei. Heine was not the only Paris correspondent of the paper. Along with him worked his old university friend Dr. Donndorf, who took care of the regular daily service, whereas Heine contributed only pieces on important events or characterizations of significant tendencies of the political and social life of France. In this department Heine advanced to the foremost rank of European journalists.

Heine himself later admitted that he undertook his task of writing on French affairs too early and without adequate preparation. He had read French newspapers in Germany, but the great debates of the period of restoration had interested him little. His chief interest was directed to writings on the French Revolution of 1789, the Convention, and Napoleon. He knew little of what happened in France between 1815 and 1830; he did not know the new French poets, and was quite ignorant of a philosopher of the stature of Auguste Comte; on the other hand, he was profoundly impressed by the philosophy of Count Saint-Simon even while in Germany and saw in it the most important key to the understanding, not only of France, but also of urgent questions of life in general. In it Heine saw a possibility of mediating the conflict between his democratic tendencies and his awareness that, as a poet, he was an exceptional person, between his acceptance of reason and the requirements of his romantic nature. Doubtless Heine looked upon Saint-Simonism with the eyes of a German romanticist, as did also Rahel Varnhagen, who was similarly, at the end of her life, deeply impressed by the teachings of Saint-Simon and his disciples. But Heine also sensed in Saint-Simonism what was actually new, an appreciation of economic forces, an effort to deduce from the general economic and intellectual situation conclusions appropriate to the new social order.

Among these conclusions were demands for a new class of leadership and a new sexual morality. Heine regarded both with sympathy. Saint-Simon declared that the old ruling classes, the nobility of war and the clergy, had forfeited their importance through modern development and must be supplanted in the social esteem which they enjoyed by a new ruling class composed of leaders in science, industry and technology. This was music to the ear of Heine, who had declared war on the aristocracy of birth and the clergy. No less cheerfully did Heine accept the Saint-Simonist idea that the spirituality of Christianity must be united with the sensual joy of the ancients and that from this synthesis a new pantheistic (more correctly, pan-entheistic) religion must be created, whose ideals should be of a thoroughly earthly character and capable of realization in this life. Such a synthesis, as a necessary reaction against ascetic overemphasis of Christian worship of the spirit, promoted, less according to Saint-Simon himself than according to his disciples, a justification of the "pagan joy in the senses," a "rehabilitation of matter," an "emancipation of the flesh." This point in the Saint-Simonist doctrine was of paramount importance to Heine and sufficed to make him an adherent of the school. Other points he accepted with more or less reservation; still others left him indifferent or met with his disapproval.

Claude-Henri de Saint-Simon (1760-1825), who from 1777 to 1781 fought with great distinction for the cause of American independence and who died in great poverty, found only few but enthusiastic adherents in his lifetime. At first these formed a scientific debating club, which gradually developed into a religious community. They felt themselves to be apostles of a religious founder; in part, they constructed a sketchy, systematic outline of this religion, and in part they introduced into it thoughts which were more or less alien to its doctrine. In consequence, quarrels soon arose among the disciples, although when Heine arrived in Paris, there was still unity among them. Their propaganda availed itself of influential journals, some of which were read even abroad. Their effectiveness reached its high point immediately after the July Revolution. A great many artists and scholars, such as the musicians Franz Liszt and Felicien David, the novelists George Sand and Emile Souvestre, the painter Raymond Bonheur, and the historian Augustin Thierry, joined it. Carlyle and John Stuart Mill were interested in its social ideas, but rejected its religious aspirations. Masses of people thronged to the Sunday meetings of the Saint-Simonists in Paris and in many capitals of the French departements, until at the beginning of 1832, the police dissolved the association and the courts sentenced its leaders to prison terms.

Saint-Simonism wished to establish a new church and a new science and to penetrate all departments of life with its ideas. It regarded religion as an essential factor in social reform, and industry as a principal instrument of the new social structure.

High regard for industrial work was one of the most important principles in Saint-Simonist education. But here Heine retained his old standpoint. Even in England he had been frightened by advancing industrialization. He could not follow the Saint-Simonists in seeing a blessing for mankind in increasing large-scale industrialization. Of Saint-Simonist efforts to promote popular welfare by modernizing banks and credit systems, by railroads and canals, Heine did not so vehemently disapprove; but the details of such plans did not interest him. Many disciples of Saint-Simon, who had been the first to conceive the idea of a Panama canal, attained leading positions in French economy after the movement collapsed. Prosper Enfantin, later chief engineer of the Rothschild railway companies, provided the impulse for the construction of the Suez Canal. The largest French corporate banks were founded by former Saint-Simonists. Heine saw an inconsistency in the fact that men who had called themselves socialists, themselves became capitalists. But, in contrast to Marxist socialism, Saint-Simonism was never hostile to capital, and it entrusted social reform not to the initiative of the proletariat but to that of industrialists, bankers, and statesmen. The Saint-Simonists hoped that universal free trade would result in world peace and the peaceful union of all peoples. Their radical wing did indeed engage in revolutionary agitation among the workers, but they rejected the idea of the class struggle.

Even in Germany, Heine had been preoccupied with Saint-Simonism. The earliest traces of it are noticeable in the Town of Lucca. As he remarked to the German socialist Karl Gruen, he made connections with the leaders of the Saint-Simonists in the first twenty-four hours of his stay in Paris. He retained a lasting friendship with several of them, such as the social philosopher Pierre Lerroux, the national economist Michel Chevalier, and the high priest of the Saint-Simonist religion, Prosper Enfantin. There were many Jews among the Saint-Simonist leaders, such as Olinde Rodriguès, called "the living tradition," because he alone had been personally close to Count Saint-Simon; his brother Eugène Rodriguès; the brothers Isaac and Emile Pereire, who later became successful competitors of the

Rothschild banking house; Leon Halévy; and Gustave d'Eichthal.
But it was precisely with the Jewish Saint-Simonists that Heine's
relations were less cordial.

The ideas of Saint-Simon and his disciples had a far more
powerful effect upon Heine's spirit than did those of Hegel. He
himself was mistaken concerning the importance of the Saint-
Simonist influence, because pantheism seemed to him essential
to both, and hence the two sources frequently merged in his
recollection. Thus he repeatedly stated that Hegel had taught
him that man is a god; whereas this doctrine is utterly alien to
Hegel. On the other hand, Prosper Enfantin, who dedicated his
book On Germany to Heine, said that God is "in the spiritual
aspect, Man, the Ego, Reason."

From Saint-Simon, Heine adopted the terms "spiritualism"
and "sensualism" to designate human tendencies and tempera-
ments. He accepted Saint-Simon's concept of Christianity in
which the teaching of the Gospels is less accented than is the
"dualism of body and soul" which Christianity inherited from
Judaism and developed to an enhanced degree. But, under the
influence of Saint-Simonism and upon this basis, Heine reached
a more favorable judgment of Christianity, which initiated a
wholesome reaction against the materialism and the cult of crude
power of the ancients; however, this reaction had now gone too
far and had made an opposing reaction necessary. With Saint-
Simon, Heine transfers paradise from the beginning of human
history to the future, and he divides world history into "organic"
and "critical" epochs. Organic epochs are for Saint-Simon the
period from Antiquity to the appearance of Socrates, and the
Middle Ages from 600 to 1500. Critical epochs are the decline
of Antiquity and the modern period after Luther's reformation.
Heine accepted this classification with slight deviations. Furthermore, Heine was at one with the Saint-Simonists in regarding
the political constitution of the people as of less importance
than its spiritual, intellectual and economic conditions. But
Heine's temperament was not in consonance with this theoretic
view. He was repeatedly seized by political excitement. Even
revolutionary movements, whose aims he disapproved, aroused

his lively sympathy when he recognized in the bearers of these movements readiness to sacrifice, courage, and loyalty to conviction. On the other hand, the defenders of the regime with which Heine was in theoretical agreement and for whose preservation he was essentially concerned were not spared his mockery if their personality and their deportment displeased him. Aesthetic viewpoints doubtless influenced Heine's political judgments.

Even before Heine had acclimatized himself to French conditions in Paris, he began his reportage on French political affairs. It was quite natural—no other journalist of standing would have done otherwise—for him to replace his lack of personal knowledge and practical orientation by the reading of Parisian newspapers. In point of fact, he borrowed many parts of his French Affairs from such newspaper articles. Occasionally, he took these over substantially without change, only adapting them to his style. In this practice he relied almost exclusively upon the papers of the opposition, the legitimists and the republicans. Hence, Heine's reports frequently give a distorted picture of the facts. Heine conceived the July Revolution of 1830 as a continuation of the Revolution begun in 1789. That was correct insofar as France again acknowledged the ideas of 1789 through the new revolution. But the preponderant majority of Frenchmen did not wish to go beyond the constitution of 1791, which had proclaimed the constitutional monarchy. They had no desire for a restoration of the republic of the National Convention. Heine's conclusions concerning Mirabeau show that his opinion was basically the same. But his feeling was different. He charged the regime of Louis Philippe with inconsistency and complained that the French bourgeoisie had bilked the people, who had won the victory, of the fruits of their victory. To be sure, the regime of Louis Philippe, with its plutocratic suffrage, was easily vulnerable to attack. But in the general view of European liberalism of the time, it was dangerous and unstatesmanlike to grant suffrage to persons who were economically dependent. For a long time afterwards general suffrage was regarded in Europe as a political weapon of dictatorship, and was in fact used as such by Napoleon

and Bismarck. Only much later did general suffrage become a
weapon of democracy in Europe. But in his polemic against the
bourgeois kingship, Heine laid no great weight upon this principal objection, for he was little concerned with extension of the
suffrage. His main charge against Louis Philippe was that the
latter had made no use of Revolutionary ideas in his foreign
policy and was too anxiously concerned to maintain peace. It
was only in the crisis of 1840 that Heine gave up his belief in
the power of Revolutionary propaganda as a weapon of French
foreign policy and realized that a Revolutionary France was not
superior to the great powers in combination. His hatred of
England, furthermore, led him to agitate against the Anglo-
French entente. This misguided step was of service neither to
the cause of France nor to that of European liberalism.

In his judgment of internal French politics, Heine was at first
too easily led by the Saint-Simonist and the republican opposition. The Saint-Simonist leadership, which was completely surprised by the turn of events, enjoined neutrality upon its adherents during the battles of the July Revolution. Subsequently
they explained that the occurrence of the Revolution was "indeed a benefit, but not the hoped-for social revolution." Heine
adopted a similar view in Paris. He also accepted the legend
created by the republican agitation, that the bourgeoisie had
taken no active part in the street fighting of July; the opposite was
true, but when Heine came to Paris the legend had already been
widely credited. He also failed to appreciate the character and
purposes of the dominant party of "Doctrinaires." He regarded
them as visionaries and theoreticians. In actual fact they were
opportunists. Their political program, called the "Doctrine,"
aimed at a compromise solution of the conflict between pre-
Revolutionary and Revolutionary France. They were no "be-
trayers of the Revolution," as Heine thought, but wished to
achieve a compromise between the interests of the conservative
and progressive classes of the population, and they had publicly
formulated their "Doctrine" even before the July Revolution.
The bourgeois king, Louis Philippe, in his theory of the juste

milieu, represented the same point of view, which was antipathetic to Heine because it was of the nature of a compromise.

Despite these inadequacies, Heine's French Affairs constitutes, not only a brilliant literary contribution, but also a great work of political and historical analysis. The handicaps of a newcomer did not prevent him from picturing the popular mood, depicting the spiritual atmosphere of Paris with accurate color, and presenting living characterizations of leading personalities even though these bear the subjective tints of Heine himself. Some of his descriptions, like his account of the outbreak of the cholera, are uncontested masterpieces of reporting contemporary events.

Heine was soon forced to give up his reporting. On April 21, 1832, Friedrich von Gentz, the confidant of Metternich, wrote a letter to Baron von Cotta in which he protested with the greatest vehemence against the collaboration of an "accursed adventurer like Heine, whom I would let pass, even love, as a poet." Cotta could not but yield to this pressure. Heine understood fully the constraint under which his publisher labored, and continued his good relations with him. He supplied the Allgemeine Zeitung with anonymous notes and other material, but it was only eight years later, and under different circumstances, that he could resume his reporting for this periodical.

When I came to Paris in the summer of 1831, I was astonished at nothing more than the picture exhibition which then opened, and although very important political and religious revolutions claimed my attention, I could not refrain from writing first of the great revolution which had taken place here in the realm of art, of which the most significant manifestation was to be seen in the *Salon* I mentioned.

No less than my other countrymen, I entertained the most unfavorable prejudices against French art, and especially against French painting, whose latest development was quite unknown to me. But there is a peculiar kinship between France and painting. It, too, followed the social movement and was eventually rejuvenated along with the people. This, however, did not take place as directly as in the sister arts of music and poetry, which had begun their transformation even before the Revolution.

—French Painters. Postscript

In art I am a supernaturalist. I believe that the artist cannot find all his types in Nature, but that the most significant types are simultaneously revealed in his soul as the inborn symbolism of inborn ideas.

—French Painters. Decamps

I hear it at this instant, as I write—hear it without—that harsh and horrid sound, more threatening and bewildering than ever, that maddening confusion of noise; drums are beating, weapons rattling and ringing, a rising flood of men with delirious sufferings and curses; for the mob of Paris whirls through the narrow streets and howls, "Warsaw is fallen! Our advance guard has fallen! Down with the Ministry! War to Russia! Death to Prussia!" It is hard for me to remain quietly seated at the table and write my poor paper on art, my peaceful criticism of pictures, to an end. And yet, should I go forth into the street and there be recognized as a Prussian, my brain may be so crushed in by some hero of July that all my ideas on art will be flattened; or I may get a bayonet-thrust in the left side, where my heart is already bleeding of itself; and worst of all, I may be put into the guard-house as a foreign disturber of the peace.

In such rioting all thoughts and pictures become confused and repel one another. The Goddess of Freedom of Delacroix meets me with a changed countenance, almost with anguish in her wild eyes. Miraculously changed is the picture of the Pope by Vernet. The old and feeble vicegerent of Christ seems all at once to be young and vigorous, and rises smiling on his chair, while his sturdy bearers are apparently opening their mouths to sing *Te Deum laudamus*. Then the dead Charles assumes another face in sudden change, and looking closer, I behold no king, but murdered Poland in the black coffin, while Cromwell stands no more before my eyes, but the Czar of Russia, a noble,

opulent form, quite as grand as he seemed to me to be years
before in Berlin, when he stood beside the King of Prussia on
the balcony and kissed the latter's hand. Thirty thousand Berlin
folk, longing for anything resembling a show, shouted "Hurrah!"
and I thought in my heart, "God be gracious to us one and all."
I knew the Sarmatian proverb, "Kiss devoutly the hand which
you cannot cut off."

Ah! I would that the King of Prussia had allowed only his left
hand to be kissed and grasped the sword with his right, and
therewith met the most dangerous enemy of our native land, as
duty and conscience required him to do. Since those Hohenzol-
lerns have assumed the duty of Lords Warden of the realm in
the north, they should guard the Marches against aggressing
Russia. The Russians are fine people, and I am ready to love and
respect them, but since the fall of Warsaw, the last bastion which
separated them from us, they have moved so close to our hearts
that I am getting alarmed.

God be merciful to us all! Our last bastion is fallen, the
Goddess of Liberty turns pale, our friends lie on the ground, the
Roman High Priest rises, laughing wickedly, and aristocracy
stands triumphant by the coffin of the popular cause. . . .

It is, even on so-called peaceful days, very hard in Paris to turn
one's mind away from what goes on in the streets, and indulge
in wistful private dreams. And though Art blooms more luxuriantly in Paris than elsewhere, we are still disturbed in its enjoyment at every moment by the rude rush and roar of life; the
sweetest tones of Pasta and Malibran are jarred by the cries for
help of bitter poverty, and the intoxicated heart, which has just
drunk eagerly from the inspiring cup of Robert's color, is immediately sobered by the sight of public misery.

—French Painters. Delaroche

On September 6 and 7, 1831, Warsaw was stormed by the
Russians, and thus the fate of the Polish insurrection was sealed.
The fall of Warsaw aroused strong popular feeling in Paris. The
republican press accused Louis Philippe of having left the Poles
in the lurch. Prussia, whose king was the father-in-law of Czar

Nicholas I, had supported the Russians in suppressing the Polish insurrection. Czar Nicholas was regarded as "the handsomest man in Europe." In his Journey from Munich to Genoa, Heine had approved of Russia's war against Turkey, and had celebrated the Czar as the "gonfaloniere of freedom," for he then regarded the democratization of Russia as more probable than that of aristocratic England. Heine had discussed the pictures of Eugène Delacroix ("Freedom Leads the People to Battle"), Horace Vernet ("Gregory XVI"), Paul Delaroche ("Cromwell at the Corpse of Charles I"), as well as "The Reapers," and other pictures of Leopold Robert in his French Painters. Malibran and Pasta: famous coloratura sopranos.

Royalist as I am by native inclination, I have become one in France out of conviction also. I am convinced that the French cannot endure a republic, neither the constitution of Athens, nor that of Sparta, and least of all that of North America.

—French Affairs, 2

The sufficiently well-known book-dealer Frank, who has all kinds of misguided projects for periodicals in his head, is still lurking here . . . and the *Allgemeine Zeitung* is the constant target of his calumny and machination. When the first article of the *Affairs* appeared, he was disturbed about its elevated tone, which in itself pleased him well enough, but not in the *Allgemeine Zeitung*, and he committed the treachery of printing a mutilated, exaggerated and falsified translation of it in the *Tribune* with some introductory words, implying that this correspondence was directly influenced by the Austrian government. This maneuver was concerted with the local German Jacobins, who wished straightway so to compromise me, whom they had bruited abroad as the author of that article, that I should be forced to declare myself either for or against them; I had previously omitted to do the first out of conviction and the second out of discretion. I am not the man to submit to force, and their only effect will be that, out of disgust of Jacobin dishonesty, I shall write even more moderately than ever. What you write me about Boerne quite agrees with my opinion, but prudence does not allow me to utter it, for at this period of reaction it would be interpreted as a piece of cowardly insurance.

—To Baron Johann Friedrich von Cotta
Paris, January 20, 1832

Tribune: Organ of the republican party, edited by Armand Marrast. Heine first visited Boerne in Paris on September 26, 1831. They at once fell into differences of opinion on politics, which were at first taken lightly by Heine but very seriously by Boerne. From their first reunion in Paris onwards, Boerne gave voice to hostile expressions concerning Heine, of which the latter was promptly informed. In the spring of 1832, matters came to an open breach between them.

I happened to be in the Saint-Simonist hall when the royal procurator caused it to be closed, and promptly went to Donndorf who is reporting the matter in the *Allgemeine.*

—To Baron Johann Friedrich von Cotta
Paris, January 25, 1832

The republicanism of the *Tribune* people is annoying to me, and I can already see the time coming when they will assail me even more bitterly than others as a defender of the institution of kingship. But it serves the kings right; they would not listen to the liberals who combated only the nobility and the rule of the clergy, and now they have the bloodiest Jacobinism at their throats. In the end nothing will be left them but to wrap themselves in their purple robes and to go down at least with dignity. We moderates will go down with them and, in so doing, expiate the sin that in our opposition did not at times spring from the purest motives.

—To Johann Friedrich von Cotta
Paris, March 1, 1832

For some days, boundless confusion has reigned in Paris because of the cholera; almost all of my acquaintances from Germany and England have departed. I, too, would have gone, were it not that in the popular mood created by the cholera very important things may happen. If the cholera advances, mad things may happen here. The disaffection of the poor classes has no limits.

—To Johann Friedrich von Cotta
Paris, April 2, 1832

During the cholera epidemic in Paris, Heine selflessly nursed his ailing cousin Carl, the son of Salomon Heine.

Wishing to visit a close acquaintance one day, I arrived just as they were placing his corpse in the hearse. Then the sad fancy seized me to return the call which he had once paid me, so I took a coach and accompanied him to Père la Chaise. Having arrived in the neighborhood of the cemetery, my coachman stopped, and I, awaking from my reverie, could see literally nothing but sky and coffins. I was among several hundred vehicles bearing the dead, which formed a queue or train before the narrow gate, and as I could not escape, I was obliged to pass several hours among these gloomy surroundings. Out of ennui, I asked my coachman the name of my neighbor-corpse, and—woe the chance!—he named a young lady whose coach had, some months before, as I was going to a ball at Lointier, been crowded against mine and delayed just as it was today. There was only this difference, that then she often put out of the window her little head, decked with flowers, her lovely, lively face lit by the moon, and manifested the most charming vexation and impatience at the delay. Now she was quite still. . . .

One may learn at deathbeds how to die, and then await death with calmness, but to learn how to be buried in graves of quicklime, among cholera corpses, is beyond my power. I hastened to the highest hill of the cemetery, whence one may see the city spread out in all its beauty. The sun was setting; its last rays seemed to bid me a sad good-bye; twilight vapors covered sick Paris as with a light-white shroud, and I wept bitterly over the unhappy city, the city of freedom, of inspiration and of martyrdom, the savior-city which has already suffered so much for the temporal deliverance of humanity.

French Affairs, 6

Mirabeau is now regarded as peculiarly the representative of that first phase of the Revolution which began and ended with the National Assembly.

As such, he has become a popular hero. He is discussed daily; he is seen chiselled and painted everywhere; he is set forth in all French theaters in all his forms, poor and wild, loving and hating, laughing and gnashing his teeth—a reckless, bankrupt god, to whom heaven and earth belonged, and who was capable of gambling away his last fixed star and his last louis-d'or at faro; a Samson who tears down the pillars of the state to bury his yelping Philistines in the ruins; a Hercules who at the parting roads of life accommodates himself to both ladies, and who recreates and refreshes himself in the arms of Vice from the exertions of Virtue. . . .

And it is by the very same moral contradictions of his nature and life that Mirabeau was the representative of his age, which was likewise so reprobate and so sublime. . . .

But far more important than the oratorical power of the man was that which he said. This we can now judge most impartially, and see from it that Mirabeau most thoroughly understood his time; that he knew not only how to tear down but how to build up, and that he understood the latter better than the great masters who are today still busy at the work. In the writings of Mirabeau we find the chief ideas of constitutional monarchy such as France needed. . . . Mirabeau was the herald of that constitutional monarchy which, in my opinion, was the desire of his day, and which, more or less democratically formulated, is now needed by us in Germany.

It was this constitutional monarchy which did the greatest injury to the Count's reputation; for men of the Revolution, who did not understand him, saw it as desertion and thought he had sold the Revolution. In their abuse of him they rivalled the aristocrats, who hated him because they knew that Mirabeau,

by destroying their business of privileges, would save and re-
juvenate the kingdom at their expense. But just as the wretched
conduct of the privileged class repulsed him, so the coarseness
of the demagogues disgusted him all the more because they, in
the mad unrestrained manner which we know so well, already
preached the Republic.

—French Affairs, Appendix to 6

*This justification of Mirabeau is Heine's own defense against
the charges of the republicans, and again defines his political
viewpoint.*

I am in as great need of your and Frau von Varnhagen's sympathy now as ever I was at the beginning of my career, for I
stand as much alone in the world now as I did then. It is only
that I now have more enemies, which is always a comfort, to
be sure, but hardly a sufficient one. You can now write to me
even more frequently, if you like, without fear of compromising
interceptions. I am now on a peaceful footing with all existing
elements, and if I do not as yet disarm, it is only because of the
demagogues, against whom I had and still hold a difficult position. These people, enemies to all moderation, wanted by all
means to force me to abandon my tribunate when I would not
consent to share their madness. But I had no inclination to do
so. Now, thank heaven, the cholera has rid me of many a
troublesome fellow, that is, fear of the cholera. It was not out of
courage that I did not flee from Paris when the panic broke out;
to tell you the truth, I was too lazy. Boerne had wanted to go
away long ago, and it was unjust to ascribe his departure to fear.
However, I had not seen him for a fortnight before, for we were
on very bad terms. He had let loose upon me certain Jacobin
intrigues which I did not like at all. I think he's crazy. That
my articles in the *Allgemeine Zeitung* please you is a comfort
to me; I am not sure of their value. . . . I am now much occupied
with the history of the French Revolution and with Saint-
Simonism. I shall write books about both, but I must still study
a great deal. Still, during the last year the spectacle of party

activity and the manfestations of Saint-Simonism have taught me much, for example, the *Moniteur* of 1793 and the Bible. All I need at present is health and a living free from care. I have had a number of opportunities to obtain the latter, but always under conditions which were repugnant to me, not as a patriot but as a decent man. What you write me with reference to Saint-Simonism is quite in accord with my own view. Michel Chevalier is my dear friend, one of the noblest men I know. That the Saint-Simonists have withdrawn is perhaps advantageous to the doctrine itself; it will now come into cleverer hands. In particular the political portion, the teaching on property, will be worked out better. As concerns myself, I am really interested only in the religious ideas, which only need to be uttered and they will sooner or later come to life. Germany will fight most vigorously for her spiritualism; "but the future is ours."

—To Varnhagen von Ense
Paris, mid-May, 1832

Boerne, the former police registrar of Frankfort-on-the-Main, is now rushing into such a sans-culottism of thought and expression as has never yet been experienced in Germany. . . .

In his conversations, Boerne's mounting political madness was less striking, for it was related to the passions which raged in his immediate environment, which were always ready to strike and, in fact, not seldom did strike. When I visited Boerne for the second time in the Rue de Provence, where he is permanently quartered, I found in his salon such a menagerie of people as can scarcely be found in the zoo. In the background there cowered a number of German polar-bears, who smoked tobacco, kept almost complete silence, and only occasionally flung out certain native expletives in the deepest *basso profundo*. . . . It is hard to conceive how this man, otherwise so sensible, can let himself be talked down by the crudest babbling and misguided into the most desperate expectations! . . .

That Paris propaganda consisted rather of crude hands than of fine heads; those were gatherings of laborers of German speech. . . . Here, by means of passionate speeches in the temper of the Rhenish-Bavarian *Tribune,* many natures were made fanatic. And since republicanism is so simple a thing, easier to understand, for example, than constitutional monarchy, which presupposes much knowledge, it did not take long before thousands of German workingmen turned republican and preached the new faith. . . . Perhaps Boerne's spoken word was much more powerful than Boerne's written speeches. . . . He spoke very well, a binding, convincing, popular, bare, artless speech, quite in the manner of the Sermon on the Mount. I have heard him speak, indeed, only a single time; it was the first and last time I attended the meeting.

But that one time was sufficient. On this occasion, dear reader, I would fain make a confession that you do not expect. Perhaps you think that the highest ambition of my life has always been to become a great poet, to be crowned on the Capitol as Messer Francesco Petrarca once was; nay, it was rather the great popular speakers that I always envied. For my life I would gladly have delivered an eloquent address in public places, before a varied gathering, an oration which would stir up or assuage passions and always produce an instantaneous effect. Yes, between ourselves I will confess that in that stage of youthful inexperience when the most comical desires assail us, I often imagined myself in such a role. I wish by all means to be a great speaker, and like Demosthenes I sometimes declaimed by the lonely seashore when wind and waves roared; thus lungs are exercised and accustomed to speak in the midst of the great tumult of a popular gathering. . . . In short, I left nothing undone, so that, if a great revolution would one day be staged among us, I should be able to step forth as a German popular speaker. But, ah, even at the first trial I observed that in such a tragedy I could never more play my favorite role. Nor, if they were yet alive, could Demosthenes or Cicero or Mirabeau step forward as speakers in a German revolution, for at German revolutions there is smoking. Think of my horror when I attended the above-mentioned meeting in Paris. I found all the saviors of their country with pipes in their mouths, and the entire hall was so filled with bad fumes that it caught me square in the chest, and it would have been plainly impossible for me to utter a word.

I cannot endure tobacco fumes, and I observed that the role of a great orator in a German revolution, after the manner of Boerne and Company, was not suited to me. I observed in general that the career of a German tribune was not strewn with roses, and least of all with fragrant roses. . . .

Was it virtue or madness that brought Ludwig Boerne to snuff up that vile reek with ecstasy and to revel so delightedly in plebeian filth? Who can rede us the riddle of this man, who was brought up in delicate silks and later proclaimed his inward distinction by proud bearing, and then towards the end of his days suddenly cracked into vulgar accents and the banal manners of a demagogue of the lowest stripe? Was he pricked by his country's distress to so horrifying a pitch of fury, or was he seized by the dread anguish of a life lost? Yes, perhaps that was it; he saw that during his whole life, with all his intellect and all his moderation, he had achieved nothing either for himself or for others; and so he veiled his head, or, to use the language of the people, he pulled his cap over his ears, and refusing to see or hear anything further, flung himself into the howling abyss. That is always the one recourse left to us when we have reached that hopeless stretch where all flowers are faded, where the body is weary and the spirit vexed. I would not engage that under similar circumstances I should one day not do the same. Who knows—perhaps at the end of my days I shall overcome my repugnance to tobacco fumes and learn to smoke and deliver the most unwashed harangues to the most unwashed audience.

—Ludwig Boerne, 3

Rhenish-Bavarian Tribune: Deutsche Tribuene, *published by Dr. Georg August Wirth.*

I am vexed every time I enter the Bourse, the beautiful edifice of marble, built in the noblest Greek style and consecrated to the most contemptible business—to petty trading in government bonds. It is the most beautiful building in Paris. Napoleon erected it, and in the same style and proportions he also built a temple to Glory. Unfortunately, the temple to Glory was never finished; the Bourbons changed it into a church and dedicated it to the repentant Magdalen. But the Bourse is perfect in its completed splendor, and to its influence we may ascribe the fact that its nobler rival, the Temple of Fame, is still unfinished and still remains, as if in disgraceful derision, dedicated to the repentant Magdalen. Here, in the vast space of the high-arched hall, here is where the hucksters in government bonds, with all their repulsive faces and disagreeable screams, heave and hum like a restless sea of self-centered greed; and where, amid wild billows of human beings, the great bankers dart up, snapping and devouring like sharks—one monster preying on another; and where, in the gallery, even speculating ladies may be seen, like birds of prey watching on a cliff. Yet it is here that those interests are at home which in this our time decide peace and war.

Therefore the Bourse is of such importance for us publicists. Yet it is not easy to grasp accurately the nature of those interests according to every influential event, or to appreciate the results justly. The rates of state paper and of discount is of course a political thermometer, but one would be deceived if he believed that this thermometer indicated the highest degree of any of the great questions which now agitate humanity. The rise or fall of funds does not indicate the rise or fall of the liberal or servile parties, but the greater or lesser hopes entertained for the pacification of Europe, for the maintenance of affairs as they are, or rather for the maintenance of those conditions on which the payment of the interest on the public debt depends.

From this limited point of view, the speculators on the Bourse are, as regards anything which may happen, greatly to be admired. Undisturbed by any intellectual or sentimental feeling, all their faculties are directed to the practical, and it is with almost animal instincts that they, like weather-frogs, divine whether any event which is apparently a promise of peace may not be a cause of future storms, or whether a great disaster may not in the end confirm general tranquillity. When Warsaw fell, no one asked what evil would result from it to humanity, but "Will the victory of the knout discourage the stirrers-up of disorder—that is, the friends of freedom?" The affirmative to this question caused a rise in securities. . . .

Neither existence nor non-existence, but peace or disturbance is the great question of the Bourse. The rate of discount regulates itself accordingly. In restless times money is uneasy; it retreats into the coffers of the rich as into a citadel, remains retired, and the rate of discount rises. In peaceful times money becomes free from care and confiding; offers itself cheaply, shows itself publicly, and is very affable—discount is low. By which we see that an old *louis d'or* has more intelligence than any man, and can best tell of approaching war or peace. It may be that from such close intercourse with money all the gamblers on the Bourse have gained a kind of political instinct, and that while of late the most profound thinkers only expected a war, they remained quiet of soul and believed in the maintenance of peace. If you asked of any of them his reasons for such security, then, like Sir John Falstaff, he would give none on compulsion, but always declared, "That is my idea."

—French Affairs, 8

The coldest indifference was manifested at the burial of Périer, as had been the case at his death. It was a spectacle, like any other; the weather was fine, and hundreds of thousands of people were afoot to see the funeral as it slowly passed along the Boulevard to Père-la-Chaise. Smiles were on many faces; on others, the dullest, every-day expression; on most, simply ennui. Of course, there were innumerable troops, though they hardly suited the hero of the pacific system of disarmament. . . . The multitude regarded it all with strange apathy, showing neither hate nor love. It was the enemy of all enthusiasm who was buried, and the convoy was Indifference. . . .

My neighbors who saw the procession spoke of the obsequies of Benjamin Constant. As I have been in Paris but a year, I only know the grief which the people felt on that day from descriptions. Yet I can imagine what such popular suffering must be, since I saw not long afterwards the burial of the former Bishop of Blois, that is, the Grégoire of the Convention. There were, indeed, no grand officials, no infantry or cavalry, no empty mourning-coaches full of court-lackeys, no cannon, no ambassadors with gay liveries, no official pomp. But the people wept. Signs of sorrow were on every face, and though it rained like bucketfuls from heavens, all heads were uncovered, and the crowd harnessed itself before the hearse, and drew it to Mont Parnasse. Grégoire, a true priest, fought during his whole life for freedom and equality of men of every color and of every faith; he was always hated and persecuted by the enemies of the people, and the people loved him and wept when he died.

—French Affairs, 8

Casimir-Pierre Périer, born 1777, died of the cholera in 1832. As French premier, he defended the policy of the juste milieu with great energy, suppressed internal insurrection, and pursued a peaceful foreign policy. Benjamin Constant (1767-1830): Liberal politician, opponent of Napoleon and the Bourbons. Henri Grégoire (1750-1831) endeavored to obtain equal rights for the Jews of France. Heine could not know that Simon van Geldern, "the Oriental," (his great-uncle) had supplied Grégoire with helps for his studies of Jews and Judaism.

When I went yesterday to the Bourse to throw my letter into the post-box, the whole race of speculators was standing between the columns and before the broad stairway. And, as the news had just been received that the defeat of the patriots was certain, the sweetest contentment was seen in every face—one might say that the whole Bourse smiled. Amid the roar of cannon the funds shot up ten per cent. That is to say, they fired at five o'clock—at six the attempted Revolution had been quelled. Then the newspapers could communicate as much information as they pleased. The *Constitutionnel* and the *Débats* seem to a certain degree to have correctly understood or hit upon what has happened; but the color and measurements are incorrect. I have just come from the theater of the strife of yesterday, where I convinced myself how difficult it would be to get at the whole real truth. This theater is one of the greatest and most densely inhabited streets of Paris, that is, the Rue Saint-Martin, which, beginning at the gate of that name on the Boulevard, ends on the Seine at the Bridge Notre Dame. At both ends of the street I heard the number of the patriots—or, as they are called today, the rebels—who fought there estimated at from five hundred to a thousand; but in the middle of the street the sum became less, and in the very center it was reduced to fifty. "What is truth?" said Pontius Pilate.

—French Affairs: Daily Bulletins
Paris, June 7, 1832

In the course of General Lamarque's funeral, a republican uprising broke out in Paris on June 5. There is a detailed description of it in Victor Hugo's Les Misérables.

I journeyed over the greater portion of the northern French coast while the news of the death of young Napoleon was being disseminated there. I found, wherever I went, a marvellous grief among the people. . . .

In a certain respect Napoleon was a Saint-Simonist emperor. . . . I found most frequently in peasants' homes the picture of the Emperor visiting the hospital at Jaffa or lying on his deathbed at St. Helena. Both of these bear a striking likeness to the pictures of that Catholic religion which is now dead in France. In one of these, Napoleon resembles a Savior who seems to cure the afflicted with the pest by a touch; in the other, he is himself dying the death of expiation.

We who have adopted a different symbolism see in the martyrdom of Napoleon at St. Helena no expiation in the sense here indicated, for the Emperor there did penance for his most fatal error, for his faithlessness to his mother, the Revolution.

—French Affairs: Daily Bulletins
From Normandy

The Duke of Reichstadt died on July 22, 1832. Immediately after his birth, in 1811, he had been named King of Rome by his father, Napoleon I.

I write these lines in the former residence of the Duke of Normandy, in the ancient town where there yet remain so many monuments which remind us of the history of the race once so renowned for its heroic wanderings and love of knightly adventure, and now so notorious for its love of litigation and craftiness in trade. In yon castle once dwelt Robert the Devil, whom Meyerbeer has set to music; on that market-place the Maid of Orleans was burnt—that great-hearted girl of whom Schiller and Voltaire have sung; in that cathedral lies the heart of Richard, the brave king who was called *Coeur de Lion* for his lion heart; from this soil sprang the conquerors of Hastings, the sons of Tancred, and so many other flowers of Norman chivalry; but it all concerns us but little now, when we are more busied with the question, "Has the peaceful system of Louis Philippe taken root in the warlike soil of Normandy? Is the new citizen-kingdom well or ill couched in the old heroic cradle of the English and Italian aristocracy, in the land of the Normans? This I can now briefly answer. The great landed proprietors, chiefly noble, are Carlists; the well-to-do workers and farmers are Philippistes; while the lower classes despise and hate the Bourbons, loving, to a lesser extent, the gigantic memories of the Republic, but for the greater part, the brilliant heroism of the Empire.

—French Affairs: Daily Bulletins
Rouen, September 17, 1832

I am living through many great things in Paris; I am watching the history of the world with my own eyes. I consort *amicalement* with its greatest heroes, and some day, if I am given life, I shall be a great historian. I have had little fortune lately in the writing of *belles lettres*. The whirlpool in which I am swimming is too great for me to be able to be free to work in poetry. I have missed fire with a novel; but I shall probably publish some fragments in a collection which I am going to prepare this winter, and in

which I shall also include the *Rabbi*. I have written few poems.
. . . I am more industrious than I was, for the simple reason that
I need six times as much money in Paris as in Germany.

—To Friedrich Merckel
Dieppe, August 24, 1832

If any one asks you how I am, tell him "like a fish in water,"
or rather, tell people that when one fish in the sea asks another
how he is, he receives the reply: "I am like Heine in Paris." . . .
I spent two months by the sea, as I do every year, and for the first
time have been bored with it. I now go to the opera diligently,
I am a partisan of Louis Philippe; my cheeks are ruddy; two
fingers of my left hand are crippled; I wear colored coats and gay
waistcoats.

—To Ferdinand Hiller
Paris, October 24, 1832

Ferdinand Hiller (1811-1885) was a composer.

I have just received the preface, in which I appear before the
eyes of all Germany as a wretched flatterer of the King of Prussia. . . . I am distraught with vexation. . . . Precisely because the
cause of liberalism is faring so ill, everything must be done. I
know that I shall be barring myself from Germany forever if the
preface appears; but appear it must, exactly as in the manuscript.

*The preface to French Affairs was mutilated by the censorship.
Heine published it as a separate brochure, and thus brought
about an irremediable break with the Prussian government.*

When we shall have brought it so far that the great mass of
the people really understand the present, they will no longer
allow themselves to be goaded by the hireling writers of the aristocracy to hatred and war; the great confederation of races, the
Holy Alliance of nations, will be formed; we shall not need, out
of mutual mistrust, to feed standing armies of many hundred
thousand murderers; we will use their swords and horses for

ploughs, and so attain to peace, prosperity and freedom. My life has been consecrated to this active duty—it is my service. . . .

I cannot pass by these resolutions of the Diet without comment. I shall not try to refute their official defender, much less, as has been often done, seek to demonstrate their illegality. As I very well know who the persons were who prepared the document on which those resolutions were based, I do not doubt that it—that is to say, the Confederation Act of Vienna—contains the most legal rights to any despotic caprice. . . .

In virtue of my academic authority as Doctor of Both Laws, I solemnly declare that such a document, prepared by faithless agents, is null and void; in virtue of my duty as a citizen, I protest against all the inferences which the resolutions of the Diet of June 28th deduced from this worthless paper; in virtue of my power as popular publicist or speaker, I lodge my complaint against those who prepared it, and accuse them of abusing the confidence of the people, of lèse-nationality and of high treason to the German people.

—Preface to French Affairs
Paris, October 18, 1832

The decrees of the Federal Diet of June 28, 1832, subjected the Diets of the separate German constitutional states to the supervision of the general Diet. This was tantamount to a fundamental negation of the idea of constitutional monarchy, which was admitted at the Vienna Congress of 1815. Shortly thereafter, ordinances concerning press, political associations, popular gatherings, universities, and the like, were made considerably more rigorous. Heine attacks not only these ordinances but their alleged basis in law, the proceedings at Vienna.

I speak of His Majesty Friedrich Wilhelm, third of the name, King of Prussia, ruler of the Rhine, to whom I was transferred as subject in the year of grace 1815, with several million other Rhinelanders. As may be well supposed, my consent to this was not asked. I was exchanged, I believe, against a poor East Frisian whom I had never seen, who had never initiated me into his former feelings of devotion to the royal Prussian government, and who perhaps was made so unhappy by the exchange that he now lies buried as a Hanoverian. I, however, have surely not been made happy by that Prussian press-ganging, and all that I have gained by it is the right most humbly to remind that monarch that he should, according to his promise, graciously bestow on us a representative constitution.

—From the records of the censorship officials at Hamburg, where a number of pages of Heine's manuscript of his Preface are preserved

I am still unable to write to you. As soon as I take up my pen to say a word to you, my head turns dizzy and my heart is torn. And I am otherwise so calm, self-control itself.

But things are at present happening in my life which would move a stone. This morning I received the news of the death of my uncle van Geldern at Duesseldorf, where he died at a time when I must feel this misfortune more profoundly than at any other. Ah, my dear Varnhagen, I feel now the meaning of the Roman saying: "Life is warfare." So I stand in the breach and see my friends falling round about me. Our good friend has fought doughtily, and has well earned her laurels.

—To Varnhagen von Ense
Paris, March 28, 1833

Rahel Varnhagen died March 7, 1833, shortly after the death of her brother and sister-in-law, Ludwig and Friederike Robert.

You have no idea what a storm is raging about me at present. I have the *juste milieu*, the hypocritical Catholic Carlist party, and Prussian spies about my ears. My *French Affairs* has appeared in French, together with my preface complete and unabridged. The preface has also been published by Heideloff in German, and is probably also in Leipzig by this time, where you will see it. I would send it to you if I were not afraid that you might be compromised. Take care. There is no safety here. Several Germans were arrested here last Sunday, and I am afraid that

I may be arrested at any moment. Perhaps my next letter will be dated from London. I am impressing all this on you to urge you to be careful and moderate. Keep as calm as is possible at this moment. . . . Dissemble. Do not be afraid of being misjudged: neither have I ever feared this. The publication of the Preface at this moment of general anxiety will surely teach the public to trust me in the future even if my piping sounds all too mild. At the proper time I shall blow a mighty trumpet blast, and am at this moment occupied in composing certain vigorous selections for the trumpet. . . .

Rest assured that I understand you, and do therefore prize and honor you. You stand higher than all others, who only understand the Revolution superficially and do not grasp the profound questions raised by it. These questions are concerned neither with forms nor persons; neither with the introduction of a republic nor the limitation of a monarchy; but with the material well-being of the people. The spiritual religion which has prevailed hitherto was wholesome and necessary as long as the greater part of men and women lived in wretchedness and had to find comfort in another worldly religion. But since it has become possible through the advance of industry and economics to extricate men from their material wretchedness and give them blessedness on earth, since then—you understand me. And the people will understand us when we tell them that now they shall eat beef every day instead of potatoes, and shall work less and dance more. Rely upon it, men are not donkeys.

I write these lines in the bed of my pretty friend who will not let me go this night for fear I should be arrested.

—To Heinrich Laube
Paris, July 10, 1833

Heinrich Laube (1806-1884) was an outstanding author of the "Young Germany" literary movement which was inspired by Boerne and Heine, but directly also by Saint-Simon and Hegel; in its struggle for liberal ideas it attached itself more closely to the movement for national unity than was agreeable to Heine. Of all the leaders of the "Young Germany" movement, Laube was the only one who maintained personal and literary relationships with Heine; they were close friends until differences of opinion concerning the Revolution of 1848 caused their alienation. Subsequently Laube became an epoch-making stage director.

The beginning of this letter, which ends with acquiescence to Saint-Simonism, is characteristic of Heine's political tactics, which he retained unaltered through all his periods of struggle. Just as Heine believed he could win the confidence of the government by occasional "moderation" and so relegate earlier radical attacks to oblivion, he also believed he could overcome the displeasure of democrats at such "moderation" by new and sharp attacks upon the government. A well considered strategy underlay this tactic of Heine's, corresponding to his unique position as "democratic royalist." Heine, who had studied and approved Lafayette's position during the first French Revolution, believed, like Lafayette, that, in the vicissitudes of war, he could, by varying his own attitude, end the ups and downs of the autocratic and democratic tendencies and thereby attain a compromise in consonance with his basic political ideas. He was confident that he could always grasp the moment precisely suitable for such a procedure. But the weakness of his tactics was that he underestimated the memory of those he irritated; these would never forgive him, even if Heine believed that he had done everything possible to conciliate them. This error regarding the consequences of his political statements frequently misguided Heine to steps towards right or left which imperilled his political reputation.

The German Spirit: Warning

Heine's intention to write books on the history of the French Revolution and on Saint-Simonism (see p. 297 f.) was never carried out. But he used the studies he had undertaken to this end to achieve a modern and European viewpoint in his investigations of the history of the German intellect. Heine's books, The Romantic School and Religion and Philosophy in Germany, both originally written for French readers and first published in French translation, received their peculiar mould by reason of their author's interest in the French Revolution and in Saint-Simonism.

In writing these books Heine had several aims. In the first place, after the numerous occasional, fragmentary, or aphoristic statements in his earlier writings, he wished to give a precise and coherent account of his personal attitude to the most important tendencies and manifestations of German spiritual life. He doubtless used manuscripts which he had brought to Paris from Germany in which he had worked out such an account as preparation for the professorship at Munich which he had hoped for. But the point of view from which the material in the published books is considered and judged is determined neither by the discussions conducted upon these themes in Germany, nor by the value judgments of German liberalism. Here Heine speaks not as a German historian or statesman for whom the fate of his own people stands at the center of his theoretical and practical interests, but rather as a European. He acknowledges and emphasizes his German nationality, to be sure, but the fate of European civilization is of greater moment to him than the national life and aspirations of Germany. Merits and weaknesses of German mind and character are therefore judged from the point of view whether and to what degree they may be useful or harmful to the progress of European civilization. Within this framework Heine took occasion to give more or less forthright expression to his artistic judgments and to his sympathies or antipathies to individual personalities.

Secondly, Heine intended these books as a warning to Europe, and in particular to France, against the danger that would come from Germany, and to offer those menaced a defense against these dangers by providing orientation in historical premises.

Heine's third objective was an urgent warning directed to French poets, artists and writers. Heine had come to Paris just one year after the great bataille romantique, which ended with the victory of Romanticism, had been fought. Heine thought this was mistaken. In his view the French were and had always been

born classicists and rationalists. His account of German Romanticism and related efforts were intended to retard the further
advance of the romantic spirit in France.

The future of European civilization could be secured, in
Heine's view, only by the realization of the ideas of the French
Revolution and the repulse of all attacks directed against these
ideas. At that time, Heine was convinced that Saint-Simonism
constituted the continuation and formulation of these ideas. For
the ideal of harmonious reconciliation between sensualism and
spiritualism, historical reality must be used as a gauge, and this
would reveal the champions of spiritualism as defenders of political and social reaction.

In elaborating this point of view, Heine's historical intuition
sometimes failed him, and he is not everywhere supported by
adequate factual knowledge. In view of the general level of historical research in his day, errors were inevitable. Above all, paral-
lels which Heine draws between Luther's reformation, Kant's
position, and the French Revolution, are today recognized as
untenable. But many details in Heine's account show how his
study of the French Revolution sharpened his historical vision
when he came to examine German intellectual history on the
basis of this knowledge.

Heine's two books proclaim their European character also by
the fact that they mark a break with the basic ideas of the German concept of history prevailing at the time.

At that time in Germany, Hegel and his disciples, as well as the
"historical school," conceived of literature, art, law and the form
of the state as manifestations of a hypothetical "folk-spirit,"
which is effective in all individuals who belong to one and the
same people from the beginning of history. At the same time,
reactionaries and revolutionaries in France regarded cultural
achievement in all departments as an expression of "society,"
which is not a hypothetical, mythical principle but a tangible
reality to which all classes and professions, the courtesan as well
as the mathematical philosopher, the aristocracy as well as the
proletariat, belong—the solitary poet as well as the stock broker,
the priest as well as the atheist. Along with Balzac, Heine is the

first great European writer who sought to give form to these connections; if almost all other great writers of contemporary France sensed them or recognized them, or dealt with individual aspects of them, none was so thoroughly imbued by them in his life and work as were Balzac and Heine. Even Heine's French Affairs shows the beginning of this new sociological view of history, which is further developed in the Romantic School, and then configured in Heine's last poems.

Heine attained no definitive standpoint with these two books. The declaration of war against Romanticism was to be followed several years later by Atta Troll, the "last free forest-song of Romanticism"; the triumph over the supposed victory of sensualist pantheism over the biblical concept of God was to be followed by an even more basic conversion, accompanied by a formal recantation of views which Heine had expressed in the other books (see pp. 428-30).

Heine always felt, and at times was quite clear about it, that predilection for Romanticism was deeply rooted in his personality. His nature was inclined to fantasy, to losing himself in dreams, which he regarded as a kind of revelation of a higher reality, as means of enlarging the knowledge possible in a waking state. His spirit was always ready to associate impressions of reality with mythological reminiscences of all kinds. He loved historical retrospect and contemplation. But as poet, thinker and politician, he remained the fighter for freedom, equal rights and progress. In this respect he diverged sharply from the literary movement of German Romanticism, which, after a brief youthful efflorescence of ideas of world citizenship and freedom, became nationalistic and reactionary. Disappointment at this turn often drove Heine to radical opposition against all Romanticism. But in his innermost feelings he clung to the conviction that one could love revery, the past, contemplation, beauty and chivalry without forfeiting the present and future, progress and freedom.

Heine's experience with German Romanticism hampered his understanding of French Romanticism. French Romanticism followed a path opposite to German. From being royalists and conservatives, the French romanticists soon became liberals, demo-

crats, republicans and socialists. Sympathy with poverty and
wretchedness, defense of persons defamed and ejected from society, is common to all French romanticists. This would have
assured them Heine's sympathy, as would their consciousness
that the Revolution begun in 1789 would proceed further, their
restlessness in anticipation of great social overturns, their zeal for
new systems of social organization. But the effect of certain
alienating elements was stronger. Heine felt, and not unjustly,
that the formal breach of the romanticists with the linguistic tradition of the classicists was not very thoroughgoing. He reproached them with clinging to the alexandrines which he de-
despised. He was further repelled by the fact that French
romantic poetry minimized pagan mythology or rejected it entirely. He was most alienated by the fact that the French romanticists were religious and, along with their concern with freedom,
preached a strict morality, even those who fought against the antiquated conventions of sexual morality. Although French Romanticism is by no means wanting in satire, irony or grotesque
fashioning, and Victor Hugo loves stark transitions from the
sublime to the ridiculous, their poetic pronouncements show a
dominating solemnity, a pathetic rhetoric, which provoked
Heine's mockery. His own mingling of pathos and irony was basically different from the transformations and contrasts of mood
which French Romanticism felt as a breach with the classical
tradition. Hence, of the French poets of his day, Heine esteemed
most highly Alfred de Vigny and Alfred de Musset, who had a
unique position. On the other hand, with all their esteem of
Heine, the French romanticists recognized that the contradictions of his nature were incomprehensible, if not provocative, to
them.

Hence, Heine's warning of German Romanticism had no success with the French writers of his period.

His political warnings were regarded in the French Chamber
of Deputies, but only later, shortly before his death. They were
completely understood only in the age of the two world wars.

Though in France only Roman Catholicism is understood by

the word Christianity, I must specially emphasize that I only speak of the former. I speak of that religion in whose first dogmas there is the damnation of all flesh, and which not only allows the spirit power over the flesh, but will also kill the flesh to glorify the spirit. I speak of that religion by whose unnatural demands sin and hypocrisy really came into the world, in that by the condemnation of the flesh the most innocent sensual pleasures became sins and because the impossibility of becoming altogether spiritual naturally created hypocrisy. I speak of that religion which, by teaching the doctrine of the casting away of all earthly goods, and of abject dog-like humility and angelic patience, became the most approved support of despotism. Men have found out the real life and meaning of this religion, and do not now content themselves with promises of supping in Paradise; they know that matter also has its merits, and is not all of the devil, and they now defend the delights of this world, this beautiful garden of God, our inalienable inheritance. And therefore, because we have grasped so entirely all the consequences of that absolute spiritualism, we may believe that the Christian Catholic view of the world has reached its end. . . .

Yet we do in no wise deny the good results which this Christian Catholic view of the world established in Europe. It was necessary as a wholesome reaction against the cruelly colossal materialism which had developed in the Roman realm and threatened to destroy all spiritual human power. . . . The flesh had become so arrogant in this Roman world that it required Christian discipline to chasten it.

—The Romantic School, 1

Heine's attempt to except Protestantism from his polemic against spiritualism rests upon faulty premises. In this respect Lutheran dogmatism differs in no way from the Catholic. In deference to authority, Luther went much further than Catholicism and Calvinism.

It was not by division into two realms that Rome perished. On the Bosphorus, as by the Tiber, Rome was devoured by the same

Jewish spiritualism, and here, as there, Roman history was that of a long death agony which lasted for centuries. Did murdered Judaea, in leaving to Rome its spiritualism, wish to revenge itself on the victorious foe, as did the dying centaur who craftily left to the son of Jupiter the deadly garment steeped in his own blood? Truly Rome, the Hercules among races, was so thoroughly devoured by Jewish poison that helm and harness fell from its withered limbs, and its imperial war-voice died away into the wailing cadences of monkish prayer and the soft trilling of castrated boys.

But what weakens old age strengthens youth. That spiritualism had a wholesome effect on the too sound and strong races of the North. The too full-blooded barbarous bodies were spiritualized by Christianity, and European civilization began. That is the praiseworthy and sacred aspect of Christianity.

—The Romantic School, 1

His turn to Saint-Simonism separated Heine from Judaism further than did his baptism. At this period of his life he emerges publicly as a radical opponent of Jewish tradition and view of life. In part this opposition is caused by factual errors concerning the nature and history of Judaism, but in greater part by tactical considerations. In his depreciatory judgments of Judaism, Heine sees a means of combating Christianity even more effectively than he could by an exclusive polemic against Christianity. Inasmuch as he combats Jewish and Christian religion alike as outgrowths of spiritualism, he believes that he can discredit Christianity by classing it with Judaism. If reducing Christianity to the single basis of ascetic denial of life is questionable, the presentation of Judaism as an ascetic religion is wholly untenable. To be sure, ancient Judaism emphasized its sharp opposition to the fertility cults of the neighboring Semitic religions with their ritual prostitution and unbounded sexuality, yet it not only countenanced lawful sexual relations but even prescribed them. Celibacy was condemned and barrenness stigmatized. Neither biblical nor post-biblical Judaism preached denial of life. On the contrary, the daily ritual ordained thanksgiving to God for enjoy-

ment of earthly life. Asceticism played a far slighter role in Judaism than in Christianity and most other religions. Unlike Heine, most other opponents of Judaism have attacked it rather for excessive "earthiness." Moreover, Heine himself, in the two books which document his campaign against spiritualism, was not consistent in his representation of Judaism as a religion of denial of life (see p. 377). Nor was Heine able to make his thesis harmonize with the facts in his efforts to exempt Protestantism from the charge of exaggerated spiritualism and to strike at the Catholic Church alone.

Leo X, that splendid Medici, was as zealous a Protestant as Luther, and just as there was a Latin prose protest in Wittenberg, so they protested poetically in Rome in stone, color and otta-verime. And do not the mighty marble images of Michelangelo, the laughing nymphs of Giulio Romano, and the joyous intoxication of life in the verses of Master Ludovico Ariosto form a protesting opposition to the old, gloomy, worn-out Catholicism? The painters of Italy waged a polemic against priestdom which was perhaps more practical than that of the Saxon theologian. The blooming, rosy flesh in the pictures of Titian is all Protestantism. The limbs of his Venus are more thorough theses than those which the German monk pasted on the church door of Wittenberg. It was as if men felt suddenly freed from the force and pressure of a thousand years; most of all, the artists again breathed freely as the nightmare of Christianity seemed to spin whirling from their breasts.

—The Romantic School, 1

Luther had opposed the Roman Church not because it was too spiritual but because it had become too worldly for him. Heine also fails to notice that Italian art and poetry of the century preceding the Reformation was even gayer and more sensual than that of the sixteenth century.

But what was the Romantic School in Germany?
It was nothing else than the reawakening of the poetry of the

middle ages. . . . This poetry proceeded out of Christianity, it was a passion flower sprung of the blood of Christ.

—The Romantic School, 1

I have classed freedom of thought and Protestantism together, but I hope that, though I belong in Germany to the Protestant Church, I shall not be accused of partisan feeling for it. I have truly classed freedom of thought and Protestantism together without partisan feeling, and indeed there is a friendly relation between them in Germany. In any case, they are closely connected; in fact, like mother and daughter. And if we can reproach the Protestant Church with many fearful instances of narrow-mindedness, it must be admitted, to its immortal credit, that it permits free inquiry into Christianity, and has freed minds from the yoke of authority, so that bold research could strike roots, especially in Germany, and learning and science develop independently. German philosophy, though it now claims equality with the Protestant Church, and will even take precedence over it, is always its daughter.

—The Romantic School, 1

German Protestantism certainly did not abolish authority, but replaced the authority of the Pope by another authority which it designated "the word of the Bible." For two centuries after the advent of Luther, German Protestantism hampered free research in religion and the sciences, whereas in Catholic countries like Italy and France research was able to develop. Luther invoked the exclusive authority of the Bible, while he rejected rational interpretations of its text. Steeped in medieval psychology of language, he believed that the word penetrated human consciousness like an act of grace. Luther thought little of human understanding and reviled it in the coarsest terms. German philosophy is the daughter, not of Protestant theology, but of French and English philosophy. Only the gradual penetration of western European enlightenment shook the intolerant rule of Lutheran theology. On the other hand, it is true that from about 1750 onwards many German Protestant theologians, always indeed a minority, put themselves at the service of enlightenment, and that the majority of the great German philosophers of the late eighteenth and early nineteenth centuries originally studied theology or were the sons of evangelical pastors. Shortly after Heine published the above conclusions regarding the friendship between freedom of thought and Protestantism, Hengstenberg, the leader of Protestant orthodoxy, protested very vehemently against Heine's activity. Hengstenberg's charges contributed more to the prohibition of Heine's writings by the German Diet than did Menzel's polemic which Heine branded as a denunciation.

And here I cannot refrain from correcting a remark with which the editor of *Europe Littéraire* accompanied these pages. He wrote that "to Catholic France, German literature must be presented from a Protestant point of view." I objected in vain that there was no Catholic France; that I did not write for a Catholic France; it was quite sufficient for me to mention that I myself belonged to the Protestant Church in Germany. This mention, while it only expressed the fact that I have the pleasure of being paraded in a Lutheran Church register as an evangelical Christian, still left me free to express any opinion in scholarly works, even if it contradicted the Protestant dogma—whereas the editor's assertion that I wrote my essays from a Protestant point of view implies that I am fettered by dogma. All in vain. The editor of *Europe* could not grasp subtle Teutonic distinctions, and they went unnoticed. I mention this, partly lest I should be accused of inconsistency, partly, too, lest I incur the ridiculous suspicion of attaching any value to clerical-religious distinctions.

Since the French do not understand the language of our schools, I have used, in referring to the existence of God, words with which the French have been familiarized by the apostolic zeal of the Saint-Simonists, and as these phrases set forth by meaning quite nakedly and distinctly, I have preserved them in the German version. Aristocrats and priests, who have of late dreaded the power of my word more than ever and have on that account sought to defame me, may distort and falsify those expressions, so as to make me appear guilty of materialism, or even of atheism; they may make me out a Jew or a Saint-Simonist, they may accuse me before their mob of all conceivable heresies, but no cowardly prudence shall ever seduce me into disguising my views of divine things with the ordinary ambiguous phrases. And my friends, too, may blame me because I do not more ingeniously disguise my thoughts, that I recklessly unveil the most delicate subjects, that I thereby irritate— But neither the ill-will of my foes nor the petty cunning of my friends shall ever restrain me from expressing myself straightforwardly as to that weightiest question of mankind, the essence of God.

I do not belong to the materialists, who make the spirit body; rather I give bodies back their spirit. I spiritualize them again—I sanctify them.

I do not belong to the atheists who deny. I affirm.

The indifferentists and so-called clever folk, who will not express themselves plainly as to God, are really the ones who deny Him. Such tacit denial is now actually becoming a social offense, since through it false conceptions are countenanced which have hitherto always served despotism as a support.

The beginning and end of all things is in God.

—Preface to the First Edition of the Romantic School

This was published in Paris, in 1833, under the title Romantic School: On the History of Modern Belles-Lettres in Germany.

When Heine wrote the two books, the Romantic School *and* History of Religion and Philosophy in Germany, *he was convinced that Catholicism was completely dead. Protestantism he conceived as a step in the direction of the Revolution, as a preliminary to the philosophy of German idealism, in which he saw a phenomenon parallel to the French Revolution of 1789. Martin Luther was celebrated by Heine as an early champion of this revolutionary effort for liberation from the pressure of the Catholic view, as a pioneer of pantheism.*

As was very soon to become apparent, Catholicism lost its power neither in the nineteenth nor in the twentieth century. On the contrary, its political influence, its social activity and its claim to control cultural life have ever grown stronger. On the other hand, later research recognized that the liberalizing picture of Luther which Heine here sketches is unhistorical. Luther by no means acknowledged grounds of reason as criteria of biblical interpretation, as Heine here assumes. Luther's demand for "free proof" of Holy Writ, which Heine celebrates, was very different from a defense of the individualistic and rational criticism which was practiced by the humanists. Luther reviled human reason with coarse abuse. The heart of his teaching is precisely that human reason is incapable of recognizing truth by virtue of its own strength, and that the redemption of sinful humanity is to be sought exclusively in trust in divine grace. Heine's view that Luther combated the "legitimacy of the Son," that is, denied the divinity of Jesus, is quite mistaken. The doctrine of the Trinity, of Deity united in Father, Son, and Holy Ghost, is as much a cardinal dogma of Protestantism as of Catholicism. Finally, Heine was wrong in claiming Luther for democracy. The Lutheran Church, whose supreme bishop is the prince, is neither democratically organized nor has it made its congregations democratic. Until late in the nineteenth century and afterwards, it continued obedience to princely absolutism and regarded resistance to secular rulers as a sin. Heine would have had far more reason to hail Calvinism as a preparation for democracy. But this direction in Protestantism was almost wholly ignored by Heine. He speaks only of the Puritans, and of these always unfavorably, as enemies of art, as "Jews."

At the same time, Heine's point of view, vigorously as it is stated, is by no means unified and consistent. Though he generally sees in Luther's Reformation a stride away from Judaism, he says at one point: "Religion itself became different; the Indian-Gnostic element disappears, and we see how the Judaean-Deistic element in it again comes to the fore"—and this he regards as an advantage. But in point of fact, Luther, relying upon the Apostle Paul, again emphasized the "Gnostic element" more strongly and he was very far from a deistic concept of God. At the end of his life, Heine further developed the idea of the kinship between Luther and Judaism which he here assumes.

Heine's concept of German Romanticism is also variable.

Primarily he sees in it an antagonism to rationalism, a reaction against political and cultural advance; but now and again also a return to the paganism of the ancient Germans, which he conceives to have been pantheistic. As such, Romanticism appears to him in the highest degree revolutionary.

In fine, from this time forward, especially since the natural sciences have made such great progress, miracles cease. . . . At least in the case of Saint-Simonism, which is the newest religion, no miracle has occurred, with this exception, perhaps, that an old tailor's bill left owing by Saint-Simon himself, was paid by his disciples ten years after his death. I still see before me the worthy Père Olinde rising with enthusiasm in the Salle Taibout and exhibiting to the astonished congregation the receipted tailor's bill.

—Religion and Philosophy in Germany, 1

Père Olinde: Benjamin Olinde Rodriguès (1795-1851), economist. He assisted Saint-Simon financially, and so restrained him from suicide. Upon his deathbed, Saint-Simon declared Rodriguès his spiritual heir and successor.

The political revolution, based on the principles of French materialism, will find in the pantheists not opponents but allies; allies, however, who have drawn their convictions from a deeper source—from a religious synthesis. We promote the welfare of matter, the material happiness of nations, not, like the materialists, out of contempt for the spirit, but because we know that the divinity of man reveals itself also in his corporeal form, that misery destroys or debases the body, God's image, and that thereby the spirit likewise is involved in ruin. The great word of the Revolution pronounced by St. Just, *Le pain est le droit du peuple*, is translated by us, "Bread is the divine right of man." We are fighting not for the human rights of the people, but for the divine rights of humanity. In this and in much else we differ from the men of the Revolution. We do not wish to be *sans-*

culottists, nor frugal citizens, nor unassuming presidents; we are for founding a democracy of terrestrial gods, equal in glory, in blessedness and in sanctity. You demand simple modes of dress, austere morals and unspiced pleasures; we, on the contrary, desire nectar and ambrosia, purple mantles, costly perfumes, luxury and splendor, dances of laughing nymphs, music and comedies. Be not therefore angry with us, virtuous republicans! To your censorious reproaches we reply in the words of Shakespeare's character:—"Dost thou think, because thou art virtuous, there shall be no more cakes and ale?"

The Saint-Simonists comprehended and desired something analogous; but the soil was unfavorable and they were repressed, for the time at least, by the surrounding materialism. They have been better appreciated in Germany, for Germany is now the fertile soil of pantheism. This is the religion of our greatest thinkers, of our best artists, and in Germany Deism, as I shall presently explain, was long ago theoretically destroyed. No one says it, but every one knows it: pantheism is the open secret of Germany. We have, in fact, outgrown Deism. We are free, and we want no thundering tyrants; we have reached majority and can dispense with paternal care. Neither are we the work of a great mechanician. Deism is a religion for slaves, for children, for Genevese, for watchmakers.

—Religion and Philosophy in Germany, 2

Shakespeare: Twelfth Night II, iii. Genevese: A hit at Rousseau and his pupil Robespierre, whose homilies on virtue were unsympathetic to Heine. This dismissal of the republicans and the aristocratic, sensual turn in Heine's revolutionary program aroused serious misgivings in Boerne and the other German republicans. On the Jewish side, emphatic protests came from Berthold Auerbach and Gabriel Riesser.

Happy Frenchmen, who have heard nothing of all this! You have remained ignorant of even the existence of those tattling evangelical journals in which the pious fishwives of the Protestant Church so lustily abused one another. Happy Frenchmen, who can form no idea of the malice, the pettiness, the bitterness with which our evangelical clergy can traduce one another! You know that I am no partisan of Catholicism. In the present state of my religious convictions there still survives, not indeed the dogmatism, but the spirit of Protestantism. I still retain, therefore, my partiality for the Protestant Church; and yet must I honestly confess that nowhere in the annals of the Papacy have I discovered anything so contemptible as might be found in *The Berlin Evangelical Church Record*. The most dastardly knavery of the monks, the meanest intrigues of the cloister, are noble and generous compared to the Christian exploits of our pietists and orthodox Protestants during their combat with the hated rationalists. You Frenchmen have no idea of the hatred that is displayed on such occasions; for the Germans are more vindictive than the peoples of Latin origin.

The reason is, they are idealists even in their hatred. We do not hate each other as you French do about outward things, because of wounded vanity, on account of an epigram, or of an unreturned visiting-card; no, we hate in our enemies the deepest, most vital possession they have, their thought. As in your love so in your hatred, you French are hasty, superficial. We Germans hate thoroughly, lastingly. Too honest, perhaps too unskilful, to revenge ourselves by speedy perfidy, we hate till our last breath.
—Religion and Philosophy in Germany, 2

Heine's profession of being "partisan on behalf of the Protestant Church" is in open contradiction to his declarations (see p. 318 and p. 323). The term "Protestantism" does not derive from Luther. It became current after the evangelical princes and magistrates of the Reich cities entered a protest (protestatio) against the decree of the Reichstag of Speyer of 1529. This was a political act, and no profession of liberty of thought or conscience. Like Heine, Goethe too on the one hand designated himself a "pagan," a "determined non-Christian," and, on the other hand, interpreted the word "Protestantism" quite unhistorically as the "right to protest."

As Luther had overthrown the Papacy, so Mendelssohn over-threw the Talmud; and he did so after the same fashion, namely, by rejecting tradition, by declaring the Bible to be the source of religion, and by translating the most important part of it. By these means he shattered Judaic, as Luther had shattered Chris-tian, catholicism; for the Talmud is, in fact, the catholicism of the Jews. It is a Gothic cathedral, overladen, no doubt, with childish and superfluous ornament, yet awakening our astonish-ment by its heaven-aspiring, gigantic proportions. It is a hierarchy of religious laws, often relating to the most fanciful and ridicu-lous subtleties, but so ingeniously superimposed and subordi-nated, each part sustaining and supporting another, and so ter-ribly consistent as to form an awe-inspiring, colossal whole.

Christian Catholicism once overthrown, the catholicism of the Jews, the Talmud, must also succumb: for the Talmud had henceforth lost its significance; it served merely as a bulwark against Rome, and it enabled the Jews to offer as heroic a re-sistance to Christian Rome as formerly they had offered to pagan Rome. And they have not only resisted; they have been victori-ous. The poor Rabbi of Nazareth over whose dying head the pagan Roman inscribed the scoffing words, "King of the Jews," even this King of the Jews in mockery, thorn-crowned and clad in ironical purple, became at last the God of the Romans, and before him they had to bend the knee! As heathen Rome had been, so Christian Rome was vanquished and has even become tributary. If you have a mind, dear reader, to betake yourself on one of the first days of the quarter to the Rue Lafitte, No. 15, you will there see a lumbering carriage draw up before the high doorway, and from it steps down a stout man. He mounts a staircase leading to a small room in which is seated a younger fair-headed man, though he is really older than he looks—a man with the distinguished, negligent air of a *grand seigneur*, underlying which, however, there is something so solid, so pos-itive, so absolute, that he might be thought to have all the world's wealth in his pocket. And truly he has all the world's wealth in his pocket, for his name is Mr. James Rothschild, and the stout man is Monsignor Grimbaldi, legate of His Holiness the Pope, in whose name he brings the interest on the Roman loan, the tribute of Rome.

Of what use, now, the Talmud?

—Religion and Philosophy in Germany, 2

The parallel which Heine draws between the Talmud and Catholicism is as untenable as is his account of Moses Mendelssohn's position with reference to the Talmud. In the Judaism of the epochs in which the Talmud possessed equal divine authority with the Bible there was no institution which could be compared with the centralized power of the Roman papacy. Even talmudic sages of great personal authority, who possessed a more or less limited local power, were never in position to subject Jews of other territories to their authority. No priestly privilege prevented a Jew from study of the Talmud. The right of free discussion was unqualified in principle in talmudic Judaism. Moses Mendelssohn by no means overthrew the authority of the Talmud. His German translation of the Bible had a different purpose from Luther's. Mendelssohn's importance in the history of Judaism by no means consists in his having promulgated a new concept of the Jewish religion. He was no religious reformer. Later Jewish Reform could not invoke Mendelssohn for its innovations. Mendelssohn marks an epoch in the history of Judaism because he was the first Jew of modern times who exerted cultural influence in Germany and in the non-Jewish world through his writings in German and obtained recognition. Furthermore, by means of his book, Jerusalem, he demonstrated to the non-Jews of the world that the Jewish religion was not an omnium gatherum of superstitions, as even Immanuel Kant, before reading the book, and Lessing, before closer acquaintance with Mendelssohn, had believed. Mendelssohn believed that there need be no conflict between his Jewish religious convictions and the ideas of the Enlightenment. But as a religious Jew, he was no Deist. Spinozist pantheism seemed to him as inconsistent with his faith as with the cultural ideal of the Enlightenment. When the philosopher Friedrich Heinrich

Jacobi insisted that Lessing, in a conversation with him, had declared himself a pantheist and an adherent of Spinoza, Mendelssohn was greatly perturbed. Although he was gravely ill, he wrote his counter-blast To the Friends of Lessing, which he completed shortly before his death.

Later, Heine changed his notions of the Talmud:

> Yes, his father led him early
> To the Talmud, and threw open
> For his benefit, that famous
> School of fighting, the Halacha,
>
> Where the athletes dialectic,
> Best in Babylon, and also
> Those renowned in Pumpeditha
> Did their intellectual tilting.
>
> He had here the chance of learning
> Every art and ruse polemic;
> How he mastered them was proven
> In the book *Cosari*, later.
>
> But the lights are twain, and differ,
> That are shed on earth by heaven;
> There's the harsh and glaring sunlight,
> And the mild and gentle moonlight.
>
> With a double radiance also
> Shines the Talmud; the Halacha
> Is the one, and the Hagada
> Is the other light. The former
>
> I have called the school of fighting;
> But the latter, the Hagada,
> I will call a curious garden,
> Most fantastic, and resembling

Much another one that blossomed
Too in Babylon—the garden
Of Semiramis; 'mongst wonders
Of the world it was eighth.
                    —Hebrew Melodies: Jehuda ben Halevy
                                        Margaret Armour

*According to Heine's view, which was shared by many in the
twentieth century, Kant's* Critique of Pure Reason *removed every
basis for faith in a personal God by its refutation of the onto-
logical, cosmological, and physicotheological proof for the existence of God, whereas his* Critique of Practical Reason *gives up
his "revolutionary intractability" by making concessions to belief
in God. This view is today generally recognized as false. Six years
after the appearance of the* Critique of Practical Reason, *which
allegedly involves Kant's recantation of the revolutionary standpoint of the Pure Reason, he was warned by an order of the Royal
Prussian Cabinet against his "falsification and depreciation of
many principal and basic teachings of sacred Scriptures and
Christianity." In Kant's system, the* Critique of Practical Reason
is of no less importance than the Critique of Pure Reason. *On
the contrary, Kant teaches the "primacy" of practical reason,
which regulates the will and the actions of men, over theoretical
reason. Kant rocked the bases of speculative theology and dogmatic philosophy by demonstrating that knowledge rests solely
on experience and he shows where speculation passes beyond the
limits of what may be experienced. The idea of God is thus not
attacked—nor is it in the* Critique of Pure Reason. *According to
Kant, ideas are the guiding lines of thought and action without
which human life becomes the unintelligent play of instincts.
Ideas transcend the possibility of experience, but in contrast to
the dogmatic speculations overthrown by the* Critique of Pure
Reason, *ideas of practical reason are not assailable, for they are
directed not to knowledge of existence but to moral conduct, to
action. They are "imperatives," "postulates," without which
civilization and the peaceful association of men is impossible.
One such "postulate of practical reason" is God. This concept of*

God, which lays all emphasis upon action and not upon reflection upon the nature of God, is incontestably related to the
Jewish concept. Hence Kant's philosophy, and in particular his
ethics, attracted many Jewish thinkers in Germany, and among
them many Jewish theologians also. Of these, many have even
erased the distinctions, which nevertheless do exist, between the
Kantian philosophy of religion and the religion of Judaism.

After repeated and careful study of Kant's chief work, I fancied
myself able to recognize everywhere in it evidences of his polemic
against these proofs of the existence of God; and of this polemic
I might speak at greater length were I not restrained by a religious
sentiment. The mere discussion by any one of the existence of
God causes me to feel a strange disquietude, an uneasy dread
such as I once experienced in visiting New Bedlam in London,
when, for a moment, losing sight of my guide, I was surrounded
by madmen. "God is all that is," and doubt of His existence is
doubt of life itself—it is death.

—Religion and Philosophy in Germany, 3

Our first romanticists were, in fact, moved by a pantheistic
instinct, which they did not themselves comprehend. The sentiment, which they mistook for a yearning towards the Catholic
Mother Church, was of deeper origin than they suspected. Their
veneration and affection for the traditions of the Middle Ages,
for the popular beliefs, the *diablérie*, the sorcery, and the witchcraft of former times—all this was a suddenly reawakened,
though uncomprehended, predilection for the pantheism of the
old Germans, and, in its foully stained and spitefully mutilated
form, what they really loved was the pre-Christian religion of
their ancestors.

—Religion and Philosophy in Germany, 3

German philosophy is an important fact; it concerns the whole
human race, and only our latest descendants will be in a position
to decide whether we are to be praised or blamed for having first
worked out our philosophy and afterwards our revolution. It

seems to me that a methodical people, such as we are, must begin with the Reformation, must then occupy itself with systems of philosophy, and that only after the completion of these could it pass to the political revolution. I find this sequence quite rational. The heads that have first served for the speculations of philosophy can afterwards be struck off by the revolution for whatever object it pleases; but philosophy would not have been able to utilize the heads struck off by a revolution that preceded it. Give yourselves no anxiety, however, ye German republicans; the German revolution will not prove any milder or gentler because it was preceded by the *Critique* of Kant, by the *Transcendental Idealism* of Fichte, or even by the Philosophy of Nature. These doctrines served to develop revolutionary forces that only await their time to break forth and to fill the world with terror and with admiration. Then will appear Kantians, as little tolerant of piety in the world of deeds as in the world of ideas, who will mercilessly upturn with sword and axe, the soil of our European life in order to extirpate the last remnants of the past. There will come upon the scene armed Fichteans whose fanaticism of will is to be restrained neither by fear nor by self-interest; for they live in the spirit; they defy matter like those early Christians who could be subdued neither by bodily torments nor by bodily delights. Yea, in a time of social revolution these transcendental idealists will prove even more pertinacious than the early Christians; for the latter endured earthly martyrdom in the hope of attaining celestial blessedness, whilst the transcendental idealist looks on martyrdom itself as a vain show, and is invulnerable within the intrenchment of his own thought. But most of all to be feared would be the philosophers of nature, were they actively to mingle in a German revolution and to identify themselves with the work of destruction. For if the hand of the Kantian strikes with strong unerring blow, his heart being stirred by no feeling of traditional awe; if the Fichtean courageously defies every danger, since for him danger has in reality no existence; the Philosopher of Nature will be terrible in this, that he has allied himself with the primitive powers of nature, that he can conjure up the demoniacal forces of old German panthe-

ism; and having done so, there is aroused in him that ancient
German eagerness for battle which combats, not for the sake of
destroying, not even for the sake of victory, but merely for the
sake of the combat itself. Christianity—and this is its fairest
merit—subdued to a certain extent the brutal warrior-ardor of
the Germans, but it could not entirely quench it; and when the
Cross, that restraining talisman, falls to pieces, then will break
forth again the ferocity of the old combatants, the frantic Ber-
serker rage whereof Northern poets have said and sung so much.
The talisman has become rotten, and the day will come when it
will pitifully crumble into dust. The old stone gods will then
arise from the forgotten ruins and wipe from their eyes the dust
of centuries, and Thor with his giant hammer will arise again,
and he will shatter the Gothic cathedrals. When ye hear the
trampling of feet and the clashing of arms, ye neighbors' children, ye French, be on your guard, and see that ye mingle not in
the fray going on amongst us at home in Germany. It might fare
ill with you. See that ye take no hand in kindling the fire; see
that ye attempt not to extinguish it. You might easily burn your
fingers in the flame. Smile not at my counsel, at the counsel of a
dreamer, who warns you against Kantians, Fichteans, Philosophers of Nature. Smile not at the fantasy of one who foresees in
the region of reality the same outburst of revolution that has
taken place in the region of intellect. The thought precedes the
deed as the lightning the thunder. German thunder is of true
German character: it is not very nimble, and rumbles along
somewhat slowly. But come it will, and when ye hear a crashing
such as never before has been heard in the world's history, then
know that at last the German thunderbolt has fallen. . . . There
will be played in Germany a drama compared to which the
French Revolution will seem but an innocent idyl. . . .

As on the steps of an amphitheater, the nations will group
themselves around Germany to witness the terrible combat. I
counsel you, ye French, keep very quiet, and, above all, see that
ye do not applaud. We might readily misunderstand such ap-
plause, and, in our rude fashion, somewhat roughly put you to
silence. For, if formerly in our servile, listless mood we could

oftentimes overpower you, much easier were it for us to do so in
the arrogance of our new-born enthusiasm for liberty. Ye yourselves know what, in such a case, men can do; and ye are no
longer in such a case. Take heed, then! I mean it well with you;
therefore it is I tell you the bitter truth. Ye have more to fear
from a free Germany than from the entire Holy Alliance with all
its Croats and Cossacks. . . .

What you are really accused of I could never understand.
Once, in a beer-cellar at Goettingen, I heard a young Old-Ger-
man assert that it was necessary to be revenged on France for
Conradin of Hohenstaufen, whom you beheaded at Naples.
Doubtless ye have long since forgotten that: we, however, forget
nothing. . . . In any case, I advise you to be on your guard. Happen what may in Germany, though the Crown Prince of Prussia
or Dr. Wirth should attain supremacy, be ye ever armed; remain
quietly at your post, your weapons in your hands. I mean it well
with you, and I was seized with dismay when I heard it said
lately that your Ministry proposed to disarm France.

As ye are, despite your present romantic tendency, a born
classical people, ye know Olympus. Amongst the joyous gods
and goddesses quaffing and feasting of nectar and ambrosia, ye
may behold one goddess, who, amidst such gaiety and pastime,
wears ever a coat of mail, the helmet on her head and the spear
in her hand.

She is the goddess of Wisdom.

—Religion and Philosophy in Germany, 3
(Conclusion)

In 1268, Conradin, the last male heir of the medieval imperial
house of Staufer, was defeated by Charles of Anjou in the Battle
of Tagliacozzo, taken captive and then executed. Even Luther
based his hatred of the French on the memory of this incident.
So did many German historians of the nineteenth century, who
put themselves at the service of nationalist propaganda.

Old Fontenelle may have been right when he said: "If I held
all the truths of the universe in my hand, I would be very careful

not to open it." I, for my part, think otherwise. If I held all the truths of the world in my hand, I might perhaps beseech you instantly to cut off that hand; but, in any case, I should not long hold it closed. I was not born to be a gaoler of thoughts; by Heaven! I would set them free. What though they were to incarnate themselves in the most hazardous realities, what though they were to range through all lands like a mad bacchanalian procession, what though they were to crush with their thyrsus our most innocent flowers, what though they were to invade our hospitals and chase from his bed the old sick world—my heart would bleed, no doubt, and I myself would suffer hurt thereby! For alas! I too am part of this old sick world, and the poet says truly, one may mock at his crutches yet not be able to walk any better for that. I am the most grievously sick of you all, and am the more to be pitied since I know what health is; but you do not know it, you whom I envy.

—Religion and Philosophy in Germany, 3

Mathilde

The most important literary productions of Heine's Saint-Simonist period are the fragmentary novel From the Memoirs of Herr von Schnabelewopski *and the* Florentine Nights, *as well as a number of lyrical poems in which the "emancipation of the flesh" is celebrated.*

In the Memoirs of Herr von Schnabelewopski, *which Heine intended as a literary pendant to the coarsely sensual scenes of the old Dutch painter Jan Steen, there is intertwined the story of "little Simson," who, as champion of Jewish monotheism, is fatally wounded in a duel with a Fichtean—a novelistic parallel to the fate of Deism as Heine represented it in the essays in* Religion and Philosophy in Germany.

In the Florentine Nights *the author's mouthpiece (called Enrico in the original form and Maximilian in the published work) gives a dying woman an account of the pleasures of life and love. Here Heine refrained from any reference to Deism, pantheism, Judaism and Christianity. Rather is his glance di-*

rected to the interlacing of reality and the dream world, to the mingling of fantasy and irony, gaiety and grimness, in his own soul, and upon the psychology of the artist whose outer and inner life diverge widely from one another. Heine often emphasized that the artist leads a double life; but seldom did he succeed in expressing this view with such brilliance and élan as in the account of Paganini in this novel, which embraces "sensualism" and "spiritualism" with equal sympathy.

Most poems in the Various cycle represent Heine's "Saint-Simonist lyric," as does the long poem Tannhaeuser. In these poems love is no longer, as it was in the Book of Songs, the cause of great suffering, but rather a source of joy and of pleasure. In place of a single beloved on whom the happiness or the misery of the poet depends, we have a whole gallery of pictures on Parisian ladies, who are examined by the poet with the air of a connoisseur; these ladies may indeed bring him momentary ecstasy, but cannot shatter his security. The Tannhaeuser poem suggests satiety in joy of life; but after a transitory yearning for "bitternesses," it decides for persistence in the joy of pleasure. It is a veiled confession of the poet who had sought in vain to free himself from his tie to "Mathilde."

While Heine still believed that he could follow one love adventure with another in Paris and sang of the alternation of his loves with undisguised satisfaction, he met a girl who never released him until his death. She was nineteen years old, and she sold shoes in a shop which belonged to her aunt. Her name was Crescence Eugenie Mirat; she was born and brought up in the little village of Vinot not far from Paris, perhaps as the natural daughter of some prominent man who did not trouble about this child. Her oral expression was ready; she could read and write; but her education extended no farther. Her beauty and the flare of her temperament enthralled Heine. But soon he had grounds to complain of her moods and of her inconsiderateness in all economic matters. "Mathilde," as Heine called her, was kindly, helpful, selfless to the point of neglecting her own household duties, and—had no understanding of the limitations of Heine's means. Heine became acquainted with her in October 1834.

Mathilde became his mistress, but exacted a promise that he would not desert her. For her part, Mathilde took no other lover, either before her tie with Heine or after his death. From 1836 onward, Heine and Mathilde were regarded as man and wife by their friends and acquaintances. In September 1841, on the eve of his duel with Salomon Strauss, the husband of Boerne's friend Madame Wohl, Heine entered into a church marriage with Mathilde, who was a devout Catholic (see p. 341).

Mathilde Heine has been very variously judged. Some close friends of the poet praised her character, her charm and her love for Heine warmly. Others were repelled by her intense temperament and her appetite for clothes. Heine recognized all of her merits and weaknesses precisely. He felt it no great disadvantage that Mathilde had only a very faint notion of his significance as a poet. That amused rather than pained him. He was more sensitive to her want of understanding for his economic situation. But both he and others often exaggerated Mathilde's extravagance. Compared with the budget of other writers living in Paris, Heine's was very modest, and a large proportion of his expenses was accounted for by his illness. To this Mathilde had to accommodate herself of necessity. She never drove Heine into debt. Nor did Heine suffer from the fact that, by her want of education and her inconsiderate expression of her antipathies, Mathilde barred his access to the bourgeois families of France; his social intercourse, as long as he was in health, had a Bohemian character. He loved his wife, devoted his best powers to her, and had no greater anxiety than to secure her future after his death.

How am I to excuse my silence! And you are friend enough to insinuate kindly that your letter has been lost! No: I will confess the truth. I received it right enough, but at a time when I was up to my neck in a love-affair, from which I have not yet extricated myself. Since October, nothing has been of the least importance for me that has not been connected with the affair. I have neglected everything, seen no one, and at best a sigh has escaped me when I thought of my friends—and I have often sighed to think that you might misunderstand my silence, but I could not bring myself actually to write. And that is all that I can tell you now: for the rosy waves are roaring round me so loudly, my brain is so bemused by the storm of the scent of flowers, that I am not in a fit state to write to you intelligently.

Have you read the Song of Songs which is the Song of Solomon? Well, read it again, and you will find in it all that I could tell you today. . . .

Read the Song of Songs of King Solomon: I call your attention to the fellow.

—To August Lewald
Paris, April 11, 1835

August Lewald (1792-1871), a German writer of Jewish origin, was a convert first to Protestantism and then to Catholicism. He became acquainted with Heine in Hamburg and visited him in Paris.

To distract Heine from Mathilde, the Princess Cristina de Belgiojoso invited him to her estate, Jonchère, where the poet spent several weeks. At the same time, the Princess took a step towards consolidating Heine's financial situation. Upon her request, her and Heine's friend, the historian Mignet, obtained of Premier Thiers a warrant for a state pension for Heine to the sum of 4000 francs (see p. 346). But Heine's passion for Mathilde was stronger than his high regard for the Princess, whose beauty, wit and strength of character filled him with admiration but left him cold.

My address is: H.H., chez la Princesse Belgiojoso, Chateau de la Jonchère, par Ruel (Banlieue). Here I have been living for some time in rustic tranquillity, which is frequently enough interrupted by gay society. The beauties of nature are benefiting me—some weeks ago I experienced a rather painful mishap. I will tell you about it orally, gracious lady, and even now I can see you smilingly console me.

—To Baroness James de Rothschild
Jonchère, June 1835

For four months my life has been so stormily tossed about, and in particular during the last three months, the waves of life have struck so violently at my head, that I could scarcely think of you, much less write you. Fool that I was, I thought that the period of passion was over for me, that I could never again be sucked into the whirlpool of raging humanity, that I was peer of the eternal gods in serenity, rationality and moderation—and look! again I stormed like a man, and indeed like a young man. Now, thanks to the indestructible force of my nature, my soul is again assuaged, my excited senses are again tamed, and I am living cheerfully and calmly at the castle of a beautiful friend in the vicinity of Saint-Germain, in an amiable circle of outstanding persons and outstanding personalities.

I believe that my spirit is now purified of all dross; my verses will grow more beautiful, my books more harmonious. So much I know: at this moment I have a true repugnance of everything unclear and ignoble, of everything commonplace and sulky.

—To Julius Campe
Paris, July 2, 1835

I am one of those people who have a horror of anything that disturbs my mind and avoid it as much as possible. Ah! in spite of the greatest care, an overpowering emotion seizes us often enough and robs us of that clearness of vision and thought which I dislike surrendering. As soon as our senses are troubled and our minds shaken we are no longer the fellows of the gods. This fellowship—I may confess it now—I have for long enjoyed. I went my way in peace and in the light; but for the last nine moons great storms have burst upon my soul, and long, long shadows beset me on every side. This confession will explain my present inactivity to you. I am still engaged in lulling the disturbances in my soul, and if I do not reach the light of day, at least I am issuing from black night.

I received your letter but I was not able to see the bearer of it, for I was in the country at Saint-Germain at the castle of the most beautiful, the most noble and wittiest of women, with

whom, however, I am not in love. I am condemned to love only
the most humble and foolish—imagine what torture for a man
of so much pride and intellect!

—To Heinrich Laube
Boulogne-sur-Mer, September 27, 1835

Juliet lives upon the surface:
She is French, and shallow-hearted;
But, to look on, how delightful
And enchanting is my Juliet!

For her glances are a lovely
Net of sunbeams in whose meshes
Captive hearts, like little fishes,
Writhe with tenderness and longing.

—Atta Troll, ch. 1
Margaret Armour

Mathilde was also called Juliet in Heine's circle.

Lo! my wife so dear and kind,
Wife most lovely and beloved,
Has my breakfast ready waiting;
White the cream, the coffee brown.

And she pours it out herself,
Joking, smiling, and caressing,
In all Christendom so sweetly
Not another mouth can smile.

And a voice so flute-like only
Can be heard among the angels,
Or, on earth, if there's another,
'Mongst the sweetest nightingales.

Pretty hand, so lily white!
How her dreamy hair in ringlets

Frames her charming, rosy features!
Aye, her beauty is perfection.

Yet today I first bethought me
—I know not why—a wee bit smaller
Ought her swelling waist to be,
Aye, a tiny wee bit smaller.
> —In the Morning Early. Love Verses
> Margaret Armour

I have been living very pleasantly in Paris lately and Mathilde brightened life for me with the consistent inconsistency of her whims. . . . Herr ——— said so much to her in praise of my writings that she had no rest until I went to Renduel and got the French edition of the *Travel Pictures* for her. But scarcely had she read a page of it than she grew pale as death, trembled in all her limbs and begged me for God's sake to shut the book up. She had happed upon a love passage and, being jealous, she would like me never to have paid homage to any other before the commencement of her dominion: indeed, I had to promise that henceforth I will address no love phrases to any ideal woman in my books.

> —To August Lewald
> Coudray, May 3, 1836

You will have received through Herr ——— the pretty tapestry which Mathilde worked for you. She showed me by this troublesome and laborious work that she was very industrious and therefore faithful to me in my absence. She must have had as little lack of wooers as Penelope, who gave her husband when he returned a far more dubious proof of her loyalty. Or do you think that Madame Ulysses did really unravel at night the web which she spun during the day? She told this to the old man when he was surprised that there was no work done. The drab had spent day and night with her suitors and had only spun intrigues.

You will hardly believe with what loving industry Mathilde worked at the tapestry when she knew that I intended it to be a present. We are both very happy living together, that is, I do not have a moment's peace day or night. I have ever been of opinion that in love one must *possess*, and I have always been an opponent of the theory of renunciation; but there is this much of good in Platonic love—that it does not prevent a man dreaming by day and sleeping by night, and in any case it is not very expensive.

—To August Lewald
Paris, January 25, 1837

Since my return from Havre, Mathilde's conduct has been so exemplary that I began to be anxious for her life. Such radical transformation is customarily an omen of death. For eight long days she was able to stay home and be satisfied with a simple *pot au feu*. No thought of theater—too expensive. She herself remade her old dresses to save getting new ones for the winter. Finally she became seriously ill and I had to take her to a nursing home where she is well cared for and will remain until spring (the whole carnival!). . . .

So I have my complete freedom this winter; *je jouis de ma pleine liberté, et je m'en abuse même.*

I go to the theater often, to my great delight!

—To Johann Hermann Detmold
Paris, January 16, 1838

Johann Hermann Detmold, lawyer, art-critic and politician, Reich Minister of Justice in 1848, often gave Heine effective assistance in his quarrel with Salomon Heine's family and with literary and political opponents. Detmold, who was converted to Protestantism from Judaism, was among Heine's closest friends during the last part of his life.

I announce today an event which I have already kept back from you for several days—my marriage with the most beautiful and pure creature, who has for years been by my side under the name of Mathilde Heine, and has been honored and regarded as my wife, and has only been besmirched with contemptuous epi-

thets by a few dirty-minded Germans of the Frankfort Clique—
I carried through this vindication of her honor by legal and
ecclesiastical authority at the same time as I was conducting the
affair of my own honor.

—To Julius Campe
Paris, September 5, 1841

I also invoked the sanction of the Church for my marriage
because my wife, who is a strict Catholic, would not have considered herself properly married in the eyes of God without such
a ceremony; and for no consideration would I shake this dear
being's belief in the religion which she has inherited. . . .

Although I myself was a free-thinker, I permitted no word
derogatory to religion to be spoken in my house. In the midst of
Paris, I lived like a steady, commonplace townsman; and therefore when I married I desired to be wedded under the sanction
of the Church, although in this country the civil marriage is
fully recognized by society. My free-thinking friends were vexed
at me for this, and overwhelmed me with reproaches, claiming
that I had made too great concessions to the clergy. Their cha-
grin at my weakness would have been still greater had they
known the other concessions that I had made to the hated priest-
hood. As I was a Protestant wedding a Catholic, in order to have
the ceremony performed by a Catholic priest it was necessary to
obtain a special dispensation from the archbishop, who in these
cases exacts from the husband a written pledge that the offspring
of the marriage shall be educated in the religion of the mother.
But, between ourselves, I could sign this pledge with the lighter
conscience since I knew the rearing of children is not my spe-
cialty. I will crown my confessions by admitting that, if at that
time it had been necessary in order to obtain the dispensation of
the archbishop, I would have bound over not only the children
but myself. But the ogre of Rome, who, like the monster in the
fairy tales, stipulates that he shall have for his services the future
births, was content with the poor children who were never born.
And so I remained a Protestant.

—Confessions

On August 31 I married Mathilde Crescentia Mirat, with whom I have been in daily contention for more than six years.

But she has a noble and pure heart, and is as kind as an angel, and during the many years of our association, her conduct was so irreproachable that she was praised as a model of decency by all friends and acquaintances.

—To Charlotte Embden
Paris, September 13, 1841

My wife comports herself very well, thank God. She is a thoroughly honest, decent, kindly creature without deceit or evil. Unfortunately, her temperament is very irregular, her moods uneven, and frequently she irritates me more than is good for me. I am still very deeply devoted to her, and she is still the most essential requirement of my life—but that will sometime cease, as all human feelings cease in time, and I look forward to that day with grim apprehension. I shall then only feel the burden of her moods without the alleviating sympathy. At other times, I am tormented by anxiety for the helplessness and fecklessness of my wife in case I die, for she is as inexperienced and helpless as a three-year-old child.

—To Betty Heine
Paris, March 8, 1842

My wife is a good, natural, cheerful child, cheerful as only a Frenchwoman can be, and she does not permit me to sink into melancholy dreams to which I am too much inclined. . . . For eight years I have loved her with a tenderness and passion which borders on the fabulous.

—To Maximilian Heine
Paris, April 12, 1843

My wife behaves quite well, does not squabble too often, but is always a spendthrift. It is only with trouble and pressure that I make out, but I do make out, and the cares pass.

—To Charlotte Embden
Paris, January 23, 1844

My wife is in general a seemly and lovable woman, and if she does not cackle too loudly, her voice is a resounding balm to my wounded soul. I love her with a passion which towers over my sickness, and in this emotion I am strong, however lame and weary my limbs are.

—To Maximilian Heine
Paris, December 12, 1848

Mathilde is too amiable, and her failings spring from her kindly heart, so that I myself cannot be angry with her even in her most foolish extravagances and other follies. Without her, life would have no interest at all for me; she helps me bear the painful burden which I should certainly cast off if I were alone.

—To Betty Heine and Charlotte Embden
Paris, February 5, 1851

Mathilde's generosity becomes the reverse of a virtue in her, for it has no measure and no consideration. But it is better to have an extravagant angel than a stingy devil. Yet even angels sometimes make life hell. If this is only rarely the case, if the hours of hell are only scattered, we can still be happy.

—To Gustav Heine
Paris, March 21, 1851

My wife cares for me and nurses me like an angel; nevertheless she does not give up membership in a sex which the dear God did not create with reason.

—To Gustav Heine
Paris, July 15, 1851

To the Angels

'Tis Thanatos, the dread indeed!
He comes upon a pale white steed;
I know the trample of his horse;
He comes to ravish me by force.
He has me now! To leave Matilda so!—
My heart can scarce conceive such utter woe.

She who was wife and child in one
Will orphan, widow, be anon,
When to the shadowy land I pass!
Here, in this world alone, alas!
I leave my wife, my child, who lay
Trusting and true upon my heart, here stay.

Ye angels, hearken from on high!
O hear my pleading, hear my cry!
The wife I love protect and save,
When I am in the dreary grave.
Guard her, for she is like you, pure and fair;
Take my poor child Matilda to your care!

By all the tears that, grieved in heaven,
To mortal sorrows ye have given,
By the dread word pronounced, when known,
In shuddering fear by priests alone,
By your own loveliness and mercy mild,
Ye angels, guard Matilda, guard my child!
                              —Romancero 2, Lazarus
                                    Margaret Armour

"*By the dread word . . . by priests alone*": Shem ha-m'forash,
*the name of God, which, during the second Jewish common-
wealth, might be pronounced only once in the year, on Atone-
ment Day, and by the High Priest.*

I nominate Mathilde Crescence Heine, née Mirat, my law-
fully wedded wife, with whom for many years I have spent my
days good and evil, and who has nursed me during my long and
terrible illness, to be my universal legatee, I bequeath to her all
my property whatsoever, and without qualification or limitation,
all that I possess or may possess at my demise and all my rights
in any property in the future. . . .

At present I feel the greatest regret that I have not provided
better for the proper maintenance of my wife. . . .

I believe I have the right to regard my cousin, Carl Heine, as the natural protector of my widow. . . . Specifically, I ask him to have paid to her annually after my death, not the half of my pension, but the entire pension undiminished, as I drew it during the lifetime of his father. My uncle treated her with love and consideration, and in this respect also I believe my request is justified.

—Heinrich Heine's will of
November 13, 1851

After Heine's death, Mathilde lived in deep retirement, until her own death in 1883. With respect to Heine's literary remains she was not always well advised by her French friends and counselors. But her grief for the deceased husband, whom she loved without being capable of appreciating his poetic significance, and her piety to his memory were recognized as genuine and upright by all who knew her during her widowhood and were not prejudiced by irresponsible gossip.

The French State Pension

Despite his literary success, Heine fell into financial difficulties from which he saw no escape. Heine was not extravagant, though on occasion he was willing to spend more for good food and amusement than his income warranted. He was generally frugal as regards his daily needs. But he was open-handed to fellow countrymen who were in straits in Paris, and more than once his trust and his willingness to help were consciencelessly exploited, so that he himself fell into the greatest embarrassment. Shrewder policy with his publisher Julius Campe might doubtless have considerably augmented his income; but especially in his dealings with Campe Heine always exercised great restraint, although he knew that Campe paid writers of lesser standing better. Several times he let Campe have important publishing rights for a ridiculously small sum because he urgently needed money for some momentary need. His removal from Germany prevented Heine from exploiting his journalistic talents and thus augmenting the income which he drew from his books. Moreover, he was loath to undertake work not in his main line of interest and seldom did so; frequently he rejected very attractive offers. French periodicals published more of his contributions than those of other foreigners, but not nearly enough to assure a minimal existence. With Salomon Heine he was on such bad terms at this time that increments from that source could hardly come into consideration.

At the intervention of the Princess Belgiojoso, who was aware of Heine's straitened circumstances, the historian Mignet made overtures to the French premier, Adolphe Thiers, to obtain a state subvention for Heine. This took place in April 1835, and it may be assumed, though it is not entirely certain, that Heine could avail himself of an annual subsidy from the French government to the amount of 4,000 francs when the Diet's prohibition (see p. 356) threatened to cut him off from all income from Germany. But this subsidy was only a small fraction of what Heine, or any other writer in Paris, required for a bare livelihood.

The grant of this pension involved no sort of political conditions; Heine retained his freedom of action as a publicist. Nevertheless, at this time Heine withdrew from the political field to the realm of history, philosophy and religion. He neither thought of returning to political journalism in the foreseeable future nor had Thiers any intention to employ him for political purposes. What was involved was an offering of honor to a distinguished guest of France. When Thiers' ministry fell, the retiring premier requested his successor and opponent, Guizot, to continue Heine's pension. So did all succeeding governments, until the Revolution of 1848. After the end of the July monarchy, the government of the second French Republic withdrew Heine's pension, as it did all others, and in the Revue Retrospective published a list of many hundreds of persons who had received subsidies from secret funds of the monarchy of Louis Philippe. Among them were many who had rendered service to that regime, but there were others who, like Heine, remained free of any obligation. When Heine resumed his political reporting in 1840, his criticism spared neither Thiers nor Guizot. He even

*made a sharp attack upon Thiers, to whom he owed his subsidy,
for his attitude in the question of the Jews of Damascus.*

The *Revue Retrospective* has for some time been delighting
the republican world by the publication of documents from the
archives of the preceding regime, and among others, it has made
public the accounts of the Ministry of Foreign Affairs during the
administration of Guizot. The circumstance that the name of
the undersigned is entered there with considerable sums has
given wide room for suspicions of the most odious character and
for perfidious constructions for which there was no justification
in the *Revue Retrospective*. They have served a correspondent
of the *Allgemeine Zeitung* as a foil for a charge whose substance
is that the ministry of Guizot purchased my pen for the definite
purpose of defending the measures of his regime. The editor of
the *Allgemeine Zeitung* appends a note to that correspondence
suggesting that I may have received this stipend not for what I
wrote "but rather for what I did not write." The editorial staff
of the *Allgemeine Zeitung* which for twenty years has had ample
opportunity, by reason not so much of what it has published as
of what it has not published of my work, to observe that I am
not a servile writer who can be paid for his silence—the aforesaid
editorial staff might have spared me that *levis nota*. I am direct-
ing these lines against the editor's note, rather than against the
correspondent, and I wish to explain as clearly as possible my
relations to the Guizot ministry. I am induced to do so by higher
interests, not by the petty interests of personal safety, not even
by those of honor. My honor is not in the hands of just any
newspaper correspondent, nor can even the best of newspapers
be its tribunal; I can only be tried before the assizes of literary
history. Not even then will I allow magnanimity to be interpreted and disparaged as cowardice. No; the support which I
received from the Guizot ministry was not tribute. It was only
support; it was—I will give it its proper name—the generous alms
which the French people bestowed on so many thousands of
foreigners who had been more or less gloriously compromised
in their native countries by their zeal for the cause of the Revolu-

tion and had taken refuge by the hospitable hearth of France. I applied for this charity shortly after the deplorable decrees of the Diet had appeared which endeavored to ruin me financially, as the chorus leader of a so-called Young Germany, by imposing an interdict not only on existing writings but also upon anything that might subsequently come from my pen, and in this way robbed me of my fortune and my livelihood without judgment and without right. The reason for the payment of this charity being entered into the accounts of the Ministry of Foreign Affairs and of its pension fund, which is not subject to public control, lay in the circumstance that the finances of other departments were at that time too heavily burdened. Perhaps also the French government did not wish patently to support a man who had always been a thorn in the flesh of the German embassy and a man whose expulsion had so often been demanded. It is well known how and why my Royal Prussian friends had plagued the French government with such demands. But M. Guizot obstinately refused to expel me, and paid me my pension regularly every month without fail. He never asked the smallest service in return. When I waited upon him, soon after he had taken the portfolio of foreign affairs, and thanked him for having authorized the continuation of my pension in spite of my radical complexion, he replied with sad kindness: "I am not the man who can refuse a German poet living in exile a piece of bread." It was in November 1840 that M. Guizot said these words to me, and it was the first and last time in my life that I had the honor of speaking to him. I have given the editor of the *Revue Retrospective* evidence to prove the truth of the foregoing declaration, and with the authentic documents which are accessible to him he should now make clear, as befits French loyalty, the meaning and origin of the pension in question.

—Heinrich Heine
Paris, May 15, 1848

Heine's declaration was published by the Allgemeine Zeitung on May 23, 1848. Its chief editor, Gustav Kolb, in whose absence the correspondence directed against Heine had been accepted, disavowed the editorial notice which had accompanied it. The Revue Retrospective discontinued before it could accede to Heine's demand that his allegations be confirmed. Heine was therefore constrained to deal with the matter once more.

Though I might very well have alleged that the pecuniary assistance which was assigned to me as an *allocation annuelle d'une pension de secours* might be considered as a high recognition of my literary reputation, as I had been notified with the most delicate courtesy, I still unconditionally attributed that pension to national magnanimity and political fraternal affection, which showed itself as beautifully here as evangelical pity ever did of old. There were very eminent men among my ex-colleagues who only called that aid a subvention; beggarly proud knights, who hated all sense of obligation, called it a loan to be subsequently repaid to the French Government with good interest; but I bowed myself to dire need and called it by its right name. . . .

Life in Paris is so expensive, especially when one is married and has no children. There dear little playthings are a pastime for the husband—sometimes for the wife—so that they need seek no amusement, which is so expensive, out of doors. And then I have never learned the art of feeding the hungry with mere words, and all the more because nature has endowed me with such a healthy, hearty appearance that no one would believe in my sad need. The poor, who have hitherto been liberally aided by me, laughed when I said that I myself must in future starve. Was I not the relation of all possible millionaires? Had not the *generalissimus* of all millionaires, had not this *millionairissimus* called himself my friend—his friend? I could never make my clients understand that the great millionairissimus called me his friend because I never asked him for money. Had I done so, the friendship would soon have been at an end. . . .

So it came to pass that calumny had free play when it did not ascribe the motives which induced me to accept the pension in question to natural wants and requirements. I remember that at that time many of my fellow-countrymen, among them the most

determined and intellectual Dr. Marx, came to me to express
their displeasure over the slanderous article in the *Allgemeine
Zeitung*, advising me not to reply by a single word, since they
themselves had already declared in German journals that I had
certainly accepted the pension received with a view to supporting
my poor partisan associates more effectively. The like was asserted by the then publisher of the *Neue Rheinische Zeitung*,
as well as the friends who formed his general staff. I, however,
returned my thanks for their kind sympathy, and assured these
friends that they had erred; that I could very well use the pension
for myself, and that I myself would answer the malicious anonymous article in the *Allgemeine Zeitung*, not indirectly through
my friends, but directly over my own name.

I will here opportunely mention that the editors of the French
ephemeral publication the *Revue Retrospective*, from which the
correspondent of the *Allgemeine Zeitung* drew his statements,
wished to express their dislike of such citation in a formal defense, which would, however, have been quite superfluous, as
the most superficial glance at that French publication would
amply show that it was quite innocent of any calumny on my
reputation; but the existence of that journal, which appeared in
irregular issues, was very ephemeral, and it was lost in the wild
whirlpool of the time, before the intended defense could appear. The editor-in-chief of that *Retrospective Review* was the
bookseller Paulin, a brave and honorable man, who had shown
himself for twenty years as very ready to assist and serve me, and
through business relations and mutually intimate friends we had
opportunities mutually to regard and respect each other. . . .

The editors of the *Allgemeine Zeitung* certainly knew nothing
of that French publication before they printed the charming
article on corruption. In fact, the most superficial examination
would have revealed to them the refined malicious cunning of
their correspondent. It lay in this, that he accused me of being
in union with persons who were as distant and different from me
as a Cheshire cheese is from the moon. In order to show that the
Guizot Ministry practiced corruption, not only by giving away
offices, but also by bestowing money, the above-mentioned Re-

view had published the budgets, receipts and expenditures of
the department which Guizot represented, and there was it
shown that every year enormous sums were assigned for expenses
not mentioned; and the accusing publication had threatened to
give in subsequent numbers the names of persons who had received the money. Owing to the sudden cessation of the Review,
the threat was not carried out, which we deeply regretted, since
everybody else could have seen how we had never taken part in
the secret munificence which proceeded directly from the Minister or from his secretary as a gratuity for certain services. A
marked distinction should be drawn between so-called *bons du
ministre*, or the secret service funds, and the *pensions* with which
the Minister finds his budget already charged, and to whom
certain sums are annually allotted for support. . . . Among the
men who were thus aided, we saw exiles from all parts of the
world, fugitives from Greece and San Domingo, Armenia and
Bulgaria, Spain and Poland, high-sounding names of barons,
counts, princes, generals, ex-ministers, and even priests, all
equally constituting an aristocracy of poverty, while on the treasury lists of other departments poor devils less pretentious were
paraded. . . .

Before November 29, 1840, when Guizot assumed the Ministry, I had never had the honor to see him. For the first time, one
month later, I paid him a visit to thank him that the business
branch of his department had received orders from him that my
yearly pension should continue to be paid monthly under the
new Ministry as before. That visit was the first and last which I
in this life ever paid to the illustrious man. In the conversation
with which he honored me, he expressed with deep feeling and
warmth, his high esteem for Germany, and this recognition of
my native land, as well as the flattering terms in which he spoke
of my own literary productions, were the only coins with which
he bribed me. It never occurred to him to ask any service of me.
. . . Since that interview I have never seen M. Guizot, nor
even his secretary, nor any one who worked in his bureau. Only
once did I learn that M. Guizot was often and urgently impor-
tuned to banish me from Paris. It is not without laughing that I

think of the pitiful figures which those claimants would have cut if they had known that the Minister from whom they begged for my expulsion was actually paying me a pension.

—Retrospective Declaration, August 1954
Lutetia, 2

Neglect of Naturalization

I will now recklessly admit that I never was naturalized in France, and that my naturalization, of which so much was said, was all a German fiction. I know not what idle or crafty head invented it. Several of my fellow-countrymen declared that they had scented it out from authentic sources; they referred to them in German newspapers, and I confirmed the error by silence. My dear literary and political adversaries at home, and many very influential intimate friends here in Paris, were led astray by this and believed that I was protected by a French citizenship from many vexations and machinations wherewith the friends who are here submitted to an exceptional jurisdiction can be so easily persecuted. By this amiable error I escaped much ill-will, and also many contributions to industrials who had turned their privileges to good account in business conflicts. The condition of a foreigner who is not naturalized becomes in Paris in the long run as unpleasant as expensive. He is imposed upon and vexed, mostly by naturalized foreigners who are stimulated by their acquired rights to misuse them most discreditably. Impelled by irritated precautions, I once fulfilled the formalities which bound me to nothing, yet which left me in a condition, in case of need, to acquire the right of naturalization without delay. Yet I had always a secret antipathy definitely to complete this act. And owing to this hesitation, and to a firmly rooted dislike to naturalization, I came into a false position, which I must regard as the cause of all my troubles, vexations and mistakes during my twenty-three years' residence in Paris. The income of a good office would have fully covered the cost of expensive housekeeping, and the wants of a not so much extravagant as a naturally free manner of living; but without naturalization all state

service was closed to me. My friends placed before me great
honors and fat sinecures, and there were examples enough of
foreigners who had risen in France to the most brilliant grades
of power and of honor. And I, I venture to say, should have had
less to strive than others with local envy, for no German had
ever gained to such a high degree as I the sympathy of the
French, whether in the literary world or in the best society; and
it was not as patrons, but as friends that the first and best sought
my company. The chivalrous Prince who was nearest the throne,
and who was not only a distinguished military leader and statesman, but who also read the *Book of Songs* in the original, would
have gladly seen me in the French service, and his influence
would have been all-sufficient to advance me in such a career. I
never shall forget the amiable kindness with which once, in the
garden of a princely woman friend, the great historian of the
French Revolution and of the Empire, who was then the all-
powerful President of the Council, took my arm, and, while
walking with me, fully and earnestly impressed it on me that I
should tell him what my heart desired, and he would pledge
himself to obtain it. Even now the flattering ring of that voice is
in my ear; I still scent the perfume of the great magnolia tree by
which we passed, and which rose with its noble alabaster-white
and stately flowers in the blue air, as magnificently and proudly
as did then, in the days of his prosperity, the soul of the German
poet.

Yes, I have spoken the word. It was the foolish pride of the
German poet which kept me even *pro forma* from becoming a
Frenchman. It was an idealistic whim from which I could not
free myself. As regards that which we call patriotism, I was
always a free-thinker, but I could never free myself from a certain dread that I should do anything which might seem, even
only half-way, as a breaking loose from my native land. Even in
the mind of the most enlightened there remains a little *alraun*
root of the old superstition which will not be banned away. One
does not like to speak thereof, but it sends its folly into the most
secret corner of our soul. The alliance which I contracted with
our dear Frau Germania, the blonde savage, was never happy. I

can well remember certain moonlight nights when she tenderly
pressed me against her vast breasts with their virtuous nipples;
but there was only a certain number of these sentimental nights,
and towards morning there came over us an unpleasant gaping
coolness, and then began no end of quarrelling. And we lived
apart at bed and table; yet it never came to a real separation. I
never could bring my heart really to separate from my domestic
trouble. Every desertion is hateful to me, and I never could
part from a German cat or dog, however intolerable I found its
fleas and fidelity. The smallest sucking-pig of my fatherland cannot complain of me as to this. Among the aristocratic and brilliant sows of Perigord who discovered truffles and feed thereon,
I never denied the modest little grunters who at home in the
Teutobergian forest grub on native acorns from a plain wooden
trough, as their pious ancestors did when Arminius slew Varus.
I have not lost a bristle of my Germanism, not a bell from my
cap, and I have always the right to fasten on it the black-red-gold
cockade. And I still have the right to say to Massmann, "We
German donkeys." Had I let myself be naturalized in France,
Massmann might have replied, "I am still a German ass, but thou
art one no longer"—and then he would have thrown a scornful,
mocking somersault which would have broken my heart. No, I
have never exposed myself to such disgrace. Naturalization may
do for other people; a tipsy lawyer from Zweibrücken, a silly fellow with iron brow and copper-nose, may, to get a place as schoolmaster, give up a native land which knows nothing of him, and
will know nothing ever; but that will not do for a German poet
who has written the most beautiful German poems. It would be
a horrible and mad thought for me to have to say that I am a
German poet and also a naturalized Frenchman. I should seem
to myself to be like one of those monsters with two heads which
are exhibited in fairs. It would annoy me terribly in writing
poetry if I thought that one head began to scan in French turkey-
cock pathos the most unnatural Alexandrines, while the other
poured forth its feelings in the inborn, true, natural meters of
the German language. And oh! just as repulsive to me as the
measures are the verses of the French—this perfumed dirt! I can

hardly bear their altogether scentless better poets. When I study that so-called *poésie lyrique* of the French, then I recognize the grandeur and glory of German poetry, and then I dare imagine that I may boast of having gained my laurels in this field. We will not yield a single laurel-leaf, and the mason, when he is called on to decorate our tombstone with an inscription, should expect no protest when he engraves the words: "Here lies a German poet."

—Retrospective Declaration,
Lutetia, 2

The "knightly prince": the Duke of Orleans, eldest son of Louis Philippe, who met with a fatal accident in 1842. The princess: Cristina Belgiojoso. Massmann: Hans Ferdinand Massmann, German philologian, patriot, and promoter of athletics, who obtained the professorship at Munich for which Heine had hoped; he is mocked in the Travel Pictures, Atta Troll, and several of Heine's poems.

The registers of the Paris police show that Heine did in fact only enter a première demande, which corresponds to what are called "first naturalization papers" in the United States.

V

THE STRUGGLE FOR CONSCIENCE

For Freedom of Art

On December 10, 1835, the German Federal Diet ordained
that "the penal and police regulations of their country and the
existing statutes against misuse of the press would be applied
with full severity against authors, publishers, printers and dis-
tributors of writings of the literary school known under the designation 'Young Germany' or 'Young Literature,' to which, specifically, Heinrich Heine, Carl Gutzkow, Heinrich Laube,
Ludolph Wienbarg, and Theodor Mundt belong." Some days
later Boerne's name was added to the list of writers to be prosecuted. Furthermore, the spread of their works by the book trade
or by lending libraries was to be prevented. The prohibition also
applied to works that might appear in the future. It was provoked
by denunciations published by the evangelical theologians Hengstenberg and Wolfgang Menzel, the former allies of Heine
and Boerne. Writers on the list who resided in Germany
were arrested. Economic ruin as well as police prosecution
threatened all.

The measures of the German government against Heine and
the other writers affected attracted great attention all over
Europe. The measures planned could not be carried out permanently in their full severity, but their initial onset must have
made Heine and his publisher very anxious.

In the beginning, at any rate, Heine did not take the danger
seriously. He believed that a Protestant state like Prussia might
well hamper political opposition, but would not be capable of
suppressing religious discussion.

I adjure you by all that you hold dear, even if you do not take
sides in the war which Young Germany is waging, at least maintain a very protective neutrality and do not provoke this young

group with a single word. Distinguish sharply between political and religious questions. In political questions you can make as many concessions as ever you like, for political state-forms and governments are only means; monarchy or republic, institutions democratic or aristocratic, are things indifferent, so long as the struggle over the first principles of life, over the idea of life itself, has not been settled. Only later does the question arise of what means can best contribute to the realization of this idea in life, whether by monarchy or republic or aristocracy or even absolutism—and I have no very great aversion to the last. By keeping the questions apart, the scruples of the censorship can also be allayed; for discussions of religious principles and morality cannot be suppressed without annulling all Protestant freedom of thought and freedom of judgment. . . .

Even without these suggestions you will perhaps have gathered why I have always entrenched myself in the Protestant shelter, just as you can easily understand the vulgar cunning of my opponents who would relegate me to the synagogue—me, the born opponent of Jewish-Mohammedan-Christian Deism. . . .

Your question regarding my return to Germany pained me deeply; unwillingly do I confess that this voluntary exile is one of the greatest sacrifices that I must offer to thought. If I returned, I should have to take up a position which might expose me to all possible misinterpretation. I wish to avoid even the appearance of the unbecoming. So far as I know, no government can have anything against me. I have kept my distance from all the agitations of Jacobinism. . . . From all sides friendly expressions reach my ear through the diplomats in Paris, with whom I am on very good terms. But all these are grounds to keep me from returning home rather than to induce me to do so.

—To Heinrich Laube
Boulogne-sur-Mer, November 23, 1835

This letter was written after the appearance of Menzel's denunciation, but before the issuance of the decree of the Diet. In writing the following letter, also, Heine was not yet clear about the situation.

I do not take the whole prosecution of "Young Germany" so seriously. You will see: a great boast and little roast. If I should really be put on a proscription list, I believe that nothing more than *démarches* would be required on my side to free me of it. All that is intended is to humble me. Prussia cannot dare do that unheard of thing of prohibiting books that are not yet written; besides public discontent there would be ridicule. I will not let myself be outfaced, and am of the opinion that the bolder a front one shows, the more easily can those people be handled. In danger the most dangerous thing is fear. In the consciousness of not having written anything against the government for four years, and of having separated myself, as is notorious, from Jacobinism—in a word, with a right good loyal and royal conscience I will not be so cowardly as to disavow the young people who are politically innocent. . . .

If the Prussian government should really be misguided to that madness of proscription, I believe I can elude its decrees more easily than anyone. I believe I write well enough so that at need I could omit my name from the title-page.

—To Julius Campe
Paris, January 12, 1836

To the Diet:

I am much troubled by the Resolution which you passed at your thirty-first sitting of 1835. I confess, gentlemen, that the greatest astonishment is allied with this feeling of uneasiness. You have accused me, tried me, judged me, without giving me a hearing on paper or by word of mouth, without any one being commissioned to defend me, without any summons being sent to me. The Holy Roman Empire, to which the German Union is successor, did not so comport itself in similar cases. Dr. Martin Luther, of glorious memory, could appear before the Reichstag provided with a safe-conduct and defend himself freely and openly against all charges. Far be from me the presumption of comparing myself with that highly esteemed man who has won for us freedom of thought in religious matters; but the disciple is fain to invoke the example of the master.

If, gentlemen, you will not grant me a safe-conduct to defend myself in person before you, then do you grant me at least the right of free speech in the German Press and withdraw the interdict that you have placed upon everything that I may write. These words are not in protest, only in petition. If I do protect myself against anything, it is against public opinion, which might regard my enforced silence as a confession of criminal tendencies, or as a disclaimer of my writings. As soon as free speech is granted to me, I hope to show conclusively that my writings are not the fruit of irreligious or immoral caprice, but of a truly religious and moral synthesis, a synthesis long honored not only by a new literary school, called "Young Germany," but by our most celebrated writers, poets as well as philosophers. But whatever, gentlemen, you may decide in answer to my petition, you may rest assured that I shall ever obey the laws of my country. The accident of my living outside your jurisdiction will never lead me to use brawling language; I honor in you the highest authority of a beloved country. The personal security which my sojourn abroad affords me happily permits me, gentlemen, to offer assurances of my deepest reverence with appropriate humility without fear of being misunderstood.

—Paris, Cité Bergère No. 3, January 28, 1836
Heinrich Heine
Doctor of Both Laws

The Diet did not deign to answer Heine's epistle. Heine very soon had to realize that the "Protestant refuge," of which he expected so much in his letter to Laube, could afford him no secure defense. He had also believed that his appeal to the example of Luther would make an impression on the Prussian government. But the Prussians were much more embittered by his religious than by his political criticism. Prussia not only anticipated the prohibition of the Diet with similarly sharp measures, but it even caused its envoy at Paris to threaten all French newspapers which printed contributions from Heine with a ban within the territory of the Prussian state. This pressure was futile, to be sure, but the financial effects of the prohibition in Germany were so much the more pressing as Heine had shortly before guaranteed a loan for a friend to the sum of 20,000 francs, and now had to make good since the friend was unable to pay. He could only meet the indebtedness by transferring to Campe the rights for a collected edition of his works for a period of eleven years. At this critical juncture the Prussian government made a solution available by an offer to permit the circulation of Heine's works if their author should submit to Prussian censorship. Campe was prepared to agree to this proposal; but Heine immediately realized that it would seriously compromise him in public opinion. Rejection of the Prussian offer was for him a point of honor, and he insisted upon the withdrawal of the manuscripts which Campe had already turned over to the Prussian censorship officials.

Heine now regarded his situation as very grave. The most important sources of his income threatened to dry up. Besides, he correctly apprehended a grave danger to political and artistic freedom in the agreement of reactionary German governments with German nationalism which fought under a liberal or democratic mask. Hence, he undertook to chastise Wolfgang Menzel who had theretofore been a champion of liberalism.

I perceived long ago that there is no going straightforward with verse, and therefore I turned to good prose. But as fine weather and spring sunshine and the charm of May do not go very far in prose, I had to discover new matter for my new form. I hit upon the unhappy idea, therefore, of occupying myself with ideas, and I pondered the inner meaning of appearances, the ultimate bases of things, the destiny of the human race, and the means by which people can be made better and happier, and the like. My natural enthusiasm for these things made it easy for me to handle them, and I was soon able to set down my thoughts in very beautiful and excellent prose. But, alas! when I had got so far in my writing, I was forbidden to write. You know the Resolution of the Bundestag of December 1835, by which an interdict was laid upon all my writings. I wept like a child! I had taken so much pains over the German language, with the accusative and dative, and had learned how to string words together so beautifully, like pearls, and had such pleasure in that occupation, which shortened for me the long winter evenings of my exile—indeed, when I was writing in German I could imagine that I was at home with my mother. And now I am forbidden to write! . . . If it is distressing enough that I, a poet of Germany, must live in exile, it will surely give every feeling man double pain that I am now, in addition, robbed of my literary property, my slight poet's wealth, that could at least protect me from physical misery in a foreign country.

I say these things with sorrow but not with discouragement. Whom should I accuse? Not the princes, for, as an adherent of the monarchic principle, a believer in the sanctity of kingship, as I have shown myself since the July Revolution, despite the dangerous bellowing of my environment, I would not truly afford any assistance to accursed Jacobinism by any particular complaints of my own. Nor can I complain to the Councils of the princes because, as I have discovered from the surest sources, many of the highest statesmen have deplored with commendable sympathy the exceptional situation in which I was placed, and have promised prompt assistance. Yes, I know it well, and it is only because of the slow pace of business that this assistance has not yet been legally brought to the light of day; perhaps while I write these very lines something of the sort will be promulgated in Germany in my favor. Even my decided opponents among German statesmen have given me to understand that the severity of the above-mentioned decree of the Diet were not meant to affect one's complete writings but only the political and religious portion; the poetic portion may express itself unhampered in poems, dramas, novels, in that pretty play of the fancy for which I possess so much genius. I could almost come to believe they wished to do me a service and force me not to squander my talent on thankless themes.

I am far from claiming all German virtues, and least of all the kind of honesty which is regarded as a special sign of Germanism.

I have told many a fool to his face that he was a sage; but I did it out of politeness. I have scolded many a sensible man for being an ass, but I did it out of hatred. Never have I purposely employed equivocation, anxiously awaiting the issue in politics or in private life, and never at all has pitiful self-seeking lain at the basis of my words. Of Menzel's politics in matters of politics I may not speak here; for politics' sake. . . .

Herr Menzel did not attack me personally, and I have no personal grudge against him. But we were once good friends and he has often assured me of his love for me. He has never reproached me with being a bad poet, and I praised him, too. I was pleased with him and I praised his work in a journal which did not long survive my praise. I was very young then, my greatest amusement was to put fleas under the microscope and demonstrate their size to people. Herr Menzel, on the other hand, put Goethe under a diminishing glass—and that gave me a childish pleasure too. . . .

Lack of knowledge and the need to conceal this lack perhaps produced most of Herr Menzel's mistakes and rascalities. If he had understood Greek it would not have occurred to him to oppose Goethe. Unluckily, Latin too was not his forte, and he therefore had to stick closer to the German. . . .

I only say this in order to point out the germ and origin of his Teutomania, not to annoy him, and I must repeat that in general I do not speak of him from spite or animosity. If there is harshness in what I say, it is not my fault. It is necessary to show the public what relationship it has with that hectoring hero of the national idea, that guardian of all that is German, who is forever casting slurs upon the French, and who has declared that we poor writers of Young Germany are Frenchmen and Jews. As for his "Jews," that is of no importance. We do not seek the alliance of the mob, and a man of culture knows quite well that people who are accused as enemies of Deism can have no sympathy with the synagogue. One does not turn to the faded charms of the mother when the daughter, growing old, no longer pleases. But that we should be represented as enemies of Germany, who have betrayed the Fatherland to France, was a trick as cowardly as it was knavish.

There are perhaps some honest haters of the French in this mob who mistake us so wretchedly and accuse us with such perverse humor because of our sympathy for France. Others are old mastiffs who still bark as they did in 1813 and whose very clamor is evidence of our progress. . . . But most of those haters of the French are rogues who simulate that hatred of set purpose. . . . France is now our natural ally. Anyone who does not realize this is stupid. One who does realize it and still combats it is a traitor. . . .

Whoever has lived out his days—the damp, cold days and the long black nights—in exile, whoever has gone up and down the hard stairs of a strange land, will understand why I repudiate the aspersion upon my patriotism more angrily and at greater length than all the other calumnies which have been preferred against me for so many years and which I have borne proudly and patiently. . . .

I would like to defend, not myself, but my writings against the accusations of atheism and immorality. But this is not possible unless I were allowed to develop my views of religion and morality from the vantage point of a synthesis. I am in hopes that I shall be allowed to do this.

—On the Denunciators

In addition to his political and financial pressures, Heine was now troubled by serious anxiety concerning his physical state. His illness affected his eyes, and for a time it seemed as if he were threatened with total blindness. Since he was not able to work, he undertook a journey to Sweden. In his enforced inactivity, he was assailed by doubts as to whether it was sensible to continue the struggle.

For a fortnight I have been wishing to write you to ask a favor. I was on the point of going to Naples, and I thought of asking you for some letters of introduction in that city. But on the eve of my departure I learned that the cholera was raging at Naples also and creating havoc. Only fools would go to meet useless danger, and consequently I very sensibly remain in the Provence. I do not wish to "see Naples and die." . . .

Today is October 30, and snow covers all the roofs of Aix, and even the statue of good King René, which I can see from my window. . . . What a great monarch was this King René! In the library I have seen his prayer book, with the initial letters colored by his own hand. As you see, I learn as I travel. I have also visited the Baths where the Romans bathed. I have seen the delightful Madonna by Chastel, a great sculptor who died at the public hospital. Not far from the church which contains this master-piece is the Rue Belgarde; there, near the Belgarde gate, on the left, is the humble nursery in which one of the noblest sons of the Revolution first saw the light of day. I have also inspected the cathedral and the curiosities on display there, for example, the four Roman columns which belonged to a temple of Apollo and which now support the roof of a Christian baptistry. See how even the stones submit to the necessity of serving the vic-tors, though they have not the excuse of our human needs, being vexed neither by hunger nor thirst nor vanity.

Should I, dear lady, proceed to make my peace, an ignoble peace, with the powers beyond the Rhine, in order to be able to leave my exile and this tiresome predicament which is worse than utter indigence? The temptations, alas, have been growing for some time. But have I not greater freedom than those who are styled Brutus or Regulus? No! I am no Regulus; I have no yearning to be cradled in a hogshead studded with spikes. I am no Brutus; I would never plunge a dagger into my poor belly to avoid serving the Prussians. No, with such a choice I should not kill myself, but turn beast. But what price these idle words— which might make you believe that the man who wrote them has succumbed to great unhappiness—the unhappiness, dear Prin-cess, of being unworthy of your friendship. Nay, Princess so fair and so compassionate, it is only that I am ill at this moment, an illness rather of the spirit than of the body. Jaundice is now eating at my heart, and all my feelings and all my thoughts are stained with that murky yellow which you observed in my person on the eve of my departure, when I was making my farewells at La Jonchère.

You would have a correct notion of the sad state of my moral health if you knew what reaction recently took place in my spirit with respect to the religious doctrines of which I am known to be an antagonist. My opinions are in contradiction to my feelings; upon my head I wear a garland of roses, but there is pain in my heart. I thirst for moral unity, for harmony between my opinions and my feelings; I must pluck all the rose petals from my garland, and leave only a crown of thorns, or I must extirpate all sufferings from my heart and supply their place with new gladness. But, alas! in vain do I fight the sufferings; they are girt in armor, and the keenest weapons of reason are blunted against them. . . .

You are the most complete person that I have found on earth. Indeed, before I knew you I imagined that a creature like you, endowed with all perfection, physical and spiritual, could exist only in fairy tales, in the dreams of the poet. But now I know that the ideal is no vain chimaera, that there is a reality to correspond to our sublimest ideas; and when I think of you, dear Princess, I sometimes cease doubting another divinity which I have been in the habit of banishing from my dreams.

—To Princess Belgiojoso (in French)
Alix, October 30, 1836

When I lay deathly sick at Paris not long ago and in my sleepless nights of fever made a muster of all my friends to whom I could confidently trust the execution of my last wishes, I found that I did not possess two such upon earth and believed that I could really count only on you, and perhaps a little on my brother Max. Therefore I turn to you today, and the friend to whom I have not written for years receives a letter from me asking him for money. I am by a most tragical circumstance in such a need of money as you can scarcely imagine, while I am far away from the few resources left to me after the shameful robbery practiced upon me by private persons and public governments. . . .

As for my solvency, I must tell you straightway that my affairs are at present in such a bad way that only a fool or a friend would lend me money now. I broke with my uncle the millionaire, angrily, some time ago; I could not stand his meanness any longer. My French friends in their amiable frivolity have led me into heavy losses. Others have exploited me. I am not allowed to publish anything in Germany but tame poems and innocent tales, and yet I have very different things lying in my desk; that my pen should have been confiscated without trial is an encroachment upon the most indisputable rights of property, of literary property; it is flat robbery. But these people have succeeded in ruining me financially.

I do not know, my dear Moser, if I am as much to you as I used to be. I only know that I have lost nothing of my own intrinsic value. If this were the case I should not now be in terrible need of money; at least, I should take refuge with people of another sort. Do not believe what is said of me; judge me by my actions. You should not believe in any article which is not signed by myself. I am attacked and reviled by Jews and Christians alike; the Jews are up in arms against me because I did not draw the sword for their emancipation in Baden, Nassau and other little hole and corner states. O the shortsightedness of them! Only before the gates of Rome can Carthage be defended. Have you, too, misunderstood me?

I write you these lines from Avignon, the former residence of the Popes and Petrarch's Muse. I love the one as little as the other. I hate the Christian lie, in poetry as in life.

—To Moses Moser
Avignon, November 8, 1836

Heine had broken with Moser because of the latter's attitude in the battle with Platen: see p. 253.
Heine's health improved, and the prohibitions also were lightened. But in return he fell into a series of quarrels, with writers

of the right as of the left, which lasted more than five years. Heine was attacked with special sharpness by Carl Gutzkow, who had shared Heine's disabilities resulting from the measures against Young Germany, and by Arnold Ruge, the radical neo-Hegelian. Gutzkow's antagonism was the more injurious to Heine in that Gutzkow was in close association with Campe. All these feuds, in which Heine was reviled and persecuted as poet, politician and private individual, produced a feeling of solitude and of alienation from Germany. Hostile remarks made by German emigrants and by a considerable portion of the German Press also made his stay in Paris uncomfortable, though there was scarcely any change in the benevolent attitude of the French.

Before matters came to an open conflict between Heine and Gutzkow, Gutzkow had read the manuscript of Heine's cycle of poems entitled Various in Campe's publishing house, and in a letter urged Heine to leave the poems unprinted, for publication of them would completely ruin his literary position. He claimed to speak in the name of the young generation of German poets, and warned Heine of their discontent. Heine postponed printing the poems for some years, but did not allow Gutzkow's threats to thwart his independence.

You may be right in thinking that certain poems in it might be used by my opponents; for they are as hypocritical as they are cowardly. . . . I do not think I shall have to reject a single one of these poems in later editions and I shall print them with a good conscience, as I would print the Satiricon of Petronius or the Roman Elegies of Goethe, had I written those masterpieces, and like the Elegies my poems are not food for the masses. You are on the wrong tack in this connection. Only cultured minds, which can take an intellectual delight in the artistic treatment of a wicked and all-too-natural subject, can find pleasure in these poems. Very few Germans are able to express an individual judgment of these poems since the subject of them, the abnormal amours of a madhouse such as Paris, is unknown to them. The autonomy of art is called in question, not the moral needs of a respectable married citizen of a corner of Germany.

My motto is: "Art for Art's sake, Love for Love's sake, and Life for Life's sake."

What you say about the younger off-shoots of our literature is very interesting. However, I am not afraid of the criticism of these people. If they are intelligent then they know that I am their best prop, and they must praise me as their own in their attack on the ancients. If they are not intelligent—then they are certainly not dangerous! I am not nearly so careless as you think. I am trying to fortify my mind for the future; not long ago I read the whole of Shakespeare, and now, by the sea, I am reading the Bible. As for public opinion of my earlier writings, it depends so much upon a sequence and concurrence of things that I cannot have much to do with it myself. But I do honestly confess that the great interests of European life always interest me far more than my own books—*que Dieu les prenne en sa sainte ét digne garde!*

—To Carl Gutzkow
Granville, August 23, 1838

The principle of "Art for Art's sake" and of the autonomy of art was actively debated in French literature during the first years of Heine's residence in Paris. Heine's friend, Théophile Gautier, was one of the firmest adherents of this theory, whereas the majority of French romanticists subordinated art to religious or humanitarian ideals. Insofar as the principle had representatives in Germany, they attached themselves closely to Goethe's formulation of the relationship between art and life.

I am for the autonomy of art, which should be the handmaid of neither religion nor politics, for it is in itself its own aim, like the world itself. Here we encounter the same narrow-minded or one-sided reproaches which Goethe had to endure from the pious brethren, and, like him, so must Victor Hugo bear the unjust accusation that he has no enthusiasm for the ideal, that he is without moral basis, that he is a cold-hearted egoist.

—The French Stage, 6

What is to be understood by the word character?

Character is the property of a man who lives and works in the definite peripheries of a definite view of life, identifies himself with them, and never falls into contradiction with his thought and feeling. In the case of very extraordinary spirits who tower above their age, the crowd cannot therefore know whether or not they possess character, because the large crowd has not sufficient vision to oversee the peripheries within which those lofty spirits move. . . .

The principle that the character of a writer can be discerned from his manner is not unqualifiedly correct; it is applicable only to that mass of authors whose pens are guided only by momentary inspiration and who rather hearken to than command the word. In the case of artists, that principle is not admissible, for they are master of the word, manage it for any purpose they desire, fashion it according to their caprice, write objectively: their character is not revealed in their style. . . .

"They have eyes and see not, ears and hear not, they have noses and smell not"—these words may very well be applied to that dull crowd which will never comprehend that without inner unity no spiritual greatness is possible and that the thing which must properly be called character is among the most essential attributes of the poet.

The distinction between character and poet has in fact proceeded from Boerne himself, and he himself has elaborated those detestable conclusions which his adherents retail against the writer of these pages. In the *Paris Letters* and in the articles of the *Réformateur* there is already a deal of chatter about my lack of character as a poet and the characterlessness of my poetry, and the most venomous insinuations wind and curve through these writings. Not with definite words but with all manner of hints, I am here suspected of the most equivocal mind if not of total mindlessness. . . .

Whether what I have created in this life is generally good or bad, we shall not argue. Enough that it was great; that I knew from the painful extension of soul out of which these creations proceeded—and I knew it also from the puniness of the dwarfs who stood before it and blinked dizzily upward—their vision could not reach to the summit and they only bumped their noses on the pedestal of these monuments which I have planted in the literature of Europe, to the eternal glory of the German spirit. Are these monuments quite without taint, are they wholly without fault or sin? Truly, neither on this point will I say anything definite. But the exceptions which these petty people take to it only demonstrate their own prettified limitations. . . .

—Ludwig Boerne, 5

As in his expressions concerning Goethe, so also in his judgment of other writers, Boerne betrayed his Nazarene limitations. I say Nazarene to avoid using either "Jewish" or "Christian," though both expressions are synonymous for me, and I use them to designate, not a faith, but a nature. "Jews" and "Christians" are for me closely kindred terms in contrast to "Hellenes," by which name, again, I designate no definite people, but a direction of spirit and a view of the world, innate as well as acquired. In this connection I might say that all men are either Jews or Hellenes, men with ascetic, art-hating drives seeking spiritualization, or men with joy in life, pride in development, and realistic nature. Thus there have been Hellenes in the families of German preachers, and Jews who were born in Athens and perhaps descended from Theseus. Here one can truly say that the beard does not make the Jew, nor the braid the Christian. Boerne was thoroughly Nazarene; his antipathy to Goethe proceeded directly from his Nazarene nature; his later political exaltation was based upon that stark asceticism, that thirst for martyrdom which is found among republicans generally, which they call republican virtue and is so little different from the earlier Christians' yearning for immolation.

—Ludwig Boerne, 1

Heine's book on Boerne aroused a storm of indignation in German leftist circles. His rejection of republican radicalism and his avowal of the independence of artistic creation brought upon him the charge of being without conscience. Particular objection was made to Heine's remarks about Boerne's private life, especially about his relationship to Jeanette Wohl, who was married to Salomon Strauss. Strauss tried to bring Heine to account and spread the report that he had boxed Heine's ears on the public streets of Paris. There followed a vigorous polemic waged in the newspapers by both parties, and a duel between Strauss and Heine in which the latter was wounded. Shortly before this duel, on August 31, 1841, Heine was married to Mathilde in order to secure her for any eventuality. Later, in a letter of December 22, 1845, to Dr. L. Wertheim, Heine declared that even at the time of his duel with Strauss he had become convinced that his aspersions with regard to Mme. Strauss-Wohl rested on false information and that he was prepared to omit the passages in a new edition of his book on Boerne. But no new edition of the book was printed in Heine's lifetime. The book was a failure and brought him much new enmity. Only very few of his friends, above all Varnhagen von Ense, publicly took his part.

In the midst of these corroding quarrels and vexatious provocations, Heine produced a masterpiece of sovereign humor, fanciful and realistic description of landscape, political and literary satire, and free poetic sensibility—the animal epic Atta Troll. He received the inspiration for this work in the bathing resort of Cauteret (Hautes Pyrenées), where he took the cure in the summer of 1841. In the figure of a dancing bear who escapes from his attendant and wishes to incite a revolution of bears against men, but is killed by treachery and cunning, Heine makes fun of poetry of political tendentiousness and of radicalism. But the fable of the bear is raised by colorful descriptions and manifold reflections above its polemical purpose into a "free forest-poem of Romanticism," to a fanciful midsummer night's dream, as Heine himself rightly characterized the poem. It is one of the most graceful compositions ever written in the German language.

My Atta Troll was written, as I say, in the late autumn of 1841, at a time when the great pother, in which my enemies of every complexion had conspired against me, had not quite worn itself out. It was a very great pother, and I should never have believed that Germany could produce so many rotten apples as were thrown at my head at that time! Our Fatherland is a blessed land: no lemons, no golden oranges grow there, and the laurel only comes forth maimed on German soil, but rotten apples abound in plenty, and all our German poets have sung a song of them. In that pother in which I was to lose both my crown and my head, I lost neither, and the absurd accusations with which attempts were made to incite the mob against me have fallen flat without my having to stoop to defend myself against them. Time undertook to justify me, and I have to recognize gratefully that the respective governments of Germany have in this respect put me under an obligation. The orders of arrest, which yearn for the return of the poet at every station on the German frontier are renewed every year at Christmas time, when the jolly little candles glitter on the Christmas tree. The way being rendered so insecure, it is quite impossible for me to travel in German territory, and therefore I celebrate my Christmas abroad, and shall end my days abroad, in exile. The doughty champions of Light and Truth, who accused me of inconsistency and servility, go about in safety in the Fatherland like prosperous servants of the state or dignitaries of a guild, or habitués of a club when of an evening they take refreshment patriotically in the wine of Father Rhine and the oysters of Schleswig-Holstein.

I have mentioned the date of the composition of *Atta Troll* with a special object in view. At that time, so-called political poesy was in full flower. "The opposition sold its skin and became Poetry." The Muses received strict orders no more to gad about in idleness and wantonness, but to enter into the service of the Fatherland as huckster-women of liberty or as washer-women to the Christian-Germanic nationality. There arose in the bardic grove of Germany that vague, fruitless pathos, that futile misty enthusiasm which, scorning death, plunged into an ocean of commonplaces. . . .

Talent was at that time a very uncomfortable possession, for it brought its owner into suspicion of want of character. Envious impotence had, after a thousand years of grubbing away for it, found its great weapon against the arrogance of genius: it found an antithesis between talent and character. It was almost flattering to the great masses to hear it maintained that honest men are as a rule very bad musicians, while good musicians are usually very far from being honest men, but that honesty and not music is the primary thing in the world. An empty head now bragged with authority of its full heart, and convictions were trump. I remember a writer of that time who accounted it an especial merit that he could not write: for his wooden style he won a silver cup.

By the immortal gods! I had to defend the inalienable rights of the intellect then, especially in poetry. As this defense was the great business of my life, I have not lost sight of it in the present poem, and the diction as well as the matter of it was a protest against the plebiscites of the political tribunes. And the very first fragments of *Atta Troll* which were printed roused the gall of my "character" heroes, my Romans, who accused me not only of literary but also of social reaction, and even of flouting the most sacred ideas of humanity. As for the aesthetic value of my poem, I gladly surrendered it to its fate, as I do now; I wrote it for my pleasure and the joy in the fanciful dream-fashion of that romantic school in which I passed the most pleasant years of my youth —and ended by cudgelling my schoolmaster. In this way, perhaps, my poem is reprehensible. But thou liest Brutus, thou liest Cassius, and thou too liest, Asinius, when you maintain that my satire touches those ideas which are the precious acquisition of mankind, those ideas for which I myself have so lustily fought and so much suffered. No: just because those ideas do ever present themselves to the poet, large and with a most splendid clarity, he is seized with an irresistible desire to laugh when he sees how roughly, how cruelly and awkwardly those ideas are apprehended by his limited contemporaries.

—Preface to Atta Troll
Paris, December 1846

Steps in the Return to Judaism

Heine's pagan-pantheistic hedonism, which drove him to combat Judaism and finds its conclusion in his opposition of Nazarenes and Hellenes, did not long maintain sole dominion in Heine's spirit, although it never wholly lost its attraction for the poet's mind. The fascination which the sensual conception of life exercised upon Heine remained strong to his last days, all the stronger, indeed, since his physical weakness made him an involuntary ascetic. Heine's intellect nevertheless soon recognized the weakness of the position which he had assumed in his battle against the "religion of spiritualism." The enthusiasm which he shared for a time with Prosper Enfantin for the "emancipation of the flesh" soon tacitly disappeared. Heine, who could not endure it if any man cast a lover's look at his Mathilde in a restaurant or theater and in such cases let fly in blind rage without regard for the number and strength of the opposition, could not long fail to realize that it would throw a peculiar light upon him if he should publicly preach a doctrine against which he defended himself with wild energy in his private life as a husband. Even on the adequacy of the aesthetic view of life Heine became more dubious the deeper his vision penetrated into the political, social and economic transformations of his time. His increasing knowledge taught him that the life of man demanded other attributes besides a sense of the beautiful and capacity for sensual enjoyment. Thus Heine attained an esteem for the Jewish moral law which had previously been alien to him. In the end, after he had so vigorously fought against "spiritualism," Heine found it necessary, in the preface to Atta Troll, to defend the "eternal rights of the spirit" against absence of spirit. He was forced to recognize that his depreciation of the spiritual in favor of the sensual and instinctive injured no one more than himself. This new realization made only slow progress in Heine's spirit, and was hampered by lasting conflict with his sensual tendencies; but it did gain ground despite much backsliding. At the end of 1838, Heine's friend, the famous orientalist Salomon Munk, asserted that Heine was again approaching Judaism. About this time, Heine attained to a new understanding of Jewish religiosity and morality by a renewed reading of the works of Shakespeare, and in particular The Merchant of Venice. The Jews still remained to him an "abstract people"—which is certainly not true of the picture that an unprejudiced study of the Old Testament yields; similarly the assumption of moral kinship between Jews and Germans must remain subject to question. But precisely this assumption shows how far Heine had removed himself from the standpoint of his Saint-Simonist period. Even more, Heine's prophecy of woe, whose truth the Hitler regime has confirmed more literally than the famous prophecy of the horrors of the German Revolution (see pp. 330 ff.), shows that he had left paganism and pantheism behind and conceived a stronger sympathy for religions which acknowledge a personal and transcendental God.

We may remark in Jessica a certain timid shame, which she cannot overcome when she must put on a boy's dress. It may be that in this we recognize the remarkable chastity which is peculiar to her race, and which gives its daughters such a wonderfully lovely charm. The chastity of the Jews is perhaps the result of an opposition which they always maintained against that Oriental religion of sense and sensuality which once flourished among their neighbors, the Egyptians, Phoenicians, Assyrians and Babylonians in rankest luxuriance, and which in continual transformation has survived to the present day. The Jews are a chaste, temperate, I might say an abstract race, and in purity of morals they are most nearly allied to the Germanic races. The chastity of the women among Jews and Germans is perhaps of no real value in itself, but its manifestation makes the most fascinating, charmingly sweet and deeply moving impression. It is touching even to tears when we read that, after the defeat of the Cimbri and Teutones, the women begged Marius not to give them over to the soldiery, but to make them slaves in the temple of Vesta.

It is indeed wonderful what a deep elective affinity prevails between both races, Jews and Germans. This chosen alliance did not originate in a historical course, because the great family chronicle of the Jews, or the Bible, was used by the whole Germanic world, nor because both races were from early times foes to the Romans and were thereby naturally allies; it has a deeper ground, the two being so much alike that one might regard primeval Palestine as an Oriental Germany, just as one might regard the Germany of today as the home of the Holy Word, as the mother-soil of prophetdom, as the citadel of the Holy Spirit.

But it is not Germany alone which bears the physiognomy of Palestine; all Europe raises itself to the Jews. I say raises itself, because in the beginning the Jews had the modern principle in themselves which is at the present day developing itself for the first time among the peoples of Europe.

Greeks and Romans held as if inspired to their native soil—to the Fatherland. The later Northern immigrants to the Graeco-Roman world were attached to the persons of their chiefs and, instead of antique patriotism, the Middle Ages witnessed the faith of vassals and loyalty to princes. But the Jews always held to and reverenced their Law, or an abstract conception, like our new cosmopolite republicans, who care neither for the country of their birth nor the persons of princes, but regard laws as leading principles or the highest. Yes, cosmopolitanism sprung from the land of Judaea alone, and Christ, who, despite the displeasure of the above-mentioned Hamburg grocer, was a real Jew, actually founded a propaganda of cosmopolitanism. As for the republicanism of the Jews, I remember having read in Josephus that there were in Jerusalem republicans who opposed the royally-inclined Herodians, fought them fiercely and called no man master, and hated Roman absolutism most bitterly. Freedom and equality was their religion. What madness!

—Shakespeare's Maidens and Women: Jessica

In fact, with the exception of Portia, Shylock is the most respectable person in the whole piece. He loves money, he does not conceal it—he cries it aloud in the public market-place. But there is one thing which he esteems above money, it is satisfaction for his injured feelings—the just retribution for his unspeakable insults. . . . No, Shylock loves money, but there are things which he loves more, among others his daughter. . . . Excluded from public life and Christian society, and forced into the narrow consolation of domestic happiness, there remain to the poor Jew only family feelings, and these come forth from him with the most touching tenderness.

—Shakespeare's Maidens and Women: Jessica

Has perhaps the faith in that extra-mundane thunder-god whom Moses preached become the fixed idea of a whole race, so that, though they have for two thousand years suffered from it by being put in strait-jackets and doused with cold water, yet for all that would not give it up. . . .

I will here by no means deny the value of that fixed idea, but I will only say that those who have it are much too weak to manage it, and therefore, being oppressed by it, have become incurable. What tremendous martyrdom have they suffered from it! What greater martyrdoms await them in future! I shudder at the thought and an infinite pity ripples through my heart. During the whole Middle Ages, till today, the predominant view of all things was not in direct contradiction with that idea with which Moses burdened the Jews, lashed it into them with holy straps, and cut it deeply into their flesh—in fact, they did not differ materially from Christians and Mohammedans, not by an antagonistic synthesis, but only by analysis and shibboleth. But if Satan, or the sinful pantheism—from which may all the saints of the Old and New Testament as well as the Koran protect us!— should ever be victorious, there will fall on the heads of the poor Jews a tempest of persecution which will far surpass all their previous sufferings.

—Shakespeare's Maidens and Women: Portia

The Jews are the people of the spirit, and whenever they revert to their principle they are great and majestic and put their coarse oppressors to shame and overcome them.

—Ludwig Boerne, 4

The Defense of the Jews of Damascus

In the Syrian city of Damascus there had disappeared, on February 5, 1840, the Capuchin monk, Thomas, and his servant. No trace of either was found. According to the report of the Austrian consul Merlato, the missing monk, who had lived in Damascus since 1806, was generally popular among the inhabitants, but had also acquired many enemies in consequence of his arrogance, frivolity and want of moderation. There arose a suspicion against the Jews of Damascus, not without the complicity of the French consul Ratti-Menton, that they had slain the Capuchin in a ritual murder. The government of the Vice-Regent Mehemed Ali of Egypt, which occupied Syria at the time, initiated proceedings against the Jews and extorted confessions from them by means of torture. Since France had supported the Vice-Regent in the eastern crisis of 1840, the French premier Thiers failed to discipline his consul at Damascus, although he saw through his dubious role. The majority in the French chamber of deputies similarly hesitated upon this occasion, which involved large matters of policy, to take a stand on behalf of righteousness and humanity. But in England, which sharply opposed the French policy in the current eastern crisis and was supported in its views by Austria, Prussia and Russia, the proceedings against the Jews of Damascus aroused great indignation. Moses Montefiore personally undertook to assist the Jews of Damascus. Before his departure for Syria he was fêted in a great gathering by the city of London. In France, Isaac Adolphe Crémieux was the first statesman of any standing who spoke on behalf of the persecuted Jews. For a long while he was quite alone. Only later did other French Jews also say a word on behalf of their Syrian co-religionists. Crémieux, too, went to Damascus, in order to defend the Jews there at their trial. He and Montefiore procured the release of the surviving defendants by a firman of Mehemed Ali.

Heine supported Crémieux's action from the beginning with great energy and without fear of consequences for his personal existence. The articles in defense of the Jews of Damascus which *appeared in the* Allgemeine Zeitung *exposed him to the danger of displeasing Thiers, to whom he owed his state pension (see p. 346), and to the charge that he was working against the interests of the state which afforded him asylum.*

I count on the columns of the *Allgemeine Zeitung* if the persecution of the Jews in Syria shall come before the tribunal of Mehemed Ali in Alexandria; the matter will offer great interest.

—To Gustav Kolb

Paris, March 15, 1840

The Paris newspapers of today present a communication from the Imperial-Royal Austrian consul in Damascus to the Imperial-Royal general consul in Alexandria in relation to the Jews of Damascus, whose martyrdom recalls the darkest times of the Middle Ages. . . . Meanwhile the executioner tortures, and on the bench of martyrdom the Jew confesses that, as he needed some Christian blood wherein to dip his dry Easter bread at the approaching Passover festival, he had for this purpose slaughtered an old Capuchin! The Turk is stupid and vile, and gladly places his apparatus of bastinado and torture at the service of Christians against the accursed Jews; for he hates both sects, regarding them as dogs, and calls them by such an honorable name, and he doubtless rejoices when the Christian Giaour gives him an opportunity with some pretence of justice for maltreating the Jewish Giaour. . . .

Fanaticism is an infectious evil, which spreads under the most varied forms, and finally rages against them all. The French consul in Damascus, Count Ratti-Menton, has brought evil things to pass, which have excited a general cry of horror here. It is he who inoculated the East with the Western superstition, and disseminated among the mob of Damascus a work in which Jews were accused of murdering Christians. This writing, which snorts with hatred, which Count Menton received from his spiritual friends for dissemination, was originally taken from the *Bibliotheca Prompta a Lucio Ferrario*, and it is distinctly asserted in it that the Jews in celebrating the feast of the Passover used the blood of a Christian. . . .

The present Minister of Foreign Affairs, M. Thiers, who lately attempted to appear not only as a man of humanity but also as a son of the Revolution, has shown a singular indifference as regards the occurrences in Damascus. . . .

Paris, May 14, 1840

But while the shrewd President of the Council shows that he knows how to tickle and profit from the national vanity of our dear Kechenaeer, the gaping gossips of the Seine, he shows himself very indifferent, and more than indifferent, in a matter where, not merely the interests of a country or of a race, but those of humanity itself are concerned. Was it want of liberal feeling or of shrewd sense which induced him to publicly take the part of the French consul who played the most shameful part in the tragedy at Damascus? No; M. Thiers is a man of great insight and humanity, but he is also a statesman; he has need not only of revolutionary sympathy, he wants aid of every kind; he must *transact*; he wants a majority in the Chamber of Peers; he can use the clergy as a Government aid, that is to say, that branch of clericals who, as they have no longer any hope of anything from the old Bourbon line, have wisely linked themselves unto the new. . . . Count Montalembert, the calmest member of the pious crew, who has also been, since the first of March, the running attendant of M. Thiers, is the visible mediator between the son of the Revolution and the fathers of the Faith, between the former editor of the *National* and the present editor of the *Univers*, which does all things possible to persuade the world in its volumes that the Jews eat old Capuchins and that the Count Ratti-Menton is an honorable man. This Count Ratti-Menton, a friend, or perhaps only a tool of the friends, of Count Montalembert, was formerly French consul in Sicily, where he was twice bankrupt and was driven out. Then he was consul in Tiflis, where he also had to leave the field, and that indeed for things not over-honorable. This only will I remark, that, at the time, the Russian Minister to Paris, Count Pahlen, gave Count Molé, the

French Minister of Foreign Affairs, firm notice that unless Count Ratti-Menton were recalled from Tiflis, the Imperial Prussian government would know how to drive him out in disgrace. The stick with which men fain would poke a fire should not be made of such vile, rotten wood.

Paris, May 27, 1840

In fact, we would rather praise than blame the Jews of Paris *if* they, as the North German journals preferred to declare, showed such great zeal and pity for their unfortunate brothers-in-the-faith in Damascus and shunned no pecuniary sacrifice for the honorable rescue of their slandered religion. But such is not the case. The Jews in France have been emancipated too long for the bond of their race not to have become loose and slack; they have all been sunk in—or to express it more correctly—have been raised to French nationality; they are Frenchmen like the rest, and have fits of enthusiasm which last for twenty-four hours, and, when the sun is warm, for even three days—and this holds for the better among them!

Many among them still observe the Jewish ceremonial rites, the external cult, in a mechanical way, without knowing why, out of old habit, but without a trace of inner faith; for the witty leaven of Voltairian criticism has worked as destructively in the synagogue as in the Christian church. Among the French Jews, as with other Frenchmen, gold is the god of the time, and industry is the prevailing religion. . . .

We must in justice admit as regards the great rabbi of the *rive droite*, Baron Rothschild, that he has shown a greater sympathy for the house of Israel than his scripturally-learned antagonist, the great rabbi of the *rive gauche*, M. Benoit Fould, who—while his brethren in the faith are tortured and strangled in Syria at the instigation of a French consul—made, with all the imperturbable calmness of a Hillel, a beautiful speech in the French Chamber of Deputies on the conversion of *rentes* and discount rates at the Bank.

The interest which the Jews here take in the tragedy of Damascus reduces itself to very minute manifestations. The Israelitish

Consistoir assembled and deliberated in the lukewarm fashion of all such bodies, and the only result of its deliberations was the opinion that the legal documents of the trial should be published. M. Crémieux, the celebrated lawyer, who devotes his magnanimous eloquence not only to Jews but to the oppressed of every faith, and all doctrines of every age, undertook the publication in question; and, with the exception of one beautiful woman and a few young literary men, M. Crémieux is the only person in Paris who actively busied himself with the affairs of Israel. At a great sacrifice of his personal interests and scorning every lurking fraud, he boldly met the vilest insinuations, and even offered to go to Egypt should the trial of the Damascene Jews be there held before the Pasha Mehemed Ali. . . .

The financial power of the Jews is indeed great, but experience teaches us that their greed is still greater. One of the most highly prized members of the religious community here—in fact, he is esteemed, or estimated, at about thirty million francs—M. Wilhelm de Romilly, would not give a hundred francs should any one ask him to contribute to a fund for rescuing his great race. . . .

When I, not long ago, turned over the *Histoire des Juifs* by Basnage, I had to laugh heartily at the naïveté with which the author replied to his enemies who accused him of having been paid by the Jews, utterly denying it, and sadly adding: *Le peuple juif est le peuple le plus ingrat qu'il y ait au monde!* . . .

And here I must make a remark, perhaps the bitterest of all. Among the baptized Jews are many who, out of cowardly hypocrisy, abuse Israel more vilely than do its born foes. And in the same fashion, certain authors, in order not to recall their origin, express themselves badly as to Jews, or are silent. That is a well-known, sadly ridiculous fact.

Paris, June 3, 1840

The reporter of the *Leipziger Zeitung* and of the smaller North German papers did not tell any direct untruths in joyfully declaring that the French Press, on this occasion, showed no special sympathy for Israel. But the honorable soul wisely took care not to lay bare the ground for this fact, which simply consisted in this, that the President of the Ministerial Council, M. Thiers, from the beginning took the part of Count Ratti-Menton, the French consul at Damascus, and the editors of all the papers which are under his control in this matter simply express his views. There are, it is true, many honest, indeed very honest, people among these journalists, but they now obey with military discipline the command of that generalissimo of public opinion, in whose ante-cabinet the order for the day is given out every morning; and certainly they cannot look one another in the face without laughing. . . . In his morning audiences, M. Thiers assures his hearers with the air of deepest conviction that it is perfectly settled that the Jews drank Christian blood at the Passover feast, *chacun à son goût*; all the reports of witnesses confirm the fact that the rabbi of Damascus butchered *pater* Thomas and drank his blood—his flesh was probably eaten by the minor officials of the synagogue—in which we could behold a sad superstition, a religious fanaticism which still prevails in the East, while the Jews of the West have become much more humane and enlightened, and many of them distinguish themselves by freedom from prejudice and good taste. . . .

A few days ago, M. Benoit Fould raised an inquiry as to the conduct of the French consul at Damascus. I therefore withdraw the reproach which escaped me in my last letter regarding that deputy. I never doubted the intelligence or the intellectual powers of M. Fould, and I regard him as one of the greatest minds of the French Chamber, but I did doubt his disposition or feelings. I very willingly let myself be put to shame when I have done people wrong and they refute it by their deeds. The question of M. Fould manifested great shrewdness and dignity. Very few journals have given extracts from his speech; the Ministerial sheets have suppressed even these, but published in all the more detail the opposing ideas of Thiers. In the *Moniteur* I have read them all. The expression, *La religion à laquelle j'ai l'honneur d'appartenir*, must strike a German vividly. The reply of M. Thiers was a masterpiece of malice and deceit. By evasion and by suppressing what he knew, and by seemingly taking pains to withhold other details, he succeeded most admirably in making his adversaries appear to be in a suspicious position. To hear him speak, one could really believe that Capuchins' flesh was the standing dish among Jews. But no, O great writer of history but very small theologian, in the East as little as in the West does the Old Testament allow its believers such dirty food. The disgust of the Jews for such bloody relish is altogether peculiar to them; it shows itself in the first dogmas of their religion, in all their sanitary laws, in their ceremonies of purification, in their fundamental views of what is clean and unclean, in the profoundly cosmogonic revelation as to material purity in the animal world, which also constitutes a physical ethic, and which was not in the least understood by Paul, who rejected it as a fable.

—Allgemeine Zeitung, 1840
Lutetia, 1

The Paris newspaper Le National *was the organ of the Radical Party before 1840.* L'Univers *was the newspaper of the Catholic ultramontane party.* Rive droite, rive gauche: *Two railroads were opened between Paris and Versailles whose shares were active on the Exchange. That on the right bank of the Seine was controlled by the Rothschild banking house, that on the left bank was controlled by the banking house of Fould. Heine frequently jested that the French Jews were divided into two sects, of one of which Chief Rabbi Rothschild was the head, and of the other Chief Rabbi Fould.*

I have suggested to my friend Crémieux to apply directly to the *Allgemeine Zeitung* in any cases where he may have any rectification to communicate from Alexandria. If this should happen, I hope that the *Allgemeine Zeitung* will not refuse my friend its support, out of affection for me and regard for its own dignity.— The article against the unfortunates of Damascus was certainly not written by Heilbronn, but by a certain Prussian, Baron Katt, and contains lies which require correction.

—To the Management of the *Allgemeine Zeitung*
Paris, October 1, 1840

Anticipations of the Revolution

Heine's letters on Damascus constitute a portion of the series of articles with which he resumed his activity as Paris correspondent of the Allgemeine Zeitung from 1840 to 1843. These articles which, in a carefully worked-over and completed form, appeared as a book under the title Lutetia, in 1854, show Heine as a keener observer and profounder expert of the popular life, politics and art of the French capital, than French Affairs had done. His glance embraces a far larger area of French culture than he did in his earlier book, which he himself had dismissed as the work of a novice. His judgment is grown mature, his knowledge of conditions and persons enriched. But even during his new period of activity as a correspondent, Heine learned much. The crisis of 1840 brought France, which supported the Viceroy of Egypt in his ambitious plans and actions against the Sultan, into serious conflict with England, Austria, Russia and Prussia, and it was forced to withdraw before the superior coalition; this had a very sobering effect upon Heine, for he had previously believed in the irresistible power of the revolutionary national feeling of the French. At the same time, he attained an acuter perception of the significance of economic matters, the influence of finance on policy, and the increasing might of proletarian movements, whose development he followed with equivocal feelings.

Herr von Rothschild is, in fact, the best political thermometer; I will not say weather-frog, because the word is not sufficiently respectful. And surely one must have respect for this man, be it only out of the respect which he inspires in others. I like best to visit him in his banking-house, where I can as a philosopher observe how people—and not only God's chosen, but all other kinds—bow and duck before him. There you may behold such a twisting and bending of backbones as the best acrobat could hardly equal. I have seen people who, when they drew near the great Baron, shrank up as if they had touched an electric battery. Even while approaching the door of his private office many experience a thrill of awe such as Moses felt on Mount Horeb when he saw that he stood on holy ground; and even as Moses took off his shoes, so more than one courtier or broker would fain remove his boots before entering the private office of M. de Rothschild, were he not afraid that the odor of his feet might embarrass the Baron. That private office is indeed a remarkable place, which inspires sublime thoughts and feelings as does the sight of the sea or of the starry heavens. We see here how small man is and how great is God! For gold is the god of our time and Rothschild is his prophet.

—Lutetia, 32

Here I would only take time to remark that our German preachers of freedom are as unjust as they are foolish when they attack the house of Rothschild with so much intensity and bloodthirstiness because of its political significance, because of its effect upon the interests of the Revolution, in a word, because of its public character. There are no stronger promoters of the revolution than these same Rothschilds . . . and what may sound even stranger: these Rothschilds, the bankers of kings, the princely money-baggers whose very existence would be most gravely imperilled by an overthrow of the European system of states, nevertheless bear in their nature the consciousness of their revolutionary mission. Specifically this is the case of the man who is known under the unassuming name of Baron James, and in whom the entire political importance of the house of Rothschild is now subsumed after the death of his illustrious brother from England. This Nero of finance, who has built his golden palace in the Rue Lafitte whence he rules the Exchanges as unlimited Imperator, like his sometime predecessor the Roman Nero, will in the end be the violent destroyer of the privileged patriciate and the founder of the new democracy. Once, several years ago, when he was in a good mood and we were walking arm in arm quite familionaire, as Hirsch Hyacinth would say, and were gadding about the streets of Paris, Baron James explained to me quite clearly how he himself had fulfilled the first prerequisite and pioneered the road for social advance everywhere by his system of government bonds.

I see in Rothschild one of the greatest revolutionaries who have founded modern democracy. Richelieu, Robespierre and Rothschild are for me three terrifying names, and they connote the gradual destruction of the old aristocracy. Richelieu, Robespierre and Rothschild are the three most fearful levellers in Europe.

That one virtually drowns in music here, that there is virtually no single house in Paris in which one can save himself from this noisy deluge as in an ark, that the noble art of sound floods our entire life—all of this is for me a perilous sign, and frequently I am seized with an unhappiness which borders on a most morose unfairness to our great maestri and virtuosi. Under these circumstances no very joyous hymn of praise can be expected from me for the man whom fashionable society, particularly the world of hysterical ladies, is at this moment exalting with a mad enthusiasm, and who is in fact one of the most remarkable representatives of the musical movement. I am speaking of Franz Liszt, the gifted pianist. Yes, the genius is here again and is giving concerts which have a magic bordering on the fabulous. Beside him all pianists vanish, with one single exception—Chopin, the Raphael of the pianoforte. In fact, with this sole exception, all other pianists whom we have heard in innumerable concerts this year are only pianists, they shine through the skill with which they manage the stringed wood; in the case of Liszt one no longer thinks of difficulties surmounted, the piano disappears, and only music is revealed. In this respect, Liszt has made the most marvelous progress since we heard him last. With his merits he combines a tranquillity which we previously missed in him.

—Lutetia, 33

Is it true that Meyerbeer will not allow his new opera to be presented if Mlle. Loewe is not engaged? Has Meyerbeer made the fulfilment of public wishes depend on so petty a condition? Is he really so extremely modest that he imagines that the success of his new work depends on the more or less complaisant throat of a prima donna?

When I last had the honor of seeing him, I was horrified by his wretched appearance. . . . May heaven grant our maestro better health and may he himself never forget that the cord of his life is so lax and the scissors of the Parcae so sharp. May he never forget what important interests are involved in his recovery. What would happen to his fame if he himself, the celebrated master, should (Heaven long forfend it!) suddenly be snatched from the scene of his triumph by death? Will his family continue that glory of which all Germany is proud? The family will surely not lack for material means, but it will for intellectual means. Only the great Giacomo himself, who is not only director-general of music of all royal Prussian musical institutions, but also the conductor of the Meyerbeer fame—only he can direct that monstrous orchestra. He nods his head and all the trumpets of the great journals resound in unison; he blinks his eyes and all the violins of praise fiddle for all their worth; he gently moves his left nostril and all the editorial-flageolets flute their sweetest melodies of flattery.

—Lutetia, 33

And yet, is Guizot really the man who is able to avert the impending disaster? There are, indeed, united in him the generally separated qualities of the most profound sagacity and an iron will; he would defy all storms with his antique firmness, and avoid dangerous sunken rocks with a most modern shrewdness; but the quiet tooth of the mice had gnawed too many holes in the bottom of the French ship of state, and Guizot, as he himself well knows, is powerless against this inner evil, which is far more dangerous than aught without. There lies the danger. Subversive or destructive doctrines have in France taken too strong a hold of the lower class; people are no longer contending for equal political rights, but for equality of enjoyment of the blessings of this earth; and there are in Paris about four hundred thousand roughs who only await the word of command to realize the idea of absolute equality which broods in their rude brains.

—Lutetia, 37

I am much afraid of the atrocities of a government by the proletariat, and I confess that I have become a conservative out of fear.

—To Gustav Kolb
Paris, January 27, 1841

Communism is the secret name of the terrible antagonist which sets proletarian rule with all its consequences in opposition to the *bourgeois régime* of today. It will be a terrible conflict—how will it end? *That* only the gods and goddesses can tell who know the future. This much we know, that communism, though it be at present little discussed, and now yearns away its life in forgotten garrets on wretched straw-pallets, is still the gloomy hero to whom a great if transitory part is assigned in the modern tragedy, and which only waits its cue to enter on the stage. We should never lose sight of this actor.

—Lutetia, 45
July 20, 1842

It is too bad that you did not always give me a free hand in the *Allgemeine Zeitung* and sometimes rejected my definite and repeated prophecies about socialism, which were at that time disregarded, as chimaeras or indirect propaganda! It must be admitted that I was among the few who judged the future correctly. Nor has anything surprised me. But much did distress me and, like all prophets, I have suffered most.

—To Gustav Kolb
Paris, August 21, 1851

My horror of communism has nothing in common with the fear of the lucky businessman who is afraid for his capital, or with the indignation of prosperous tradesmen who fear that their sharp dealings will be hampered; no, I am rather troubled by the secret anxiety of the artist and scholar, for we see our whole modern civilization, the laborious achievement of so many centuries, the fruit of the noblest efforts of our predecessors, threatened by the victory of communism. Carried away by the stream of a generous impulse, we may sacrifice the interests of art and science, even our own particular interests, to the general interest of suffering and oppressed people; but we can never conceal from ourselves what we must expect as soon as the great crude mass which some call the People and others call the Mob, and whose legitimate sovereignty has long since been proclaimed, attains to actual rule. The poet in particular feels a mysterious horror at the thought of this awkward sovereign assuming the rule. We would willingly sacrifice ourselves for the people, for self-sacrifice is among our most refined pleasures—the emancipation of the people was the great task of our life, and we have wrestled for it and endured nameless wretchedness at home and in exile—but the pure and sensitive nature of the poet strives against any close personal association with the people, and even more are we horrified at the thought of its caresses, from which God preserve us! . . .

Ah, the People, this poor king in rags, has found flatterers who empty their cauldron of incense much more shamelessly than the courtiers of Byzantium and Versailles. These coarse lackeys of the People incessantly praise its excellences and its virtues and cry out in transports: "How beautiful is the People! How good is the People! How intelligent is the People!"—nay, ye lie. The poor People is not beautiful; on the contrary, it is very loathsome, but this loathsomeness comes from dirt, and will disappear with it as soon as we build public baths where his Majesty the People can bathe gratis. A small piece of soap could do no harm, and we will then see a People which is neat and proper, a People that has washed. The People, whose kindliness is so highly praised, is not kindly; it is frequently as evil as other potentates. But its evil comes from hunger; we must provide that the sovereign People always has food, and as soon as its Majesty is properly pastured and satisfied, it will benignly and graciously smile, quite like the others. His Majesty the People is likewise not very intelligent; it is perhaps more stupid than the others, it is almost as beastly dumb as its favorites. Love and confidence it grants only to those who speak the jargon of suffering or howl, while it hates every brave man who addresses it in the language of reason in order to enlighten and refine it. . . . The reason for this perverseness is ignorance, and this national evil we must seek to eliminate by public schools for the People, where instruction can be imparted to it along with appropriate sandwiches and other sustenance, gratis. And if everyone in the People shall be put in position to acquire any knowledge he likes, then you will soon see an intelligent People. Perhaps it will eventually become as educated, as cultured, and as witty as we are, namely, as you and I are, my dear reader.

—Confessions

A legislative chamber must be composed of compact masses of different parties, or else the whole parliamentary machine cannot act. Should every deputy bring a special different and isolated opinion to market, there could never be a vote which could be in any way regarded as the expression of a common will; and yet the most essential condition of the representative system is that such a common will shall manifest itself. Like all French society, the Chamber is decomposed or cracked into so many splits and splinters that there are in it no two men who quite agree in their views. . . . But what will be the end of all this fine splitting, this dissolution of all the connecting links of thought, this *particularism*, this extinction of all mutual intelligence, which is the moral death of a race? What led to this state of affairs was the culture of material interests, selfishness and money.

—Lutetia, 39
Paris, December 28, 1841

The French have a short memory and soon forget their best-founded fears. Therefore they appear so often as actors—yes, and as leading actors—in the stupendous tragedy which the good Lord suffers to be played on earth. Other races have their great periods of movement, their history, only in their youth, at the age when they throw themselves without experience into action; for in later and riper years reflection and the weighing of consequences restrain nations, like individuals, from rash deeds, and it is only external pressure, not the pleasure in their own will, which drives them into the arena of general history. But the French always keep the light-heartedness of youth, and no matter what they may have done or suffered yesterday, today they think no more about it; the past is effaced from their memories, and the dawning day drives them on to new deeds, new daring, and new suffering. They will not grow old, and they believe perhaps that they will retain their youth by clinging to juvenile folly, heedlessness and generosity—yes, generosity.

—Lutetia, 50
Paris, July 29, 1842

What use to the French of all of their deftness, of all of their skilful and adaptable character, if they forget so quickly what they have done! They have no memory, and that is their greatest misfortune. The fruit of every deed and of every misdeed is lost through oblivion.

—Lutetia, Appendix
Paris, July 20, 1843

For the generosity with which he treated me I owe a great debt of gratitude to M. Guizot. But when my faith in his firmness towards the royal demands was shaken, and when I saw that he was dominated mischievously by the will of Louis Philippe, and understood the dreadful wrong-headedness of his autocratic obstinacy and morbid egoism, gratitude would have had no power to hold my words in check, and I should certainly have pointed out, respectfully but mournfully, the mistakes by which the too-yielding Ministry, or rather the crazy king, were leading the country and the world to ruin. But my pen was gagged by sheer physical incapacity. I am only able now to make public the real cause of my silence and *not*-writing.

Even if I had felt the desire to publish only a line in the *Allgemeine Zeitung* against the unholy system of government of Louis Philippe, it would have been impossible for me, for the very simple reason that the prudent king had, before the 29th

November, taken precautions against such a possibility of attack by a correspondent, by securing his august self, by making the then censor of the *Allgemeine Zeitung* at Augsburg not only a knight, but also an officer of the French Legion of Honor. However great then was my predisposition towards the king, the Augsburg censor found that I did not love him enough, and struck out every disparaging word and prevented the publication of many of my articles on the royal policy.

—Lutetia: Retrospective Declaration

August 1854

The ministry of Guizot-Soult was formed on November 29, *1840.*

Visit to Hamburg

In Paris, Heine repeatedly gave expression to his longing to see his mother again and to his nostalgia for Germany.

Anno 1839

O Germany, so far, so dear,
    Thy memory dims mine eye with woe!
This merry France seems sad and drear,
    Her lightsome folk a burden grow.

'Tis reason only, cold and bare,
    In witty Paris that is crowned—
O foolish bells! O bells of prayer!
    Yonder at home how sweet ye sound!

These men how mannerly! And yet
    Their courteous bow I take amiss.—
The rudeness that of old I met
    Where I was born, was joy, to this.

These smiling women! For their lives
    They chatter like a turning mill!

Give me the silent German wives,
　　That go to bed demure and still.

Here round and round in frantic chase
　　Things whirl as in a dream, and move!
There all seems nailed into its place,
　　And glides along the ancient groove.

The watchman's horn, I hear it blow:
　　Familiar, faint, from far it hails;
The watchman's song, I hear it grow
　　And mingle with the nightingale's.

Those were the poet's golden times,
　　'Neath Schilda's oaks of shadowy boon;
Where once I wove my tender rhymes
　　From the violet's breath and the light o' the moon.

　　　　　　　　　　—Margaret Armour

Night Thoughts

The thought of Germany at night
Drives slumber from my pillow quite;
My mind recalls the day of parting,
And hot, resistless tears are starting.

The years have come, the years have passed,
Since, mother dear, I saw thee last;—
Twelve years have gone—gone unreturning—
Yet grows my longing and my yearning.

My yearning and my longing grow,
That mother has bewitched me so;
I think of her as of no other,
May God preserve her, dear old mother!

The dear old dame, she loves me so!
In trembling lines her letters show,

By signs that cannot be mistaken
How deep her mother's heart is shaken.

Of her I think where'er I stay;
Twelve long, long years have passed away;
Twelve years 'mong strangers have distressed me.
Since to her true heart she has pressed me.

Ah, Germany lives evermore,
It is a land sound to the core,
With oaks and lindens firmly rooted;
Whene'er I wish I can salute it.

For Germany I should not care
So much, were not my mother there;
For it no trouble need I borrow,
But she I love may die tomorrow.

Ah, since I left my native land
Death touched with unrelenting hand
My early friends, aye, many perished
Whom in my youth I fondly cherished.

And if I count the shadowy crowd
My heart in anguish throbs aloud;
Could I these mournful figures banish,
I should have rest. Thank God, they vanish!

Thank God! Athwart the window-pane
Serene French daylight shines again;
In comes my wife, like morn in gladness,
And smiles away my German sadness.

—Frank Siller

In the same year, 1843, when this poem was written, Heine
decided to venture the journey to Hamburg in order to visit his
mother and sister and make a new agreement with Campe. Since
entry into Prussia was forbidden him, he travelled by way of

Brussels and Bremen. He returned through Prussian territory. This return journey in the opposite direction is described in the epic Germany: A Winter's Tale. Except for Salomon Heine, who was ailing but received his nephew cordially, the poet found all his relatives in good health and spent happy days with them. He also visited old friends, like Christian Sethe. From Campe he received a new contract by which Campe obtained publication rights for all of Heine's writings for an unlimited period and engaged to pay the poet, and after his death, his widow, an annual royalty of 2400 francs from 1848 onwards.

The literary fruit of this journey, Germany: A Winter's Tale, is humorous travel description with sharp satire against Prussia and its new king, Friedrich Wilhelm IV, who summoned the romantic spirit to his assistance against the contemporary liberal current. Heine did not forebear to include romantic allusions in his declaration of war against political romanticism, in order to make his mockery of the king, who had ruled since 1840, the more effective. He also reached back to the doctrine of Saint-Simon in order to give his satire a social basis, and in the midst of his playful tones there are feeling echoes of social complaint and of the battle for intellectual freedom. The liberals and the democratic German nationalists are attacked no less sharply than the King.

I travelled here only with a view of visiting my relatives and hurried through Germany as quickly as possible and wished to come back to Paris as quickly and directly, for my wife had given me only one month's furlough. Hence, I have made no overtures to the respective German governments and have no guarantee of security. Why should I make inquiries? That in itself is a concession, and I will truly make none. Not the Prussian government but I am the offended party, unjustly injured in matters of my private property—and should I then make humble inquiry whether I would suffer no personal affront if I came to Berlin?

—To Varnhagen von Ense
Hamburg, November 9, 1843

The Prussian government had issued an order of arrest against Heine for "insults to royalty and instigation to discontent." When later the poet wished to consult the friend of his youth, the famous physician Dieffenbach, in Berlin because of his illness, the Prussian Minister of Interior informed him that he would cause Heine to be arrested immediately upon his crossing the border. In Hamburg Heine was safe from arrest. His return journey through Prussian territory was made in strict secrecy and great haste.

Have also made many verses on my journey; they come with great ease when I breathe German air.

—To Julius Campe
Paris, December 29, 1843

I have been well of my eye-trouble for a month now. Before that I was almost blind—could not write and, what was worse, could not read. You have no idea of the uneasiness which devoured me. Happily my big poem was almost finished. . . . The whole brew speaks out about the present state of affairs in Germany in a bold and personal fashion. It is politico-romantic, and I hope will give the death-blow to the prosaico-bombastic poetry of "tendency."

—To Julius Campe
Paris, April 17, 1844

I wrote the following poem in January of this year in Paris, and the free atmosphere of that place breathes in many a strophe more acutely than I myself like. I took pains at once to modify and soften what seemed incompatible with the German climate. Nevertheless, when I sent the manuscript to my publisher in Hamburg, in March, many doubts had to be carefully balanced. I had to undertake the fatal business of revision again, and it may well have happened that the more serious tones were more muted than was necessary, or that the tinkle of humor became too obstreperously gay. From some naked thoughts I again wrested their fig-leaves in hasty impatience, and perhaps I have offended

squeamish ears. . . . But what I foresee with even greater apprehension is the outcry of the Pharisees of nationalism who now
share the antipathies of the government, enjoy the affection and
high esteem of the censorship, and can set the tone in the daily
press where it is possible for them to attack their own opponents
who are at the same time the opponents of their supreme rulers.
Our hearts are fortified against the displeasure of these heroic
lackeys in their liveries of black, red and gold. I can already hear
their beery voices: You even blaspheme our colors, you despiser
of the Fatherland, you friend of the French, to whom you would
yield the free Rhine! Calm yourselves. I will regard and respect
your colors when they merit it, when they shall no longer be an
idle or servile sport. Plant the black, red and gold banner upon
the heights of German thought. Make it the standard of free
humanity, and I will offer up my best heart's blood for it. Calm
yourselves. I love the Fatherland as well as you. Because of this
love I have spent thirteen years of my life in exile, and because
of this love I return to exile, perhaps forever. At least without
whining and without drawing down the corners of my lips in a
grimace of suffering. I am the friend of the French, as I am the
friend of all men if they are good and reasonable, and because
I myself am not so stupid or so evil that I could wish that my
own Germans and the French, both the chosen peoples of
humanity, should break each other's neck to the advantage of
England and Russia and to the malicious joy of all the squires
and parsons of this globe. Be calm. I will never yield the Rhine
to the French, for the very simple reason that the Rhine belongs
to me. Yes, it belongs to me by inalienable right of birth. I am
the free son of the free Rhine; my cradle stood upon its banks,
and I see no reason why the Rhine should belong to others than
the children of its own country.

—Preface to Germany: A Winter's Tale

Heine wrote this preface in Hamburg September 17, 1844; this
time he had arrived by boat from Le Havre accompanied by
Mathilde. At his earlier sojourn in Hamburg, in 1843, the numerous changes in the economic and political situation of Germany

interested him so intensely that he determined to study them
more thoroughly on a second visit and to embody his new impressions in a book. He was prevented from doing so by a new
onset of his eye-trouble which forced him to long inactivity in
Hamburg. Nevertheless, he personally saw to the printing of the
New Poems despite his physical handicap. This second collection
of Heine's poems which contained beside the previously suppressed cycle Various (see p. 367), several ballads and romances
which soon grew famous, as well as satirical political poems of
unexampled power, appeared in the autumn of 1844, and immediately came into such demand that upon his return to Paris
Heine heard that a second edition was already in request.

VI

THE MATTRESS CRYPT

The Quarrel about the Inheritance

On December 23, 1844, shortly after the poet returned to
Paris, Salomon Heine died. The relations between uncle and
nephew, which had long, especially from 1835 to 1837, been
strained, had lately taken a turn for the better; this was due not
least to Mathilde, who understood how to win Salomon Heine's
good will. Salomon Heine had granted his nephew an annual
pension of 4800 francs. According to the testimony of the composer Giacomo Meyerbeer, who was present at the agreement in
Paris and overheard the negotiations, this pension was regarded
as lifelong. But in Salomon Heine's will there was no mention of
it. The will only made the poet a single bequest of eight thousand
marks. Salomon Heine's son and heir, Carl Heine, refused to continue the pension, for the will imposed no obligation upon him
to do so. It was not greed which determined this attitude. In
view of the thirty millions which he had inherited, the pension
was a trifle. He rather wished to use the opportunity to constrain
the poet to silence on family matters. Heine had often spoken of
the manuscript of his memoirs, in which he intended to charac-
terize his contemporaries, and he had several times imprudently
remarked that in these memoirs he would smite his uncle and
those attached to him "with the long whip of satire." Carl Heine
therefore wished to pay the pension only as a voluntary stipend
on the condition that any literary expression concerning the
family should be submitted for his approval before publication.
Heinrich Heine was unwilling to submit to this censorship. He
was so provoked by his uncle's will and his cousin's attitude that
he suffered something like a stroke, and in this condition lost
sight of the boundaries between what was useful and morally
permissible in the steps which he took to assert the unqualified
obligation of the pension. When, after repeated vain efforts

at litigation against the executors of the estate at Hamburg, he finally realized that his situation was legally hopeless, he sought to exert moral pressure upon his relatives and to make them submit by threats and by the effects of public opinion. In this campaign Johann Hermann Detmold and young Ferdinand Lassalle were helpful, whereas his publisher Campe and the Prince Hermann von Pueckler-Muskau sought to prevail upon Carl Heine to yield by peaceful means. But Carl Heine resisted the pressure of the press as well as the friendly addresses. He exploited Heine's depressed situation mercilessly, and by his inflexible stubbornness forced the poet to yield to the conditions he had made. Thereafter Carl Heine not only paid the pension but, after the outbreak of his serious illness, assisted the poet far beyond his obligations. After two years of bitter conflict a reconciliation of the two cousins took place. But Heine could never forgive his Hamburg relatives their conduct. In it he saw an affront to his genius, a treacherous attack, and this notion contributed greatly to the grim color of his picture of the world which prevails in his last poems. Even the poet's most forbearing judge cannot agree that Heine behaved well in this family quarrel. But Heine doubtless believed that his cause was just, and, if the excitement of struggle had brought his lurking sickness to an open outbreak, it is understandable that Heine should have burdened his relatives with blame for his hopeless sufferings, though without real grounds.

Yesterday evening I received your letter. You can easily imagine what a horrible night I spent. My brain trembled in my head. I cannot yet hold two ideas together. Although I was prepared for the event, it shocked me so deeply that I have not been so much moved since the death of my father. I wonder that with all your vexation you were able to write me immediately. . . .

I wrote him as late as yesterday, although I had a premonition of the misfortune. Give me as many details as you can about his last moments. This man played so great a role in my life's history; he will be described unforgettably. What a heart! What a head! About his final arrangements I have long been free from care.

He told me enough of them himself, or gave clear enough indications. I would give my last shilling if I could have kept him
five more years, or even three more years; yes, I would even give
half of the years remaining to me for such a cause. And how
affectionately he treated my poor mother. To me he said many
harsh things, and last summer he even struck me with his cane
in his excitement. Heavens, how gladly I would again receive
my strokes. If I could only weep! . . . Yes, I know it is true that
I have lost him, but I cannot yet believe it.

—To Charlotte Embden
Paris, December 29, 1844

*His sister's letter had contained news of Salomon Heine's
death. Shortly thereafter the poet learned the contents of the
will. Thereupon Heine turned first to his publisher Campe.*

I know that you are my good friend in spite of our late differences, and in the most delicate matter I turn to your practical
wisdom. You will easily understand the matter. I am sending
you two letters; one is from Carl Heine, which please keep safely.
You see what it is proposed to do with me. I believe that if I
allow myself to be gagged my pension will be paid as before.
They want to keep me under control, to say nothing about the
will and take no action against the Foulds, Carl Heine's wife and
mother-in-law, whose interests I have crossed. Then I am sending you a letter to Carl Heine; read it and keep the copy for me.
Please send the original in a sealed envelope to Carl Heine. I am
writing in great haste. You will see that I am beginning to fight
to the death, and in addition to the courts will win public
opinion to my side in case Carl Heine does not give in. I will
have my rights, even if I must seal them with my death. . . . In
a few days I will send you power of attorney for a lawyer, then
I will send you relevant papers in evidence; in a word, I will act
without delay, although I am ill and wretched and can scarcely
hold pen in hand. But what a misfortune! I gave no provocation.
What dung-carts of filth!—though I am used to that; but others
are not used to it, and perhaps will think it over before they give

the signal to provide the mob with an orgy. I am prepared for anything—embittered by things unheard of.

—To Julius Campe
Paris, January 8, 1845

In great need, you can always count on receiving a letter from me. Perhaps you have already heard from Hamburg what a great misfortune has befallen me. I do not mean my uncle's death, but the way in which he thought of me. I had long expected, from many indications, that he had been induced to believe that I should squander any large sum or that the government would confiscate it. My pension was a settled thing. Speaking candidly, I did not hope for any large remembrance in his will, but only that my pension should be increased. Seven days after his death, on the 30th, I received a long letter from Carl Heine, apparently written on the day of the funeral, in which Carl, otherwise my most considerate friend, informed me in the harshest terms that my uncle had left me only 8000 marks in his will, that nothing was said of a pension, but that he himself would give me an annual stipend of 2000 francs, on condition that, if I write anything about his father, I must first submit the manuscript for examination. Yesterday I wrote him a letter with deliberate contempt, and informed him I should take action at law. . . . Perhaps they expected that I should come to them supplicating, and then would receive the money as formerly. But I believe that threats are a better tactic here and will produce better results. My action at law is no threat; I can make it good. But if I give earnest of what I will do, they will grow tired and give in. The press must do its best to help me in intimidation; the first mud flung at Carl Heine, and especially at Adolphe Halle, will be effective. These people are not used to filth, while I can endure whole carts of it; like flower beds, they only facilitate my digestion. I leave it to your prudence, therefore, to insert a series of little articles in the papers which are read in Hamburg, in which my uncle is defended against the charge of having wished to provide for me otherwise than by his will, and saying how they believe that they have the whip hand of me and threaten not to pay my

pension any more if I give public expression to what I think
about the will and the intrigues which have been set afoot against
me. It is easy to win public opinion to the side of the poet against
the millionaires.

—To Johann Hermann Detmold
Paris, January 8, 1845

*Detmold carried out Heine's injunction. His skill was greatly
admired by the poet, but did not achieve the desired results.
Heine planned to travel to Hamburg himself to supervise the
suit more closely, but his health prevented.*

I hope Campe has written to you on the state of affairs and
that you have already taken steps to bring influence to bear for
me, partly through the press, partly through direct intimidation.

The press must employ intimidation, specifically with reference to Adolphe Halle, who wishes to become a senator. If you
have anyone in Hamburg whom Halle respects, hasten to urge
him to tell Halle to put an end to the spectacle of which the pro-
logue only has so far been played. I am accessible to any honorable declaration, even to a petition to pacify offended pride;
paper, a printed display, are of no consequence to me; a man who
has plenty of glory can yield a little on a point of honor. But I
must have my pension, uncurtailed and irrevocable and unqualified by conditions. Act upon what you know.

Contemnere mundum
Contemnere se ipsum
Contemnere contemni,

as the old monks used to say, and I have come to this saying
through disgust, disgust with life, contempt for men and the
press, sickness, Mathilde. It is a desolate miasma, a weariness of
thinking, a yawning—my pen falls from my hand.

—To Johann Hermann Detmold
Paris, January 13, 1845

My friend, Herr Lassalle, who brings you this letter, is a young man of the most distinguished intellectual gifts; he has the soundest learning, the widest knowledge, the greatest perception that I have ever encountered; he combines the most splendid imaginative quality with an energy of will and a skill in affairs which simply astound me, and if his sympathy for me does not perish, I expect very active assistance from him. In any case I have been very glad to know such a combination of knowledge and capacity, of talent and character. . . . Herr Lassalle is so distinctively a child of these modern days, which refuse to take any account of that renunciation and modesty with which in our day we dawdled and twaddled more or less hypocritically. The new generation wishes to enjoy and to make good in the visible; we old fellows used to bow down humbly before the invisible, aspired to the kisses of shadows and the scent of blue flowers, and renounced and blubbered; and yet we were happier than those hard gladiators who go so proudly to meet death in combat. The thousand-years' dominion of romance is at an end, and I myself was its last fairy king, and I was deposed. If I had not hurled the crown from my head, and donned the smock, they would have beheaded me summarily. Four years ago, before I turned apostate, I still had a longing to play about with my old dream comrades in the moonlight—and I wrote *Atta Troll*, the swan-song of the dying period, and I dedicated it to you. It was your due, for you were my chosen brother-in-arms in play and in earnest. Like me, you have helped to bury the old times and have acted as wet nurse to the new—aye, we have brought them up and are afraid—we are like the poor hen who has hatched a duck's eggs and is horrified to see her young brood plunge into the water and swim comfortably. . . .

You see, my dear friend, how vague and uncertain I am. This weakling mood has its roots in my illness; if the paralysis, which cramps my chest like an iron band, disappears, my old energy will come forth again. But I fear that the trouble will last a long time. The treachery which was practiced against me in the bosom of my family, when I was unarmed and trusting, came upon me like a flash of lightning from a clear sky, and injured me almost fatally. Whoever considers the circumstances will see in it a murderous assault: sneaking mediocrity which, consumed with envy of genius, waited for twenty long years, had at length attained its hour of victory.

—To Varnhagen von Ense
Paris, January 3, 1846

The great agitator Ferdinand Lassalle (1825-1864) travelled to Berlin to work for Heine there. He persuaded the Prince von Pueckler-Muskau and Alexander von Humboldt to intervene in Heine's favor.

Today I will confine myself to thanking you. Never has anyone done so much for me. Nor have I found anyone in whose action so much feeling and so much clarity of understanding are combined. You have full right to be bold; we others only usurp this divine right, this heavenly privilege.

—To Ferdinand Lassalle
Paris, February 10, 1846

In May 1846, Heine's condition took such a turn for the worse that the newspapers reported his decease. This caused Carl Heine to make peace with him and acknowledge the pension. The promise and reconciliation took place at a visit in Paris in 1847.

Unfortunately my condition, which has grown considerably worse since the end of May, has become so serious now that I am afraid. . . . My organs of speech are so paralyzed that I cannot speak, and I have not been able to eat for four months because of the difficulty of chewing and swallowing and the complete loss of taste. I am dreadfully emaciated, my paunch has dwindled, and I look like a withered, one-eyed Hannibal. . . .

I know that I am past saving, but that I can last out in wretchedness and agony for a while, one or at most two years. . . .

My mind is clear, and even creative, but not so splendidly cheerful as it was in the days of my happiness. God forgive my family for their sins against me. It was not the money, but my moral indignation over the most intimate friend of my youth and my own blood relation not honoring his father's word, that has broken my heart, and I am dying of it.

—To Julius Campe
Paris, September 1, 1846

Since I wrote this will a reconciliation has taken place between me and my cousin Carl Heine, and the expressions I employed in recommending my surviving spouse to him are today no longer appropriate; for when I spoke to him of this matter yesterday, he shamed me by the reproach that I could have had the least doubt that he would take adequate care of my widow, and with the most affectionate readiness he undertook the obligation of paying my wife after my death half the sum of my pension throughout her life. He here again displayed all of his noble nature, all his love, and when he gave me his hand as a pledge of his solemn promise, I pressed it to my lips, so deeply was I moved and so greatly did he at that moment resemble his deceased father, my poor uncle, whose hand I had so often kissed as a child when he showed me some kindness.

—Postscript to the Will of September 27, 1846
Paris, February 26, 1847

My whole broil with Carl arose, as he himself told me, from conversations about me which Lottchen had had with Therese and which the latter, apparently beside herself with untimely threats, communicated to Carl. I have never chided her with it, but I know once and for all that her cleverness does not stand the test and can be more dangerous than stupidity.

—To Gustav Heine
Paris, December 17, 1850

The pension under discussion has by no means been withdrawn or diminished after the decease of my uncle Salomon Heine of glorious memory, and was always correctly paid to the penny and farthing. The kinsman who is burdened with this pay-

ment has, since my illness took a turn for the worse, also caused
extraordinary quarterly remittances to be made which, paid
simultaneously with the pension, increase the sum to almost
double. By a generous stipulation in favor of my beloved wife,
who will lose her earthly support at my death, this same kinsman
has further banished the bitterest of all cares from my sickbed.

> —Correction, April 15, 1849
> Allgemeine Zeitung, April 25, 1849

> Seized at nights by fury blazing,
> Clenched fists I brandish raging,
> Breathing threats: its strength depleted,
> Sinks my arm, my anger cheated.
>
> Soul and body both unhingèd,
> Death now takes me, unavengèd;
> Blood-kin none with anger bitter
> Left behind to wage vendetta.
>
> Ah, 'tis blood-kin and none other
> Who to death me now deliver,
> Wreak the bloody deed of guile,
> Lay me low by treason vile.
>
> Siegfried-like: to lay me low
> Shrewd they strike a guided blow;
> Cunning kinsman lightly spies
> How the wounded hero dies.
>
> —From the Mattress-Crypt, 5

With lips they kissed me, false hearts within,
Courteously poured me juice of the vine—
With poison mingled it, fell and malign—
So did my kith, so did my kin.

Melts from my bones my flesh, my skin,
I cannot raise me whence I recline,

They have subtly robbed me of youth divine—
So did my kith, so did my kin.

A Christian I, and the sacred verse
Fast enjoins: Hence ere I die
Dutifully, brotherly, I forgive you all.

But my bile turns—with a hearty curse
I'd liefer maledictions on you call:
God curse and damn you be my cry.

—From the Mattress-Crypt 2

The Revolution of 1848 and Its Consequences

The French February Revolution of 1848 brought the July
Monarchy of Louis Philippe to the end which Heine had frequently foretold. But Heine could take no satisfaction in the
fulfilment of his prophecy. After the fall of the House of Orleans
he became more clearly aware how closely he was bound up with
the principle of parliamentarian monarchy, little as he had approved individual measures of that monarchy. He could not
develop any friendliness towards the Second Republic; and this
was not merely because his state pension had been withdrawn.
He saw in this revolution a stride towards a socialist republic,
towards the rule of communism, and he retained this conviction
even after the overthrow of the workers' insurrection in June
1848. For a while Heine was sympathetic to Louis Napoleon,
after whose coup, he was moved to write the essay Waterloo in
which he enthusiastically hails the restoration of the Bonaparte
dynasty. But the personality of the new Emperor, Napoleon III,
could not inspire him with lasting confidence. Heine could summon even less enthusiasm for the German revolution of 1848
than for the French. In it he saw—correctly and with greater insight than both his contemporaries and subsequent historians—
an outbreak of nationalist, not democratic, tendencies. Thus the
pessimistic view of the world which Heine had conceived as a
result of his bitter experiences in the quarrel over the inheritance

*was confirmed by impressions of political, social and economic
life.*

Paris, March 3. I have not yet been able to write you about
the events of the three great February days, for my head is quite
stunned. Incessant drumming, shooting, and *Marseillaise*. The
latter, that never-stopping song, near bursts my brain, and that
crew of ideas dangerous to the state which I have kept incarcerated there for many years has again burst loose. To dampen
somewhat the excitement which seethed in my mind I occasionally hummed to myself some pious tune from home, as for
example, *Heil Dir im Siegerkranz* or *Ueb' Du nur Treu und Red-
lichkeit*—but in vain. The devilish dago song drowned out all
better sounds in me. I was afraid that the demonic sounds of
revelry would soon reach your ears also, and that you too would
experience its alluring power. The song which the Pied Piper of
Hamelin whistled must have sounded something like that. Does
the great Author repeat himself? Is His creative power exhausted? Had he not already presented the drama, which he
vouchsafed us last February, eighteen years ago, also in Paris,
under the title the "July Revolution"? But a good play can be
seen twice. In any case, it is improved and augmented, and moreover the conclusion is new and was received with thunderous
approval. I had a good place from which to watch the spectacle;
I had, in effect, an orchestra stall, for the street in which I happened to find myself was barred at both sides by barricades. I was
only barely able to get back to my residence. Here I had full occasion to admire the talent which the French display in the construction of their barricades.

Paris, March 10. . . . What an elegant piece is that circular, or
rather that manifesto, of M. de Lamartine! What a holy and
conciliatory gravity exudes from his words, assuaging the wounds
of the present and banishing anxiety of the future! This man is
truly a prophet; he has the language and the insight. With astonishment and with dizziness we look upward to the lofty figure
who, in a year, has soared to such greatness before our eyes. In
the beginning he was only a poet, of the first rank to be sure, but

not particularly surpassing the rest of us. I esteemed him highly for the perfection of his form and the harmonious unity of his emotions and thoughts (two properties entirely lacking in his rival, Victor Hugo, and yet essential for attaining immortality) —but I regard as fatal in Lamartine's poetry that spiritualism, that so-called Platonic love, which I had already found intolerably repugnant in the *Canzoni* and sonnets of his ancestor Petrarch, and which I have combatted my life-long in verse and prose. It was only when I heard Lamartine's political speeches that I rejoiced in his political fellowship. . . .

—Allgemeine Zeitung, March 9-15, 1848

Alphonse de Lamartine (1790-1869), outstanding poet of French Romanticism, was a member of the Chamber of Deputies from 1834 and one of its most brilliant orators. He spoke on cultural questions as well as on economic problems, and represented the standpoint of the radical opposition to the government. After the fall of Louis Philippe, he became leader of the provisional government and Minister of Foreign Affairs. Lamartine's circular mentioned by Heine is directed to the diplomatic representatives of France abroad, and aims to allay the fears of other governments that the French republic of 1848 would endeavor to resume the policies of the first French republic. Lamartine emphasized the peaceful character of the new government and its intention to live at peace with European monarchies. At the election for president, Lamartine was defeated by Louis Napoleon and retired from public life. Heine's opposition to the "spiritualism" of French Romanticism was well known to Lamartine. He was one of the few French writers who rejected Heine completely. Later Heine expressed unfavorable judgments upon Lamartine as a statesman.

The spectacle has brought me low physically and morally. I am so discouraged as I have never been before. I wish to live very quietly now, and not trouble myself about anything any more. The tumult broke out in the midst of the crisis of my cure, and I lost not only money but also health. If things here take an even worse turn I will depart, with my wife or alone. I am very vexed. In Germany things may not be more comfortable, nor have I any great eagerness to go there. . . . My wife is behaving very well. If she does not behave well, I will now give her her liberty, as all kings give their peoples theirs; she will then see what comes of liberty. You have no notion of the misery which prevails here. The whole world is becoming free and bankrupt.

—To Betty Heine
Paris, March 30, 1848

Heine soon gave up any thought of leaving France without Mathilde. On September 6, 1848, he wrote to his sister: "But it won't do, for my wife speaks no German, and without her life would not be possible, or, at least, not comfortable."

You can easily understand my feelings at the revolution which I saw taking place before my very eyes. You know that I was no republican, and you will not be astonished at my not having become one. The present doings and hopes of the world are foreign to my heart. I bow to Fate because I am too weak to defy it, but I may not kiss the hem of her garment, to use no balder expression. . . . You will not be surprised at my having been terribly moved for a moment, and having had a cold, prickly feeling all over my back and arms. Well, it has passed. But it was very hard to see old Roman faces all about me, and to have pathos the order of the day, and Venedey a hero of the time. Gladly would I fly the turmoil of public life that so oppresses me to the imperishable springtime of Poetry and imperishable things, if only I could walk better and were not ill.

—To Alfred Meissner
Paris, April 12, 1848

Alfred Meissner (1822-1885), a German-Bohemian writer, was very close to Heine during the last years of his life. Jacob Venedey (1805-1871), a democrat and a political refugee in Paris, was later a leader in the German revolution of 1848. Despite political an-

tagonism, Heine did him much service, but frequently made fun of his activity, as for example, in Kober I.

Dearest Sister: My wife desires that I no longer keep you under too great illusions, which have been necessary for my mother's sake, concerning the state of my health, so that you will not be too greatly shocked at news of my death. But that, dear child, I hope will not happen very soon, and I can still drag out a dozen years as I am, unfortunately. For a fortnight I have been so crippled that I have to be carried about like a child; my legs are like cotton. My eyes are horribly bad. But at heart I am well, and my brain and digestion are good. I am well taken care of, and I lack for nothing to meet the great costs of this illness. . . . Now you know where you are. I would have been glad to visit you this summer; perhaps I shall see you next spring, or perhaps you will come here next year. This year I am really glad not to see you here because of the pother of world revolution, which you doubtless have to endure there as well as we here. Yes, we are living in a miserable time, and I could wish for a reunion with you in health and happiness and not for a few sick seconds. But will I grow better? God alone, who directs all things for the best, knows. . . . We shall keep my sickness secret from Mother as before.

> Shadow-love and shadow-kisses,
>   Shadow-life—you think it strange!
> Fool! Did you imagine this is
>   Fixed and constant; free from change?
>
> Everything we love and cherish
>   Like a dream, goes hurrying past;
> While the hearts forget and perish,
>   And the eyes are closed at last.
>
> —To Charlotte Embden
> Paris, June 10, 1848

His intention to keep his sickness secret from his mother Heine carried out to the end with great care. He succeeded in making his mother believe that he was suffering only eye-trouble.

Concerning current events I say nothing; it is universal anarchy, world hugger-mugger, divine madness become visible.

—To Julius Campe
Paris, July 9, 1848

It is very hard to be confined to a mattress while all the world is on foot and things march onward. The news which I receive from my country increases my anguish. At this moment, when I should have pursued my life's work with the greatest energy, I am condemned to idleness, and I cannot even respond to the cries of distress of my friends who request the customary assistance. Our enemies have the upper hand in Germany. The so-called national parties, the fanatics of Germanism, are strutting about in their overweening conceit, as ridiculous as they are coarse; their rodomontades are incredible. They dream of nothing but their turn at playing the prime role in world history, of rallying to German nationalism its lost tribes from the east and the west; and if you carelessly give them Alsace they will not fail to demand Lorraine also, and heaven knows where they would put a period to their Teutonic pretensions. War is their desire, and on this point they sympathize with our princes, who ask for nothing better than to turn against the foreigner the warlike and pugnacious ardor of their own rebellious subjects. I have received very sad news from the Rhine. The most devoted friends of France who have been working for twenty years to undermine the Prussian power in the Rhine provinces no longer venture to fight against the invasion of national spirit, and they have hoisted the colors of the German Empire.

—To J. J. Dubochet (in French)
Paris, August 20, 1848

Dubochet, book-dealer and publisher, was friendly with Heine, Thiers and Mignet.

Germany rises against France in a political bacchanal. Everything goes well with us along the Rhine, and the most advanced communist may find the realization of his ideas. Yes, we enjoy communism, in fact, if not in name, for we have all arrived at equality of fortune, for no one longer possesses anything.

—To Francois Mignet
Paris, January 17, 1848

Here everything is chaos. Everyone has a solution in his pocket; cash money would give more pleasure. There are long watery speeches in Parliament, but no spirit of God hovers over the waters. Chamber and President are afraid of one another and fall upon their knees to one another, like the Moor and Papageno. I am heart and soul for the President, not merely because he is the nephew of the Emperor, but because he is a fine fellow and can counteract a great evil by the authority of his name; like Louis Philippe, Louis Bonaparte is a miracle vouchsafed the French. Whether he can maintain himself is another question. For these people fear nothing and look only to the hour. . . . I am often distressed to think that Lindner and Lebret are no longer alive to see the renewed glow of empire through Louis Napoleon. What dithyrambs their old hearts would have sung! How often I think of the past, my dear Kolb!—when we still went about in pinafores in idyllic Munich.

—To Gustav Kolb
Paris, April 21, 1851

Lindner and Lebret were Heine's colleagues in the editorship of the Politische Annalen *(see p. 236f).*

On December 2, 1851, Louis Napoleon's coup, which made him President for ten years with dictatorial powers, took place. The form of the republic was not formally abolished.

Dearest Mother:
Since the greatest excitement is at this moment again reigning in Paris, and there was much bloodshed yesterday and the day

before, I hasten to inform you that I am well and beyond the area of danger. My illness at least gives me the advantage of not getting involved in the party struggle; if I were well, I should be liable at any moment to be maimed or even shot to death. My wife can unfortunately not be kept back from sticking her nose out on the street at every tumult, and yesterday she was in the midst of fire. Unfortunately, I can give no orders in France; the necessary authority is lacking in my own house as everywhere else.

I fear things will go badly with Louis Napoleon. Unfortunately he has not understood that the French do not indeed love the republic, yet still wish to keep it. One does not easily allow something that costs so much to be taken away.

—To Betty Heine
Paris, December 5, 1851

What I have thought of the President here for a year and a day you know. . . . Now everyone sees that I judged him correctly and that he has disguised himself. . . . He was really the lion in the ass' skin which he stripped off early one morning to the terror of the whole menagerie in the Chamber. How far his *coup d'état* can be justified by the provocation of that Chamber is hard to determine. Those fools constantly pricked and nagged at the hero who wielded the shining sword of executive power in his hands, whereas they had only its legal scabbard. Their blindness was inconceivable, and I did not wonder at what happened. But my heart bleeds nevertheless, and my old Bonapartism cannot resist the woe which overwhelmed me when I surveyed the consequences of that event. The beautiful ideals of political morality, legality, civic virtue, freedom and equality, the rosy-dawn dreams of the eighteenth century for which our fathers so heroically marched to death and which we no less heroically dreamed after them—there they lie at our feet, trodden down, scattered, like the sherds of a porcelain bowl.

—To Gustav Kolb
January 13, 1852

We now have the entire Empire here, which is very agreeable
to me.

—To Gustav Heine
Paris, October 14, 1852

I write you nothing about Politics, for things are too confused here. Despite my temper, which is well known to you, I
would not venture to publish my present views in the *Allgemeine*.

—To Gustav Kolb
Paris, March 22, 1853

*Heine's avowal of Bonapartism, which follows, was first pub-
lished after his death. Heine had intended to weave into his
Confessions reflections on the Battle of Waterloo and its consequences, after Louis Napoleon was proclaimed Emperor of the
French as Napoleon III, on December 2, 1852, exactly a year
after his coup. But Campe's vigorous objection prevented the
section on Waterloo from being printed during Heine's lifetime.
In it Heine again emphasizes his view that the defeat of
Napoleon I was a misfortune for democracy and a regression for
the ideas of the Revolution, and in the accession of Napoleon III
to the throne he saw the revenge of Waterloo.*

I do not need to emphasize particularly that only on December 2, 1852, did the French people receive complete satisfaction
by which the wounds of its injured national feeling could be
cicatrized. I feel this triumph deep in my soul, for I once felt
such deep distress at the fall. I myself am a veteran, a cripple
with heart affronted, and I understand the jubilation of the poor
peg-legs. Moreover, I have the malicious joy of reading the
thoughts in the countenances of our old enemies who put a
good face on a bad game. It is not a new man who now sits upon
the French throne, but it is the same Napoleon Bonaparte whom
the Holy Alliance declared in contempt, against whom it waged
war, and whom it thought it had dethroned and slain. But he

still lives, he still rules—for as once in ancient France the king never died, so in the new France the king does not die, and by the very fact that he suffers himself to be called Napoleon III, he protests against the appearance that he had ever ceased to rule; and by the fact that foreign powers acknowledge our current Emperor by that name, they reconcile the French national feeling by a recantation of their earlier affront, as shrewd as it is just.

—Waterloo: Last Poems and Thoughts

Return to Judaism

It was not his great illness which first aroused in Heine the belief in the God of his ancestors. Even long before he was chained to his bed he recognized the precariousness of the ideas which he had adduced for his hostile stand against the Jewish religion. The realization that the religious tradition of Judaism had developed human properties for which neither the Hegelian philosophy nor Saint-Simonism, neither the Greek cult of beauty nor modern sensualism, offered an equivalent, matured gradually in Heine, having repeatedly to struggle with backsliding, particularly since, in consequence of his slight knowledge of Jewish sources, he could for a long while see Judaism only through the spectacles of Christian authorities. A decisive turn in Heine's spiritual development is marked by his intensive study of Michael Sachs' book on Religious Poeetry of the Jews in Spain which appeared in 1845. Here, for the first time, the unfalsified spirit of Judaism was opened up to Heine. The book acquainted him with poets in whom he admired not only the delicacy of feeling, the rich and mobile spirit, the abundance of ideas, but also their gravity and the stature of their temper, their immersion in the truths of the Jewish religion. After having long believed that Judaism and artistry were incompatible with one another, Heine was turned to another mind by the Spanish Jewish poets and their interpreters. In the period of the Kulturverein, when he was working at the Rabbi of Bacherach in order to glorify the past of Judaism, he had already come to admire the heroism of the Jewish martyrs; but the cause for which they underwent martyrdom remained indifferent to him. He believed that even as a "contemner of all positive religions" he could sing the hymn of praise to Jewish heroism, just as other poets, and he himself on other occasions, had glorified Greek, Roman, or medieval Christian heroes; nevertheless, he must have felt that this placed him in an untenable position. Now he saw that post-biblical Judaism had produced, not only great poets, but poets who were and remained believing Jews, and whose biblical and talmudic education made their spirit, not only sensitive, receptive and inventive, but also steadfast in suffering and stalwart in temptation. Under this impression Heine read and re-read the Old Testament with new perception, independent of Christian authorities; and he also began to write the first poems of the Romancero, when the fatal illness broke upon him in full force. The sufferings which Heine had to endure in this illness strengthened the faith in the God of his fathers which had already been awakened. According to the affirmations which Heine made to the numerous visitors to his sickbed, he owed to his faith the spiritual strength which preserved him from utter despair and enabled him to compose the great poems of his last years with members lamed and eyes blinded. With these poems he surpasses the Book of Songs, to which he owed his world-fame for power of language, for wealth of thought, and for perspectives in world history.

Heine's conversion to the God of Judaism by no means connotes conciliation with the world and with his personal fate. The melancholy experiences of the quarrel over the inheritance and of contemporary political history were by no means extinguished by Heine's recognition of the omnipotence of the biblical God. His bitterness at the world and people persisted; but in the faith in God whose ways are unsearchable, Heine found a possibility of preserving the tranquillity of his own spirit despite suffering and corruption. Heine's last poems proclaim the transitoriness of beauty, the doubtful worth of glory, and the inexorable brutality of life's struggle. They present a world in which "heroic blood fails, and the worst cause prevails." They contain his confession of defeat by the terror of life, and they demonstrate the triumph of his spirit, vigilant to the last hour, over horror and misery. He bows to the will of God, for in faith in God he finds a firm hold-fast which enables him to endure hard suffering. But he does not refrain from expressing his own dissatisfaction with the events that embittered his life. Nor does his shrill laughter abate even in moments of profoundest possession; nor does his mockery re-tire before what he avows to be most high and holy. The soul of the moribund poet oscillates in the broad range between humility and impertinence, enthusiasm and irony; he glorifies the beauty of the Sabbath and the spiritual heroism of Judah Halevi, yet in the Disputation he refutes the rabbi as well as the monk. But the mockery of the Disputation is not Heine's last word. Heine's re-turn to Judaism did not imply his re-entry into the synagogue; what it did bring in his last years, along with the acknowledge-ment of the God of the Old Testament, was an altered and more favorable concept of the Jewish people. After the Romancero was completed, he deepened his Jewish knowledge by tireless study, despite physical handicaps, and he began to speak with greater reverence of the "Jews, the work of the Master Workman."

In my sleepless nights of torment I compose beautiful prayers, which I do not cause to be written down, and they are all ad-dressed to a very definite God, namely, the God of our fathers. . . . But what will be said of me in heaven? I can already see how many an angel of conviction will express himself contemptu-ously: Here we see this quite characterless person who, when things go badly for him, causes a petition to be made through old women to the same Deity that he vilely scorned in his days of health.

—To Maximilian Heine
Paris, December 12, 1848

At the risk of being accused of loutishness, I shall no longer keep from you the great event of my soul. I have deserted Ger-man atheism and am on the eve of returning to the bosom of beliefs most commonplace. I begin to perceive that a very little touch of God can do no harm to a poor man, particularly when he has been lying upon his back for seven months.

—To François Mignet (in French)
Paris, January 17, 1849

In the May-month of last year I had to lay me down and I have not risen from my bed since. In the meanwhile—I shall confess it candidly—a great transformation has taken place within me: I am no longer a divine biped, I am no longer "the freest German after Goethe," as Ruge called me in healthier days; I am no longer the Great Pagan No. 2, who used to be compared to Dionysus wreathed with vine, whereas my colleague No. 1 was given the title of the Archducal Weimar Jupiter; I am no longer a Hellene, rejoicing in life and somewhat full-bodied, who laughed contemptuously at gloomy-minded Nazarenes—I am now only a poor deathly-sick Jew, a withered picture of misery, an unhappy man.

—Correction, Paris, April 15, 1849
Allgemeine Zeitung, April 25, 1849

For Ruge see p. 431.

That there is a heaven, my dear Max, I am now quite certain, for I have such great need of one in my pains on earth. Farewell, my dear brother, and may the God of our fathers keep you. Our fathers were gallant lads: they humbled themselves before God and were therefore so stubborn and contemptuous to earthly powers. I, on the contrary, turned an impertinent face to the Lord and was crawlingly humble before men—and therefore am I now laid low like a trodden worm. Praise and glory to God in the highest!

—To Maximilian Heine
Paris, May 3, 1849

My religious convictions continue the same and I feel good about it. So much evil has been done me which I am no longer in position to recompense; I therefore turn the liquidation of my whole life over to dear God.

—To Maximilian Heine
Paris, January 9, 1850

The stories that are told abroad of my present religiosity and pietism have been mixed with much foolishness and even more wickedness. There has not been so great a change in my religious feelings, and the only inner event of which I can definitely and with self-awareness report to you, consists in the fact that a February Revolution has transpired in my religious views and thoughts also; in place of an earlier principle, which had previously left me quite indifferent, a new principle has emerged to which also I do not cling very fanatically and by which my state of mind cannot be suddenly transformed. To make the matter clear to you in a single word, I have given up the Hegelian God, or rather the Hegelian godlessness, and in its place again given preference to the dogma of a real and personal God, who is outside nature and the human being. This dogma—which can be carried out as consistently as our Hegelian synthesis—the ancient Magi had already presented with the greatest profundity, according to the testimony of Neoplatonist fragments; and later, in the Mosaic sources, it is presented with an enthusiasm of truth and an eloquence which is surely not to be found among our modern dialecticians. Hegel has sunk very low in my estimation, and old Moses is in the ascendant. If I only had his prophets along with Moses.

—To Heinrich Laube
Paris, January 25, 1850

"To have Moses and his prophets": A student expression for "being in funds."

I have not become a hypocrite, but I will not play tricks with God; as I deal honestly with men, so will I with God also; and from everything that was produced in my earlier period of blasphemy I have plucked out the fairest poisoned flowers with firm hand, and in my physical blindness have perhaps at the same time thrown many an innocent flower that grew side-by-side with them into the fire. When they were crackling in the fire—I confess it—I experienced some strange moods; I knew not whether I were hero or madman, and I heard the ironic, consoling voice of some Mephistopheles whispering: "God will pay you for that more than Campe, and thou need'st not torture thyself with printing, or haggle with Campe before publication, as for a pair of trousers." Ah, my dear Campe, I wish you believed in God, even though it were only for one day; your conscience would then tell you with what ingratitude you are treating me at a time when I am burdened with such horrible misfortune. . . . Do not be alarmed at the phrase "blessing the temporal"; it is not meant pietistically. I do not mean that I confuse the temporal with the divine, for however near I may come to the Godhead, heaven is a long way from me; do not believe the rumors going about that I have become a pious lambkin. The religious upheaval which has taken place in me is purely spiritual, more an act of my thought than of holy feeling, and my sickbed has very little to do with it, as I am absolutely conscious of myself. I have come by great, exalted and terrible thoughts.

—To Julius Campe
Paris, June 1, 1850

What is publicly reported of my sickness is insignificant in comparison with my actual sufferings. And I bear it all with religious patience. I say religious, because I cannot altogether dismiss what is being said of my present faith. But I must assure you in this connection that there are great exaggerations on the subject, and that I do not remotely belong to the so-called pious souls. The main thing is that I have long felt a great repugnance for German atheism, have long cherished better convictions with reference to the existence of God, but have waited a long while before manifesting these things, perhaps to give dear God a pleasant surprise.

—To Gustav Kolb
Paris, April 21, 1851

A grave without peace, death without the privileges of the dead, who need spend no money nor write letters and books. It is a sad condition. I was long ago measured for my coffin and my obituary, but I am so slow in dying that it is almost as tiresome for myself as for my friends. But patience; everything has an end. You will one morning find the booth shut up where the puppet-shows of my humor often delighted you. . . .

Lying on one's death-bed, one becomes very sensitive and sentimental and desirous of making peace with God and man. I confess that I have scratched and bitten and have been not exactly a lamb. But, believe me, those highly esteemed lambs of meekness would comport themselves less piously were they possessed with the teeth and claws of the tiger. I can boast that I have only rarely made use of those actual weapons. Since I myself stand in need of God's pity, I have granted an amnesty to all my enemies; many beautiful poems, which were directed against very exalted and very humble persons, have been included in the present collection. Poems which contained only the barest aspersion upon the good God Himself have most scrupulously been consigned to the flames. It is better that the verses should burn than the versifier. Yes, I have made my peace with the creation and the Creator, to the great distress of my enlightened friends, who reproached me with this backsliding into the old superstitions, as they preferred to call my return to God. Others, in their tolerance, express themselves more bluntly. The entire high clergy of atheism pronounced its anathema upon me, and there are fanatical parsons of unbelief who would gladly break me upon the wheel to make me acknowledge my heresy. Fortunately, they have no other instrument of torture at their disposal besides their writings. But I will admit everything even without torture.

Yes, I have returned to God like the prodigal son after I had long kept swine among the Hegelians. Was it the *misere* which drove me back? Perhaps a ground less miserable. I was overcome by divine home-sickness and was driven by it through woods and valleys, over the most dizzy mountain paths of dialectics. On my way I found the God of the Pantheists, but I had no use for him. That poor creature of dreams is interwoven and overgrown with the world, really incarcerated in it, and stares at you without will and without power. To have a will one must be a person; and to manifest it, one must have his elbows free. If one desires a God who is able to help—and that is after all the chief thing—one must accept his personality, his transcendence, and his holy attributes, his goodness, his omniscience, his justice, and the like. The immortality of the soul, our persistence after death, is then thrown into the bargain just as the butcher throws some good marrow-bones into the shopper's basket gratis if he is pleased with his customer. In the language of French cuisine, these good marrow-bones are called *la réjouissance*, and they are used for brewing excellent broths which are very strengthening and refreshing for the poor and suffering sick. That I do not refuse such *réjouissance*, and that it rather agrees with me, no feeling person would hold against me.

I have spoken of the God of Pantheism, but I cannot refrain from remarking that he is not really a God, for the Pantheists are only atheists ashamed, who are less afraid of the thing than the shadow which it casts on the wall—its name. In Germany, during the time after the Restoration, most people played the same fifteen-years' comedy with God as the Constitutional Royalists in France, being for the most part republicans at heart, played with the kingdom. After the July Revolution the mask was removed on both sides of the Rhine! Since then, but especially after the fall of Louis Philippe, the best monarch who ever wore the constitutional crown of thorns, the opinion took shape here in France that there are only two forms of government, absolute monarchy and republic, and rational criticism and experience maintain that one must choose one of the two and that the compromises lying between are impossible and corrupting. In the same way, a view arose in Germany that one must choose between religion and philosophy, between the revealed dogma of faith and the latest conclusions of speculation, between the absolute God of the Bible and atheism.

The more decided a mind is, the more easily does it become

the victim of such dilemmas. For my part I cannot preen myself on any separate advance in politics; I adhere to the same democratic principles to which I was devoted in my earliest youth, and for which I have glowed ever more ardently. In theology, on the other hand, I was guilty of retrogression, for I have returned to the old superstition of a personal God. It cannot be hushed up, as many of my enlightened and well-meaning friends have attempted to do. But I must expressly contradict the rumor that my retrogression has led me to the steps of any Church or to its bosom. No, my religious convictions and opinions have remained free from any Church; I was neither lured by the chime of bells nor dazzled by altar candles. I have neither played with symbolism nor renounced my reason. I have forsworn nothing, not even my old pagan gods, from whom I have indeed turned, though we parted in love and friendship. It was in May 1848, on the day when I went out for the last time, that I took farewell of my dear idols to which I prayed in the days of my happiness. I was hard put to it to crawl as far as the Louvre, and I almost broke down when I entered the great hall, where the blessed Goddess of Beauty, Our Dear Lady of Milo, stands on her pediment. At her feet I lay for a long time and wept so as to move a stone to pity. And the Goddess looked down on me so compassionately and yet so desolately as though she would say: "Seest thou not that I have no arms and therefore cannot help thee?"

—Postcript to Romancero
Paris, September 30, 1851

My ancestors belonged to the Jewish religion; I have never been proud of this origin, for I have often enough felt humiliated when I was taken simply as a human being—while Hegel had me believe that I was a god! I was so proud of my divinity, and I believed myself so large, that when I passed through the Saint-Martin or Saint-Denis gate, I involuntarily bowed my head, fearing that I would bruise myself on the arch. It was a fine period, now long past, of which I can never think without sadness, when

I compare it to my present state when I am lying miserably on my back.

—To Saint-René Taillandier (in French)

Paris, November 3, 1851

I ask that my funeral should be as simple as possible, and that the expenses of my interment should not exceed the amount of those of the least important citizen. Although I belong to the Lutheran confession by the act of baptism, I do not desire that the ministers of that Church should be invited to my burial; and I object to any other sort of priest officiating at my funeral. This objection does not spring from any sort of free-thinking prejudice. For the last four years I have renounced all pride of philosophy and returned to religious ideas and feelings. I die believing in one God, the eternal Creator of the World, whose pity I beseech for my immortal soul. I regret having sometimes spoken of sacred things without due reverence in my writings, but I was led astray more by the spirit of the time than by my own inclination. If I have unwittingly offended against good morals and the morality which is the true essence of all monotheistic doctrines of faith, I do ask pardon of God and man. I forbid any speech being made at my grave-side, either in German or French. At the same time, I express a wish that my fellow countrymen, however happily the destinies of our native country should shape themselves, should never carry my ashes to Germany. I have never cared to devote my personality to political mummery. It has been the great task of my life to work for a sincere understanding between Germany and France and to upset the plots of the enemies of democracy, who exploit international prejudices and animosities to their advantage.

—Will of November 13, 1851

The older Jews, who were very feeling people, cherished the belief that one must not eat anything tasty in the presence of a child without giving him a bite of it, for fear that the child might lose a drop of blood, or as they put it, out of *zaar lechayim*, which is more expressive than the word *rachmones*. Your noble heart, dear Baron, seems to have remained true to this magnanimous superstition, and whenever fortune has particularly favored you in your colossal enterprises, not only your immediate friends, but also the poet, that big child, have received something to swallow.

—To Baron James de Rothschild
Paris, January 15, 1852

In 1851 and 1852 Heine destroyed by fire a number of manuscripts which were inconsistent, or could not be made to correspond, with his new religious views. Heine was confronted by the special problem of new editions of works already printed whose statements he could no longer espouse. This was above all the case with Religion and Philosophy in Germany, in which the Saint-Simonist point of view is dominant. When a second edition became necessary Heine at first wished that it be not issued. But this would have injured the interests of his publisher Campe more than his own. Furthermore, failure to issue a new edition would have led to misinterpretations of another kind. After long reflection Heine decided upon an unrevised reprint, but provided a preface which is tantamount to a total recall of the basic views of the book.

Under all circumstances an honorable man retains the inalienable right to avow his errors openly, and I shall here exercise this right without embarrassment. Hence I declare without subterfuge that everything in this book that has to do with the great question of God is as false as it is foolish. As foolish and as false is also the assertion, mimicked from the schools, that Deism in theory is destroyed, and that it now only drags out a miserable existence in the material world. No, it is not true that the *Critique of Reason*, which has destroyed the arguments for the existence of God, familiar to mankind since the time of Anselm of Canterbury, has likewise made an end of God himself. Deism lives, lives its most living life; it is not dead, and least of all has it been killed by the newest German philosophy. This fine-spun Berlin dialectic is incapable of enticing a dog from the fireside, it has not power to kill a cat, how much less a God. I have in my own body had experience how slight is the danger of its killing; it is continually at its work of killing, and yet folks remain alive. The doorkeeper of the Hegelian school, the grim Ruge, once obstinately maintained that he had slain me with his porter's staff in the *Halle Chronicles*, though at that very time I was strolling along the boulevards of Paris, healthy and gay, and more unlike dying than ever. Poor worthy Ruge! He himself, at a later period, could not restrain the most honest outburst of laughter when I made him the confession, here, in Paris, that I had never so much as seen that terribly homicidal journal, the *Halle Chronicles*; and my full, ruddy cheeks, as well as the hearty appetite with which I swallowed oysters, convinced him how little like a corpse I looked. In fact, in those days I was still healthy and sleek, I stood in the zenith of my fat, and was as arrogant as Nebuchadnezzar before his fall.

Alas! a few years later, a physical and mental change began to take place. How often since those days have I thought of the history of the Babylonian king, who esteemed himself as no less than God, but who, having miserably fallen from the summit of his infatuation, crawled like an animal on the ground and ate grass—which would no doubt be salad! This story is to be found in the grandiose and splendid book of Daniel, a story which I recommend to the edifying contemplation, not only of the worthy Ruge, but to that of my far more unregenerate friends, these godless self-gods, Feuerbach, Daumer, Bruno Bauer, Hengstenberg, and whatever else be their names. Besides this one, there are indeed many other beautiful and noteworthy narratives in the Bible which would be worthy of their attention, as, for example, just at the beginning, there is the story of the forbidden tree in Paradise and of the serpent, that little *Privatdozent* who lectured on Hegelian philosophy six thousand years before Hegel's birth. . . .

In my latest book, *Romancero*, I have explained the transformation that took place within me regarding sacred things. Since its publication many inquiries have been made, with zealous importunity, as to the manner in which the true light dawned upon me. Pious souls thirsting after a miracle, have desired to know whether, like Saul on the way to Damascus, I had seen a light from heaven; or whether, like Balaam, the son of Beor, I was riding on a restive ass, that suddenly opened its mouth and began to speak like a man. No; ye credulous believers, I never journeyed to Damascus, nor do I know anything about it, save that lately the Jews there were accused of devouring aged monks of the order of St. Francis; and I might never have known even the name of the city had I not read the Song of Solomon, wherein the wise king compares the nose of his beloved to a tower that looketh toward Damascus. Nor have I ever seen an ass, at least any four-footed one, that spake as a man, though I have often enough met men who, whenever they opened their mouths, spake as asses. In truth, it was neither a vision, nor a seraphic revelation, nor a voice from heaven, nor any strange dream or other mystery that brought me into the way of salvation; and I owe my conversion simply to the reading of a book. A book? Yes, and it is an old, homely-looking book, modest as nature and as unaffected a book that has a work-a-day and unassuming look, like the sun that warms us, like the bread that nourishes us; a book that seems to us as familiar and as full of kindly blessing as the old grandmother who reads daily in it with dear, trembling lips, and with spectacles on her nose. And this book is called— quite briefly—"the Book," the Bible. Rightly do men also call it the Holy Scriptures; for he that has lost his God can find Him again in this Book, and towards him that has never known God it sends forth the breath of the Divine Word. The Jews, who ap- preciate the value of precious things, knew right well what they were doing when, at the burning of the Second Temple, they left the gold and silver implements of sacrifice, the candlesticks and lamps, even the breastplate of the High Priest adorned with great jewels to their fate, but saved the Bible. This was the real treasure of the Temple, and, thanks be to God! it was not left a prey to the flames or the fury of Titus Vespasian, the wretch who, as the rabbis tell us, met with so dreadful a death. A Jewish priest, who lived at Jerusalem two hundred years before the burning of

the second temple, during the splendid era of Ptolemy Phila-
delphus, and who was called Joshua ben Siras ben Eliezer, has
written down for us, in a collection of apophthegms, or *Mesha-
lim*, the thought of his time about the Bible, and I will here
impart to you his beautiful words. There is in them a sacerdotal
solemnity, and yet they are as refreshing as if they had but yesterday welled forth from a living human breast; and the words are
as follows:

"All this is the Book of the Covenant made with the Most
High God, namely, the Law that Moses commanded as a precious treasure to the house of Jacob. Wisdom floweth therefrom
as the water of Pishon when it is great, and as the water of Tigris
when it overspreadeth its banks in spring. Instruction floweth
from it as the Euphrates when it is great, and as Jordan in the
harvest. Correction breaketh forth from it as the light, and as the
water of the Nile in autumn. There is none that hath ever made
an end of learning it, there is none that will ever find out all its
mystery. For its wisdom is richer than any sea, and its word
deeper than any abyss."

—Preface to the Second Edition of Religion
and Philosophy in Germany
Paris, May 1852

*Arnold Ruge, publisher of the Hallische Jahrbuecher, in which
he published an "anti-romantic manifesto" in 1839, was the principal spokesman of the "Hegelian left" or "neo-Hegelians," who
split off from the "Hegelian right," the politically conservative
and religiously orthodox Hegelians, after the appearance of David
Friedrich Strauss' Life of Jesus (1835). Ruge was a democratic
republican, but a determined opponent of socialism. During
Heine's "Hellenic" period, he attacked him sharply, but later
became an admirer, and called him "the freest German after
Goethe" (see p. 421). The philosopher Ludwig Feuerbach (1804-
1872) declared that ideas of God, spirit and immortality are
formed out of the needs of rational man, who shapes God after
his own image. Feuerbach is also the first German representative
of Existentialism. Karl Marx, "the Socialist," published the*

Deutsch-Franzoesischen Jahrbuecher *with Ruge, but then quar-*
reled with his associate. The writer Georg Friedrich Daumer
(1800-1875) was known as a translator of oriental poetry and as
author of books on the genesis of Judaism and Christianity,
which were based on very curious hypotheses. He was later con-
verted to Catholicism. Bruno Bauer (1809-1882) was disciplined
as a Privatdozent of Protestant theology because of his radical
views; he was an outspoken antagonist of Christianity and even
more of Judaism, and later collaborated on the extremely con-
servative Kreuzzeitung. *The orthodox Protestant theologian,*
Ernst Wilhelm Hengstenberg, Heine included in the series of
atheists only out of mischief.

Joshua ben Siras ben Eliezer: Heine means Jesus ben Sirach
whose book was written about 135 B.C.E. He was not a priest.

The reawakening of my religious feelings I owe to that sacred
book; for me it became as much a source of healing as an object
of the most devout admiration. It is strange! during my whole
life I have been strolling through the various festive halls of philosophy, I have participated in all the orgies of the intellect, I
have coquetted with every possible system, without being satisfied, like Messalina after a riotous night; and now, after all this,
I suddenly find myself on the same platform as Uncle Tom. That
platform is the Bible, and I kneel by the side of my dusky brother-
in-faith with the same devotion. . . .

Previously I had not much admired the character of Moses,
probably because the Hellenic spirit was predominant in me, and
I could not pardon the lawgiver of the Jews for his hatred of the
plastic arts. I failed to perceive that Moses, notwithstanding his
enmity to art, was nevertheless himself a great artist, and possessed the true artistic spirit. Only, this artistic spirit with him,
as with his Egyptian countrymen, was applied to the colossal and
the imperishable. But, unlike the Egyptians, he did not construct
his works of art from bricks and granite; he built human pyramids
and carved human obelisks. He took a poor shepherd tribe and
from it created a nation which should defy centuries; a great, an
immortal, a consecrated race, a God-serving people, who should

serve as a model and prototype for all other nations: he created Israel. With greater right than the Roman poet, may that artist, the son of Amram and the midwife Jochebed, boast that he had builded him a monument more enduring than bronze.

I have never spoken with proper reverence either of the artist or of his work, the Jews; and for the same reason—namely, my Hellenic temperament, which was opposed to Jewish asceticism. My prejudice in favor of Hellas has declined since then. I see now that the Greeks were only beautiful youths, but that the Jews were always men—strong, unyielding men—not only in the past, but to this very day, in spite of eighteen centuries of persecution and suffering. Since that time I have learned to appreciate them better, and, were not all pride of ancestry a silly inconsistency in a champion of the Revolution and its democratic principles, the writer of these pages would be proud that his ancestors belonged to the noble house of Israel, that he is a descendant of those martyrs who gave the world a God and a morality, and who have fought and suffered on all the battle-fields of thought.

The history of the Middle Ages, and even that of modern times, has seldom enrolled on its records the names of such knights of the Holy Spirit, for they generally fought with closed visors. The deeds of the Jews are just as little known to the world as is their real character. Some think they know the Jews because they can recognize their beards, which is all they have ever revealed of themselves. Now, as during the Middle Ages, they remain a wandering mystery, a mystery that may perhaps be solved on the day which the prophet foretells, when there shall be but one shepherd and one flock, and the righteous who have suffered for the good of humanity shall then receive a glorious reward.

You see that I, who in the past was wont to quote Homer, now quote the Bible, like Uncle Tom. In truth, I owe it much. It again awakened in me the religious feeling; and this new birth of religious emotion suffices for the poet, for he can dispense far more easily than other mortals with positive religious dogmas. He possesses grace, and to his spirit the symbolism of heaven and earth is open; he requires no churchly key. The silliest and most contradictory reports are in circulation about me concerning this. Very pious but not very wise men of Protestant Germany have urgently inquired if, now that I am ill and in a religious frame of mind, I cling with more devotion than heretofore to the Lutheran evangelical faith, which, until now, I have only professed after a lukewarm, official fashion. No, dear friends, in that respect no change has taken place in me, and if I continue to adhere to the evangelical faith at all, it is because now, as in the past, that faith does not at all inconvenience me. I will frankly avow that when I resided in Berlin, I, like several of my friends, would have preferred to separate myself from the bonds of all denominations, had not the rulers there refused a residence in Prussia, and especially in Berlin, to any who did not profess one of the positive religions recognized by the State. As Henry IV once laughingly said: "Paris is well worth a mass," so I could say, with equal justice, "Berlin is well worth a sermon." Both before and after, I could easily tolerate the very enlightened Christianity which at that time was preached in some of the churches of Berlin. It was a Christianity filtered from all superstition, even from the doctrine of the divinity of Christ, like mock-turtle soup without turtle. At that time, I myself was still a god, and no one of the positive religions had more value for me than another. I could wear any of their uniforms out of courtesy, after the manner of the Russian Emperor, who, when he vouchsafes the King of Prussia the honor to attend a review at Potsdam, appears uniformed as a Prussian officer of the guard.

Now that my physical sufferings, and the reawakening of my religious nature, have effected many changes in me, does the uniform of Lutheranism in some measure express my true sentiments? How far has the formal profession become a reality? I do not propose to give direct answers to these questions, but I shall avail myself of the opportunity to explain the services which, according to my present views, Protestantism has rendered to civilization. From this may be inferred how much more I am now in sympathy with this creed.

At an earlier period, when philosophy possessed for me a paramount interest, I prized Protestantism only for its services in winning freedom of thought, which, after all, is the foundation on which, in later times, Leibnitz, Kant and Hegel could build. Luther, the strong man with the axe, in the very nature of things, had to precede these warriors, to open a path for them. For this service I have honored the Reformation as being the beginning of German philosophy, which justified my polemical defense of Protestantism. Now, in my later and more mature days, when the religious feeling again surges up in me, and the shipwrecked metaphysician clings fast to the Bible—now I chiefly honor Protestantism for its services in the discovery and propagation of the Bible. I say 'discovery,' for the Jews, who had preserved the Bible from the great conflagration of the sacred temple, and all through the Middle Ages carried it about with them like a portable fatherland, kept their treasure carefully concealed in their ghettos. Here came by stealth German scholars, the predecessors and originators of the Reformation, made their way there stealthily, to study the Hebrew language and thus acquired the key to the casket wherein the precious treasure was enclosed. . . .

Yes, the world is indebted to the Jews for its God and His word. They rescued the Bible from the bankruptcy of the Roman Empire and preserved the precious volume intact during all the wild tumults of the migration of races, until Protestantism came to seek it, translated it into the language of the land and spread it broadcast over the whole world. This extensive circulation of the Bible has produced the most beneficent fruits, and continues to do so to this very day. The propaganda of the Bible Society has fulfilled a providential mission which will bring forth quite different results from those anticipated by the pious gentlemen of the British Christian Missionary Society. The latter expect to elevate a petty, narrow dogma to supremacy, and to monopolize heaven as they do the sea, making it a British Church domain— and lo, without knowing it, they are demanding the overthrow of all Protestant sects; for, as they all draw their life from the Bible, when the knowledge of the Bible becomes universal, all sectarian distinctions will be obliterated. . . .

To the observant thinker it is a wonderful spectacle to view

the countries where, since the Reformation, the Bible has been
exerting its elevating influence on the inhabitants, and has impressed on them the customs, modes of thought and tempera-
ments which formerly prevailed in Palestine, as portrayed both
in the Old and in the New Testament. In the Scandinavian and
Anglo-Saxon sections of Europe and America, especially among
the Germanic races, and also to a certain extent in Celtic countries, the customs of Palestine have been reproduced in so
marked a degree that we seem to be in the midst of the ancient
Judaean life. . . .

The readiness with which these races have adopted the Judaic
life, customs, and modes of thought is, perhaps, not entirely
attributable to their susceptibility of culture. The cause of this
phenomenon is, perhaps, to be sought in the character of the
Jewish people, which always had a marked racial affinity with the
character of the Germanic, and also to a certain extent with that
of the Celtic races. Judaea has always seemed to me like a fragment of the Occident misplaced in the Orient. In fact, with its
spiritual faith, its severe, chaste, even ascetic customs—in short,
with its abstract inner life—this land and its people always
offered the most marked contrasts to the population of neighboring countries, who, with their luxuriantly varied and fervent nature of worship, passed their existence in a bacchantic dance of
the senses.

At a time when, in the temples of Babylon, Nineveh, Sidon
and Tyre, bloody and unchaste rites were celebrated, the description of which, even now, makes our hair stand on end, Israel sat
under its fig-trees, piously chanting the praises of the invisible
God, and exercised virtue and righteousness. When we think of
these surroundings we cannot sufficiently admire the early greatness of Israel. Of Israel's love of liberty, at a time when not only
in its immediate vicinity, but also among all the nations of antiquity, even among the philosophical Greeks, the practice of
slavery was justified and in full sway—of this I will not speak,
for fear of compromising the Bible in the eyes of the powers
that be. . . . To this very day the Saxon peasant uses the beautiful

and touching aphorism: "A hundred years of wrong do not make a single year of right."

The Mosaic Law, through the institution of the jubilee year, protests still more decidedly. Moses did not seek to abolish the right of property; on the contrary, it was his wish that every one should possess property, so that no one might be tempted by poverty to become a bondsman and thus acquire slavish propensities. Liberty was always the great emancipator's leading thought, and it breathes and glows in all his statutes concerning pauperism. Slavery itself he bitterly, almost fiercely, hated; but even this barbarous institution he could not entirely destroy. It was rooted so deeply in the customs of that ancient time that he was compelled to confine his efforts to ameliorating by law the condition of the slaves, rendering self-purchase by the bondsman less difficult, and shortening the period of bondage.

But if a slave thus eventually freed by process of law declined to depart from the house of bondage, then, according to the command of Moses, the incorrigibly servile, worthless scamp was to be nailed by the ear to the gate of his master's house, and after being thus publicly exposed in this disgraceful manner, he was condemned to lifelong slavery. Oh, Moses! our teacher, Rabbi Moses! exalted foe of all slavishness! give me hammer and nails that I may nail to the gate of Brandenburg our complacent, long-eared slaves in their liveries of black, red and gold.

—*Confessions*

Exodus 21.1-6 describes the ceremony to which a slave is submitted if he elects to remain with his master after the expiration of his stipulated term of service.

Miserere

I do not envy Fortune's sons
    Their life—I envy sore
The swift and painless ease with which
    They pass and are no more.

In splendid raiment, laugh on lip,
  And on their head a crown,
While seated at the board of life
  The sickle mows them down.

In festal garb, with roses decked
  That had not time to fade,
These favorites of Fortune fall,
  And reach the realms of shade.

Dead men of gallant mien are they,
  Unwasted by decline.
To court they're bidden welcome by
  Tzaritza Proserpine.

I envy them their happy lot!
  For seven years have I
In anguish tossed upon the ground,
  And yet I cannot die!

O God! cut short this torment vile,
  And let me buried be;
I have no gift for martyrdom,
  As thou must surely see.

At Thy inconsequence, O Lord!
  Forgive me if I wonder;
To sour a poet born so glad—
  It surely is a blunder.

This pain has dulled my mirth of soul,
  Grief makes in me her home;
And if the sorry jest goes on,
  I'll join the Church of Rome.

And then like other saints I'll whine,
  And din Thee to Thy cost—

And so the best of humorists,
    To letters will be lost.

                —From the Mattress Crypt
                Margaret Armour

Matilda plucked a posy gay;
With pleading hand I waved away
Her smile, her flowers,—I shudder so
When I behold sweet flowers ablow.

They speak so plain the thought I shun:
Fair life and I no more are one.
In the dark land that waits for me
My poor unburied corpse should be.

When flowers I smell I fall aweeping;
Of all this world has in its keeping—
Love, beauty, sun and laughter fain—
The tears alone to me remain.

I used to sit and watch entranced
The rats that in the opera danced;
And now I hear the horrid shuffling
Of rats and moles in churchyards scuffling.

O fragrant flowers! to my sight
Ye bring a chorus, ballet bright,
Of perfumed memories old and sweet—
Lo! up they spring with dancing feet,

In short and fluttering skirts come flashing,
With castanets and cymbals clashing;
But all the laughter, dallying, wooing
But shows the darker my undoing.

Hence with the flowers! I cannot bear
The scents that mind of days so fair;

Those pranks and revels long ago—
To think on them's to weep for woe.—
                    —From the Mattress Crypt
                        Margaret Armour

I was ordained, O lamb, to be
A shepherd and a shield to thee.
I gave thee of my bread to eat,
With water from the fountain sweet.
When cold and loud the winter storm,
Upon my bosom thou wert warm;
In my embrace I held thee fast.
When chill and fierce the winter blast,
When wolf and torrent, rivals dread,
Howled in their dark and rocky bed,
Thou didst not shake or start affrighted.
Even when the blazing levin blighted
The tallest pine—upon my breast
In sleep untroubled thou didst rest.

My arm is feebler than of old;
Pale Death draws nigh. From sheep and fold
And pastoral things I must away.
O God, within Thy hands I lay
The staff Thou gavest.—Do Thou keep
My lamb when I am laid asleep
Beneath the grass—preserve untorn
Her flesh from every wounding thorn.
Oh, guard her fleece from briars keen,
And bogs defiling and unclean;
Spread everywhere before her feet
The greenest pasture spring sweet;
And free from sorrow may she rest
As once she slumbered on my breast.
                    —From the Mattress Crypt
                        Margaret Armour

Within the hour-glass I can see
  The dwindling sands run low.
My sweet, my angel wife, from thee
  Death tears me; I must go.

He tears me from thy arm, sweetheart,
  No longer can I fight,
My soul must from my body part,
  She dies from sheer affright.

In the old house where she would be
  Death will not let her live;
She trembles, "Whither?"—like a flea
  Imprisoned in a sieve.

I cannot change by tears or strife
  What Fate has fixed forever,
And soul and body, man and wife,
  When strikes the hour, must sever.

—From the Mattress Crypt
Margaret Armour

Hallelujah

Sun, moon, and stars on heaven's height
Bear witness to Jehovah's might,
And, when above the righteous gaze,
They sing to the Creator's praise.

I have no need to look so high,
For on the earth, at hand, there lie
Full many works with wonder fraught,
That, here below, the Lord hath wrought.

Yea, worthy folk, I humbly turn
My gaze to earth, and there discern

The gem of God's creative art,
His masterpiece: the human heart.

The sun in all his glory bright,
The moon that shines so soft at night,
The gleaming stars, the splendor dire
Of comets with their tails of fire—

They suffer, one and all, eclipse,
And, like so many farthing dips,
Before the heart grow pale and wan
That flames within the breast of man.

The world in miniature it holds,
The woods, the meadows, and the wolds,
The wilds which savage breasts infest,
Such as the heart too oft molest.

Here rivers rush and torrents leap,
Here yawn the precipices deep,
Midst gardens gay, and fields whose grass
Now feeds the lamb, and now the ass.

Here fountains of pure water spring,
And nightingales complaining sing:
To please the lovely roses pine,   ∕
Until they die of a decline.

Nor is there any lack of change,
So ample is the weather's range—
Today, the land by sunshine kist,
Tomorrow, grey with autumn mist.

The flowers drop their petals sweet;
The stormy winds tempestuous beat;
At last the snow begins to fall,
And streams and lakes are frozen all.

Now is the time for wintry sport;
The feelings to their masks resort:
In drunken folly dance along,
Among the masquerading throng.

'Tis true, amid those pleasures vain
There mingles oft a secret pain;
'Mid masquerade and music gay,
They sigh for bliss that's passed away.

A sudden crack.—Nay, start not so!
It is the ice that breaks below.
The crust gives way, which, smooth and chill,
Had bound our hearts so long for ill.

Lo! what was cold and sad is gone;
And Spring—ah, joy!—returns anon:
The season fair of all delight
Love's magic wand awakens bright!—

Great is the glory of the Lord,
In heaven, on earth, alike adored.
Loud songs of praise to heaven's King,
And hallelujahs I will sing.

Man's heart He formed so fair and sweet,
And then to make His work complete
He breathed therein from heaven above,
His breath divine, whose name is love.

Hence with the lyre of ancient Greece,
And let the wanton muses cease
Their dances lewd! In worthier ways
I'll sing to the Creator's praise.

No pagan music shall be mine;
But David's pious harp divine

With strings melodious shall prolong
The hallelujahs of my song!
                    —From the Mattress Crypt
                    Margaret Armour

I am publishing my works in French with Michel Levy *frères*, who have been recommended to me as publishers. I had the choice between them and another publisher, who was once a *bonnetier*, that is, he was a manufacturer of cotton nightcaps, and I chose the first, perhaps because they were the seed of Levi. I believe that M. Levy is none the less for that an honest man, and even if I were to make a fatal mistake, I should be the last to be influenced by the old prejudice against Jews. I believe that if one helps them to make money they are at least grateful, and will take advantage of one less than their Christian colleagues. The Jews have been left with a great instinctive civilization through an unbroken tradition of two thousand years. I think they have been able to play such a part in European culture, just because they have had nothing to learn in the matter of feeling, and only needed to come by scholarship.

                    —To Joseph Lehmann
                    Paris, October 5, 1854

Heine had become friendly with Lehmann in the days of the Kulturverein.

Nothing is more repulsive to me than those usual condolences, that cruel and barbaric custom, which permits anyone at any hour he likes to wrest the bandage from our wounds and to irritate our anguish by empty turns of speech. To me such condoling, whining, luke-warm, chattering comfort is far more deadly than the shrieking howls of pagan dirges; and I can see how truly human, how delicate in feeling, is the pious usage of the old Jews who sat silently down by the mourners and after a while, again without saying a word, departed.

                    —To Baroness Betty de Rothschild
                    Paris, December 10, 1855

Heine died on February 17, 1856. His burial is thus described by Ludwig Kalisch in his book, Paris Life, which appeared in 1880:

"We had assembled in the residence of the poet, and, when the coffin was carried out of the chamber, we were seized by indescribable pain. We felt the great loss which Germany had suffered by the death of the poet. Among the French who accompanied the corpse along with us were Mignet and Théophile Gautier. Alexandre Dumas joined us on the way. He had seen the funeral approaching from his hansom and first discovered Heine's death from seeing his coffin. He dismounted immediately and, visibly shocked, followed the procession to the cemetery. Silently we walked behind the bier, and as silently we watched the coffin sink into its grave."

INDEX OF NAMES